The Collected Works of
Sardar Vallabhbhai Patel

VOLUME I
(1918–1925)

ADVISORY COMMITTEE

The Collected Works of
Sardar Vallabhbhai Patel

VOLUME I
(1918–1925)

The Kheda Non-Cooperation Movement, Nagpur Flag Agitation and Borsad Satyagraha

Chief Editor

P.N. CHOPRA

KONARK PUBLISHERS PVT LTD
New Delhi • Seattle

KONARK PUBLISHERS PVT LTD
206, First Floor, Peacock Lane,
Shahpur Jat,
New Delhi-110 049
Phone: +91-11-41055065, 65254972
Email: india@konarkpublishers.com
Website: www.konarkpublishers.com

Konark Publishers International
8615, 13th Ave SW,
Seattle WA 98106
Phone: (415) 409-9988
Email: us@konarkpublishers.com

Second Impression 2015

Cataloging in Publication Data—DK
Courtesy: D.K. Agencies (P) Ltd. <docinfo@dkagencies.com>

Patel, Vallabhbhai, 1875-1950.
[Works]
The collected works of Sardar Vallabhbhai Patel / chief editor, P.N. Chopra.
15 volumes cm
Reprint. Originally published: 1990.
Includes indexes.
Contents: volume 1. 1918-1925 — volume 2. 1926-1929 — volume 3. 1930-1931 — volume 4. 1932-1934 — volume 5. 1 January 1935-31 December 1935 — volume 6. 1 January 1936-30 June 1937 — volume 7. 1 July 1937-31 December 1938 — volume 8. 1 January 1939-31 March 1940 – volume 9. May 1940-December 1942 — volume 10. 1 January 1943-31 December 1946 — volume 11. Special volume — volume 12. 1 January 1947-31 December 1947 — volume 13. 1 January 1948-31 December 1948 — volume 14. 1 January 1949-31 December 1949 — volume 15. 1 January 1950-31 December 1950.
ISBN 9789322008444 (set)

1. India—Politics and government—1919-1947. I. Chopra, Pran Nath, editor. II. Title.

DDC 954.035 23

Typeset by The Laser Printers, New Delhi, and printed at Thomson Press (India) Ltd.

प्रधान मंत्री

Prime Minister

FOREWORD

We shall forever remain indebted to the great leaders who fought for the liberation of our motherland. Among these leaders, Sardar Vallabhbhai Patel retains a special place in our hearts and minds because of the success he achieved in uniting our country.

To compile the life and work of a stalwart like Sardar Patel is indeed a humongous task. I commend the editors and publishers for compiling the *Collected Works of Sardar Patel.*

The speeches and writings of this great son of India will continue to inspire us in our task of nation-building.

(Narendra Modi)

New Delhi
08 May, 2015

प्रधान मंत्री

Prime Minister

FOREWORD

We shall forever remain indebted to the great leaders who fought for the liberation of our motherland. Among these leaders, Sardar Vallabhbhai Patel retains a special place in our hearts and minds because of the success he achieved in unifying our country.

To compile the life and work of a statesman like Sardar Patel is indeed a humongous task. I commend the editors and publishers for compiling the *Collected Works of Sardar Patel*.

The speeches and writings of this great son of India will continue to inspire us in our task of nation-building.

(Narendra Modi)

New Delhi

08 May, 2015

Contents

Publisher's Note

Sardar Vallabhbhai Patel was one of the founding fathers of the Republic of India. As a leader of the Indian National Congress party, he made significant contributions to the freedom struggle and in the transfer of power at the time of India's independence. As the first Home Minister and Deputy Prime Minister of India, he made a unique contribution in the integration of all the princely states into a united nation and also established the all-India civil services (IAS, IPS, etc.) which became the administrative backbone of modern India.

Since there is a renewed interest in understanding the enormous contribution of Sardar Patel, this reprint of the 15 volume set compiled from various journals, periodicals and letters will come in handy. This set, first published in 1990, is exceedingly useful in understanding the life and times of Sardar Patel.

New Delhi,
10 January 2015

Foreword

THE ONE NAME that stands out most prominently when one thinks of the unity and integrity of India is Sardar Vallabhbhai Patel. I am not sure if anybody among the leaders of the Indian National Congress would have handled it so well, so effectively and so efficiently. His strength, his imagination, his determination, his sagacity and more than his patriotism and his appreciation of the necessity that India should be one united integrated whole in order that as one nation it may grow in stature from strength to strength from poverty to affluence, in one word a strong nation, which would stand in the front rank of nations and lead them. He knew that unless the Princes numbering 562 merged their states into the Indian Union, one Indian Nation would be impossible. The manner and method he adopted for this noble purpose was an abject lesson unrivalled in world's political history. He cajoled, he flattered, he threatened. Most of them were made to realise that if they did not fall in line, their own subjects would rise against them as Indians. They would not only lose their popularity, they would also lose their identity. Some of the Princes were misled to think that as British paramountcy had ended, they were free and reverted to their original sovereignty. The feeling of the majority of the Princes was so much against it that many of them, specially those of Travancore, Mysore and Bhopal, waited till the last bastion, viz. Nizam's Hyderabad have had to face a police-cum-military action which was brief and complete. This achievement of making one integrated and united India was almost entirely of Sardar's.

One great quality of Sardar is often missed. That is his human approach to problems and human kindness and sympathy. I can quote many instances. The one most pronounced is the way in which he saw to it that after the Princes agreed on his advice or otherwise to merge their States into our Union, standard of life to which they were accustomed from birth was continued at the same level. That this good arrangement was changed after his death to their disadvantage is another matter.

One shudders at the thought what would have happened if these states had not been merged in. Not only India would have been politically not one but torn up into fragments with each bit having different governments, different laws, indeed different in everything, making it impossible for its sustained growth and development socially, politically, economically, culturally, an India weak in every way. This is where Sardar's greatness lies.

While this is so, many friends have been feeling that there is no attempt at publishing Sardar's life and achievements for except the publication of his correspondence by that well-known journalist Durga Das, who is known by his book *India From Curzon to Nehru and After,* a good publication indeed.

Dr. P.N. Chopra, former Editor, *Indian Gazetteers,* Government of India and Chief Editor of *Who's Who of Indian Martyrs* and *Towards Freedom* Project and myself used to meet quite often as friends and in one of these meetings he mentioned this subject and we agreed that such a publication is a dire necessity to keep records straight, just and correct about the struggle and achievement of India's freedom. We agreed on this publication as while works on other leaders, Mahatmaji, Pandit Nehru, Dr. Rajendra Prasad, Abul Kalam Azad and others were being published, not to publish Sardar's life and work was a lacunae. This is its result.

A Committee was formed with Dr. Chopra as Member-Secretary and myself as Chairman, Shri Hitendra Desai and Shri N.C. Chaturvedi as Vice-Chairmen and important Members of Parliament and Chief Ministers, Governors and well-known Vice-Chancellors as advisors. I am proud to say that with their co-operation, help and advice and with the untiring efforts of Dr. Chopra, we have been able in such a short span of time to bring out the first Volume of Sardar Patel's Collected Works.

I am equally happy to say that in response to my appeal for financial help, the Chief Ministers of Karnataka, Andhra Pradesh, Gujarat, Maharashtra, Uttar Pradesh, Madhya Pradesh, Himachal Pradesh and Governors of Mizoram and Punjab have not only expressed full sympathy with this work, but some of them have already sanctioned and paid some amount. I am expecting similar help from other Chief Ministers. We are thinking of putting up a Memorial in Delhi in Sardar's name in which everything about Sardar will be found—a library, a museum, a sufficiently commodious hall for meetings, some rooms for boarding of scholars, etc. We have requested the Central Government to allot us the building, 1 Aurangzeb Road, where Sardar lived as Deputy Prime Minister incharge of Home Affairs, from where he worked and brought about the integration of the States into the Indian Union for this purpose. I am very happy to say that the response has been sympathetic and expect necessary orders to be passed soon.

We also propose to approach the public for help for this work of great national importance and hope we will receive generous help to commemorate the name of Sardar Vallabhbhai Patel who was not only very much responsible for integrating and uniting India but in building up and organising the Indian National Congress during the entire period of the struggle for freedom. The nation is ever grateful to the Great Sardar. Let the future generations remember him with admiration, respect and gratitude.

Chitradurga, Karnataka
January 1990

S. NIJALINGAPPA

Introduction

ALMOST A DECADE before the foundation of the Indian National Congress, Vallabhbhai Jhaverbhai Patel was born on October 31, 1875, in a peasant family at Nadiad, a town in Kheda district from which his mother Ladbai hailed. His father Jhaverbhai, a small farmer with 10 to 12 acres of land in Karamsad village, was a sturdy, upright and straightforward man of independent nature to whom the village folk flocked for advice and succour in times of distress. It is said that Jhaverbhai took part in the Great Revolt of 1857 under the Rani of Jhansi and was later taken prisoner by the Holkar of Indore. He was an expert in chess and at a game so impressed Holkar that he released him and he returned to Karamsad after an absence of about 3 years. Vallabhbhai inherited from his father the skill to organise and plan a campaign or a movement at the opportune movement.

To this unassuming and humble parents, India owes a deep debt of gratitude for having given to the nation two of its greatest leaders—Vithalbhai and Vallabhbhai—and in spite of their adversity educated and trained them so well that they were unrivalled in their respective spheres of activity. Hard working and conscientious from his very childhood, Vallabhbhai helped his father in the fields along with his studies in the local primary school at Karamsad. Jhaverbhai, Vallabhbhai's father, was a deeply religious man and being a follower of Swaminarayan sect he would visit the temple at Vedtal twice a month. Vallabhbhai imbibed the teachings of this sect and following in the footsteps of his father, fasted twice a month till he was at Karamsad. However, this seemed to have been a transitory phase as later on he did not display any religious convictions for this sect. It was but natural that these early impressions left an abiding impact on his mind and, to quote his biographer N.D. Parikh, "Vallabhbhai afterwards used to speak with great admiration of Sahajanand Swami and his disciples and generally the purity of life led by them and by the *sadhus* of former days. He recognised the great moral influence this cult had on the lives of thousands of men and women of all classes and in particular of the uneducated backward classes." It is interesting to note that Vallabhbhai also inherited from his father another trait which has been commented upon by all those who came into contact with him, *viz.* the habit of walking to and fro, while talking to someone or when he happened to be in pensive mood. For his secondary education, he had to go to Petlad, at a distance of about 14 kms from his native village of Karamsad, which he had to traverse on foot, every week carrying the foodgrains which he cooked himself. But soon he was able to organise a group of schoolmates and they would by turn bring the necessary foodstuff from the village and thus devote more time to studies.

Reminiscing on his school days, Vallabhbhai once wrote: "As far as I remember, I yielded to none in the captaincy of mischief or of sly attempts to hoodwink one's elders. As far as I can recall, however, it was almost always in a good cause—of course, a good cause from my own point of view. I took to studies as seriously as I took to play cheerfully. I had no patience with an indifferent teacher and never spared a lazy one. As children, we had our own methods of correcting our teachers and we fully exploited all the subtleties of the manoeuvres which only children can. I can vividly recall one particular incident. My teacher at school had got annoyed because I persuaded the class to make fun of him for being late. He prescribed a task for me as a punishment. I came to the school next day without any task done. The following day I was asked to do twice as much. Days went by without the task being done and the punishment increased doublefold for each day, that went by until it was my task to write out the sums 200 times. I wrote on the plate just the figure 200 and took it to my teacher with an innocent air. The teacher asked me where the *padas* (in Gujarati that means both sums and buffaloes) were, I told him, 'I could write only 200 when the *padas* (buffaloes) ran away'. The teacher was all sound and fury. I was presented before the Headmaster who instead of punishing me took the teacher to task for not knowing the correct method of prescribing tasks."

A few other incidents bear it out that he was a born campaigner and a leader since his school days. When Vallabhbhai was only in 6th standard he came into clash with a teacher who was in the habit of using his rod too frequently and punishing the students rather harshly. Once he imposed a heavy fine on a young student which he could hardly afford to pay. Vallabhbhai could not stand this injustice and persuaded all the students of the school to abstain from attending their classes. The strike went on and the young Vallabhbhai even made arrangements for their stay in a local *dharamshala*. On the third day, the Principal had to yield, sent for the student leader Vallabhbhai and assured him that the students would not be punished severely in future. Though he could not stand inhuman treatment or injustice from any quarter, his love and respect for his teachers was proverbial. It is related that one of his teachers in the High School stood as a candidate in the Municipal elections. His opponent was a rich person with considerable resources and influence and was sure of victory against a humble teacher. He boasted that if he would lose the election he would get his moustache shaved. Vallabhbhai could not stand the humiliation of his teacher and the vanity of his opponent. He took up the challenge on behalf of his teacher and organised the campaign with such resoluteness and methodical manner that his teacher came out victorious with a thumping majority. He was determined to take the matter to its logical end by organising a procession of about 50 students who accompanied by a barber went to the residence of the vanquished hero and asked him to abide by his promise.

The son of a sturdy *Kisan*, Vallabhbhai had inherited not only his father's strong physique but also his iron nerves for which he was known since his school days. He was reputed for his courage, endurance and unflinching determination. He had a boil during his school days, the remedy for which, in those days, was only a puncture by a barber with a red hot iron rod—a painful operation indeed. The barber could not muster the courage to do so. The young Vallabhbhai took the red hot iron rod from the barber's hand and applied it to the boil himself without a trace of uneasiness on his face. We see these traits of his character—of suffering physical and mental agony stoically never allowing anybody to know about it. While in London he had to undergo an operation for taking out of a guinea worm from one of his legs. While the doctor was taking it out, it broke midway and a portion remained inside which had to be taken out, causing unbearable physical pain to the patient. The doctor was naturally worried but the patient insisted that the doctor should take it out without worrying about the suffering he would have to undergo. The Sardar, as he came to be known later on after the historic Bardoli Satyagraha of 1928, went through the agonising and painful process without taking chloroform and did not show any signs of suffering which enabled the doctor to finish his job satisfactorily and expeditiously. To quote the former Prime Minister Morarji Desai, his contemporary, ardent follower and admirer, Sardar Patel "maintained his spirit until his life's end as I could see when I was with him in Yervada Jail in 1941. He was suffering from intestinal trouble and the intestines were having a reverse movement and the pain of it was visible even to others. And yet he not only took no service from any of us but got up early in the morning before others and served tea to his companions without any sign of inconvenience or pain."

In his school days as a boy and later on throughout his life, Vallabhbhai's path was strewn with innumerable obstacles but he never let his equanimity of mind to be disturbed and removed the obstacles, whether thrust by man or nature. He had given ample proof of it in his school days when he found a stone of a considerable size obstructing the path to Petlad where he was studying. While his colleagues went ahead without caring to remove it, Vallabhbhai sweat himself to dig it out and made the path smooth.

Few would realize now the hard way, unlike some of his contemporaries such as Gandhiji, Motilal Nehru, Jawaharlal Nehru, Tej Bahadur Sapru and others, Vallabhbhai had to get his early education and it was quite natural that he was already 22 years old when he passed his matriculation examination. He had been a witness to the sufferings of his peasant folk and was determined to fight for justice and fairplay which was only possible if he was a master of himself. He, therefore, decided to be a lawyer and after passing the District Pleader examination, he started practice at Godhara where his elder brother Vithalbhai had already made a name for himself. He was soon involved in the case of a teacher against an influential person who had engaged the services of a well-known pleader with whom the judge was also on friendly terms. While on an inspection of the site of the incident with the Judge and the lawyer, Vallabhbhai had to suffer the ignominy of being made fun of by both of them for having taken up this weak case, as he was a briefless lawyer. Vallabhbhai kept his cool (and did not lose his temper) 'figures'. If there is any difference between words and figures, the banker will not pay the amount and he will return the cheque with the remark 'Amount in words and figures differ'. In case the banker finds that the amount in words is less than the amount mentioned in figures, and pays such lower amount, the customer cannot find fault with the banker.

If the alteration is apparent, a banker will not honour such cheques. However, if the banker pays such cheque, he will be held liable and will not get the statutory protection. If an alternation has been skillfully executed in such a way that the banker cannot find out, the banker can escape from his liability as he is innocent. However, if the customer has drawn a cheque carelessly, leaving blank spaces and if some unscrupulous person has taken advantage of such a situation, the banker cannot be held liable.

3. *Place :* The cheque should be drawn at the specified branch of the bank. If the consumer has used any other cheque leaf other than the one supplied to him, the banker will not honour the cheque. In case the place of payment is altered, it is considered to be material alternation.

4. *Number of Parties :* A customer may draw cheque in the names of more than one person. Strictly speaking, all should jointly present the cheque for payment at the bank. However, a banker may pay to one of the parties if the cheque is signed by all the payees. But if any of the payee's name is removed or added without any authorisation of the drawer, it amounts to material alteration and such cheque should not be paid.

5. *Removal of Crossing :* If crossing is to be removed, the drawer can cancel the crossing by writing across 'Pay Cash' with his full signature. Such cancellation of crossing enables the holder of the cheque to receive cash through the counter.

6. *Converting an Order cheque into a Bearer cheque :* The significance of the bearer cheque is that the banker can pay the amount of the cheque to any one who presents such cheque for payment. But if it is an order cheque, the banker should ensure that the cheque is paid to the right person. While a bearer cheque may be converted to an order cheque, an order cheque can be converted into a bearer cheque only by the drawer. If any other person converts an order cheque into a bearer one, with out the authority of the drawer, it becomes material alteration.

Alternations permitted by Law

1. The Negotiable Instruments Act of 1881 permits the following :

(a) As per Sec. 125, open cheque/ uncrossed cheque can be crossed by any one for safety. General crossing may be converted into a special crossing.

but at the next appearance in the Court, he narrated the talk they had proving thereby that the Judge and the opposing lawyer were friends and the former was prejudiced and therefore pleaded for the transfer of the case. It was not only agreed to but he also won it and henceforward his clientage increased manifolds. He had to take up another case at the behest of his father who was greatly agitated as an arrest warrant against Swaminarayan Maharaj, Yogna Purshottamdasji Maharaj had been issued in case of some temple property. In a sarcastic way Vallabhbhai asked his father how could anybody dare to issue warrant against the great Swami "who has the power to get deliverance for us all". In any case he got the case settled out of court.

Vallabhbhai was a criminal lawyer *par excellence.* Quite studious and thorough in handling cases, he soon became a reputed lawyer at Borsad. To quote Babubhai J. Patel, "His robust commonsense, courage, foresight, unruffled temperament and understanding of human psychology, helped him considerably in his profession." Soon he came into clash with a British Magistrate who had the strange habit of insisting on the witnesses to look at a mirror instead of the Court or the lawyer. Vallabhbhai raised objection to it as it had no legal sanction. The Magistrate refused to yield. Vallabhbhai took the matter to the higher authorities at the District Court and included the name of the Magistrate as a witness. The Magistrate got panicky and agreed to give up this practice.

Vallabhbhai was not content with his lot as a local lawyer. He had set his eyes on acquiring a higher position for which he wanted to go to England to be a barrister. Vallabhbhai himself confessed at a meeting about his craving for higher education as well as his eagerness to imitate the British in all possible ways in his youth and to quote him, "While introducing me, Shri Mohanlal has said that once upon a time, I used to imitate the British and their ways closely. That is quite true. It is also true that sports used to take up whatever spare time I had. I used to think then that for our unfortunate country it was the best policy to imitate the foreigner. I had been taught to think that the people of our country were of poor character and unworthy and that it was only the foreigner ruling over us who was good and had the ability to improve our condition. We could only be slaves. This was the sort of poison which was being instilled in our minds. I was anxious to go overseas to see the people of England who, living 5,000 miles away, were able to rule us for so long."

But Vallabhbhai knew that he belonged to a middle class family and his father could hardly afford to send him to London and therefore he worked hard as a pleader to save enough money to study for Bar-at-Law in England. It is a tribute to his capabilities and hard work that within 3 years of his setting up his practice at Borsad he could amass sufficient money to apply for admission in the Middle Temple in 1905. He wrote to the famous travel agency Thomas Cook and Sons for arranging his trip to London. As the fate would have it, when all the formalities were nearly complete, the Company's last letter addressed to him fell into the hands of his elder brother Vithalbhai who had the same initials "V.J. Patel". He was also anxious to go to London for the bar and pleaded with his younger brother Vallabhbhai to let him avail of this chance and he could go later. Vallabhbhai greatly respected his brother and whenever they happened to be together, he would look after his needs and comforts. He would serve him, wash his clothes and even cook food for him. He considered it as a privilege to be of some service to him and without a moment's hesitation agreed to his request and let him proceed abroad. As it was not enough he met all his expenses while in London and looked after his family in India. In fact, he asked his sister-in-law to stay at their house and when he found that she and his wife would not pull on amicably, he sent his wife Zaverbai to her parents for some time. During his brother's absence, he had to work hard to look after the family at home and pay for the studies of his brother abroad.

The fate now dealt a severe blow to Vallabhbhai. His wife Zaverbai whom he had married at the age of 18 and had a daughter Maniben (b. 1903) and a son Dahyabhai (b.1905) by her, fell seriously ill due to severe intestinal trouble in 1908. Vallabhbhai took her to Bombay and got her admitted in the famous Cama Hospital. She improved a little and the doctors advised operation. Meanwhile he had to leave for Anand where he had to defend a client involved in a murder case. He left word with the doctors to inform him about the date of the operation so that he could rush back. However, the condition of his wife became serious and the operation had to be performed urgently in his absence. The doctors informed Vallabhbhai about the successful operation and the consequent improvement in the condition of his wife. But the next day her condition deteriorated and she breathed her last that very day. As the destiny would have it, Vallabhbhai received the tragic news while he was arguing the case in the Court. A man of iron will, Vallabhbhai read the telegram carrying the saddest news of his life and kept on cross-examining the witness and did not disclose the contents till the court adjourned. Needless to say his client was acquitted. But at what a heavy price hardly anybody knew. He was left with a 6-year old daughter and a 4-year old son to look after. But he never wavered from his unflinching resolve not to marry again, earlier for the sake of the children and later on for devoting his whole life to the liberation of the motherland. It is a strange coincidence that all the five brothers lost their wives at a comparatively young age and they never remarried. Vallabhbhai used to call his family a "Family of Widowers".

On return of his brother to India after completing his studies in London, Vallabhbhai left for U.K. in 1910 and joined the Middle Temple Inn. With his meagre resources, he had to work hard in London too and would walk about 14 kms. daily to go to and return from the Library in the Middle Temple when he was already 35. Thousands of miles away from his home, Vallabhbhai's concern for his family was uppermost in his mind. In one of his letters dated 16 December 1910 written to his brother Narsibhai from London, he explained his helplessness and added, "While I was there I did my best for our home and looked after everything. At present I am not in a position to do anything." (Doc. 3)

"The story of Vallabhbhai's career in the Inns of Court," to quote Dr. Pattabhi Sitaramayya, "was remarkable. His practical knowledge of law gave him an easy victory over his fellow students. His studious habits and established position at the Bar in India helped to abridge his course by a year." He pursued his studies, got a first class in the finals and a prize of £50. Referring to this, he wrote in a letter to his brother on June 7, 1912. in his unassuming manner, "I have completed my examinations and have passed in the First Class. It means that I shall be coming six months earlier than usual . . . ." (Doc. 6)

As a peasant, Vallabhbhai was eager to go to the villages around London and acquire first hand knowledge which he did after his examination was over. He returned to India with flying colours. In spite of an attractive offer, made by the then Chief Justice of Bombay, of a Professorship at the Government Law School (the College was then known as "School"), Vallabhbhai having no attractions and ambitions in the first place for the Bombay legal world, preferred to come over to Ahmedabad. He wanted to make Ahmedabad a centre for his future activities. He was completely westernized and took to smoking, card playing with money stakes, etc. In the words of Pattabhi Sitaramayya, "he was not one of the early admirers of Gandhi and with his English style of dress and deportment, his children studying in a Convent as a preliminary to their being sent to England for studies, he was in every way a worshipper at the shrine of Britain. He had full play to his cynical humour which valued nothing constructive and which was adept at tearing to pieces, in common with his brother Vithalbhai, the best of endeavours in the cause of ordered progress. He had all the genius of his profession—dividing and destructive, but back of it all, there lay dormant a flair of constructive capacity, which showed itself in evolving scheme of escape for his clients and friends from dangers and difficulties seemingly baffling." Like Gopal Krishna Gokhale, Vallabhbhai also had the rare knack of achieving perfection in whatever he did. G.V. Mavalankar, lawyer, friend and a contemporary, later on Speaker of the Lok Sabha, writes about his capabilities as a barrister: "His conduct of his cases always exhibited thorough mastery of facts, a proper and correct estimate of the opponent's case and line of attack and his carefully planned defence and attack. But one great quality which struck everybody and made him the object of admiration was his fearlessness and the bluntness with which he would deal with the Court in which he was appearing. He would never allow the judge to outstep; even in the least, the limits of courtesy nor would he allow or tolerate any unfair, unjust or improper leaning on the part of the Court in favour of the police or the prosecution. . . . It is difficult, at this day, for people to realize what this meant in 1913-14, when the people and the bar carried notions different from now about respect and courtesy for authority. These notions of courtesy and respect almost savoured of flattery and servility. Vallabhbhai was far above these and never minced matters, for fear of losing practice before a particular Judge; if he happened to criticize or expose the idiosyncracies of a Judge. He was thus a great protector of the self-respect as well as the convenience of the bar and the public . . ." Mavalankar continues: "I need not multiply instances of Vallabhbhai's courage and fearlessness in the course of his legal practice. It is this quality and the training he had in the legal profession that is to my mind the basis of his success in later political life."

In those days Vallabhbhai presented a different picture altogether. As already mentioned, he had imbibed western culture and could be spotted in the Club, "a smart, youngman, dressed in a well-cut suit, with a felt hat worn slightly at an angle; with piercing and bright eyes, not given to many words, receiving visitors with a smile but not entering into any conversation, maintaining firm and pensive looks, appearing almost to look upon them with a sort of superiority complex whenever he opened his lips carrying an impression of sternness and reserve, such was the new barrister which had come to Ahmedabad for practice." At that time there were only 6 barristers in Ahmedabad, Vallabhbhai being one of them. His personality and behaviour were both a cause of attraction as well as resentment to his clients and people of Ahmedabad at large.

While imitating British manners, Vallabhbhai also took up bridge playing at the Club, and soon acquired mastery over this game which became the envy of many of his contemporaries at the Club. Mr. Wadia and his partner who till then held the field, threw a challenge to him. Vallabhbhai accepted the challenge with the condition that stakes would be quite high. Vallabhbhai proved to be more than a match and won £15 to £20 on the very first day. The game continued on the second day and Wadia was a loser again. On Mrs. Wadia's pleadings, Vallabhbhai agreed not to prolong the game further. He had achieved his purpose and humbled his opponents and his vanity and ego too.

It was during this period in 1915 that Gandhiji visited Ahmedabad, paid a visit to the Club to talk to the members. Vallabhbhai was busy playing cards when someone mentioned this to him, but he did not pay any heed to the newcomer but merely shrugged his shoulders cynically.

Meanwhile, his distinguished brother Vithalbhai had initiated himself into the public life of the country as a Member of the Bombay Legislative Council. It was difficult to combine public life with legal practice and, therefore, the two brothers decided between themselves that while Vithalbhai would wholeheartedly devote himself to public work, Vallabhbhai would continue the practice and earn enough to meet the expenses of the family. This compromise was faithfully followed by Vallabhbhai till 1917 when he too plunged into the service of the country. Recalling this episode the Sardar said in 1921, "If we want independence and if we wish to serve the country, we must be prepared to be poor. We, therefore, decided that one of us should serve the country and the other, the family. My brother gave up his flourishing practice and started on a career of public service while I bore the burden of maintaining the household. I reconciled myself by the thought that I could claim at least a share in his good things."

In 1914, the Government of Bombay amended the District Municipal Act which gave them the right to appoint Indian Civil Service Officers in the bigger municipalities. Taking advantage of it, the Government now appointed. Shillidy, a die-hard British Civil Servant as Municipal Commissioner of Ahmedabad. He was an arrogant, high-handed and ruthless officer who became a terror for the citizens of Ahmedabad. The educated classes and intelligentsia were greatly upset and wanted to teach him a lesson. As Devavrat Pathak Pravin Sheth writes: "Vallabhbhai's entry into the Ahmedabad Municipality was prior to and independent of Gandhiji. What then were the main reasons that impelled him to enter the Ahmedabad Municipality; one reason advanced was that Vallabhbhai was a match for the arrogant and overbearing British officer who was then at the head of the Municipality and needed to be controlled. The other important factor was the fighting capacity of Vallabhbhai which he had amply shown at Bar. The third factor was his trait for helping the poor and taking up cudgels on their behalf and waging a relentless struggle for a right and just cause." It was under these circumstances that Vallabhbhai was elected as a Municipal Councillor of Ahmedabad Municipality in 1917. Thus began an association which was to last for 11 long years, i.e. from 1917 to 1928 with a short break for 1922-24 when the Municipality was superseded by the Government.

Vallabhbhai's entry into Muncipality was independent of Gandhiji. As stated above, Vallabhbhai had remained aloof from Gandhiji during the period (1915-1917) but "he was watching, studying and establishing contacts". Nobody could think that in no distant future Vallabhbhai was destined to be a comrade-in-arms and trusted lieutenant of Gandhiji.

Gandhiji, after his arrival in Ahmedabad in 1915, was a familiar figure at the Gujarat Club. But dressed as he used to be in his "Kathiawadi turban, *kurta* and *dhoti,* he could not impress the members of the Gujarat Club, especially Vallabhbhai who is reported to have curtly, unceremoniously and sarcastically brushed aside any idea of ever listening to Gandhiji at the Gujarat Club." But a historical event suddenly changed his entire outlook and subsequently proved to be a turning point in his life. G.V. Mavalankar relates how Vallabhbhai came to be attracted towards Gandhi. He writes: "It was at the (Gujarat) Club that we received one afternoon the news about the heroic stand of Gandhiji in the court of the Motihari (Bihar) Magistrate who banned Gandhiji's enquiry into the conditions of labour employed by the European planters in Bihar. This was the first act in India of Gandhiji's technique of non-violent resistance. Gandhiji refused to obey the order and preferred imprisonment to abandonment of the inquiry. This act of Gandhiji electrified all of us at the Club. The late Diwan Bahadur Harilal jumped up and waving his hands exclaimed: "Mavalankar, here is a brave man and we must have him as our President." It was this occasion which attracted Vallabhbhai more to the Gujarat Sabha and his attention hitherto restricted to the Municipality, he gave more and more time to the affairs of the Gujarat Sabha. Gandhiji accepted our invitation to be the President of the Sabha and that was also the beginning of Vallabhbhai being drawn nearer to Gandhiji's activities and methods. Brave as he was, the bravery in Gandhiji found in him a ready response. This was the small beginning of the close and great association in comradeship in the service of the motherland." It changed his entire outlook and subsequently proved to be a turning point in his life. J.B. Kripalani recalls his first meeting with Vallabhbhai in 1917 at Sabarmati Ashram set up by Gandhiji and adds,

"He was then living in a modest house. Vallabhbhai invited Mahadevbhai and myself to dinner. It was a sumptuous meal. But it did not appear that it was specially prepared for us. In his life he had often to content himself with plain diet; but I have an idea that he was always partial to good food. At this first meeting, we talked of current political affairs. The talk was racy, interspersed by his humorous remarks, about men and matters."

Though Vallabhbhai was greatly impressed by Gandhiji and accepted his leadership, he refused his invitation to stay at the Ashram frankly telling Gandhiji that he could not accede to his wishes as he was not in agreement with conditions prescribed by Gandhiji for living at the Ashram. Sardar now left his practice and dedicated himself to the national service under Gandhiji's leadership. He used to say in later life that as a disciplined follower, he would give his independent and frank opinion but ultimately go by the directive of the leader. In a humorous way, he would say that he had locked his brain and given the key to Gandhiji.

Thus the circumstances forced both the brothers to plunge themselves in public service but they mutually agreed that Vallabhbhai would confine himself to work in and around Ahmedabad and Vithalbhai in and around Bombay. Whenever he visited Bombay he did not actively participate in public activities unless absolutely essential. The arrogant British Municipal Commissioner Shillidy, an I.C.S., ignored the interests of the ordinary inhabitants of the city and did not care for pressing their civic problems. His only concern was for the white people most of whom resided in the cantonment area. To one of his acquaintances he gave the right to control and manage the Suskar Tank near Kankaria for industrial use which caused pollution and was naturally detrimental to the health of the people living in the surrounding areas. While he managed to keep adequate supply of water to the cantonment area at very cheap rates, he neglected the vast majority of the people of Ahmedabad. There was criticism in the local papers and also in Gujarat Club but he ignored it with contempt. Vallabhbhai was indignant and he brought forward a resolution that as Shillidy had consistently ignored the interests of the tax-payers, and had unilaterally taken a decision on the Suskar Tank and had put his personal interests above those of the people, his services should be terminated. (Doc. 8) Gandhiji also lent support to it in a speech at a public meeting held on January 1, 1918: "We must protest for, otherwise, the officials will never know that we suffer; nor need we wait till the new elections, as it is quite likely that they may be delayed by a year." Later on, Vallabhbhai also got removed another British officer Massey who had to proceed on long medical leave and when Vallabhbhai insisted that he should produce a medical certificate, he resigned. Thus Vallabhbhai had started his experiment in non-cooperation from the Municipal Committee as Gandhiji had declared on November 3, 1917 at the meeting of the First Gujarat Political Conference: "In the running of the Local Government lies key to *Swarajya*. . . . Unless we improve the condition of our cities, *Swarajya* will have no meaning for us." To quote G.V. Mavalankar: "His spirit of service and devotion to duty were of such an exceptional character that as Chairman of the Municipal Sanitary Committee, he stuck up his residence in the city of Ahmedabad when plague (1917) was raging and refused to move out for personal safety. His was a familiar figure moving in the streets of Ahmedabad, getting the sewers cleaned and the plague-stricken areas disinfected. When friends argued, he simply looked at them, and his silence was more eloquent than his words. It appeared as if he wished to say, 'I have undertaken the duty as Chairman of the Sanitary Committee, and how can I ask safety for myself? It would be a breach of faith to the public to leave my post of duty, and how can I leave the conservancy staff of the Municipality to undergo risks of plague and seek safety for myself?'"

Vallabhbhai's greatest contribution to India's struggle for independence was in the successful application of non-violence in various struggles he waged. The Agrarian Movement in Kheda in 1918 for securing redress of the grievances of the Kheda District peasants regarding land revenue remission due to failure of crops, undoubtedly was his first experiment. About 22,000 peasants of Kaira sent a petition to the Revenue Collector to postpone the collection of revenue. But the government was adamant. Gandhiji asked Vallabhbhai to take up the cause of the farmers. Vallabhbhai now toured each and every village and exhorted the peasants not to pay any taxes. "The fight will act as a spark which will set the whole country afire", he said. (Doc. 10). He reminded them on 31st March 1918 that "The brave man, who has inspired this fight however is capable of converting the cowardly into the bravest of persons, and in India, the Kheda District is the land of brave men." (Doc. 10) Addressing the villagers of Rass village on April 18, 1918 he asked the villagers not to pay any heed to the observances of the Commissioner and unitedly stand up against repression let loose by police. (Doc. 15) In a stray pamphlet attributed to him, Vallabhbhai said: "A bitter war is on between the public and the blind administration. . . . It has auctioned many houses. . . . It has auctioned standing crops. It has threatened imprisonment. But in spite of all this the public has stood firm. . . ." (Doc. 16) In another statement Vallabhbhai said: "Our fight is for truth and that is what satyagraha means. It is a fight between the people and a blind Government." (Doc. 17) The satyagraha continued for 6 months but ultimately the Government had to yield and a settlement was arrived at and only 8% of the land revenue was to be recovered. Vallabhbhai congratulated the people of Kheda and said, "The public of Kheda have rendered great service to themselves, to the struggle for independence and to the state". He further said that, "by their courage the agriculturists of Kheda have drawn towards them the attention of the whole country. For the past six months they have shown great loyalty to truth, fearlessness, unity, firmness and self-sacrifice." (Doc. 18)

Gandhiji paid a high tribute to Vallabhbhai and said: "A leader's skill is judged by the competence in selecting his assistants for the execution of his plans. Many people were prepared to follow my advice, but I could not make up my mind as to who should be my deputy commander. I then thought of Vallabhbhai. I must admit that when I met Vallabhbhai first, I could not help wondering who this stiff-looking person was, and whether he would be able to do what I wanted. But the more I came to know him, the more I realized that I must secure his help." Vallabhbhai too has come to the conclusion that although he has flourishing legal practice to-day and is doing very important work in the Municipality, he must become a whole-time public leader. So he has taken the plunge. If it were not for his assistance, I must admit that this campaign would not have been carried through so successfully." (Doc. 20) To quote D.P. Mishra, veteran Congress leader and once Chief Minister of Madhya Pradesh: "Sardar always recalls to my mind the Indian peasant. Sardar was not only born in a peasant home; the whole make-up of his personality was that of an Indian peasant. The peasant is completely engrossed in his land. To tend it and make it productive is almost all his concern. He is practical, and knows not how to prance about on the wings of imagination. The simple wisdom of ages is all his knowledge. He is not averse to new ideas, but only when you convince him of their practical utility. He would call a friend a friend, an enemy an enemy. He has no talent for tinsel talk. If you win his trust, he will even lay down his life for you. He is peace-loving, but he will not hesitate to use force in the defence of his land." The humility of Vallabhbhai in the hour of triumph is worth recording: "I have not done anything. . . . I wish to say on behalf of my colleagues and myself that if the people of Kheda district had not given proof of their courage and tolerance, he would not have been able to achieve anything. I would, therefore, say that the honour which has been conferred on me rightfully belongs to the people." (Doc. 19) Gandhiji in his tribute to Vallabhbhai said that he had tested Vallabhbhai with fire and he had proved to be 100 per cent gold.

Vallabhbhai next took up the cause of the business community of Ahmedabad who had been asked to fill in new income-tax forms. He reprimanded the business community for not taking up the matter when it was being debated in Legislature. He asked them to read newspapers to be in touch with political developments and other legislative bills. (Doc. 21) Thus when Vallabhbhai was engaged in a relentless battle against the British authorities the country was faced with a national crisis in the wake of the passing of the Rowlatt Bills, popularly known as Black Bills, which curbed the freedom of the people. Gandhiji decided to offer Satyagraha. To begin with, he announced 30th of March 1919 and later on April 6 when *hartal* would be observed all over India. Gandhiji left for Punjab but was detained near Mathura and sent back to Bombay. Vallabhbhai led a huge procession on April 6 and openly defied law. Riots broke out in Gujarat and martial law was imposed in Ahmedabad. Vallabhbhai had already urged the traders on March 2, 1919 to prepare themselves for the struggle. (Doc. 25) On April 13, 1919, Vallabhbhai decided to bring out the *Satyagraha Akhbar* to keep the people informed about the happenings in various parts of the country, particularly Gujarat. (Doc. 28) Vallabhbhai gave up legal practice in pursuance of the five-point programme of Gandhiji and plunged himself in the Non-Cooperation Movement.

In the wake of the disturbances, following the passing of the Rowlatt Act, the Ahmedabad Municipality had levied a penalty of Rs 4,80,000 on the inhabitants of Ahmedabad. Vallabhbhai moved a resolution that the collection be deferred on the plea that the matter was under consideration of the Hunter Inquiry Committee. (Doc. 30) As Vallabhbhai refused to pay the fine, the Government resorted to attach his belongings which consisted of only a sofa-set in his drawing room which was advertised and sold. (Doc. 33) Vallabhbhai strongly condemned the British rulers for their atrocities in the Punjab, the massacre at Jallianwala Bagh and the order requiring people to dishonour India. "Not content with humiliating the Punjab, these gentlemen representing the Government considered the intolerable hardships and troubles of the people a matter of fun. The coming generations have a claim on us who are their trustees and if we leave them any heritage of insults and dishonour, of what use would all the wealth and the comforts be that we may leave to them?" (Doc. 28)

Vallabhbhai supported the Khilafat Movement and criticized the treatment meted out to Turkey and West Asian countries after World War I and said, "It has, as a matter of fact, been a heart-breaking episode for the Indian Muslims, and how can Hindus stand by unaffected when they see their fellow countrymen, thus, in distress."

Vallabhbhai had been appointed Chairman of the Reception Committee of the Fourth Gujarat Political Conference. In his spirited address, he showered praises on Lokmanya Tilak and said, "No greater fighter has arisen on political firmament than Tilak who could fight the British bureaucracy with its own weapon. His deep scholarship, his shining character, his ideal simplicity, his fearlessness, his unquestioned patriotism and most of all his call for complete swarajya, this is his legacy." (Doc. 37) Vallabhbhai collected a sum of Rs 25 lakhs for the Tilak Swarajya Fund against a target of Rs 10 lakhs.

The Congress at Calcutta started the Non-Cooperation Movement under the leadership of Gandhiji. "Swaraj within a year" became the battle-cry. On August 1, it is said, in pursuance of Gandhiji's programme of Swadeshi, the people of Ahmedabad made a huge bonfire of their foreign clothes. Vallabhbhai's barrister's robes, about a dozen suits, 250 collars, neckties and pairs of shoes were consigned to the flames. Vallabhbhai exhorted students to boycott schools and colleges. "Do not ask yourselves, 'What should I do', or 'What should happen to me', because these are the considerations of impotent men. Jump into the struggle and be prepared to do your best. That is your duty to-day." (Doc. 40)

A grass-root politician, he was quite conscious of the grave economic implications of the British policy of exporting raw materials. In a statement on December 6, 1923, he declared that the "Englishmen import cotton worth five crore of rupees from India and send us textiles made from that cotton which are worth sixty crores of rupees. The money which they got from you is utilized to appoint Commissioners and Collectors, to buy guns which are utilized to keep you under their heels." (Doc. 194)

Vallabhbhai also moved a resolution in the Ahmedabad Municipality, "to remove Government control over primary education in Municipal schools and that no formal grants should be received from Government", which was approved and forwarded to the Government. (Doc. 42) The Government retorted by forcibly getting the premises of the schools vacated. Vallabhbhai asked people not to worry as the education which the children received was only limited to a standard to make our people *patwaris,* peons, police inspectors, *tehsildars* and not for higher posts. He called upon them to be fearless as "man dies only once. The moment you are rid of fear you are free." (Doc. 46) Vallabhbhai advised people not to expect justice from the British rulers as "the man who gives justice should be impartial and independent. Even gods also are unable to give justice when they have an interest. So if you want justice, we have not to demand but snatch it from them. Independence is not granted, it has to be achieved." (Doc. 47) However, when a bomb was thrown on Lord Hardinge in Chandni Chowk, Delhi, which created great sensation throughout the country. Vallabhbhai praised the attitude of the Viceroy who declared that he did not want any retaliatory or repressive action to be taken. (Doc. 50)

The Congress held its 36th session at Ahmedabad on December 28, 1921. As Chairman of the Reception Committee, Vallabhbhai made a stirring speech and said: "We have tried to overcome our weaknesses honestly and in a definite manner. The proof, if any proof is needed, is Hindu-Muslim unity. . . . I can proudly claim that our relationship is not merely of friendship but of fruitful cooperation so that we can take the nation forward. Similarly, we have established cordial relations with Parsis, Christians and other citizens of the country." He further told the delegates that the Bardoli and Anand districts were ready for civil disobedience and would assuredly prove their mettle. (Doc. 62) Gandhiji was full of praise for making seating arrangements on the ground and providing cushioned mattresses to the President and a few others at the Provincial Conference and the Khilafat Conference. But what he appreciated most was Vallabhbhai's speech which was brief and to the point lasting only 15 minutes.

Now Gandhiji launched his non-cooperation movement as a protest against Punjab wrongs and to support the Khilafat cause. The growth of Government repression and the prosecution of the Ali Brothers added fuel to the fire. Vallabhbhai took up the cause of the Ali Brothers and in a speech on September 25, 1921 said that "even though Indians in general and Muslims in particular have been deeply hurt by the arrest of Maulana Mohammad Ali and Shaukat Ali, they have kept their feelings in check and have remained peaceful." (Doc. 56) In accordance with the Congress resolution, Vallabhbhai now made preparations for the launching of the civil disobedience in Bardoli (Doc. 60), but to his great dismay Gandhiji suspended the movement after the outbreak of violence at Chauri Chaura, a small village near Gorakhpur on February 5, 1922.

While participating in the national events, Vallabhbhai was equally involved in the affairs of the Municipality. He had already been able to weed out the proud and haughty British officers—Shillidy, Macassey, Master and Engineer Wadia—which was essential to enable him to do some constructive work for the welfare of the citizens of Ahmedabad. He had now been able to bring together a band of honest and efficient officers and workers who were to be nucleus around which he built up his party organisation in the Municipality as well as to help him in his welfare activities. However, it was too much for the British authorities and they resorted to the last weapon in their armour and superseded the Municipality in 1922.

This period of two years 1922-1924, when the Municipality was under suspension, came as a blessing in disguise to Vallabhbhai who was now free to indulge in important national affairs which ultimately helped him to be a leader of national stature.

In the meantime, a bitter controversy had arisen on the question of entry into Legislative Assembly during the 37th annual session of the Congress held at Gaya in December 1922. Some members including C.R. Das, President of the Session, and Pandit Motilal Nehru advocated "Council Entry". Vallabhbhai, as a true disciple of Gandhiji, was against Council Entry and advised that it would be in national interest if emphasis was laid on constructive work. (Doc. 70) Vithalbhai, too, was in favour of Council Entry and there used to be heated discussions between the two brothers. Gandhiji also discussed the matter with him and wrote to Vallabhbhai on 15 July 1921: "I had again a long talk with Vithalbhai. I think he understands the importance of the spinning-wheel better now. I do feel that his proper field is the Councils. He cannot go among the people, mix with them and serve. Only he has not trained himself to do so. He has trained himself with other work. It seems to me that the two kinds of work require different attitudes." Vallabhbhai had withdrawn his candidature from the Bombay Council elections in pursuance of Gandhiji's Non-Cooperation Movement. He had also withdrawn his daughter Maniben from the Convent. His decision to give up legal practice brought great hardship to the family as this was the only source of livelihood. Vallabhbhai thus sacrificed all he had and was a wholetime political worker.

After the arrest of Gandhiji in 1922, Vallabhbhai devoted all his energies to the propagation of his ideals. In an interview to the *Bombay Chronicle* (13 March 1922), he spelt it out at length, and emphasized the constructive work, particularly the Hindu-Muslim unity which was his life's aim. (Doc. 79) As General Secretary of the Gujarat Provincial Congress, he instructed all the district committees to carry on the programme of Gandhiji. (Doc. 85)

Meanwhile, in the Punjab the Akalis were carrying on a relentless struggle against the British Government. The Sikh League, inaugurated in 1919 with the avowed object of safeguarding the political and religious interests of the Sikh people, turned its attention to the mismanagement of the Golden Temple at Amritsar. Under the influence of the prevailing spirit of Non-Cooperation, resolutions were passed at a Sikh Conference in 1920, demanding control by the Sikhs themselves of their religious and educational institutions without interference of any kind from the Government. The body of Puritan Sikhs, known as the Akalis, formed the vanguard of the reforming party. They used to form *jathas* or companies which travelled from shrine to shrine in their work of reformation. Vallabhbhai was full of praise for their sacrifice and non-violent struggle and said that these brave sons of India who had won laurels in many battles "silently watched the *lathi* charge on them by the police, who were ordered by the Government which they had loyally served. . . . Akalis wore only *khadi.* In this crusade Akali women are showing great courage and enthusiasm . . . ." He further added: "Religious sacrifice which is performed in Punjab is such that even gods from heaven would like to come and watch. While the country is peaceful, Akalis have performed the great sacrifice, the honour of which Bardoli could not get. . . ."

The people inhabiting the Borsad and a part of Anand taluka were kept in terror for 6 or 7 years by a gang of two dreaded terrorists Babar Deva and Ali Miyan who committed robberies and murders. The Government was unable to capture the dacoits and blamed the people for refusing to cooperate in giving informaton about their whereabouts. Some 24 informants had been killed by the dacoits; therefore naturally they were hesitant to come forward. Under instructions from Gandhiji and Vallabhbhai, Darbar Saheb Gopaldas Desai tried to persuade the dacoits, particularly their leaders Babar Deva, Ali Miyan and others, to give up their activities which were bringing misery and suffering to many and lead a life of respectable citizens. It was true that initially they were hounded out for some small crimes and were harassed by the police. Darbar Saheb contacted the ruthless dacoit Babar Deva and at the same time approached the Government for leniency. "If you have no faith in what we say, entrust the duties of subduing the outlaws in our hands. We are sure and we promise that all the outlaws will become peaceful citizens within the end of the year and the once happy district of Kaira will again beat the grandeur of the Garden of God." (Darbar Saheb Gopaldas Desai, "To the outlaws", *The Indian Quarterly Register,* Vol. I, January-March 1924). Thus long before Jaya Prakash Narayan started his quiet and admirable movement to bring round the dreaded Chambal Valley dacoits, Vallabhbhai had initiated this process as early as 1924.

Vallabhbhai advised the dacoits if there were any, "Your life is not worth living; you will die on gallows by bullets, by a fall, but one day you are surely going to die. After having committed so many sins, go to the police station, or Government bungalow and confess your crimes, and express regret, so that your sin might recede. . . . Confessing your crime and then to die on gallows is an act of bravery. Simply hiding yourself is cowardice." (Doc. 220)

In reply to Darbar Saheb Gopaldas's appeal (9 January 1924), Babar Deva wrote: "From Kaira accept the *Ram Ram* of Babar Deva. I did not give trouble to anybody without any reason. Now I am not doing the business of dacoits. I have left dacoity. It is that by my name other dacoits commit dacoities and loot the people. But I request you not to get cheated by these dacoits. I came to Kaira for the last two days to see the collector in the evening but the collector saheb was at Borsad. Convey my *Ram Ram* to Shri Vallabhbhai-Bapu."

The police laid the blame on the villagers for not supplying the information and imposed punitive tax on 88 villages of Borsad and 14 villages of Anand Taluka. In an order dated 25 August 1923, the Government ordered that every person above the age of 16 would be liable to pay a tax of Rs 2 and annas 7 per head, irrespective of sex to enable them to post additional police. (Doc. 115)

Vallabhbhai asked the villagers to refuse to pay the punitive tax as it was the duty of the Government to protect its citizens. In the Secret Home Department File (7 December 1923), it is recorded that the *Mamlatdar* agreed that the villagers of Borsad were not in a position to pay fine. The District Superintendent of Police, however, disagreed. Collector in turn supported the contention of the *Mamlatdar* and was also not in favour of posting additional police. (Doc. 198) The Commissioner remarked that "if they ignored that agitation at this stage, it might lead to a struggle of unknown and incalculable dimensions." (Doc. 199)

Vallabhbhai was greatly moved by the atrocities committed by the police on the villages of Borsad and Anand taluka and launched a satyagraha movement in which Darbar Saheb Gopaldas Desai played a very important role. Gopaldas, a close companion of Vallabhbhai, was the ruler of Dhasa village in Kathiawar. He took part in the Kheda satyagraha: his civil and criminal powers were later taken away by the British Government and he was asked to apologize. On his refusal the Government started attachment proceedings against him. Vallabhbhai said, "His sacrifices are fit to be written in letters of gold." (Doc. 161) Though the Government started attachment proceedings ruthlessly, but the people suffered patiently. His message to the people was "Do not interfere in the work of the police. Do not get infuriated or excited even when your dearest articles are attached. . . . The key to our success lies in absolute control over thought, word and action." (Doc. 206)

Meanwhile, Sir Leslie Wilson, who had taken over as Governor of Bombay, found substance in Vallabhbhai's allegations and the tax was withdrawn. Vallabhbhai congratulated the people of Borsad on their victory. "The people of Borsad have won because their cause was absolutely true and just." However, he refused to issue any statement proposed by Gopaldasbhai. "A true satyagrahi does not make the opponent feel that punch of defeat," he said. (Doc. 217) On the other hand, he thanked the Governor Sir Leslie Wilson on the great moral courage he had shown by withdrawing the punitive tax. (Doc. 218) Gandhiji called Vallabhbhai "King of Borsad".

Vallabhbhai and Gandhiji were opposed to Council Entry but to save the split in the Congress they had agreed to the proposal of C.R. Das, Motilal Nehru, Vithalbhai and others to fight the elections and carry on the fight against the British Government from inside the Council. Gandhiji was in jail in 1923 when the tax on salt was enhanced. Vallabhbhai wrote in *Navjivan* on January 14, 1923, "The Government's decision to enhance the salt tax had made it clear that the Legislatures are altogether futile. The proposed tax was rejected by a majority vote not once but twice. Nevertheless the Viceroy ignored the majority and certified the proposal. It was but natural to hope that now at least the Members of the Legislatures would be disillusioned enough to want to quit the Legislatures." Vallabhbhai had the foresight to see as early as 1923 that the enhancement of salt tax by the Government which affected the common man could be an invaluable weapon for a future satyagraha. Gandhiji was to take up this issue later and launch a nation-wide satyagraha which shook the British Government.

An effort was made by Motilal and C.R. Das, at Gaya Congress, that the Congress should give up the boycott of British goods from its programme. But in spite of the fact that Gandhiji was in jail, Vallabhbhai and his followers got the move rejected. Referring to it, Vallabhbhai wrote on January 14, 1923 in *Navjivan:* "The Congress President Deshabandhu Chittaranjan Das had supported the proposal to give up the boycott. Leaders like Motilal Nehru and Hakim Sahib (Ajmal Khan) tried their might but in spite of that the delegates refused to give up the boycott or make it milder." (Doc. 120) In protest C.R. Das resigned from the Presidentship of the Congress and later on started propaganda against Gandhiji and blamed him for not accepting Lord Reading's offer. As Gandhiji was in jail, Vallabhbhai took upon himself to defend him and did not spare his brother Vithalbhai for supporting C.R. Das. In an article in the *Navjivan* of April 22, 1923, he wrote: "For a short time after his (C.R. Das's) release, he kept quiet on the subject of entry into the Legislatures and discoursed in public only on religious and philosophical matters. Some thought that perhaps he might retire into solitude like Aurobindo Ghosh. At an opportune moment, however, he had taken charge of the movement which had been set afoot by Vithalbhai and others. . . ." As he found little support from the public at that time, he accepted a truce for two months. But as soon as he was able to win over AICC he began the frontal attack and Vallabhbhai asked: "Had he ventured to charge Mahatmaji in this bitter manner eight months ago, would anyone had listened to him? But that would not have been Deshbandhu's way." (Doc. 131)

Vallabhbhai did not share his brother Vithalbhai's views on the question of Council Entry, and said: "Patel Saheb who is a supporter of entry into Legislature went to England and knows, therefore, the persons who have drafted the constitution. They designed the Legislatures bearing in mind that people like him would enter the Legislatures; and so they provided safeguards against possible subversive activities and thus made Legislatures practically ineffective . . . ." (Doc. 113)

Motilal Nehru, General Secretary of the Swarajya Party, in a hard-hitting speech criticized the stand of the "No-Changers" who were preparing the country for Civil Disobedience Movement and made it clear that "his party whatever happens will not desist from contesting the forthcoming elections." "In the forthcoming elections", Motilal made it clear that "our battle-cry will be mend or end the Councils." (Doc. 138) Thus he slammed the door of any compromise between Gandhiji and Vallabhbhai and their followers on the one side, and C.R. Das, Vithalbhai, Ajmal Khan and their comrades, on the other. (Doc. 138) Vallabhbhai was of the firm view that they might get some concessions but not "Swaraj". He further added that they were weakening the Non-Cooperation Movement by joining the Councils. Vithalbhai did not agree with his brother Vallabhbhai on this issue and, according to Bombay Police Secret Report (19 May 1923), he told his friends that "as the country was not prepared for civil disobedience and so by working the constructive programme alone, they were not making any progress towards Swaraj; it was therefore proposed that the

Councils should be captured." (Doc. 140) Against this, Vallabhbhai advocated mass Civil Disobedience Movement. (Doc. 142) He even asked leaders of the Council Entry to court arrest at least twice before approaching the people for votes. (Doc. 143)

Vallabhbhai was firmly of the view that by entering the Councils, they could not hope to win the Swaraj. "It cannot be said that only a handful of educated persons can defeat the Government on its own ground and in its own language." He asked the people to forget the Assemblies because they would make us totally powerless. "A man who tries to ride two horses, eventually falls to the ground and if we would do it, we would also fall." (Doc. 194)

The conflict among the members of the Swarajya Party was commented upon by Vallabhbhai on 8 January 1924, while referring to the divergent stand taken by the members of the Punjab, Madras and some others. He said, "That a bewildering confusion of thought now reigns supreme in the ranks of the Swarajya Party has, by this time, been made quite evident. It remains to be seen how far this party will succeed in maintaining coherence and cohesion in its ranks amidst such conflicting views and tendencies." (Doc. 214)

In the absence of Gandhiji, Vallabhbhai was busy organising the people for a non-violent struggle. Soon an opportunity came in 1923 when he was called upon by the Congress Working Committee to lead what later on came to be known as "Nagpur Flag Satyagraha". The genesis of the trouble lay in hoisting the National Flag on the building of the Jabbalpur Municipality on the anniversary of Gandhiji's imprisonment on March 18, 1923. The District Magistrate prohibited it and Pt. Sunderlal who took out the procession with the National Flag was arrested and sentenced to 6 months' imprisonment. Jamnalal who followed also met the same fate. Now Vallabhbhai took over and urged the people of Gujarat for volunteers. In response to his appeal, hundreds of volunteers from all over India began to pour into Nagpur and took out processions with the National Flag. In spite of brutal beatings, all volunteers remained non-violent and courted arrest. Besides Vallabhbhai had to face the criticism of Swarajists who opposed the movement. The Nagpur Provincial Congress Committee was dominated by Swarajists who made Vallabhbhai's work still more difficult. But Vallabhbhai was not to be deterred and exhorted the people of Gujarat on whom he could depend to come forward and join the struggle in Nagpur. "Oh! you residents of Gujarat. Have you heard the mysterious sound of drum beats from the holy warfield of Nagpur? Remember, the flag that was hoisted on the *pandal* of the Congress session; held on the banks of the Sabarmati in presence of Mahatma Gandhi is being dishonoured at Nagpur. . . . No country has got most precious object like this without sacrifice. Today we are fighting for retention of our flag . . . . Get yourself recruited as satyagraha soldiers, sign the pledge and march towards Nagpur when ordered." (Doc. 152)

While fighting this battle almost single-handed, Vallabhbhai felt the absence of Gandhiji, as most of other leaders were not co-operating as they—the Swarajists—were against this struggle. Vallabhbhai gave vent to his anguish in a letter to Mahadev Desai (12 July 1923): "But here we have an orchestra in which every person plays whatever tune he likes. All the English newspapers are either opposed to the struggle or are indifferent."

C.R. Das's death, a little later however, changed the situation. Sir J.H. Kerr, Governor of Bengal, informed the Viceroy, Lord Lytton on July 1, 1925 that "The fact is that his party have not yet rallied from the shock and have not yet had time to settle on any particular line of policy. . . . There was apparently some opposition from the extremist section on the ground of Sen Gupta's mode of life and his English wife, but she undertook, according to our report, to wear *khaddar* in future and to abjure drinking and European ball dancing." With the result that with Gandhiji's help he was elected unanimously (MSS Eur F160/32). The Governor also foresaw the split of the Swarajya Party into two sections viz.—the politicians and the revolutionaries.

Vallabhbhai was determined to keep religious harmony at all costs and when there were some communal disturbances, he issued an appeal on 6 October 1923 along with other Congress leaders—Lajpat Rai, Motilal Nehru, Hakim Ajmal Khan and others—stressing on the people that "if any individual or group of individuals belonging to any community commits any act of violence against or attacks the person, property or honour of women or place of worship of his fellow townsmen or helps those who indulged in such misdeeds, he is, from the religious point of view, guilty of a great sin; and that it is the duty of co-religionists of such offenders to stand up to resist these miscreants and protect those who are so attacked." (Doc. 188)

Before his departure for Nagpur to participate in the Flag Satyagraha, Vallabhbhai made an impassionate appeal to his countrymen, particularly Gujaratis, to maintain Hindu-Muslim unity at all costs. (Doc. 156) Later on Mahadev Desai, in his letter to Vallabhbhai on 24 October 1924, thus paid him a tribute that "Whatever happens to Hindus and Muslims in Gujarat, Bapu is not worried."(Doc. 244)

In between sometimes he did feel concern about his motherless son and daughter and wrote to Mahadev, "I hope you and Devdas will be able to find time to look up my children; they should not feel desolate. I cannot understand why Maniben wept. This is not the time to weep. She has plenty of courage. After giving advice to people in C.P. to go to jail, how can we cry." (Doc. 155)

Sir Leslie Wilson, Governor of Bombay, in his letter of 21st July 1925, to Lord Lytton, the Viceroy, had rejected the British assumption that the "declamation of politicians of Hindu-Muslim Unity are dishonest. These declamations seem to me to be usually the result of self-deception arising from the shallow thought and historical ignorance of these men. Apart from the outward and visible sign of religious difference between Hindu Idolatory and Mahommedan Monotheism, I gather that the true basis of disunion is economic." Lord Wilson, however, agreed with Lord Ronaldshay that the "existence of the seventy millions of Moslems in India is the most formidable obstacle in the way of those whose battle-cry is 'India a Nation'." (MSS Eur F 160/32).

Vallabhbhai organised the Nagpur Flag Satyagraha in a methodical manner asking the Congress Committees in various provinces to keep a regular supply of volunteers who were willing to court arrest and bear hardships. In the jail in those days conditions were very harsh and the prisoners had to grind corn 30 to 50 pounds per day and were provided with *chappatis* of very coarse grain which was difficult to digest. In spite of all these hardships about 1,200 persons courted arrest.

The intensity of the Flag Satyagraha movement caused grave concern in Government circles. In a Memorandum addressed to Secretary of State, dated 6 December 1923, and signed by high-ranking British and Indian officials referred to the magnitude of the Flag Satyagraha Agitation and said, "The agitation had assumed more clearly than at any previous stage the aspect of a contest between the Government established by law and the forces organised against it, and His Excellency the Governor justly summed up the position in his address to the Legislative Council in the following words: 'The Local Government regards the agitation as clearly civil disobedience, an attempt to overcome the authority of Government. . . .'" (Doc. 197)

Meanwhile, Vithalbhai started negotiations with the authorities in which Vallabhbhai was also invited on the invitation of W.M. Hailey, the Member-in-charge, Home Department, in Viceroy's Council. Both the brothers met him and the terms of settlement were arrived at. Permission was granted to the people to take out a procession through civil lines carrying the National Flag and it was also agreed to release the prisoners arrested in connection with the ṣatyagraha. Vallabhbhai came back to Ahmedabad victorious. But the British authorities were displeased with the high officials of the Central Provinces for agreeing to these conditions and even the Secretary of State expressed his displeasure over the handling of the issue. In a Secret Note dated 19 October 1923, Sir W.M. Hailey, Member-in-charge in Viceroy's Executive Council, informed the Private Secretary to the Viceroy that the C.P. Government did not inform them about the agreement to release the political prisoners. The Secretary of State took serious note of it. The Government of India placed the blame on the Central Provinces Government and informed the Secretary of State that the "Local Government should have consulted the Government of India before entering upon negotiations for it must have been obvious that their action would have repercussions far beyond their own province. . . . It is very inconvenient that news of such action should reach the Government of India and myself through newspapers. It is merely due to accident that Parliament had risen that matter did not immediately lead to very embarrassing criticism here." (Doc. 185)

Vallabhbhai was very happy over the victory and in a letter dated 1 September 1923, he informed Mahadev Desai how the entire Civil Service Club in Nagpur had become anti-Government as they saw in it "total defeat of the Government". (Doc. 172) However, Vallabhbhai made it clear that the campaign was thus directed not for the purpose of claiming an unrestricted use of public roads or for insulting the Union Jack, or for antagonising any section of the people but for cooperation. In spite of preoccupations, Shri Verma took great pains to meet the ministers concerned to get an accommodation for the Society allotted. Our special thanks are due to Shri R.K. Hegde, former Chief Minister of Karnataka and to Chaudhary Devi Lai, former Chief Minister of Haryana and now Deputy Prime Minister of India, for their financial support without which it would not have been possible to implement the Project. Shri Amar Sinh Chaudhary, Chief Minister of Gujarat, Shri Motilal Vora, former Chief Minister of Madhya Pradesh, Shri N.D. Tiwari, then Chief Minister of Uttar Pradesh and Shri N.T. Rama Rao, then Chief Minister of Andhra Pradesh, have very kindly sanctioned financial help which will assuredly help in the expeditious completion of the Project. We have also approached the Central Government for allocation of the 9 Motilal Nehru Marg opposite to 1 Aurnagzeb Road, New Delhi, where the Great Sardar lived during his tenure as Deputy Prime Minister of India and completed the merger of 500 odd States in the Indian Union. We intend to build there a suitable memorial, a comprehensive library, a photographic exhibition, meeting rooms, auditorium, etc. and also to institute an annual lecture in the memory of this Great Son of India.

To Km. Maniben, India, particularly the historians, owe a deep debt of gratitude for preserving the private correspondence of her illustrious father so meticulously. But for her the posterity would have been deprived of such an invaluable source material for writing an objective history of India's freedom struggle and later on in the unification of the country.

Dr. Prabha Chopra has helped me throughout in the completion and editing of the volume. I would also like to express my thanks to Dr. Ravindra Kumar who helped us in the collection of material for this volume. Shri A.P. Venkateshwaran and Dr. S.R. Bakshi took keen interest in the compilation of this volume. Prof. C.K. Mehta and Shri D.P. Pandey have kindly translated into English the material in Gujarati and Hindi respectively. Shri Subhash Sharma alongwith Shri Hardeep Singh took pains to type out the manuscript.

Our thanks are due to Shri Babubhai J. Patel, Chairman and Shri Nathubhai N. Naik, Director, Sardar Vallabhbhai Patel Memorial Society, Ahmedabad, for making available to us records in their possession. Shri Hitendra Desai, Managing Trustee, Navjivan Trust, has kindly extended to us all possible cooperation. Shri Yashwant Shukla, Convenor, Gujarat Vidya Sabha, has always been helpful. We are also obliged to the authorities in charge of the Ahmedabad Municipality for allowing us to look into their records.

We are indebted to Prof. B.C. Bloomfield, Director and Mr. A.J. Farrington, Deputy Director, India Office Library and Records, London, for their unstinted help and cooperation.

I would also like to take this opportunity to express my thanks to Shri K.K. Chaudhary, State Editor, Gazetteers Maharashtra; Director, Maharashtra State Archives and Director, Baroda State Archives for their cooperation. I am also indebted to Director, National Archives of India and Director and Deputy

Director, Nehru Memorial Museum and Library and their staff for permitting us to consult records in their custody.

Our special thanks are due to Shri V.C. Jain and Shri K.P.R. Nair of Konark Publishers Private Ltd., New Delhi, for undertaking the publication of *The Collected Works of Sardar Vallabhbhai Patel* with patriotic devotion and dedication.

New Delhi, P.N. CHOPRA
January 1990

Abbreviations

A.I.C.C.	All India Congress Committee
A.P.	Associated Press
A.S.P.	Assistant Superintendent of Police
B.I.P.C.	British Indian Penal Code
B.N.R.	Bengal-Nagpur Railways
B.P.C.C.	Bengal Provincial Congress Committee
C.D.	Civil Disobedience
C.I.D.	Criminal Investigation Department
C.I.O.	Central Intelligence Officer
C.P.	Central Provinces
C.P.	Communist Party
C.P.C.	Congress Provincial Committee
Cr.P.C.	Criminal Procedure Code
D.I.B.	Director of Intelligence Bureau
D.I.G.	Deputy Inspector-General of Police
D.M.	District Magistrate
G.O.C.	General Officer Commanding
H.M.G.	His Majesty's Government
I.B.	Intelligence Bureau
I.C.P.	Indian Communist Party
I.C.S.	Indian Civil Service
I.E.S.	Indian Education Service
I.G.	Inspector-General
I.N.C.	Indian National Congress
L.L.B.	Bachelor of Law
M.L.A.	Member of Legislative Assembly
P.C.C.	Provincial Congress Committee
P.S.V.	Private Secretary to the Viceroy
P.W.D.	Public Works Department
R.I.	Rigorous Imprisonment
S.P.	Superintendent of Police
T.U.	Trade Union
T.U.C.	Trade Union Congress

Abstracts of Documents

1

Vallabhbhai to Narsibhai[1] *on His Inability to Render Financial Help to Family due to Closing of Courts*

GODHRA
16 March 1901

RESPECTED NARSIBHAI,

The plague is spreading here virulently. Every day there are about ten cases and rats are dying in large numbers. It is possible that the epidemic will continue for some time. There is no work in the Courts and it appears that for the next two to three months, things will continue like this. I would, therefore, have to spend money from my own pocket to keep body and soul together. But please do not worry about it. I passed for which I am thankful to God. Good days will return and all problems would be solved. Please do not worry on my account. I had thought that when I have a good practice, I would come to visit you, but for the present I cannot. I would help you to the best of my ability. You know that I love my family and my worries have ended after my passing the examination. I am always thinking of how I should help you. God has been kind to me and even when the bad days are here, I am not losing courage. When my condition improves, you would also realise my position. For the present, I am helpless. If the plague spreads further, I would send Kashibhai. Please continue to inform me about the family and its affairs.

Please take care of father. Rest is O.K. If I can be of any service to you, please do not hesitate to tell me.

Yours affectionately,
VALLABHBHAI

[1]Narsibhai Jhaverbhai, elder brother of Vallabhbhai.

2

Vallabhbhai to Narsibhai Expressing Anguish at Financial Difficulties Facing Family

Sardar Shrino Patro[1]

BORSAD[2]
75 *January 1904*

RESPECTED NARSIBHAI,

I received your letter today. As I had to go to Nadiad for my personal work, I had written the letter and kept it with me. But suddenly because of some work I had to cancel my journey, hence yesterday I have sent the letter to Dungerbhai[3] at Nadiad. So, today he must have paid the money to Naranbhai. I had not the least idea that you must be needing it badly. I have written to return the money with interest and so you need not worry in the matter. . . you have written about the mortgage of sister's ornaments that does not behove you. Yet you are elder, and so you must have done whatever you must have thought proper. I have already written to return the money. I did not take it as a joke as you think. In a day or two you will receive the letter about the receipt of money. You have written that you are in debt. But I understand that your debt is my debt. So you write to me the names of the creditors, so I will relieve you as quickly as possible from the debt so that you heave a sigh of relief.

Second thing is now you have not to do farm work from now onwards. Only keep the account of running the household and take the expenses from us. Please don't feel bad about it, because land tilling activity of both the brothers[4] adversely affects your health. Not only that you had to put bone breaking labour, and the benefit is much less. Therefore, from today you send the account of whatever you spend and we will send the money every month.

Kashibhai has come there. Send him here immediately and make him understand, it is not good to live the life of a vagabond after he has attained maturity. I don't understand why he has left Nadiad and gone there. We are thinking of sending him to Bombay.[5] So you send him here.

If Somabhai is cured of fever, then if he is here, he will get good medical treatment and he will get much relief. Even if he is cured of fever, then also if he stays here for some time, then he will regain his health. So send him here.

If I can do anything for you, please write to me.

Yours obediently,
VALLABHBHAI

[1]In Gujarati, vol. Ill, edited by G.M. Nardurkar, 1976.

[2]Having practised in Godhra for about two years, Sardar practised at Borsad, and stayed there for about eight years.

[3]Sardar's maternal uncle Dungerbhai Jijibhai Desai.

[4]Somabhai was eldest and Narsinghbhai was second.

[5]For further studies.

3

Vallabhbhai to Narsibhai Explaining Reasons for His Proceeding to London without Meeting Him[1]

LONDON
16 December 1910

RESPECTED BROTHER NARSIBHAI,

Received your letter. I was writing letter continuously to Kashibhai, in which I had asked him to keep me informed about the news from home, and give you my news. But he does not reply.

I am quite well. Please write to me off and on giving the news on the domestic front. I have written to Dahiba[2] about Mani,[3] so Mani will stay with Dahiba.

As new law[4] came into force, out of helplessness I had to rush her hurriedly. Otherwise it was not possible for me to come here. I think all of you are offended. But it was not possible for me to come later. Therefore I had to hurry. Now if God willing the time would pass very quickly and again I shall have the good fortune to be with you and father and mother.

When I was there I did my best for our home, and looked after everything. At present I am not in a position to do anything. Tell my *pranams* to father and mother. Do write to me off and on.

Yours obediently,
VALLABHBHAI

[1]In 1909 after the demise of his wife on August 1910, Vallabhbhai left for England for studying law.
[2]Sardar's younger sister, Maniben used to stay there during holidays.
[3]Daughter Maniben.
[4]Only LL.B's from India could appear for examination for admission to Bar-at-Law.

4

Vallabhbhai Informing Narsibhai about His Passing Examination in London Standing First

Sardar Shrino Patro-3

LONDON
19 January 1911

RESPECTED NARSIBHAI,

Kashibhai does not write to me at all and I do not get any information about the family. I request you to kindly keep on writing to me and also tell Kashibhai to keep in touch.

I appeared for an examination in which I got the first place. Please pay my regards to father and mother.

I am keeping good health and you need not worry about me. With God's grace, these two years would pass quickly and I would be back.

I hope that Kashibhai is all right. Please remember me to everybody.

Respectfully yours,
VALLABHBHAI

5

Vallabhbhai to Narsibhai regarding His Return to India in a Year's Time

Sardar Shrino Patro-5

LONDON
26 April 1912

RESPECTED NARSIBHAI,

Received your letter. My health is good. I will be returning there in about a year's time. Tell (*sic*) my obeisance to father, mother and all others.

Please write to me off and on about the health of everybody. I have written several letters to Kashibhai[1] but there is no reply.

You must be well.

Remember me to everybody.

Vallabhbhai's
highest regards

[1]Kashibhai Patel, Sardar's younger brother.

6

Vallabhbhai to Return to India Six Months Earlier

Sardar Shrino Patro-3

MIDDLE TEMPLE, E.C.
7 June 1912

RESPECTED NARSIBHAI,

I have completed my examinations and have passed in the First Class. It means that I shall be coming six months earlier than usual which could be sometime in January next. January is not far and God has been kind that He reduced the period of my stay here by six months. Please inform father and mother about this and remember me to all our relatives.

I hope that everybody is well. With love to all.

Yours affectionately,
VALLABHBHAI

7

Vallabhbhai to Narsibhai about His Visit to U.K. Villages

Sardar Shrino Patro-3

LONDON
22 August 1912

RESPECTED NARSIBHAI,

Received your letter. After the results of the examination were declared, I had gone to the villages here and roamed about. Now I am back in London. I have regained my health, because of changes in the atmosphere, and being relieved of the studies. I am glad to know that father and mother are well. Now I have to spend only five months here, yet definite date of my return journey is not fixed. I will inform you when it will be fixed.

Tell all our relatives that I am well, and write to me about their wellbeing.

My respectful *pranams* to my parents.

Yours obediently,
VALLABHBHAI PATEL

8

Patel's Resolution urging Government to Remove Reactionary British Engineer in Ahmedabad Municipality

7 June 1917

Ahmedabad Municipality, Administration Report, 1916-17

The attitude adopted by the Municipal Commissioner on the question of the Suskar Tank has put the Board in a very difficult situation. It should either accept the retrograde attitude of the Municipal Commissioner and his uncivilized behaviour or take to the only other alternative which is open to it.

Mr. Shilidi had given his opinion in writing to the Government without consulting the Board and has said that the Municipal Committee does not need the tank because it is of no use to it. The Sanitary Committee's resolution that the tank belongs to the Municipality is without any foundation. In the last resolution of the Committee it has been made out as if every controversy has been decided in its favour and the application made by some taxpayers to the Municipality President is a plot on the part of the Sanitary Committee.

This Board is sorry to note that a person in the position of Mr. Shilidi who is an officer of the Municipality does not consider that 53,000 sq. yards of land, valued at not less than Rs 1 lakh, which is situated near the Kankaria Railway Station and can be very useful for a developing city like Ahmedabad where houses can be built in future, of no consequence.

The Board is sorry to note that the Municipal Commissioner did not consider it his duty to protect the proprietory rights of the Municipality. Not only that, when the Municipality tried to assert its proprietary right, he sent his letter dated 6th December, 1916 along with the resolution of the Municipality to the Government and tried to stultify the efforts of the committee. By doing this, he is guilty of putting his personal interest above those of the people.

His impudent reply, his baseless charges and his efforts to derive the resolutions of the Councillors is harmful for the Municipality as a whole. Not only that he has tried to create discontent and dissensions.

When all the papers had been put up before the President and they were in the custody of the Board, he cut off the last thirteen words of his letter to the Government and the least that can be said about it is this that his conduct was extremely objectionable.

Under these circumstances, it becomes necessary for the Board in the interest of proper functioning of the Municipality that Mr. Shilidi cannot remain as the Municipal Commissioner of this Municipality. The Board, therefore, requests the President that when the administrative report of the Municipality is sent to the Government, it should be accompanied by a copy of this resolution.[1]

[1]Commenting on that resolution the President wrote, "... It is a matter of great regret that in several matters there has been a friction between the Municipal Commissioner and the General Board of the Municipal Councillors (as represented by their majority). The General Board has resolved on the 7th June 1917 that I should forward to the Government along with the Administration Report a copy of the resolution passed by them on that date in connection with the Suskar Tank and it is my painful duty to do so. The majority in favour of the resolution was less than three-fourths of the whole number of councillors and has not therefore the force of section 186 B(93) of the Bombay District Municipal Act, 1901..." (*Administration Report,* 1916-17, Ahmedabad Municipality).

9

Vallabhbhai Justifies His Advice to Villagers Not to Pay Taxes

Prajabandhu, 27 March 1918

It is stated in the summons that I am creating difficulties in the work of revenue collection by misguiding the people. But I have neither given wrong advice nor have I incited anybody in an unjustified way; I do not think that the people have either misunderstood the situation or been made excited by me. I have given them only reasonable and right advice. I estimate the crop in my village to be a 25 per cent crop and, therefore, even in accordance with the normal rules, the people of my village are within their rights in not paying land revenue.

Mahatma Gandhi advised agriculturists of Kheda publicly at a big meeting on the 22nd March that they should of their own free will refuse to pay any money both in order to maintain their self-respect and also to prove that their case was not false. I consider that advice to be sound and therefore regard it my duty to advise other people accordingly. I do not think that in doing so I am breaking any law or encouraging bad behaviour in any way. Nevertheless, if there is any breach of law, I am prepared to undergo the requisite punishment. I must, however, tell you that the Section under which you have summoned me is not applicable to this charge. Who am I, however, to suggest that that fact is not known to you? Nevertheless, since you have invited me to attend, I have come, and I am grateful to you. Whether you will make me still more grateful by sending me to jail is for you to decide.

10

Vallabhbhai Exhorts Peasants of Kheda to Accept the Challenge

Prajabandhu, 31 March 1918

This fight will act as a spark which will set the whole country afire. Happiness cannot be obtained without undergoing trials and tribulations, and if per chance you get happiness easily, it does not last very long. A State ought to be proud of a people who are strong and determined. There is nothing to be gained from the loyalty of a cowardly and cringing public. The loyalty which you get from a fearless (*sic*) and self-respecting people is the loyalty which a Government should welcome. The Government has granted postponement for land revenue of Rs 1-3/4 lakhs out of a total assessment of Rs 23 lakhs. The first instalment has also been nearly paid. Thus only a sum of about Rs 10 lakhs remains to be paid. It might be thought that if we collected this much from Bombay or from Gujarat and paid it to the Government, the people would be saved much hardship. The brave man, who has inspired this fight however, is capable of converting the cowardly into the bravest of persons, and in India Kheda District is the land of brave men. They will not think in terms of receiving assistance in this manner. There is no real advantage to be gained from such monetary assistance. It may, of course, postpone hardship for a while. But it is only if you are prepared to face hardships now and get the Government to change its policy, that you can remove this source of hardship for all time.

11

Vallabhbhai to Lallubhai regarding Gandhiji's Visit

Sardar Shrino Vishishta Aur Anokhe Patro-2

ANATHASHRAM, NADIAD
2 April 1918

DEAR LALLUBHAI,

Mahatma Gandhi and I are scheduled to reach Odd tomorrow. Kindly make arrangements for a vehicle to wait for us at Bhajal railway station.

Secondly, please inform the people of the villages around and collect the people.[1] We want to return by the evening train. Everything must be done before that. Please do not put yourself to any inconvenience on our account. Gandhiji, as you know, does not eat any regular meals and I shall also take some fruits as he does. Do not make any special arrangements for our food.

This is something which Bhukhabhai, Motibhai and you have to do together.

Yours,
VALLABHBHAI

[1]At the peak of Kheda Satyagraha, Gandhiji was invited by the Viceroy to attend the War Conference where he urged him as a citizen of the British Empire to help in the recruitment of soldiers. Gandhiji agreed and undertook this tour. Though the people were not enthusiastic nor was Sardar Patel, but their loyalty to Gandhiji was unflinching.

12

Vallabhbhai Urges Villagers of Borsad to have Faith in Gandhiji

Prajabandhu, 13 April 1918

The Commissioner has told you about the pledge which the mill-workers of Ahmedabad took. I feel it is my duty to clear up a misunderstanding, because I was one of those who intervened in that dispute. It is not correct to say that the mill-workers were forced to break their pledge. Right from the outset it had been decided that if the mill-owners accepted arbitration, the mill-workers would accept whatever increase the arbitrators considered reasonable, and would resume work. The arbitrators were appointed. On the first day of resumption of work the workers received an increase of 35 per cent; thereafter they accepted an increase of 27-1/2 per cent on the understanding that when the arbitrators declared their award, whatever adjustment was necessary to be made in their wages to make it accord with the award will be made in due course. When this settlement was reached, our commissioner was also present. He has great regard for Gandhiji and Gandhiji too has great regard for him; so have I. In that meeting the Commissioner told the workers: "Gandhiji will give you right advice. If you follow it you will do well and will get justice." I am telling you the same that if in this matter too you follow the advice of Gandhiji, you will receive justice at the hands of this very Commissioner. If Government appoints a committee and has the facts ascertained, every thing will be simple.

13

Pratt Commissioner, Northern Division, Advises Villagers to Pay Land Revenue

Prajabandhu, 15 April 1918

I would like you to listen to me attentively and repeat to every body what I say, when you go back to your villages so that what I say to you now may come to be known throughout the district; for what I am going to say to you today is not only for you but for the whole district. You have been given much advice by Mahatma Gandhi and Vallabhbhai Saheb and other gentlemen who are working with them. They have made speeches from village to village but today I would request you to listen to me.

The rights of the agriculturists are such that they can keep the land in their possession for generations. But those rights carry with them the duty to pay regularly the land revenue assessment fixed according to law. It is only on that condition that you can continue to enjoy the possession of your land. It is the Government who determines the assessment through the instrumentality of its officers and without the intervention of any lawyer or barrister. No one but the Government has the right to fix the assessment. It is not a matter of which the civil courts can take cognizance. No one can go to a court with a complaint that the land revenue assessment is too high. The agriculturists have no legal right to demand or to insist upon the postponement of the assessment. That is entirely within our gift. We issue orders after taking into account the condition of the crop and any complaints and objections that may be raised. After the final order is passed, there is no appeal. It is not a matter for Gandhiji or Vallabhbhai, and on that particular issue your fight will be in vain. That is what I wish to impress upon you and you must pay heed to these words, not merely because they are my words, but because they represent the legal position. It is not merely my order but that of Lord Willingdon. I have in my possession his letter which says that he will accept whatever order I will pass in this matter. You must, therefore, realize that it is not just I who am talking today but His Excellency the Governor.

Mr. Gandhi is a very good man, a very holy man and he gives you advice because he believes genuinely and honestly that it is in your interest. He thinks that by not paying up the land revenue assessment, you will be protecting the poor; that is what he was telling me when he saw me yesterday. But isn't the Government the protector of the poor? Is it the duty of you to remember the days of the famine? In the famine of 1900, in the famine of 1902 caused by rats, I was the Collector of Ahmedabad and Panchmahal Districts. You will remember how many works had been opened by the Government for assisting the poor. I remember how many hundreds of thousands of rupees were spent for feeding the people, in building tanks and in giving taqavi loans. Those amongst you who are old will certainly remember those days. It is against such a Government that today your fight in this district is being waged. There is a big war going on in the world, and the circumstances are such that it is the duty of you all to give the Government every assistance. But instead of that what does the Government get from this district? Does it get assistance, or does it get opposition?

If you continue this fight against the Government it will be you who will have to bear the consequences and not these gentlemen of the Home Rule League. They will not suffer in any way. They are not the people who will go to jail. When a movement of this kind was started in Africa, Mahatma Gandhi went to jail. In this country he will not go to jail. Jail is not a fit place for him. I tell you again that he is a very good and a very holy man.

The Government does not harbour any anger against you. If children kick their parents, the parents are sad, but they do not get angry. Why must you suffer all this loss; forfeiture, *chauthai* fine, confiscation, the disruption of the *Narva*[1] right? Why do you want to destroy your property by your own hands? Do you wish to lose your *Narva* right? Do you not care for your women and children? Would you like to be reduced to the status of labourers, and what for?

I have 28 years' experience of land revenue law. Mahatma Gandhi is my friend. He came to this country from Africa only two or three years ago; he has spent the greater part of his life in Africa. He is well-versed in religion. Whatever advice he gives on the subject is sound, but in political matters, in matters concerning land and land revenue assessment, he knows very little. I know far more about these matters, and I shall be sorry to see you suffer the consequences of your ill-advised actions. I shall be sorry to see the lands of good *Patidars* confiscated. Government knows that there has been a misunderstanding regarding the rights of agriculturists. Therefore, the benevolent Government is giving you this final opportunity of listening to its advice.

I have come here to give you this advice, and I have only this to say that it is the duty of the agriculturists to pay up their land revenue dues. Do not think that our *mamlatdars* and *talatis* will collect money by seizing and selling your property. They will not take so much trouble. Our time is very valuable. They will not go to anybody's house to collect the money. I am not threatening you. You must realize that parents do not threaten but merely give advice. If you will not pay your assessment, your land will be confiscated. Many people tell you that that will not be so. But I tell you that that will be so. It is not necessary for me to take any pledge to that effect, but I have the authority to make good my words. Those who refuse to pay land revenue assessment will not get back their land. The government does not wish to retain on their books such agriculturists, nor are we anxious to include the names of such in our records of rights. Once those names have been removed they will not be re-entered.

Now, let me tell you one more thing in conclusion. If anyone, through misunderstanding or mistake, takes a pledge, he need not consider himself bound by that pledge. Such a pledge need not be kept. If you break such a pledge no one can say to you that you have sinned or have committed a mistake. The world will regard such a person as innocent. You will recollect what happened in Ahmedabad. Many of you may not read newspapers; therefore I will tell you. There was a struggle recently in Ahmedabad between the millowners and the mill hands. The latter had taken oath that they would not go back to work until they got an increase of 35 per cent in their wages. But what happened in the end? When they realized that their pledge was not reasonable they could not adhere to it, they broke it and accepted an increase of 27-1/2 per cent and resumed work. In the same way, I tell you that when you took this pledge, you made a mistake. You did it only because you forgot your duty towards the Government. You did not give full weight to the consequences of this pledge; consequences not only to yourself but to your children. Taking into account all this I ask you to think again and decide whether you should do your duty by the Government or adhere to your pledge and suffer the consequences?

[1]*Narva* is a system of land tenure peculiar to this part of Gujarat.

14

Vallabhbhai Corrects Commissioner's Observation

Prajabandhu, 15 April 1918

The Commissioner had told you about the pledge which the mill-workers of Ahmedabad took. I feel it is my duty to clear up a misunderstanding, because I was one of those who intervened in that dispute. It is not correct to say that the mill-workers were forced to break their pledge. Right from the outset it had been decided that if the mill-owners accepted arbitration, the mill-workers would accept whatever increase the arbitrators considered reasonable, and would resume work. The arbitrators were appointed. On the first day of resumption of work the workers received an increase of 35 per cent; thereafter they accepted in increase of 27-1/2 per cent on the understanding that when the arbitrators declared their award, whatever adjustment was necessary to be made in their wages to make it accord with the award will be made in due course. When this settlement was reached, our Commissioner was also present. He has great regard for Gandhiji and Gandhiji too has great regard for him; so have I. In that meeting the Commissioner told the workers: "Gandhiji will give you right advice. If you follow it, you will do well and will get justice." I am telling you the same that if in this matter too you follow the advice of Gandhiji, you will receive justice at the hands of this very Commissioner. If Government appoints a committee and has the facts ascertained, everything will be simple.

15

Vallabhbhai urges People of Kheda to remain United and Fearless during Satyagraha[1]

Navjivan, 18 April 1918

The land of this sea coast has been consecrated because Mahatma Gandhi came here today. The people of Borsad Tehsil are considered to be the most pugnacious throughout the district. The people on the sea coast are thought to be the most quarrelsome.

Now Satyagraha has been started here and we should give up mutual quarrels, robbery, cheating and other crimes. We should seek the path of justice. Whatever zeal you have, utilize it in this battle for justice. Please do not misuse your strength. Stop using the sickle for killing people. Live like brothers and be humble. Let us firmly demand our rights. Stop being afraid of the tehsildar and demand your rights with courage. You are not lower than a Tehsildar. Sometimes a Tehsildar may not have even 25 bighas of land . We do not have to help him. If you want to honour him, you can entertain him at your house but there is no need to be afraid of him. The main purpose of our fight is to rid the people of their fear and to do away with harmful customs, mutual quarrels and other troubles.

The government would create problems for you but there is no happiness without pain. The best way is to accept pain voluntarily. I know that if you are given proper guidance, you can follow the truth path. Justice is on our side in this fight. You have shown your love for Mahatma Gandhi and I am sure that you would follow the path shown by him.

What would the government do? It would attach your property, impose a fine of 25 per cent of the land revenue and may take over your lands. But do not start a riot. I have seen that when your land is being attached, you take up arms. We do not have to use any force. If the land is taken over, it is not that the whole village will lose its land. After all, you would be the one to till it. Remember that a potter puts about a maund of things on his donkey. If it is able to carry it, he increases the load to two maunds. Similarly as you carry the load, the government goes on adding to it. Throw away the load which you have been carrying so far and do not be afraid. Follow the truth and even the government would admit that the people have not been emasculated.

In the end, I would request that whatever happens, you must stick to your decision. If you do it, the name of Kheda district would find an honourable mention in the history of India. The whole of the country is looking towards you. The government would have to give justice to the people which they are demanding. If the people unite, the government will not be able to go against their wishes. If this government calls itself just, it cannot do otherwise.

Only by following this path, you would be able to ensure prosperity for the coming generations.

[1]Speech made before the villagers of Raas village on 18 April 1918 during the Kheda Satyagraha. The village is situated on the sea coast.

16

Vallabhbhai on Repression Let Loose on the Peasants of Kaira

Stray Pamphlet issued in May 1918

A bitter war is on between the public and the blind administration. The Government is determined to recover land revenue and is using all the resources at its command. It has appointed special officers and has even recruited clerks of courts for the purpose. It has issued notices and orders of forfeiture throughout the district. It has auctioned many houses. It has imposed the *chauthai* fine widely. It has auctioned standing crops. It has threatened imprisonment. But in spite of all this the public has stood firm. If the officers tried, the Commissioner came to their assistance. He threatened with dire consequences all the agriculturists at Nadiad. He read to them the Governor's letter in which permission was given for the forfeiture of land, and stopped all auctions of moveable properties. The agriculturists took all this cheerfully. But in the net result, the Government was recovering no money at all. . . so the Government gave up confiscations and re-started auctions of moveable properties. . . .

In order to give the agriculturists as much trouble as possible, even when there was other property which could be auctioned, they took charge of milk-giving buffaloes and kept them in the sun. They separated them from their little calves. This reduced the price of the buffalo by half. Even so the agriculturists adhered to their pledge patiently and bore whatever hardship they were called upon to bear. Women found it difficult to be eye-witnesses to the bad treatment that was meted out to their carefully looked after cattle. Nevertheless they showed great courage.

The longer the fight lasts the stiffer is the test which the public have to pass. But without such hardships they cannot have this unique experience. Many bureaucrats find they receive no welcome in any village. Persons who were obtaining whatever they wanted free of cost are unable now to get anything even on payment. Their attitude is beginning to change and it would seem as if they had a vague feeling that there was some truth in the people's case but they are helpless before the current policy of the Government. In such difficult circumstances if the Government oversteps the limits, is itself angered, and harasses us, we, for our part, should not act unreasonably, never be impolite or lose our temper but commiserate rather than be angry, and be always peaceful. Even the hardest heart can be conquered by love and the more the opponent is stiff the more should our affection go out to him. Only, so, shall we be able to win. That is the significance of Satyagraha.

17

Vallabhbhai Exhorts People of Kheda to Carry on Struggle in spite of Sufferings[1]

May 1918[2]

Our fight is for truth and that is what Satyagraha means. It is a fight between the people and a blind government. The government have decided to forcibly realise land revenue and the people have taken a vow that they would respectfully disregard and disobey the immoral orders of the government and if the government uses coercion, the people would accept all the troubles, but would not pay land revenue.

The officers have started attachment proceedings. Two special officers have been appointed for realization of land revenue in the Matar Tehsil. Even the employees of the courts have been put on this job. Attachment notices have been issued throughout the district and proceedings have been undertaken at the houses of prominent citizens. Eviction orders have been issued. Twentyfive per cent of the land revenue is to be realized as fines. Standing crops have been attached. The people have stood firm in spite of the danger of imprisonment and the officers have accepted defeat. It was then that the Commissioner came to their aid. All the farmers of Nadiad were summoned and threatened. The letter of the Governor was read out to them. He announced that attachment proceedings would be stopped. The Commissioner thought that the people would be frightened but when he heard the courageous reply of the farmers, he was surprised because in his 28 years of political service, he had not come across such persons. The officers issued eviction notices and when the notice forms were exhausted, they issued orders for eviction. The people welcomed these orders but did not pay a single *anna* to the government. Finally, the experienced Collector whose job it was to give justice to the people had to go and the new Collector took over. He dropped the eviction proceedings and started attaching the lands.

Attachments were carried out in all villages but the people stood firm. The farmers of Kheda district are the lovers of their cattle. They consider them as the members of their families. The wives of the farmers wake up from deep slumber in the night twice or thrice to feed their buffaloes. The cattle have shining coats and if you pinch them, you are afraid that blood will flow out. The families of the farmers depend on their cattle for sustenance. They cannot see their cattle in distress.

The officers responsible for attachments have taken full advantage of this situation. In spite of the fact that there were other household goods which could be attached, they have taken away buffaloes and other milch cattle just to cause the greatest pain to their owners. At some places, the cattle were taken away and tethered in the sun. At many places, their calves were taken away. When the cattle lay with pain and fear, the women and children of the farmers start crying. During attachment proceedings, the prices of the buffaloes fall to 50 per cent of the normal. Even so the farmers have stuck to their guns and have quietly undergone the pain. The farmers are tempted with remission of fine if they give up their stance after the cattle are taken away. Even then the farmers let their cattle be auctioned and the government which claims that it is like a kind father realises from the proceeds of the auction not only the land revenue but also 25 per cent fine. Even then the farmers invite the Mahatma to their villages. There is a sort of competition among the villages for inviting the Mahatma.

The farmers forget their troubles the moment they set eyes on the Mahatma and hear him speak. Some farmers feel obliged to the government that it has refused to postpone the realization of land revenue and thus given them an opportunity to see and hear the Mahatma. The best result of this struggle is that the people are improving their morals.

The people are no longer afraid of the officers and the Kheda farmers can look them in the face with courage. Not only that, even those poor people who had for centuries given free labour are now rid of the evil customs of *begar.*

The people have now realized that mutual differences lead to destruction. They have given up their centuries old feuds and are living in amity. They no longer go to the courts to resolve their quarrels. It is being realized by all that an unjust government can be opposed and the progress of the people lies in such opposition. Even the government has learnt a lesson from our satyagraha. The good results of our fight are evident and the people have learnt a lot from it.

As the struggle lengthens, the people are being tested. If this opportunity to undergo these troubles had not arisen, the people would not have gained much. Now is a testing time for us. The whole world is looking towards us. The officers do not get an opportunity to run the administration. People had to spend a lot of time to deposit government dues in the Tehsil offices but now the officers are going from door to door collecting those dues. They do not frighten the people but treat them humbly and also try to tempt them. There is nobody in the villages who would play host to those in power. Those who used to get things free in the villages sometimes are unable to find them even if they want to pay. There is no end to their difficulties but the people have stood firm. It appears that the officers have realized the error of their ways. It appears also that they have realized that truth is on the side of the people. But we should realise that the officers' hands are tied, placed as they are in the administrative set-up. It is but natural under the circumstances that they may overstep the limits, become angry and cause us pain. Even so, we should not deviate from the path we have chosen, should continue to be humble and should pity the officers than to be angry. We should also maintain peace. Love can melt even the hardest heart. If our love for our enemies is as great as their hardness of heart, we can win them over. That is the secret of our Satyagraha.

It is a matter of gratification that even women and children are taking interest in the Satyagraha in the villages. But we should take care to see that our youngmen do not misbehave with the officers. If we give up the path of humility, the youngmen may become impudent. If that happens, our struggle will end in defeat and not in victory.

This Satyagraha has earned a name for us in the country and it is just possible that we have awakened the feelings of mercy and justice in the heart of Mr. Pratt. If we make the slightest error now victory might elude us. My request to you is that even if the officers overstep the limits and do something improper, we should not show any ill-will towards them but should try to persuade them with love. If anything improper is being done anywhere, information about it should be sent to the headquarters of the Satyagraha.

[1]Gandhiji had gone to Bihar during the Kheda Satyagraha. Sardar Patel gave the said message to the people of Kheda district in May 1918.

[2]*Sardar Patel Ke Bhashana,* Edited by Narihari Dwarikadas Parikh and Uttam Chand Deep Chand Shah, Navjivan, Ahmedabad, 1950.

Vallabhbhai, as a student

Mother Ladbai

Birth place, Nadiad

Primary School, Karamsad, where studied

Government High School, Nadiad

Family ancestral house at Karamsad

Ahmedabad residence

As an young advocate

White leaving for London

Back home as Barrister

Famous brothers, Vithalbhai and Vallabhbhai

18

Vallabhbhai Congratulates Peasants on Success of Kaira[1] *Struggle*

Prajabandhu, 4 June 1918

The fight has come to an end but we have to say regretfully that there is no grace in the manner of its conclusion. Postponement has been agreed upon, but not in a generous frame of mind if the public had been informed about the orders, which are said to have been issued on the 25th of April, many could have been spared the hardships they had to undergo. Wherever land revenue had not been recovered, landholders apprehended severe action, and in order to avoid having forfeiture notices served on them, they abandoned their houses and lived out in the fields. Women suffered a great deal which they need not have endured. They bore insults from impertinent Circle Officers and saw with aching hearts their milch buffaloes taken away. . .The officials knew quite well that the sole reason for the struggle was that the poor did not have the ability to pay their assessment. The Commissioner refused to take notice of their difficulties and in spite of every effort, it was not possible to get his "no" converted into a "yes". His one refrain was that the law did not allow individual relief. Now the Collector says that it is well known that such individual relief can be given Well then, is it being suggested that the public deliberately and obstinately wanted to suffer so many hardships?

Perhaps the officials had been influenced by the hardships which were being endured by the public. They may well have recognised their mistake but instead of admitting freely that they had made a mistake and acting generously, they now state that relief would be given on the merits of each case, suggesting at the same time that this is what they had always been prepared to do. It is because of this attitude that we say that the settlement has not left a good taste in one's mouth.

Nevertheless we welcome the settlement since our request had been accepted. Now only 8 per cent of the land revenue remains to be recovered. Until today it was a matter of honour not to pay up the land revenue; now it will be a matter of honour to pay it up. Whoever has the means to pay, would do so and thereby show that where there is no conflict between man-made law and spiritual law, the Satyagrahi (a soldier in the battle of truth) has no hesitation in honouring man-made law. In preparing the list of those who are unable to pay up the land revenue, we should be very careful to see that no one is included who can fairly be regarded as having the means to pay.

By their courage the agriculturists of Kheda have drawn towards them the attention of the whole country. For the past six months they have shown great loyalty to truth, fearlessness, unity, firmness and self-sacrifice. We hope that they will develop these great qualities still further and bring credit to their motherland. The public of Kheda have rendered great service to themselves, to the struggle for independence, and to the State.

[1]As Secretary of Gujarat Sabha, Vallabhbhai was called upon to render relief to the victims of the floods caused by excessive rains in Kaira District in early 1917. The crops had been damaged badly and about 22,000 farmers sent a petition to the Revenue Collector to postpone collection of revenues where the yield had been less than 25 per cent. The government turned down their request on the yield was 40 per cent. Gandhiji now asked Vallabhbhai to take up the cause of the farmers. It was during this Satyagraha that Vallabhbhai changed his western dress to that of a *dhoti,* shirt and waist coat and walked from village to village asking the farmers not to cooperate with the tax-collectors. The people stood by their leader like a rock and his efforts were crowned with success. Eventually the Government postponed the collection of tax. Gandhiji in his tribute to Vallabhbhai said that he had tested Vallabhbhai with fire and he had proved to be 100 per cent pure gold. Gandhiji further added that but for Vallabhbhai the campaign would not have been a success.

19

Vallabhbhai Congratulates People of Kheda on Success of Satyagraha[1]

29 June 1918[2]

It is a custom in India to distribute the offerings made to gods and holymen to their worshippers. Mahatma Gandhi has today followed that practice. I have not done anything. There are people who have served the Ahmedabad Municipality for 20 years and more. What could I do in 18 months? I wish to say on behalf of my colleagues and myself that if the people of Kheda district had not given proof of their courage and tolerance, we would not have been able to achieve anything. I would, therefore, say that the honour which has been conferred on me rightfully belongs to the people.

For hundreds of years India has been suffering from a mortal disease. She had not so far been lucky to find a good doctor. The doctors who looked after her believed in prescribing sweet medicines. Now a sweet medicine cannot cure an incurable disease. Some people might find it strange that a person who has been fighting the government can give such advice. But let me remind you that the doctor who has arisen to cure your illness has nothing but the spirit of service of the people in his whole being. If you think that his medicine is the right one accept it. But please do not lose courage. . . . Follow the Mahatma's advice if you want that your district Kheda should arise on the political firmament of the country.

[1]On the 29th June 1918 at the time of the conclusion of the Kheda Satyagraha, an address was presented to Mahatma Gandhi. Replying to it, Gandhiji paid tribute to the role of Sardar Patel in the Satyagraha.

[2]*Sardar Patel Ke Bhashana,* Edited by Narihari Dwarikadas Parikh and Uttam Chand Deep Chand Shah, Navjivan, Ahmedabad, 1950.

20

Gandhiji's Tribute to Vallabhbhai on Success of Kaira Movement

Prajabandhu, 30 June 1918

A leader's skill is judged by the competence in selecting his assistants for the execution of his plans. Many people were prepared to follow my advice, but I could not make up my mind as to who should be my deputy commander. I then thought of Vallabhbhai. I must admit that when I met Vallabhbhai first, I could not help wondering who this stiff-looking person was, and whether he would be able to do what I wanted. But the more I came to know him, the more I realised that I must secure his help. Vallabhbhai too has come to the conclusion that although he has flourishing legal practice today and is doing very important work in the municipality, he must become a whole time public worker and serve his country. So he has taken the plunge. If it were not for his assistance, I must admit that this campaign would not have been carried through so successfully.

21

Vallabhbhai Advises Traders Not to Fill New Income Tax Forms

Prajabandhu, 25 August 1918

Merchants of nearly Forty Mahajans of Ahmedabad alongwith other merchants went to the public meeting on Friday, 23rd August 1918 at 3.30 p.m. which was held under the Presidentship of Vallabhbhai J. Patel at Wadi Dasha Shrimali Community for raising their voice against the Income-Tax forms. Both Hindu and Muslim merchants were present in big number.

In the beginning the President Vallabhbhai Patel said, "You know why we have gathered here. In today's meeting it would have been proper to have a President of merchant community instead of me, but merchants of Gujarat are afraid of pressing the demand to the Government. They even do not dare to show courage to come forward. Therefore it is the duty of the experienced persons to go to their rescue. From this viewpoint, I have accepted to preside over today's meeting. In this context you have falsified our proverb that 'Bania has foresight.' When this law was passed none of you uttered a single word and when the occasion has come for filling of the form you have become active. When the law was passed both newspapers and leaders had cautioned the government but busy businessmen did not pay any attention. It seems that from now on the merchants should also remain informed about political movement over and above the business activities. Government does not know the feeling of the people because people do not take part in political affairs. Those who take part in political affairs do not go to legislative assembly. When this law was passed in the Viceroy's Council, no representative ever expressed the difficulty of the business class. People's representation is very less in legislative assembly. Therefore, the voice of the people does not reach there. It is high time now to change this situation because new political reforms have been introduced. Therefore the business community should rise to the occasion. The business community should read the newspapers and keep themselves abreast about the proceedings of the legislature and political problems of the country. The business community is not capable to participate in the legislature, but when you would be able to develop that capacity you would be able to guard your interests. In this matter there is uneasiness in the business community. People have become sensitive in Surat, Broach, and Karachi because this law is not convenient to the traders. Government believes that people pay less tax in comparison to the income and the government does not possess any means to know the correct income. So the government like to know from the people its income for escaping from Super Tax. The traders divide their income amongst their relatives. When the government came to know about these tricks it had decided this method of filling up this form and they believe that there is a great danger in it. The traders are ready to give some more tax but they are not ready to fill up the form. It is certain that this form is not liked by them. Then what is to be done is to be thought by you. In this meeting Hindus and Muslims have gathered together is a sign of joy. It is a drawback that traders do not maintain unity till the end. We have to think about our capacity to stand together. The farmers and the people of Kheda have demonstrated the people must have a right to pay or withhold the tax. If people get united for a proper action the government cannot do any thing to the traders. Just now it is our duty to support the traders from Bombay. They have asked for justice by sending a telegram to the Viceroy and requested him to meet its deputation. So it is our duty to cooperate with them and support them.

The land in Kheda was being confiscated every year but this year there is no confiscation. This indicates the hollowness of the British justice, but justice is given to those who demand it. Traders are very selfish and therefore their unity does not last long. Besides supporting Bombay the form should be filled after one month after the decision of the Viceroy. Such an answer should be given to Collector of Income Tax. Today the condition of the traders is safe and many traders do not understand how to fill up the form. Under these conditions to confess and fill the forms and if the details be proved wrong then to be liable to punishment is dangerous. So we should not retreat from pointing out our objection.

22

Vallabhbhai asks Businessmen to be Ready for Struggle

Prajabandhu, 15 September 1918

On 4th September 1918, some businessmen went to meet the Collector along with Vallabhbhai J. Patel in connection with the Collector's invitation to discuss the difficulties experienced in filling up the new Income Tax forms. They have presented their difficulties before the Collector. After hearing the representations, the Collector asked them to give him eight days to look into the matter and also informed them to see him again on 12th September 1918.

In this context a very big meeting of the businessmen was organised to discuss further steps in the Shrimali Wadi at Shakmarket at 8.00 p.m. on last Tuesday, 10th September 1918. In the beginning of the meeting Shri Nakrabhai explained in detail the new Income Tax forms. As President of the meeting Shri Vallabhbhai said that because of the Collector's invitation he met him with nearly twentyfive businessmen. There the Collector Mr. Fox asked some of them about the difficulty in filling of the forms. Then the businessmen who were present there submitted their difficulties. Some of us desired that it is difficult to mention individual production in a joint family because who can as head of the family decide the earning of his son or brother? At the same time it is also very difficult to mention the real amount for the simple reason that if a son has declared the less production naturally on that account the head of the family will also mention the same less production for which he is considered accountable? How can a head of the family take this responsibility on his own? At the same time to own responsibility of the submission of the production of a partner will be a difficult problem. Further these new income tax forms are of such type that by filling them the secrecy of the business will be out. This means that to ask the businessmen to fill in these forms will be an act of showing distrust towards the businessmen. In reply to these problems, the Collector Mr. Fox clarified that after breaking the Income Tax Law when they go to the income tax office they are acting like a thief who after committing the theft goes to the judge for clarification and guidance. It seems from your representation that they had decided to pay less income tax. If they have any objection in filling of these new forms they could go elsewhere and stay where there was not such a law.

Now we have to think about the inappropriateness of the Collector's reply when he considers the businessmen as thieves because officers generally are of such rude temper. Now they had to think about what they had to do. Earlier they had resolved to support the Bombay Committee and it is their duty to stick to it.

Your decision of not filling of the forms was still there, that was what he understood. They had to be fearless even if there was any pressure on them from the government. This act would not be a crime. It is the privilege of everyone to ask for relaxation within the limits of the law and they had to continue to ask for the help but in the beginning they had to decide first and then have had to think about what to do if government pressurised them. Side by side they had to make provision for the expenses of the court when government by using its own powers, filed a suit against anyone. I am happy to know that the business class has become active.

At thc end of this meeting two resolutions were adopted. (1) This meeting supports the Bombay Committee wholeheartedly. (2) This meeting authorised the local committee to reply on 12th September 1918 not to fill in the forms unless the help the Bombay Committee had sought is fulfilled by the government. Both these resolutions were passed unanimously.

23

Vallabhbhai asks Collector not to Insist on Filling Income Tax Forms

Prajabandhu, 15 September 1918

Last Thursday, on 12th September 1918,businessmen alongwith Barrister Vallabhbhai Patel went to see the Collector, according to the appointment given to them by the Collector. In response to the question put to him by the Collector, Barrister Vallabhbhai Patel said that all of them had resolved in a meeting called on Tuesday last. They had decided that no businessman would fill in the new Income Tax form. He further said that since in the cities like Surat and Bombay no pressure was exercised on merchants to fill in forms. So long as the matter was not disposed of in those cities no pressure should be exercised on merchants there. It was in the fitness of things to keep the same standard everywhere. In the end the Collector declared that those merchants who would not fill in the forms would be liable to legal proceedings and then the meeting came to an end.

24

Vallabhbhai on Drought in Gujarat

Prajabandhu, 8 December 1918

Last Wednesday on 4th December 1918 at 6.00 p.m. a meeting was convened by Seth Shri Kasturbhai Manibhai at the Premabhai Hall. Seth Kasturbhai's name was proposed by Seth Ambalal Sarabhai as President for the meeting and Shri Anandshanker Bapubhai Dhruva seconded it. Seth Kasturbhai presided over the meeting.

Vallabhbhai Patel declared that the drought had created a very critical situation in Gujarat. Because of the world war, dearness had increased so much that the cost of foodgrain, fodder, and cloth had become unbearable and those who maintained themselves only on cattle, their plight had become most miserable. Cloth in general had become less costly but those who wanted to buy ordinary cloth did not find themselves in a better situation and the report prepared by Indulal Yagnik, who moved about in various districts such as Ahmedabad, Kheda, and Panchmahal etc., had been published in the newspapers. He informed them that they would have gone through those reports. He further said that in Zalod many persons had died of starvation and the conditions in other districts would be the same that was the impending danger, therefore, timely steps should be taken. And they would have to depend on the help of the government to some extent. 'Influenza' had affected the economic conditions of villagers. Many families had lost their young sons and that had rendered them helpless. Even the condition of cattle was deplorable. They were being sold in Friday Markets at throwaway prices. In this connection some of them had decided like this. First of all we should bring down the prices of grain and control it and in each district a fair price grain shop should be started. For the poor poorhouses should be organised where free food should be provided. We should stand by the government in its effort to help the weak. The poor should be given clothes because in winter their conditions will be miserable. Cattle camp should be organised for cattle and farms should be provided for growing grass, fodder, maize and millets. And further the farmers should be assisted in their work. In consultation with the government, seeds for grass etc., should be collected and distributed to the farmers without any charge and if financial position permits, grass depots should be opened. For all these activities I propose the following resolutions: This meeting of some citizens of Ahmedabad hereby resolves that in most parts of Gujarat because of drought and unprecedented dearness of grain and fodder people and cattle undergo unbearable misery. To alleviate the misery funds should be collected and a committee of the following gentry be formed. The committee is hereby authorised to increase their number, if needed.

President: Kasturbhai Manibhai
Members: (1) Mohandas Gandhi
(2) Lady Chinubhai Seth
(3) Seth Shri Ambalal
(4) Smt. Kasturbhai Manibhai
(5) Seth Mangaldas
(6) Prof. Swaminarayana
Secretaries: (1) Kasturbhai Lalbhai
(2) Vallabhbhai Patel
(3) Indulal Yagnik
(4) Krishnalal Narshihlal Desai
(5) Ganesh Vasudev Mavalankar
Treasurers: (1) Khushaldas Gokaldas
(2) Seth Amritlal Chunilal

25

Vallabhbhai asks Traders to Prepare Themselves for Movement against Rowlatt Bills[1]

Prajabandhu, 2 March 1919

This is the first meeting of the Traders in Ahmedabad and it shows that a time has come when even the traders of Gujarat should hold such a meeting. When the Great War was on, the Government told us if we helped in the war effort, independence for us would be nearer. When the Secretary of State for India came here, a representation was made to him on behalf of Gujarat. Later on the Secretary of State gave us the Reforms and meetings were held demanding that they be amended. The Great War is over but the scheme has not yet been implemented. Instead of the Reforms, India got the Rowlatt Act in return for the services it had rendered to the Empire. Such laws as the Rowlatt Act are not found in any other country. Even though there was disagreement among our leaders, they unanimously demanded in the Council that the Bill be held in abeyance. A Government member of the Council had said that the movement of the people would be according to the wishes of the leaders. The Government says that they had brought the Bill after due consideration and that the responsibility was ours. True, the leaders would decide the direction that the movement is to take. If the traders of Ahmedabad start a movement, it is a harbinger of the great movement which we propose to launch. Somebody may ask what harm the traders would come to if this Bill is passed? Firstly, there may not be any political agitation as a result of the Bill. If that is so, it does not make any difference whether we are offered any reforms or not. If some writing is considered seditious, the police would arrest us, whatever the source from which that writing has come in our possession. If we are able to prove that the writing was not for the purpose of spreading sedition, even then we would be punished and there would be no appeal against that sentence. One of the members of the Council pointed out that the provision for appeal was not to be found in England either. But there are juries in that country. First an offence has to be proved before a 12-member jury and then the case goes to another jury consisting of 9 members. If that jury unanimously holds the accused guilty, only then sentence is pronounced. In India, there is neither a jury nor any assessors. All the elected members are against this law but the Government wants to pass it and refuses to consider those representatives as the voice of the people. But it were these very representatives who were accepted as the leaders of the people when the Government wanted Rs 67.5 crore for the war effort and they were charged with the responsibility of moving a Resolution to that effect. The draft of the Bill has been referred to a Select Committee and some minor amendments might be made. Even so the main objective of the Bill will remain inviolate. That is why we have done the right thing in holding this meeting and, as a Government member has said, the leaders must launch a movement.

[1]Immediately after the end of World War I in 1918, the British Government panicked by the surge of revolutionary activity, replaced the Defence of India Act with a still harsher legislation popularly known as Rowlatt Act to curb the freedom of the people. The result was the birth of a satyagraha launched by Gandhiji with the objective of conducting an organised agitation against these 'Black Bills' all over the country. Gandhiji called upon the people to observe complete *hartal* on April 6,1919. In Gujarat Vallabhbhai led a huge procession on April 6 and openly defied law. Riots broke out in Gujarat and martial law was imposed at Ahmedabad.

26

Vallabhbhai Advises People to Disperse

Home Depu (Sp.) F. No. 521 (Pt. 3)/1919
Bombay Archives, 11 April 1919

To

The General Officer Commanding
Bombay Brigade

April 11th, 1919

. . . The Collector and the Supdt. of Police motored through the city and visited the "Prem Gate" and below is an extract from the report of the former, what they saw:—

"We found the 'Prem Gate' surrounded by a hostile crowd. A motor car drove up containing Vallabhbhai, Yagnik and Dr. Kanuga, all prominent Satyagrahis. I had some conversation with them and told them to advise the crowd to disperse which they did successfully. . ."

27

Vallabhbhai to bring out "Satyagraha Akhbar"

Prajabandhu, 13 April 1919

The news of Mahatma Gandhiji's arrest in Delhi resulted in the strike in the city. The work came to a standstill. Mills were closed. Riots broke out, firing was resorted to and the city was thrown to anarchy and confusion.

In the evening of 10th April 1919, 15,000 persons assembled on the sands of Sabarmati. The assembly was divided in three sections for convenience and each section was addressed by different speakers. Those who addressed the meeting were Indulal Yagnik, Jivanlal, Barrister Vallabhbhai Patel, Jadavji Gandhi. In each section Gandhiji's message was read out. In this meeting it was announced that on every Thursday handwritten News Bulletin *Satyagrah Akhbar* would be published by Vallabhbhai Patel without government registration.

28

Vallabhbhai Insists on Municipal Employees to Obey Commissioner's Orders

Prajabandhu, 4 May 1919

On 26th April 1919, a special general meeting of local Municipality was held under the presidentship of Raobahadur Ramanbhai. The following Councillors were present. Dr. Doshi, Mr. Natwarlal, Mr. G.K. Mavalankar, Mr. Kalidas, Mr. Vallabhbhai, Mr. Sutaria, Mr. Medh, Mr. Valiulla and others.

As suggested by Mr. Karanjawala, the last item of the Agenda was taken up and he said that the post of P.A. should be discontinued and Mr. Bhagat should be sent back to the post of P.A.'s secretary, Mr. Bhagat was not complying with the order of the Commissioner and started misbehaving with him.

In this connection Mr. Vallabhbhai Patel said that this issue was wrongly twisted in partisan attitude. The Commissioner enjoyed the powers legally given to him and all servants of the Municipality were under his jurisdiction. Interference in taking work would be detrimental. When this post was instituted we had opposed. We have to keep in mind the question of municipal expenditure. We cannot pay the person without work. In the end it was resolved that Mr. Bhagat should obey the orders of the Commissioner.

29

Vallabhbhai to His Daughter Maniben[1]

Sardar Ki Seekh[2]

AHMEDABAD
3 January 1920

MY DEAR MANI,

I received your letter this morning on my return from Amritsar today. I am glad that you are enjoying yourself. Your uncle[3] will now sail for India shortly. I am just writing to your brother[4] to come here for a few days if his school is not reopened. When are you coming here? With love,

Your affectionate father,
VALLABHBHAI PATEL

[1]The only letter Sardar Patel wrote to his daughter in English.
[2]In Gujarati published by Navjivan Publishing House, 1958.
[3]Elder brother of Sardar Patel, Vithalbhai Patel.
[4]Dahyabhai Patel.

30

Patel's Motion to Defer Collection of Damages from People of Ahmedabad Approved

15 January 1920

Administration Report Ahmedabad Municipality, 1917-1918, GRI/1918, also G.R. IV, 1920-21

Motion from Mr. V.B. Patel dated 18th November 1919 as under:

As the replies of Government in the last Council Meeting to certain questions of the Hon'ble R.S. Harilal D. Desai, on the subject matter of the order of the District Magistrate, Ahmedabad for damages, arising out of the disturbances in April 1919, show that the Hunter Inquiry Commission is to inquire into the matter, the Collection of Rs 4,80,000 by the Municipality be postponed until the report of that committee (*sic*) is out.

A copy of this resolution be sent to the District Magistrate.

Mr. Vallabhbhai proposed and Mr. Sutaria seconded that as the replies of Government in the last Council Meeting to certain questions of the Hon'ble R.S. Harilal D. Desai on the subject matter of the order of the District Magistrate, Ahmedabad, to levy compensation from the inhabitants of Ahmedabad for damages, arising out of the disturbances in April 1919 show that the Hunter Enquiry Committee is inquiring into the matter, the collection of Rs 4,80,000 by the Municipality be postponed until the report of that committee is out.

A copy of this resolution be sent to the District Magistrate.

Hon'ble R.S. Harilal put an amendment and Mr. Chahewala seconded that as the Government of Bombay has disallowed any information for discussion in the last sessions of the Legislative Council in anticipation of the results of the Disorders Enquiry Committee about the compensation orders to be levied from the inhabitants of Ahmedabad by the District Magistrate of Ahmedabad for the damage done during disturbances of April 1919 as the amount of compensation fixed needs enquiry and as the recovery at one time of the whole amount of Rs 4,48,000 is likely to embarrass the inhabitants of Ahmedabad in these hard times from whom a sum of Rs 4,06,000 has been lately recovered through other channels, the Chief Officer be requested to take steps to collect an amount equal to one time the compulsory water tax this season and to keep over the collection of remaining amount for the next season pending further instructions and inasmuch as the orders of the District Magistrate do not fix any time limit for the recovery he be requested to agree to the course proposed above.

Dr. Bhagat put an amendment and Dr. Kanuga seconded that as the Government of Bombay has in the last Legislative Council refused to give any information about the nature of the enquiry, by which the amount of compensation ordered to be levied from the inhabitants of Ahmedabad by the District Magistrate was arrived at on the ground of the Hunter Enquiry Committee as the amount of compensation fixed needs examination and as the recovery at one time of the whole amount of Rs 4,48,000 is likely to embarrass the inhabitants of Ahmedabad in these hard times when a sum of Rs 4,06,000 has been lately recovered through other channels, the collection of Rs 4,48,000 by the Municipality be postponed until the report of Committee is out and Government are pleased to give the necessary information and to reconsider the question.

Mr. Kalidas put a motion for closure seconded by Mr. K.N. Desai and on votes being taken it was lost.

Mr. Doshi proposed and Mr. Sutaria seconded that the meeting be adjourned to Monday the 19th instant at 6.00 p.m.

After Mr. Doshi put his motion Mr. K.N. Desai raised a point of order whether in view of Rule 35 read together with Rule 41, a motion of closure should not have precedence over that for an adjournment.

The Vice-president ruled that there having been no motion for closure before the motion for adjournment came, the motion for adjournment should be put to vote first.

Mr. Kalidas moved an amendment that the meeting be adjourned to 19th instant at 6.00 p.m. and in the meanwhile the Chief Officer be requested not to collect any thing in connection with District Magistrate's order.

. . . . the underground drainage which had been transferred from the charge of the Health Department to the Engineering Department in 1916, became so choked up by neglect to remove silt from it that a grave danger to the public health arose therefrom. Sullage water began to overflow in localities on the approach of Jamalpur Pumping Station and a voluminous stream of sullage overflowing in the Bhistiwad Nalla became an intolerable nuisance. . . The Municipality had to consult Mr. F.C. Taraporwala C.J.E. Retired Superintending Engineer, who very kindly went into the question and gave valuable advice. A clearing of the sewer under the circumstances had to be done at a very heavy cost which could have been avoided if proper precautions were taken by the Municipal Engineer. The Municipality instituted an inquiry into the subject and it was found that reports from the Health Department pointing out the choking up of manholes and reports from the Engineer at the Jamalpur Pumping Station asking for repairs and replacements of worn out parts were kept unheeded by the Municipal Engineer. . .

31

Vallabhbhai urges Postponement of Fine on People due to Riots after Hunter Committee Report

Prajabandhu, 18 January 1920

The special general meeting of the Local Municipality that was postponed on the last 5th (5th January 1920) met on 12th January 1920. Shri Ramanbhai presided over it in which Shri Vallabhbhai, Pestanshaw, Maneklal, Balmukund, Krishnalal, Bhagat, Harilal, and Daulatram were present. Shri Vallabhbhai proposed that the municipality should postpone the collection of Rupees forty eight thousand fine imposed on the people by District Magistrate for the compensation of the damage done in the riots of last April 1919 till the publication of the report of the Hunter Committee. For this work the Chief Officer had advised that the Board should turn into a Committee and after coming to a general consensus, a resolution should be brought forth to avoid the obstacles in discussing the rules of the meeting. The members did not like the advice and therefore it was discarded.

32

Sanitary Conditions in Ahmedabad: Patel's Report to Municipality

Municipality Committee Records, 3 June 1920

1. The first part of Water Works for the City of Ahmedabad which cost Rs 7,76,880 was completed in 1891 and handed over to the Municipality in 1892. It consisted of four supply wells of 25 feet dimension with 12", 18" and 24" connective pipes upto a Jackwell 10 feet in diameter. From the Jackwell the water was pumped by a duplicate set of pumps and engines of 90 H.P. into a reservoir 42-1/2 feet in diameter and 19 feet high supported on a masonary tower 40 feet high above the ground level. The capacity of the reservoir is 1,50,000 gallons which was considered to be equal to 1/8th day's supply at 10 gallons per head for a population of 1,20,000 persons only. The four wells were decided upto [*sic*] on the supposition that they would give a supply of 1800 gallons per minute which means a supply of 10 gallons per head to a population of 1,30,000 pumped in 12 hours. In 1891 the population was 1,48,412.

2. The maximum consumption of water in June 1892 was about 11 lacs gallons per day but was expected to reach 15 lacs within a short period. A fifth well was added at a cost of Rs 9200 to meet the insufficiency of supply.

3. The original engines and pumps were designed to deliver 13 lacs gallons in 12 hours and hence a new engine had to be added in 1898 at a cost of Rs 44,000.

4. In 1908 the daily consumption had already risen to about 35,00,000

gallons per day and the infiltration from the 5 wells was found to be sufficient to meet the demands. The stream was 650 feet from the nearest and 1200 feet from farthest well as compared with 190 from the nearest and 550 from the farthest end when the Water Works was first constructed. To augment the supply the connective pipes between Wells No. 2, 4 and 5 were in 1902 lowered 2' 6" so also Well No. 1 along with its connection with Well No. 3. Another connection from Well No. 2 to the Jackwell was also added. In 1905 a sixth supply well was added.

5. In order to meet with the increasing demand, proposals were made in 1907 to add two more wells (No. 7 and 8) and to construct a Third Jackwell and to provide an additional engine and a pump.

The distribution system was also proposed to be partly overhauled. The daily consumption of water had gone upto 45 and 3/4 lacs gallons per day in 1908 and the Municipality resolved to construct 4 more wells instead of 2 as mentioned in their project of 1907 which was estimated to cost Rs 3,50,000.

6. Another project, estimated to cost Rs 1,75,113 comprising (1) replacing of old pipes of 3" and 4" diameter by 6" and 5" together with 2400 connections, (2) construction of 2 new supply Wells (No. 11 and 12), (3) lowering of Well No. 6 and its connection with No. 5, (4) The lowering of Well No. 5 and its connection with No. 4, (5) Lowering of Well No. 4 and its connection with No. 2, was proposed.

7. The daily consumption of water had by this time gone upto 55 lacs gallons. The population in the city within the wall had increased by about 27% in 20 years and amounted to 167,000 souls and the suburban population was 50,000 souls. The suburban area got its supply from the old town mains which were consequently severely strained and there was serious loss of effective head. In order to remedy these defects it was decided that all proposals for improvements suggested since 1908 should be included in one comprehensive scheme that would be sufficient to meet with the requirements of the immediate future.

8. A supplementary scheme for Rs 1,57,000 had also been prepared by the Municipality to meet with the demands newly created by the extension of the Municipal limits. The total population for which provision is made in the comprehensive scheme prepared by the Executive Engineer is 2,45,640. The rate of supply assumed for the distributive services is at 10 gallons per head to flow in 6 hours which is equivalent to a daily supply of 20 gallons pumped in 12 hours, the total daily consumption in 1910 being 55 lacs in hot weather including the supply to the Mills and cantonment.

9. All the wells in the river bed were found in hot weather of 1912 to be capable of supplying about 4400 gallons per minute. The connecting pipes of the second line of wells were 6 feet higher than those of the third line and it was expected that the yielding capacity of all the wells combined would be much improved after the lowering of the connecting pipes of the second line.

There was also a proposal to put up a filtration gallery to be 600 feet long and in the form of a perforated steel tube 3 feet in diameter covered with 4 feet thick mantle of metal gravel and rubble etc. The total pumping capacity now provided is 9000 gallons per minute with 4 engines of which three are each capable of 1800 gallons per minute and the 4th can deliver 3600 gallons per minute and was included in the comprehensive project.

10. Another high level reservoir of the capacity of three lacs gallons was also included in the project.

11. After considerable delay and with some modifications the scheme which is henceforward called a comprehensive project was sanctioned by Government on the 17th October, 1913. The estimates sanctioned amounted to Rs 8,98,918. The Executive Engineer was directed to carry out the work which was already in progress.

12. The proposal to construct a filter gallery and of constructing 2 wells (No. 11 and 12) appears to have been abandoned.

13. In the year 1914 the river current reached farther to the west and supply of water in the well rapidly decreased so that in the month of January the Municipality had to resort to a temporary device of bringing the river current near the wells by digging a channel. Since then the Municipality spends every year about Rs 10,000 for some such temporary arrangement to maintain the present supply which is woefully deficient.

14. Soon after the Comprehensive Project received sanction of Government, important and expensive modifications were suggested by the Mechanical Engineer and the Sanitary Engineer at a time when early completion of the scheme was of vital importance. The Executive Engineer suspended the work by reason of the proposed alterations. The then Collector Mr. Painter protested against this interference and the consequent delay in the work which seriously embarrassed the Municipality.

Mr. Shonbridge, the Sanitary Engineer, insisted on his proposed alterations which meant considerable delay. The whole revised scheme including the alterations proposed (New Jackwell and Central collecting main) had to be placed before Government for sanction. A reference from the Chief Officer to Mr. Shonbridge for early preparation of the plans and estimates of the revised scheme met with a very curt reply. His reply was 'that a municipality of the size of Ahmedabad ought to employ an Engineer capable of preparing its scheme for it and it would take a long time for him to prepare the scheme even after having the necessary staff as he would then have other scheme claiming priority.' No progress was made during that period year [*sic*] and on 15th May, 1914, the revised scheme was sanctioned by Government.

15. On the 15th June, 1914, a public meeting of the citizens of Ahmedabad held in the Premabhai Hall under the Presidency of Sheth Mangaldas Girdhardas passed a resolution drawing attention of the Government and the Committee of Management to the keen and widespread dissatisfaction prevalent among the citizens at the acute and serious deficiency in the supply of drinking water. In forwarding this resolution to Government, the Collector observed that 'the urgent problem which must be settled very soon [*sic*] and that the scheme selected may be executed in the cold weather when the percolation into the supply wells can best be improved; it is hoped that a conference of all experts concerned be able to

meet in Ahmedabad in August or September and settle it, otherwise we shall again have half empty wells, idle engines and half-filled pipes and consequent crop of complaints next summer.' It appears from the forwarding letter of the Commissioner that the Committee of Management, with whom the Collector agreed, were not satisfied that the order of the Government will solve what they considered to be the most difficult problem, that is to say, of bringing the current nearer the supply wells. They submitted three alternative proposals none of which was approved by the Sanitary Engineer because of the risk of contamination of supply.

Thus all proposals for immediate increase of supply such as (1) filter gallery, (2) constructing new wells, or (3) training the river current by means of a masonary wall across a portion of the river respectively pressed by the Committee of Management were rejected.

Under these circumstances the Committee of Management got support from Government against public criticism which by the way naturally lost all its force on account of the mixing up of the opposition against the increased water rate. The Government also informed the President of the public meeting by their resolution No. 7323 of 15th September, 1914, 'that the shortage was due to causes beyond the control of the Committee of Management and officers concerned who took all reasonable measures to minimize its extent and that every endeavour is now being made by resort to special works to prevent its recurrence next hot weather.'

16. In 1915 Committee of Management handed over charge to the Municipality under this condition and it is painful to observe that in this helpless condition the Municipality has to quietly submit to the bitter attacks of people and comparative lack of interest on the part of Government.

17. It is in the fitness of things to point out here that another public meeting was held in 1917-18 under the auspices of the Gujarat Sabha and a deputation waited upon Mr. Pratt, the Commissioner N.D. This time the public were informed through the deputation that the Municipality was to blame and that as the affairs of the Municipality were managed by the Municipality, Government had nothing to do in the matter and they must look to the Municipality for proper supply and give them no peace or rest till that was done. His attitude was surprising as he knew that the scheme was in charge of the Government Public Works Department from the beginning and the Municipality had no voice in the matter. It may be mentioned here that the supply system of the Cantonment was so altered as to ensure a continuous supply and although it must be acknowledged that the supply required by the Cantonment is very small the promptness with which the complaint of Cantonment was attended to is striking.

18. The Sanitary Engineer in his letter of 2nd September, 1914, forwarded through the Mechanical Engineer, who also agreed with his views, said that if the municipality will at once commence the work of the laying of the new connecting pipes and the execution of the new Jackwell the improved supply could probably be ready for Ahmedabad before next hot weather. Several hot weathers have passed since then and yet the expectations have not been realized. The revised estimates

of the Comprehensive Scheme went up to over 12 lacs and the work is expected to take at least one more year. During recent years the conditions have become worse and the position has been well-nigh intolerable. The Municipality spends money after temporary makeshift of channel and a *bund* across the river and the Public Works Department compels the Municipality to destroy the temporary works soon after completion on the threat of delaying their works. In 1910 the daily consumption was 35 lacs gallons while the present average supply in winter and summer is 59 lacs of gallons per day.

The comprehensive scheme originated and designed in 1911 to meet with immediate future requirements based on the calculation of 20 gallons per head per 12 hours a day which can well be called famine ration will take nearly a full census period for completion if it be completed next year. It would not be out of place here to quote the opinion of the Hydraulic Engineer, Mr. Trivers Smith of Bombay, in his recent scheme of the improvement of the water supply of the city of Bombay that whereas a rate of supply for trades, Municipal, domestic and all other purposes aggregating 40 gallons per head per day was a liberal allowance ten years ago it hardly meets the bare necessities today.

19. Nearly half the city is drained and extension of underground drainage is one of the most vital needs of the city. The drained area suffers from insufficient supply more on account of its high level and drainage tanks, and the water closets being dry the sullage is not properly diluted. The result is that the pumps at the drainage station get out of order and the drains get silted. Consequently there is overflow of sullage water in the city. No city in the world can put up with such a condition. The Town planning area will have to be provided with a proper supply of water. The present population can be estimated at 300,000 and if 30 gallons per head per day can be taken as a reasonable allowance, our present requirements are 90 lacs of gallons whereas our supply is 50 lacs. The Sanitary Engineer to Government has now given his opinion for the first time in the informal conference held in the Municipal Hall about the probable yield of the wells after completion of the scheme. In his opinion the utmost that can be expected from the present system after the completion of the project would be 60 lac and can probably be raised to 70 to 80 by constructing three more wells in the river bed but he would not be prepared to say so with certainty.

20. There is again the danger of the central main getting choked with sand and if such a thing does happen there is no means to clear the main and the position would be very serious indeed.

He rejected the proposal of filter gallery which was originally in the project except that of taking water direct from the river in case the Municipality put up the requirements at 100 lacs to 150 lacs per day which by the way is nearly one half the river current in the hot weather.

21. We have given the history of what is being done from the beginning and a detailed idea of our present and future difficulties in order to impress upon all to be prepared for a bold and generous scheme. There is no doubt that our

present needs cannot be put at anything less than 90 lacs per day and we must think of temporary scheme which can take a shorter period for completion and can be relied upon in the next clear weather [*sic*] for the required supply. At the same time it is necessary to think of some scheme which would be a permanent solution of this difficult problem.

This is one aspect of the question. Another curious aspect is regarding the quality of water supply by the present system.

22. In November, 1913, Wells No. 9 and 10 had to be closed as the water was declared to be unfit for drinking purposes by the Director of Bacteriological Laboratory. This circumstance gave additional strength to Mr. Shonbridge's idea of the central collecting main with sluice valves as that scheme would enable the Municipality to cut off any well containing contaminated water from the other wells without difficulty.

23. It has also been recognized that a certain minimum distance i.e., 150 feet, is necessary between the nearest well and the river current to avoid contamination and farther the current the purer the supply but at the same time it is true that the quantity of supply is affected in proportion to the distance of the current. In monsoon almost all the wells are under water in the floods and some even when the floods pass off. It is during this period that the quality of water is said to be seriously affected.

24. In more recent years the results of repeated analysis attracted the attention of the Sanitary Commissioner and on the 8th August, 1918, Colonel Hutchinson advised the Municipality to reconsider the whole question of its water supply in spite of part capital expenditure. In his opinion the infiltration wells do not and can never be expected to yield good water during monsoon and the only proper solution of the Ahmedabad water supply is by means of mechanical filteration.

25. The Chief Officer in March last proposed the construction of two additional wells near the river current in order to improve the quantity of water. The Sanitary Committee under the circumstances advised the Board to invite a representative of the Peterson Engineering Company who should advise the Municipality on the question of the suitability of mechanical filters on the present complicated system of water supply and to prepare the plans and estimates for a temporary scheme for the immediate improvements of supply and for a permanent improvement both as regards quality and quantity. The General Board accepted the proposal of the Sanitary Committee by their resolution No. 753 dated 22-3-1920 but added that the opinion of the Sanitary Board should also be taken. In accordance with this resolution a conference between the members of the Municipal Board and the Sanitary Board was arranged during the last days of the month of May 1920 mainly with the assistance of Mr. Chattfield, the Collector of Ahmedabad. Mr. Walker, the General Manager of the Peterson Engineering Co. came here and made a clear study of our system. He was also present in the conference. The collector also attended.

26. We have already stated above the opinion of the Sanitary Engineer as regards the probable increase of supply by the completion of the scheme.

The Sanitary Commissioner who had studied the statement of analysis condemned the water and was in favour of adopting filteration system.

Mr. Walker was of opinion that the present system must be abandoned, and advised the adoption of the temporary scheme of chlorinating the water supplied by the present system together with additional water taken direct from the river by means of pipe from one of the wells to [*sic*] the current. This was considered to be the only immediate solution and the Sanitary Commissioner approved it as a temporary measure for a period of three years during which time the Municipality may be able to make up its mind for a more ambitious scheme.

27. The temporary scheme is roughly estimated to cost about Rs 23000 initial and about Rs 13000 recurring. The plant will be of use if in future mechanical filters are to be adopted. This scheme will roughly take six weeks for completion after it is sanctioned and Mr. Walker has agreed to send it in about a fortnight's time. The Sanitary Engineer also agreed that scheme may be of use to the Municipality to consider the necessity or otherwise of more expensive scheme.

28. The other scheme of adopting mechanical filters right away is not so easy. It involves a capital outlay of Rs 10 lacs and a large recurring cost of Rs 1,25,000 in addition to the present recurring cost of Rs 9300. It is expected to take three years for completion. The abnormal cost is due to the necessity of double pumping as in the absence of any catchment area or some such natural facility, a gravitation system which would be far more cheap is out of question.

29. The Hon'ble R.S. Harilal suggested that before condemning present system outright and plunging headlong into a costly scheme of this nature it would be necessary and advisable to have water analysis made on the spot for about a month so as to enable the Municipality to take the rate payers into confidence and to prepare them for additional burden. The Sanitary Commissioner saw no objection to such a course being adopted. It was also suggested that a permanent laboratory should be opened in Ahmedabad.

30. Under these circumstances we propose that the Sanitary Board be requested to depute the Board's analyst for thorough examination of the samples from various wells and taps on the spot for at least a period of three months during this monsoon as that is the most suitable period for analysis of the Ahmedabad water. He may be informed that the Civil Surgeon has kindly consented to allow the use of his laboratory but as the laboratory is not properly equipped the Board's analyst may be authorised to come here with the necessary equipment. We also propose that Government may be requested to open a permanent laboratory in Ahmedabad on the terms and conditions on which it is opened in Karachi and Poona. In our opinion a laboratory is one of the most urgent needs of the city.

33

Gandhiji Praises Vallabhbhai

Young India, 7 July 1920

All the readers of *Young India* may not know that Ahmedabad came under a heavy fine for the misdeeds of the April of last year. The fine was collected from the residents of Ahmedabad but some were exempted at the discretion of the collector. Among those who were called upon to pay the fines were income-tax payers. They had to pay a third of the tax paid by them. Mr. V.J. Patel, noted barrister, and Dr. Kanuga, a leading medical practitioner, were among those who were unable to pay. They had admittedly helped the authorities to quell the disturbance. No doubt they were satyagrahis but they had endeavoured to still the mob fury even at some risk to their own persons. But the authorities would not exempt them. It was a difficult thing for them to use discretion in individual cases. It was equally difficult for these two gentlemen to pay any fine when they were not to blame at all They did not wish to embarrass the authorities and yet they were anxious to preserve their self-respect. They carried on no agitation but simply notified their inability to pay the fines in the circumstances set forth above. Therefore an attachment was issued. Dr. Kanuga is a very busy practitioner and his box is always full. The watchful attaching official attached his cash box and extracted enough money to discharge the writ of execution. A lawyer's business cannot be conducted on these lines. Mr. Patel sported no cash box. A sofa of his sitting-room was therefore attached and advertised for sale and duly sold. Both these satyagrahis thus completely saved their consciences.

Wiseacres may laugh at the folly of allowing writs of attachment and paying for the collection of fines. Multiply such instances and imagine the consequence to the authorities of executing thousands of writs. Writs are possible when they are confined to a few recalcitrants. They are troublesome when they have to be executed against many high-souled persons who have done no wrong and who refuse payment to vindicate a principle. They may not attract much notice when isolated individuals resort to this method of protest. But clean examples have a curious method of multiplying themselves. They bear publicity and the sufferers instead of incurring odium receive congratulations. Men like Thoreau[1] brought about the abolition of slavery by their personal examples. Says Thoreau,

> I know this well, that if one thousand, if one hundred, if ten men whom I could name.—if ten *honest* men only—aye, if *one* honest man, in this State of Massachusetts *ceasing to hold slaves* were actually to withdraw from this co-partnership and be locked up in the country goal therefor, it would be the abolition of slavery in America. For it matters not how small the beginning may seem to be, what is once well done is done for ever.

Again he says,

> I have contemplated the imprisonment of the offender rather than seizure of his goods—though both will serve the same purpose, because they who assert the purest right and consequently are most dangerous to a corrupt State, commonly have not spent much time in accumulating property.

We, therefore, congratulate Mr. Patel and Dr. Kanuga on the excellent example set by them in an excellent spirit and in an excellent cause.

[1]Henry David Thoreau (1817-1862); American recluse, naturalist and writer.

34

Vallabhbhai Condemns British Atrocities in Wake of Rowlatt Bills Agitation[1]

27 August 1920

The All India Congress Committee feels that before the Congress Session is held in Calcutta in the following week, an effort should be made to ascertain the wishes of the people on the proposal to offer non-cooperation. That is why this Conference is being held. The path of non-cooperation is directly opposed to the policy which has been followed hitherto, and the question which has been placed before you is the question of deflecting the course of the popular movement in that direction. Both those who support the idea of non-cooperation and those who oppose it have been asked to attend this Conference. Both schools of thought must listen to the arguments of each other with patience. People who desire independence cannot ignore popular opinion of any shade whatever, for the objective of all parties is in the final analysis the same. The difference only arises in regard to be the methods to be adopted to achieve that objective.

In 1914 when the first World War began, it was said that England had been forced to enter the war for the preservation of the independence of smaller States and also in the name of truth and justice. Hundreds of thousands of soldiers went from India to fight in the battle-fields of Europe, Africa and Asia. Today there is hardly any part of the world in which people are as poor as India, and yet we make a present of 15 million rupees to England. England was not too certain of India's loyalty at first but later she was amazed at our wholehearted loyalty and help during the war. Our wise and able leaders were of the view that to give conditional help at a time of danger would not have been honourable. But what did we get in return for this when the war was over? We were given the Rowlatt Act which deprived us of freedom of action. When the people protested against such a tyrannical piece of legislation, the Government decided upon a policy of suppressing all resistance by force. Smarting under a sense of injustice, a section of our people in a fit of temporary insanity committed atrocities. We cannot defend these mad acts of our people. When innocent people are murdered, when Government buildings are burnt, when women are attacked, it is only to be expected that the Government would react strongly and act without moderation in taking effective and deterrent action. But Government officers exceeded all bounds of reasonableness, and the Government passed a law to exonerate those officers from the normal legal consequences of their actions. And finally, it appointed a Committee ostensibly to investigate the happenings in Jallianwala Bagh and Lahore, but actually, as has turned out, to hush up every thing.

The British Parliament is the last court of appeal for justice. There are people in this country who have greater faith in British justice than even in the existence of God. But these discussions in the British Parliament have opened the eyes of even such people. If a person who has been cherishing a stone for a long time, believing it to be a diamond, discovers one day when he goes to sell it in his time of difficulty that it is indeed nothing but a stone, can he really blame the stone? Our condition today is what it is because of the blind faith we have had in British justice. In the House of Lords, the Lords verily showed their nobility! They made little of the grave hardships and atrocities which the people of the Punjab endured. Murder of so many innocent men and women was to them nothing as compared with the honour of one callous Englishman: that officer they regarded as brave, and those innocent persons who were killed as rebels. General Dyer's intention was honest; he only made a slight miscalculation, he fired a few more rounds than was perhaps necessary and killed a large number of men, women and children, but, then did not save India? Sir Michael O'Dwyer who was mainly responsible for these atrocities was praised by the British Government for the services he had rendered to the Punjab; but the services which the people of the Punjab had rendered were forgotten.

Presumably to instil terror into the minds of people while the Martial Law was in operation, men were killed on the slightest excuse; they were made to crawl and to trail their nose in dust; they were whipped publicly; some were executed in the market place; supply of drinking water was stopped; women were allowed to be molested and maltreated; these and many other atrocious acts were performed. . . .

When the order requiring people to crawl on their stomachs was criticized in Indian Legislature by popular representatives, many members from the Government benches in replying used language, which would have done honour to a gang of gamblers and drunkards. They poured ridicule on those who had been made to crawl; even Pandit Madan Mohan Malviyaji was not spared and he was openly insulted.

Can we easily forget this attempt to dishonour India? Not content with humiliating the Punjab, these gentlemen representing the Government considered the intolerable hardships and troubles of the people a matter for fun. The coming generations have a claim on us, who are their trustees; if we leave them only a heritage of insults and dishonour, of what use would all the wealth and all the comforts be that we may leave to them? If we put up with this insult, would it be a matter of surprise if for all time to come we are despised by civilized nations?

The Turkish Empire was divided in spite of Britain's promise. The Sultan was made a prisoner in Constantinople. Syria was absorbed by France. Symrna and Thrace were swallowed by Greece while Mesopotamia and Palestine were taken possession of by the British. In Arabia, too, a ruler was created who would support the British Government. Even the Viceroy admitted that some of the conditions of peace could not but offend the Muslim community. It has, as a matter of fact, been a heart-breaking episode for the Indian Muslims, and how can Hindus stand by unaffected when they see their fellow countrymen, thus, in distress?

Some argue that as the representatives of Turkey had accepted the peace conditions, India had no right to protest. A signature given under duress only confirms an injustice, and can not take away the right to ask for justice. During the Martial Law in the Punjab, the officers who had caused the Punjabis to crawl had the impudence to put forward the strange defence that people crawled very willingly and that some indeed enjoyed it so much that they crawled not once or twice but even three times and, I suppose, had to be stopped from continuing to crawl along other streets! There were officers who claimed that people liked the Martial Law so much that they shouted victory to Martial Law and were anxious that the Martial Law should be kept on. Verily, there is no limit to credulity or wishful thinking. Could evidence of this nature take away from us the right to condemn or criticize the Martial Law and its injustice?

[1]N.D. Parikh, *Sardar Patel Ke Bhashana,* Navjeevan Publishing House, Ahmedabad.

35

Vallabhbhai's Spirited Address as Chairman, Reception Committee, Fourth Gujarat Political Council

27 August 1920[1]

On behalf of the Reception Committee and the people of Ahmedabad, I welcome you from the bottom of my heart. The meeting of this Council is normally held by the end of the year during Diwali. But because of some important and unforeseen circumstances, we needed to meet earlier. Because of the hastily organised session and, that too, during the rainy season, you might find that certain things are lacking and you might have to undergo some inconvenience for which I apologise to you on behalf of the Reception Committee.

Capital of Gujarat

Ahmedabad is the capital of Gujarat but at this time it will not be proper for me to go into its glorious history. The city is also a centre of industry and trade but its present importance is because of the fact that the Sabarmati Ashram is situated here. Mahatma Gandhi who founded this Council and brought a new life into the politics of India has given the type of importance to the city which would not have been possible otherwise. Gandhiji has been infusing the spirit of truth and *Ahimsa* through *Navjiwan* and through the *Young India.* He has been instrumental in waking up the whole country towards a life of self-respect and duty. The eyes of the country are fixed on Gujarat. Everybody looks to Gujarat for leadership.

The Late Lokmanya Tilak

The Commander-in-Chief of India's battle for Swaraj, Lokmanya Bal Gangadhar Tilak, is no longer amongst us. Who can fill his place? The basic principle of his life was: "Swarajya is my birth right and I (shall not beg for it, but) have it." He fought fearlessly for the achievement of his goal till the end of his days. No greater fighter has risen on the political firmament than Tilak who could fight the British bureaucracy with its own weapons. His deep scholarship, his shining character, his ideal simplicity, his fearlessness, his unquestioned patriotism and, most of all, his call for complete Swarajya—this is his legacy. The more we follow in his footsteps, the more successful we would be. People have forgotten the names of kings and princes but the name of Lokmanya Tilak will ever remain in the hearts of India's people. Those in power lose their authority when they die but the reign of the great patriots continues even after their death. People try to follow in their footsteps and remember them always. His love for the people was boundless and people reciprocated. A proof of it, if any proof was needed, was found in the huge public meeting held at Chopati in Bombay to mourn his death. It is our duty to pay our respects to that great man before we begin to consider the official agenda of the Council.

Khilafat and the Punjab Problem

The Congress Committee met in Banaras to consider the situation created by the Khilafat Movement and the incidents of Punjab. The Committee considered the question of non-cooperation and decided to hold a special session of the Congress to take a decision on this momentous subject. The Committee has decided that before the session is held in Calcutta next week, the people of India should carefully consider the question of non-cooperation and make their views known to the Congress. That is the reason why a session of this Council has been called earlier than normal. We must consider this question seriously. Our political movement has been going along only one direction for the past many years. The movement has gathered momentum and the great war has added to it. The path of non-cooperation is different, rather contrary from the present path and now the question is before you that we change the direction of our movement towards non-cooperation. Non-cooperation is the great battle which will begin between the Government and the people but it will remain within certain parameters. This battle would test the strength of both the parties. If both the parties follow the rules, neither of them would be the loser. He who wins will not lose. As a matter of fact, both the parties will gam a lot. The battle is as difficult as its results are desirable. It will not be an easy task to contend against a government which has defeated a powerful nation like Germany with the force of arms and superior strategy and which is now drunk with its victory. We will have to show great courage and a spirit of sacrifice for which the people will have to be educated. This is the subject which we have gathered together to discuss today. All friends, whether they are in favour of the non-cooperation movement or against it, have been invited to the council. We must not take a decision in haste or with impatience. We must hear the views of both the factions with patience. The people who want Swarajya cannot show disrespect to either of the factions because the final goal of all the parties is the same. If there is any difference of opinion it is with regard to the means we adopt in our battle. Who can doubt that the difference of opinion would be genuine? Those who are against it may be small in number but that very fact should make us hear their views with humility and consider them dispassionately. If there is no contrary view, there is no room for debate or discussion. Those who disregard the opposition because they are in a majority do not have any right to force their views merely on the basis of their majority. I request the council to take a decision on this important matter after due consideration.

India's Aid in the War Effort

When the war broke out in Europe in 1914, it was said that England had no axe to grind in it, that it did not want to fight, that Germany had thrust the war on it and it had to take to arms to defend the independence of the smaller nations and in the interest of truth and justice. Hundreds of thousands of Indian soldiers shed their blood in this war, in Europe, Africa and Asia. There would hardly be a country on the surface of this earth which is poorer than India. In spite of that India gave Rs 1.5 billion to England, raw materials worth crores of rupees and other ordnance goods. India, about whose allegiance many doubts were expressed, gave such a proof of its support for the war effort that the people of England were surprised. Our leaders accepted the Government of India's advice that no controversial matters be aired as long as the war lasted. They also accepted the Press Act, the Defence of India Act and the Seditious Meetings Act even when they were mis-applied. Nobody objected when excesses were committed during recruitment and War Loans. People were advised by everybody that they should keep quiet. The advice that India would cooperate only if the Indian and the British soldiers were treated alike was considered improper. Our wise and clever leaders found it against the grain to impose any conditions for help while the empire was in danger. It was thought that such behaviour would not behave India and the Indians believed in the liberal and just attitude of the British people and also the liberal promises made by the British Ministers from time to time. Our Muslim brothers went to the other extent in showing their faithfulness towards the Empire. The Ali Brothers who are like the two eyes of the Muslim community were detained during the war, many Muslim papers fell victim to the Press Act, even so thousands of brave Muslims fought against Turkey and laid down their lives because they believed the promises made by the British Prime Minister and other ministers.

The Reward for Sacrifice

The great war ended finally in the victory of the Empire. Let us look into what we have got. Immediately after the hostilities ended, the Government of India gave us by way of a gift the Rowlatt Act which destroys personal freedom.

It was done in the interest of India and Indians were astonished. There was a hue and cry from one end of the country to the other. At a time when the whole world was talking about the principle of self-determination, a handful of foreigners, who claim the monopoly of political sagacity, disregarded organised public opinion and bound India in the shackles of slavery. Even the advice of those who did not find it gentlemanly to impose any conditions for helping the Empire in its moment of crisis was rejected. The advice of the members of the Council who are nominated by the Government and who support the government all the time was of no avail. The whole world knows the consequences of such a thoughtless action. The people were groaning under the heels of the cruel government run by the Governor of Punjab. The policy of repression used by the government against those who oppose the Rowlatt Act merely added fuel to the fire. Mahatma Gandhi was stopped from going to Punjab and the leaders of Amritsar were whisked away by the authorities. The result was that a section of the people lost its cool because of the intense anger and in a fit of momentary madness, it committed certain excesses. We cannot defend those who indulged in such acts in anger. If the Government takes stern measures to stop such excesses and punishes the guilty, nobody can blame it. One can understand that when innocent people are murdered, government property is destroyed, churches are set on fire and women are molested, the Government would naturally be angry and if it goes beyond the limit in curbing such incidents, one can understand that it is natural. If the government's sternness had been in proportion to the excesses committed by the people, we would not have spoken against it. But the government went beyond the limits in its cruel behaviour. You cannot find any instance of such atrocities committed by a government of any civilized nation. They go beyond the atrocities which the Germans committed in Belgium. And, what is more, the government passed a law to absolve the authorities guilty of these atrocities. After that a committee was appointed to go into these incidents. Those who have faith in such committees being able to give justice quietened the people and advised everybody to have faith in the committee. When the Council, at its session in Surat, did not pass the resolution demanding the recall of the Viceroy, it was because of this consideration. But the Enquiry Committee tried to sweep everything under the carpet. The three nominated Indian members resigned from the Committee and those who had faith in the Committee had to keep quiet. Sir Chimanlal Sitalvad was thought fit to be a judge of the highest court and the Government did not place any faith in his capacity to dispense justice when the Whites and the Indians clashed. Before Sir Chimanlal was appointed to the Committee, he had expressed his views against Satyagraha. That is why nobody would be surprised at what he has said about Satyagraha in his report. The Government, however, liked only that portion of the report. It utilized that and would continue to do so. The British Parliament is the final court of justice. There are people in our country who have greater faith in British justice than in God. The Parliament, however, removed all their doubts. If a person keeps a worthless piece of stone in his possession thinking it to be a priceless jewel and tries to sell it when he needs the money, you cannot blame that piece of stone. This is the position in which people who had faith in British justice find themselves. There is no doubt that, generally speaking, where there is no self-respect involved, a British officer can give true justice. There are many examples where Indians have been killed by the Britishers under the British Government but there is not one single example where a Britisher was hanged for the crime of murdering an Englishman. The members of the House of Lords showed the mettle they are made of. They laughed at the trials and tribulations which the people of Punjab underwent. The murder of hundreds of innocent human beings was swept under the carpet so that the prestige of one cowardly British officer could be maintained. He was given accolades for his bravery and the innocent people who became his victims were called rebels. How can one believe in British justice under these circumstances? The House of Lords gave a severe blow to India's self-respect which led to clouds of despondency over the Indian horizon. It led to a situation where nobody knew which way to go and what to do. In the House of Lords, Lord Sinha advises us to forget the past. It is this Lord Sinha who when he was conferred the title spread a wave of happiness in India. We had become the believers in British justice. This shows how short-sighted we are in political matters. If an Indian is given a place in the House of Lords, does it mean that India's luck has favoured her ? If Lord Sinha had not been in that House at the time of the carnage in Punjab, could India have lost anything ? What has his presence in the House of Lords gained us ? India's and Punjab's self-respect was trampled under the British feet and instead of giving us justice, the members of that House laughed at the troubles of the people. How can we forget this. During the martial law in Punjab, a deliberate policy of genocide was adopted to spread terror, the noses of the Punjabis were rubbed into the dust, they were forced to crawl on their bellies, flogged at public thoroughfares, gallows were erected right inside the city, the city was bombarded from the air, the students were frog-marched for 16 miles, the leaders were put behind bars, atrocities were committed to create false evidence, drinking water supply was stopped, efforts were made to divide the Hindus and the Muslims, women were molested and many other devilish atrocities were committed. How can we forget all this? The Congress Committee made reasonable recommendations but they were disregarded. The officers who committed the atrocities were not sorry at what they had done. On the other hand, they were proud of what they had done. The Government had the means whereby the pain and the insults heaped on the people could be forgotten but they did not make use of that excellent opportunity. When the Central Assembly discussed the orders issued under Martial Law that people should crawl on their bellies, the supporters of the Government used a language which behoves only gamblers and drunkers. They laughed at those who were made to crawl. They did not spare any effort to insult Pt. Madan Mohan Malviya. Those who sought to defend General O'Dyer in the House of Lords and the Central Assembly, said that only his calculations were wrong and that he had saved the country from anarchy. Can we forget these things? The General is responsible for all these atrocities but the British Cabinet remembered his services to Punjab and praised him. The services which Punjab had rendered were forgotten. Punjab which had shown its allegiance to the Crown and had made the largest sacrifices in the Great War was accused, falsely, of rebellion. This was the devilish charge made against Punjab. The evidence led before the Hunter Committee does not prove that a single bullet was fired by the people at the authorities during those dark days. In spite of that the charge of the people rebelling against an army having the latest weapons is the height of impudence. I ask those, humbly, who advise us to forget the past as to what they want to teach India. If such atrocities were committed in any other country and if instead of punishing the guilty those who were the victims of atrocities were laughed at what would be the consequences? It's easy to see what would happen. Should we learn to pocket all insults? Who has the right to teach India to pocket such insults? The new generation would say about such people that if they were not born it would have been very good for the country. At least we have some rights on posterity because we are the trustees of the coming generations. If we leave a legacy of toleration for insults, what good would our property be ? If we pocket these insults, other countries would look down upon us. How can we, in that condition, claim to be the partners of the Britishers?

The Condition of Muslims

Let's see how our Muslim brothers fare. Turkey has been divided into two. The Sultan is a prisoner in Constantinople, France has gobbled up Syria. The Greeks have taken over Symarna and Thrace. Mesopotamia and Palestine have been taken over by the Britishers. They have controlled Arbistan and a puppet government has been installed there. The Viceroy has himself admitted that some of the conditions of the armistice are such that they are a cause of grief for the Muslims. In disregard of the sacred promises made by the British Prime Minister to the Indian Muslims and forgetting the susceptibilities of the Muslim community, the Allied nations put an end to the Government of the Khalifa. This injustice has deeply hurt the Muslims. That they have been the victims of injustice is admitted on all hands. What they should do under these circumstances has been decided by the Central Khilafat Committee. This Council should solve this problem too. The Hindus cannot remain neutral when the Muslims are in such a sorry state. If the Hindus want the friendship of the Muslims they must share their troubles. Some people argue that when the Turkish representative accepted the terms of the Armistice what right has India got to speak on a subject? If signatures are got under duress, an injustice does not become justice and the rights of those who cry for justice cannot be forgotten. The officers who forced the Punjabis to crawl on their bellies during the Martial Law gave a curious argument: that the people did it twice or thrice and they had to be stopped. They also argued that the people liked Martial law to such an extent that they shouted slogans like "Long Live Martial Law" and they importuned the Government for continuing it. Does this mean that we have lost the right to speak against the injustices committed during Martial Law?

NON-COOPERATION

We used all methods to stop the injustice with regard to Punjab and Khilafat. We held meetings in villages, passed resolutions, raised our voice of protest, sent telegrams and deputations, reminded the government of the solemn promises made by its Ministers but all in vain. We were convinced that the present system of getting justice is worthless. We also realized that we had taken the wrong way. But even if we consider that what is done is done and cannot be changed, we must take a decision that we would not again take to that path. Whatever we do or not do, we must take care to see that we are not deceived in future. It is the responsibility of the leaders to see whether India is allowed to go down or to take up arms to save it. The people are looking towards them. Mahatma Gandhi has shown us the path of civil disobedience. The Khilafat Committee has accepted the Mahatma's advice. This reminds me of the scene one saw at the last day's meeting of the Amritsar Congress. Mahatma Gandhi touched the sacred ground of Jalianwala Bagh, where the blood of Hindus, Muslims and Sikhs had mingled and stood in the jampacked pandal of the session, he took off his cap and said that we must cooperate, believe the liberal promises made by the Emperor and accept the hand of friendship and also to stop disbelieving what the Britishers said at that time. That Mahatma is today advising the whole country to take to the path of civil disobedience. Probably no other person has the kind of faith in the British Constitution which Gandhiji has. He is a lover of the English. Who has served the Empire as he has? The educated leaders have served the Crown because they were tempted by high office. But Gandhiji served without any considerations of self interest in the Zulu and Boer wars. Gandhiji always praises Mr. Montague for his high character and services, but he says that such people of high character are dangerous politically. Gandhiji is right, it seems. The Government which plays dirty politics is afraid of people of high character but such persons are the bed-rock of countries where clean politics is the norm. Who can serve the people as Gandhiji has done? We do not see any other way open to us. No other leader can guide us. Now when only one way is open to us, we cannot disregard it. Some leaders have issued a declaration against civil disobedience. There is no reason to doubt their sincerity when they give us this advice. When we change direction, it is possible that we would hesitate, make an assessment of the dangers ahead and in doing so, there can be differences of opinion. But all these things have been forcefully contradicted by Mahatma Gandhi in his recent speech in Madras. What more can I say? Some people think that civil disobedience is against religion. I cannot claim to be as erudite as they are but I ask them where does this religion go when you advise the people not to take part in the civil disobedience movement? We can ask humbly, Sir Narain Chandawarkar, what comes in the way of his returning the knighthood in an empire where people like Michael O'Dwyer are made knight and those like Ravindra Nath Tagore return it?

DANGERS OF NOT DOING ANYTHING

We hear people saying that there is danger in civil disobedience that there is an apprehension of riots breaking out. It is true that there is danger, but which country has easily got independence? Is there less danger in doing nothing?

If we keep quiet under the present circumstances, the people are in danger. If a patient's life is in danger and the surgeon's knife is the only remedy, the doctors would use it regardless of the danger it may pose to the life of the patient. The Muslims are a people who are zealous by nature. If they had not been advised to take to civil disobedience, bloodshed would have resulted. Has anybody considered this aspect of the matter? There is no doubt the government could have stopped that bloodshed, but that does not appear to be possible. Thousands of Muslims are migrating these days which shows how much their religious susceptibility have been hurt. Both the government and those who oppose civil disobedience should consider the consequences if the sentiments of the Muslims are not allowed to be expressed. If the opponents of civil disobedience use their intelligence and strength in advising the people to remain away from violence and do not advise them to stay away from the civil disobedience movement, they would serve the government and the people better. Has anybody given up his efforts for the betterment of the people merely because there is danger in such an enterprise? If those who built such a large empire are afraid of danger, they would not have been able to build it. There is always danger of railway accidents and ship disasters, but does it mean that people should be advised not to travel? A wise man takes all precautions against danger. The people are now awake and they know the injustice that is inherent in the laws like the Rowlatt Act and the injustices which have been committed against the Khilafat Movement. If the Government does not listen to us, the people would always lose. And if we are afraid of losing or the obstacles that come in our way, we will not be able to take the people forward. If there is danger in civil disobedience, let us find another way. Is the Khilafat Movement and the injustice in Punjab less insulting than the division of Bengal? Has India's manhood vanished?

Reforms are Useful

We have been tempted by the so-called reforms. The biggest danger is that we might be taken in by the efficacy of these reforms. But they are without any merit and will not give us any benefit. If bloodshed is harmful, these reforms would be equally harmful in the final analysis. The present government merely exploits the people and is a vehicle for their destruction. If certain British parts are replaced with Indian parts in this administrative machine, it is not going to make any difference. Will one Indian Governor take India forward? Do the British Governors not have any qualities or character? Are not people like the Hon'ble Lord Hardinge not found among them? It was he who did not harm anybody even though he was the victim of a murderous attack in Delhi's Chandni Chowk. If a few drops of the sacred Ganges water are mixed with the gutter, it does not become clean. So long as the whole system is not changed and the Government of India is not run for the benefit of Indians, no improvement is possible. So long as the interests of the foreigners have the pride of place, if the British bureaucrats are appeased and some so-called reforms are offered as a sort of a bribe, it is not going to help us. The reason is that there is no justice, no liberty and no equality which we want. Most of the Britishers look at us with contempt and enmity. What is the good of such reforms? Is there any assurance that the events like those in Punjab will not be repeated? The condition of Indians in South Africa, East Africa and Fiji is pitiable. Is it going to change after these reforms? If we are not honoured in our own country, would we get any honour abroad? And look at the heavy price we have paid for these reforms. We have been demanding for a number of years that the expenditure on the high offices in the Civil Services be reduced but before the reforms were implemented, the expenditure on I.C.S., Military and other posts went on increasing by Rs 25 crores every year. Our right to criticise this increase in expenditure has been taken away and Health and Education departments have been made over to us. The people do not want such reforms. They want to avoid hunger, insults and want to live in an air of freedom. Which among these would you be able to provide through these reforms?

Boycott of the Assemblies

The faithful Muslims have boycotted the assemblies. If they do not sit in the assemblies, who would the Hindus sit with? There is no atmosphere in which cooperation is possible; it has been vitiated and poisoned. What is the good of closing your eyes to reality? Most of the Englishmen living in India look down upon us. The English Press emits poison and the English ladies have similar views. The Englishmen want to hang those whom we revere. And those who we think should be hanged are honoured by the British. The Government was right when it issued an order that government employees should not contribute to the "O'Dwyer Fund" but does it mean that the mentality of the officers has changed? The Government forced the Collector of Dharwar to cancel his foolish circular. But does this mean that the views of the man have changed? Being a fool he expressed his real views, but how many are there who would behave similarly. It is shameful for us to pretend any partnership or friendship with the British in the circumstances. It is not that the Britishers are evil by nature, but their views and ours are different. They are different because our interests are contrary to each other's. So long as the circumstances do not change, this Council has to decide whether we should boycott the new assemblies or not.

Injustice and Atrocities

We are helping the Government in the matter of atrocities and the injustice that it is perpetrating on us. If they have taken away our freedom, we have helped them do it.

Sir Reginald Craddock proudly tells us that the Government can keep Indians under their heel with the help of two lakh Indian policemen and hundreds of thousands of Indian soldiers. This is a subject which should be duly considered by us. Our brothers who are in police service or are seeking to join it, or those who want to join the Armed forces should be told the facts of life. Our soldiers are being used by the Britishers in Mesopotamia, Syria, Palestine, Egypt and other countries to fight against the people of those countries seeking independence. The people of those countries curse us and instead of calling back our soldiers, new contingents are being sent there. This should be opposed strongly by this Council.

The Police and The People

The police should be the protectors of the people but how far they are doing their duties these days is clear to all. One hears that dacoities and robberies are being committed in many villages of Gujarat. The police are unable to protect the people. It cannot be said that the police is guilty. Most of the policemen are illiterate and the salaries which they get are too meagre to sustain them. It is natural, therefore, that instead of protecting the people, they become partners of dacoits or robbers. Sometimes they make money by committing atrocities on the people. It is not that the Government does not know it. If we take the present political situation into consideration, we would be driven to the conclusion that a time has come when we should learn to defend ourselves. We must raise corps of volunteers in all villages and train them. The Council must take a decision to that effect.

Need for Panchayat Courts

In the courts, the cases are on the increase and the people do not get justice. The blame cannot be given to those who are responsible for dispensing justice. There are other reasons into which I need not go at present, but there is need to save the people from the troubles that they face when they go to the courts. We must have Panchayat Courts at various places so that cheap and speedy justice is available to the people.

Responsibility of the Educated Class

A great responsibility rests on the educated classes. People are ignorant and they are not ready—such an excuse will not absolve them of their responsibility. People must be educated and guided to the right path. For that literacy is the need of the hour. It is the responsibility of the educated classes to educate the masses. They cannot fulfil this responsibility by going to the municipalities, local boards or assemblies in their spare time. The educated classes can easily discern the faults from which government policy suffers. When they give expression to their views about those faults, they become unpopular with the government. But merely pointing out the faults of the government is not the end of their duty. The progress of the people depends on their courage, character and the capacity to make sacrifices.

Conclusion

There are many parties amongst us. We use our mental and physical capacities to strike at each other, cannot tolerate differences of opinion nor see any good in something which is different from our views. We worsen the situation by making charges against each other. Under these circumstances, the poor people are puzzled and cannot see the right path. If we have to get justice and independence, we must look into our faults and improve them. We must have a spirit of tolerance, self-confidence and courage. We must also make sacrifices. In short, if we want justice, we must see the good rather than the bad among our rulers and must improve our character so that it approximates to British character. I pray to God that He gives us guidance and helps us. In the end, I again welcome you and request you to elect the President of this Council.

[1] *Sardar Patel Ke Bhashana,* Edited by Narihari Dwarikadas Parikh and Uttam Chand Deep Chand Shah, Navjivan, Ahmedabad, 1950.

36

Vallabhbhai Asks Indian Leaders to Give up Titles

Navjivan, 30 August 1920

I cannot claim to be as learned or to possess as deep a knowledge of religious books as these gentlemen, but I would ask them what happens to this argument when they themselves advise people not to take part in non-cooperation, to keep away from it and generally to non-cooperate with the non-cooperators? I would like to ask Sir Narayan Chandawarkar in all humility: Why does he hang on to his British title, when he knows on the one hand that the same Government has conferred a similar title on a man like Sir Michael O'Dwyer, and on the other hand that the Gita does not forbid such renunciation as an act of protest. A great poet Sir Rabindranath Tagore has already surrendered his title of 'Sir', and the person whom you regard as a prophet, worthy of the deepst respect, has surrendered his medals.

37

Gandhiji on Gujarat's Contribution to Satyagraha under Vallabhbhai's Leadership (Extracts)

Navjivan, 5 September 1920

Gujarat has played its part well. The Conference has never in the past had to face, and it will not have for a hundred years more to face, an issue as serious as the one on which it took a decision. We needed at this critical time a leader with an iron will and we found one. Everyone who reads the speeches of Mr. Vallabhbhai Patel and the venerable old gentleman, Abbas Tyabji, will readily acknowledge that they were resolute and unambiguous, but polite. The chairman of the Reception Committee stated his views in a brief but impressive speech, in the simplest Gujarati. We cannot say anything about Mr. Abbas Ali's style, since his speech was originally written in English. Other speeches were short and easy to follow. I have rarely come across or listened to presidential addresses so brief but direct as those speeches.

The Conference was worthy of the president. The resolutions it has passed leave nothing to be desired. They are categorical and are to be implemented forthwith.

The resolutions passed before now called upon the Government to do something or other; now, it is we who are to act.

The Conference has been sufficiently warned. The leaders told it of all possible dangers. It was made very clear that the people would lose their good name if they were found lacking the strength to carry out their decisions. The Conference has accepted non-cooperation unanimously, regardless of whether the special Congress votes against non-cooperation as such or against the actual programme suggested.

Gujaratis are reputed to be practical; they do not pass resolutions, carried away by emotion. If Gujarat fails to act on the resolution, it will fall in the esteem of others as much as it has risen by passing it. If Gujarat weakens in its resolve, even the country as a whole may suffer. It is a sign of wisdom, in the first instance, not to embark upon a task but, once a task is undertaken, it is one's duty always to see it through.

Gujaratis have become the trustees of Mother India's honour. May God grant them firmness.

The Conference has decided on the boycott of legislative bodies, Government schools and law-courts. It has requested title holders to renounce their titles.

If you wish to support the cause of non-cooperation and free yourselves from the yoke of the wicked Empire, do not go away at the sight of volunteers but contribute your mite. If anyone approaches you for funds on my behalf or Sardar Vallabhbhai's or on behalf of the Swarajya Sabha, do not give anything straightaway. Contribute only if you happen to know the persons. Those who do not have money on them now may send their contributions to Ahmedabad. From today, may God make you fearless, give you the strength for self-sacrifice, may He make you truthful and humble. May you fear God alone and may He rid you of your fear of other men.

38

Vallabhbhai Indignant over British Collector Ahmedabad's Observations, Demands Withdrawl

27 September 1920
(G.R. 11/1920-21) Resolution 505

A copy received of the Administration Report of the Ahmedabad Municipality for the year 1919-20 by the Collector of Ahmedabad, forwarded to the General Board for information.

Mr Vallabhbhai proposed and Mr. Krishnalal seconded that this Board strongly protests against the following unwarantable and offensive remarks of the new Collector of Ahmedabad under the heading "General Remarks" in his letter No. M.U.N.I. dated 15/18th September, 1920, and insists on his withdrawing the same.

The remarks are as under—"It is not the fault of the President that the Board has on some occasions come to rash or unfortunate decisions under the influence of the hot-headed element amongst them."

This Board refuse to consider the report till the aforesaid remarks are withdrawn.

A copy of this resolution be forwarded to the Government.

Mr. Chahewala moved an amendment seconded by K.S. Dr. Mansuri that this be noted.

Mr. Pestanshah moved an amendment seconded by Sheth that this Board considers the opinion of the Collector as expressed in the remarks, "It is not the fault of the President that the Board has on some occasions come to rash or unfortunate decisions under the influence of the hot-headed element amongst them" as objectionable and uncalled for, and regrets its inclusion in the covering letter of the Collector No. M.U.N.I. dated 15/18th September, 1920, forwarding the Ahmedabad Municipality Report to Government.

A copy of the resolution be forwarded to the Government.

K.B. Dr. Nanavatty moved an amendment that this Board has read with regrets the following remarks made by the Collector in his letter No. M.U.N.I. dated 15/18th September, 1920, and resolves that more useful purpose would have been served if they had not been made.

The remarks are as under—"It is not the fault of the President that the Board has on some occasions come to rash or unfortunate decisions under the influence of the hot-headed element amongst them."

The amendment fell through for want of a seconder.

Votes were then taken between the amendment of Mr. Pestanshah and the original proposal.

Mr. Vallavbhai [*sic*]'*s* proposal was carried.

39

Vallabhbhai Moves Resolution to Boycott Reformed Councils

Ahmedabad Municipal Committee Records
G.R. 11/1920-21, Resolution 525
2 October 1920

Motion of Municipal Councillors Mr. V.J. Patel and Mr. Krishnalal dated 2nd October 1920—

"This Board, being of opinion that in the interest of the people of this country the reformed Councils should be boycotted, resolves that no Municipal Officers or Servant should directly or indirectly take any part whatsoever in the forthcoming Council election. This does not in any way affect individual right of voting."

Mr. Vallavbhai [*sic*] proposed seconded by Mr. Thakore that this Board, being of opinion that in the interest of the people of this country the reformed councils should be boycotted, resolves that no Municipal Officer or Servant should directly or indirectly take any part whatsoever in the forthcoming Council elections. This does not in any way affect individual right of voting.

Mr. Chahewala raised point of order whether the first part of the motion is in order in view of the General Board's Resolution No. 558 dated 6-10-1920.

The President ruled that in view of the resolution of this Board dated 6-10-1920 the portion "Being of opinion that in the interest of the people of this country the reformed Councils should be boycotted," is out of the order at this meeting and therefore the following is the proposition of Mr. Vallavbhai [*sic*] before the meeting.

This Board resolves that no Municipal Officer or Servant should directly or indirectly take any part whatsoever in the forthcoming Council elections. This does not in any way affect individual right of voting.

Mr. Krishnalal moved an amendment seconded by Mr. Sutharia that this Board resolves that no Municipal Officer or Servant should be asked against his will to take any part whatsoever in the forthcoming Council elections.

40

Vallabhbhai Exhorts Students to Boycott Schools and Colleges[1]

Prajabandhu, 3 October 1920

Ever since the Special Session of the Congress was held in Calcutta and the resolution for non-cooperation was passed, the students of that city are asking the leaders what they should now do. I am happy to see that the students as a class are looking at public issues from a nationalistic point of view and I feel that it is a happy augury. The Congress has passed the Non-Cooperation Movement and the students have been asked to boycott Government schools and colleges. Every student who is imbued with a sense of patriotism and self-respect should follow that resolution. The resolution passed in the Calcutta Congress is the first of its kind under British Rule and it is clear that a great responsibility is cast on us as a result of the resolution. But it is clear that even while fulfilling that responsibility, we cannot become free without taking to the path of non-cooperation. All of you must be aware of what is happening in Punjab. The newspapers are full of those reports. You must have found out that the students in the Punjab Province had to undergo needless misery. Well-built students of Punjab have been flogged. Some of the students have been rusticated from the schools and colleges without any reason. The students are being forced to walk

18 to 20 miles in the burning sun and appear before the authorities. Those who run this kind of administration do not deserve that we should send our children to schools run by them. Your self-respect demands it. Do not be beset with apprehensions as to what would happen if you leave these educational institutions. There are 56 lakh illiterates in the country but they do not starve. Why are you afraid that you would face starvation if you boycotted the schools. You will not remain illiterate. The only thing you have to give up is your love for the degrees. I see that many people are eager to become lawyers because they are under the impression that lawyers earn huge incomes. But this is a false impression. If you want to become wealthy, you can do so if you engage in industry or trade. You see many rich people who are not even matriculates. That does not stand in the way of their becoming millionaires. The fact of the matter is that when you leave your school or college, you would be teaching a lesson to the teachers. Some people think that they should join the non-cooperation movement only after they have got the B.A. degree. Such a decision is taken only by weak minds because after graduation, a person starts looking for a job and he is unable to do anything else. If Gujarat college is emptied of students tomorrow, it will not be utilized as a venue of an exhibition of animals. We would be able to utilize those buildings under public supervision. The students of Gujarat must, therefore, take courage in their hands and boycott the schools and colleges. If you take this step instead of the others, it would be matter of pride for you. You would be able to help in bringing independence to the country. There are many such examples in Europe. The clarion call for the battle of non-cooperation has been given. The battle has been joined. Do not ask yourselves: "What should I do" or "What would happen to me", because these are the considerations of impotent men. Jump into the struggle and be prepared to do your best. That is your duty today. The time is short and Mahatmaji has yet to address you. I do not want to come in between him and you.

[1]Speech made by the Sardar on 28 September 1920, exhorting the school and college students to join the Non-Cooperation Movement.

41

Vallabhbhai Asks for Donations for Swaraj and Vidyapith

Navjivan, 11 November 1920

It is well known that these days Mahatma Gandhi is asking people to contribute to the alms. Gandhiji has always felt bad when he has to ask people to donate money. He has said that if I can get work done without money, I would never touch money. But in this *Kaliyug,* I also cannot get my work done without money.

Mahatma Gandhi has suggested to us to ask for donations from the people of Ahmedabad. He had desired to move in Ahmedabad for contributions. But because he had to run here and there for solving several urgent problems, it was not possible for him to be here on Diwali.

He has ordered us to beg for alms from people of Ahmedabad for Swaraj, and Gujarat Vidyapith. All those who live in Ahmedabad whether they might be rich or poor, man, woman or children, are requested to give according to their capacity to the volunteers, when they come during Diwali and request you to give donation. The money will be used only for Swaraj activity conducted through Mahatma Gandhi and for imparting national education through Gujarat Vidyapith, which is founded by Gandhiji. Seth Punjabhai Hirachand belonging to the firm of Nemchand Kacharubhai has been appointed as treasurer.

People are requested to give money after donation collectors are identified as our volunteers.

42

Vallabhbhai's Motion to Remove Government Control over Primary Education in pursuance of Congress Resolution Carried

Ahmedabad Municipal Committee Records, G.R. IV/1920-21
21 January 1921

Motion dated 21-1-1921 from Vallabhbhai J. Patel, Municipal Councillor, as under—

In response to the call of nation so clearly expressed by the Indian National Congress held at Nagpur, this Board resolves that with a view to remove Government control over Primary Education in Municipal Schools no further educational grants should now be received from Government. A copy of this resolution should be forwarded to Government.

Mr. Vallabhbhai moved seconded by Mr. Kalidas that in response to the call of nation so clearly expressed by the Indian National Congress held at Nagpur, this Board resolves that with a view to remove Government control over Primary Education in Municipal Schools no further educational grant should now be received from Government. A copy of this resolution should be forwarded to Government.

Mr. Chahewala raised the following points of order—

(1) Whether the reference to Indian National Congress is in order.

(2) Are the words "with a view to remove Government control over Primary Education in Municipal Schools" in order.

The President ruled that though the Municipality is not governed by the decisions of the Indian National Congress or any outside body the reference is not out of order as it suggests the reasons for bringing the motion.

With regard to the second point the President ruled that as Government have statutory control over the administration of Municipal Primary Schools, the words, "with a view to remove Government control over Primary Education in Municipal Schools" are not in order and will be deleted from the proposal before the meeting.

Mr. Vallabhbhai's proposal then stood as under—

In response to the call of nation so clearly expressed by the Indian National Congress held at Nagpur, this Board resolves that no further Educational Grant should now be received from Government.

A copy of this resolution should be forwarded to Government.

K.B. Dr. Nanavatty put an amendment seconded by Mr. Chahewala that the papers should be filed as this Board does not wish to discontinue the receipts of Educational Grants from Government.

Mr. Vallabhbhai raised a point of order whether there being no papers on the subject and the amendment being a direct negative of his motion, the amendment is in order?

The President ruled that as the amendment is a negative of only one point of Mr. Vallabhbhai's motion and includes an addition about filing papers which the President understands to file the motion the amendment is not out of order.

Mr. Nathubhai put another amendment seconded by K.S. Dr. Mansuri that it is necessary that before this Board takes into consideration the proposal to discontinue the receipt of Educational Grants from Government the financial aspect of the question should be fully investigated and laid before the Board.

The Managing Committee should therefore be requested to submit:

I. A report on the ways and means for meeting the deficit which would be caused in consequence of the Municipality's declining to receive

(*a*) The annual Government Grant amounting to half of the Municipality's expenditure on schools.

(*b*) The further annual Government Grant which the Municipality would receive on the introduction of compulsory education.

(*c*) The Government Grant equivalent to half the cost of building Municipal schools' houses on the sites to be acquired from the recent Government Grant of Rs 4 lacs on which sites the Municipality has bound itself to erect school houses.

II. Draft rules for the new tax which the Managing Committee may suggest to levy in order to meet the deficit so that before dealing with the question of discontinuing Government Educational Grants the draft rules of the tax may be adopted and notified to the public so that objections may be received.

The Schools Committee may be requested to report—

(*a*) Whether they are prepared to continue the services of the present school masters who are on the pensionable list of Government by paying leave and pension contribution as hereto; or

(*b*) Whether they decide that the Government should be requested to withdraw them after statutory six months' notice as required by proviso to section 46 of the Act. In case they decide to give notice of withdrawal it should be ascertained how many of the present staff of trained teachers are ready and willing to continue in Municipal service. They should also be requested to state how they propose to maintain an adequate strength of trained teachers without any institution of training teachers in immediate future.

Dr. Jacob put an amendment seconded by Mr. Mistri that a committee of educational experts be appointed to sketch the curriculum for the Ahmedabad Municipal Schools according to National ideal and the wants of Gujarat, and the Government Grant for Education be not given up until any individual or the public have placed at the disposal of the municipality an amount of money which is calculated to yield sufficient annual interest to carry on free Primary Education of Children of both sexes from 7 to 12 years of age.

Mr. Sutaria moved closure seconded by Dr. Bhagat and it was lost.

Mr. Krishnalal moved closure seconded by Dr. Bhagat and it was carried.

Votes were then taken between the amendments of Dr. Jacob and Mr. Nathubhai. . .

Dr. Jacob's amendment was lost.

Votes were then taken between the amendments of Mr. Nathubhai and K.B. Dr. Nanavatty. . . .

K.B. Dr. Nanavatty's amendment was lost.

Votes were then taken between the amendment of Mr. Nathubhai and the proposal of Mr. Vallabhbhai. . . .

The proposal of Mr. Vallabhbhai was carried.

43

Vallabhbhai's Proposals regarding Kilns Carried

Ahmedabad Municipality' Records IV, 1920-21
27 January 1921

Sup. Business No. 3 and 4 G.B. Resolution No. 850 of 1920-21—

Resolution No. 1195 dated 21-1-1921 of the Sanitary Committee approving of the by-laws revised by the Chief Officer: as regards kilns in view of their means of livelihood without contributing to the abatement of smoke nuisance and recommending that the potters should be at liberty to carry on their business without the interference of the executive. The Committee is not in favour of relaxing the by-laws regarding the kilns of tiles.

Motion dated 20-1-21 from the Municipal Councillor Mr. Harilal D. Saheba— "That by-laws No. 3 A under section 58-B-3 sanctioned by government order No. 4627 dated 19-4-1920 be amended so as to exempt kilns used for earthen pots used for domestic purposes."

Mr. Vallabhbhai proposed seconded by Mr. Phirozshah that in view of hardship caused to the potters as well as the inconvenience caused to the public under the present new by-laws this Board resolves that the by-laws for regulation of dangerous and offensive fumes should be so amended as to allow small kilns for making tiles within the Municipal District subject to the usual regulations. Articles of the domestic use such as *Ghadas, Matlas* should be included in the proviso to by-laws 2-A and the Legal Delegate should be requested to draft the necessary amendment in the by-laws so that early sanction of Government may be obtained.

Pending the revision of the by-laws such kilns should be allowed as described above.

The present by-laws applying to lime kilns and brick kilns should continue.

Mr. Goverdhanbhai put an amendment seconded by Sheth Maneklal that in view of hardship caused to the potters as well as inconvenience caused to the public under the present new by-laws, this Board resolves that the by-laws for the regulations of dangerous and offensive fumes should be so amended as to allow small kilns as well as kilns for making tiles within the Municipal District subject to the usual regulations. Articles of domestic use such as *Ghadas, Matlas* should be included in the proviso to by-laws 2-A and the legal Delegate should be requested to draft the necessary amendment in the by-laws so that early sanction of Government may be obtained.

Pending the revision of the by-laws such kilns should be allowed as described above.

Lime kilns specially for the purpose of heavy masonary constructions be allowed subject to their temporary use till the construction are finished outside the city walls.

The present by-laws applying to brick kilns should continue.

K.B. Dr. B.H. Nanavatty put another amendment seconded by Dr. Jacob that the papers relating to the amendment of by-laws regulating the various kinds of kilns in the city be filed.

Mr. Goverdhanbhai withdrew his amendment with the consent of his seconder.

Mr. Pestanshah put another amendment seconded by Mr. Jalaludin that in view of the hardship caused to the potters as well as the inconvenience caused to the public under the present new by-laws this Board resolves that the by-laws for the regulations of dangerous and offensive fumes should be so amended as to allow small kilns as well as kilns for making tiles within the Municipal District subject to the usual regulations. Articles of domestic use such as *Ghadas, Matlas* should be included in the proviso to by-laws 2-A and the Legal Delegate should be requested to draft necessary amendment in the by-laws so that early sanction of Government may be obtained.

Pending the revision of the by-laws such kilns should be allowed as described above.

The present by-laws restricting the distance of lime kilns to 390 ft. from the city walls should be so amended as to allow temporary permits for lime-kilns to be issued to mills and factories under construction in the extra rural [*sic*] area the permits to expire on the completion of the work.

The present by-laws applying to brick kilns should continue.

Mr. Sutaria moved closure seconded by Mr. Chahewala and it was carried.

Votes were then taken between the amendments of Mr. Pestanshah and K.B.

Dr. Nanavatty with the result that K.B. Dr. Nanavatty's amendment was lost.

Votes were then taken between the amendment of Mr. Pestanshah and the proposals of Mr. Vallabhbhai with the following result—

The proposal of Mr. Vallabhbhai was carried.

44

Vallabhbhai's Stirring Address at Bhil Conference[1] at Dohad

Bombay Chronicle, 8 February 1921

Mr. Patel began his inspiring speech in a homely manner so as to be intelligible to the illiterate Bhils.

He referred to the removal of the Guru which he termed as disgraceful on the part of the officers responsible. Government officers, he said, were trying their best to prevent the holding of the conference by all questionable means. The action of the Government by rousing the Guru at midnight and removing him by night mail without previously informing and without allowing him to see his child can be anything but brave. He rejoiced at the fact that no resistance was offered, though his most devoted followers were present in hundreds. This was a step which ensured our moral victory.

Mr. Patel continuing appealed to the people to withdraw all moral support from the Government which was responsible for numerous sins.

Appealing to Bhils, he said that they had no reason to be afraid of anybody in the world. Their wants were few, their abode was with tigers. Why need they be afraid of anything. But he said they had missed their right path by contracting the habits of drink, by occasional thefts, had no reason to be afraid of anybody in forced labour. He exhorted them to resist to the last at any cost.

[1]Speech was delivered on February 6 at Dohad.

45

Vallabhbhai Criticizes Government for Illegal Occupation of Premises to Run Schools

Navjivan, 13 March 1921

On the 8th March 1921, the Collector issued a notice to the Municipality for the vacation of these premises. The Municipality claimed its rights over them and refused to oblige. The Collector used the police in disregard of the law and the locks of the schools were broken and the premises occupied by them. Sardar Patel told the representative of *Navjivan* in an interview quoted here:

The Government has occupied forcibly three of the premises. None of them, according to my information, is owned by the Government. One was built by the Infanticide Fund, the second with the financial help of the people and, as to the third, there is a dispute about its ownership. None of the conditions of the lease have been violated by the Municipality. Even if one was to concede that the Government had any rights over the premises, its action in using the armed police to occupy them is akin to the dacoits who send threatening letters to people and extort money from them. Even a lessee who has a yearly lease on a house is entitled to a month's notice for vacation. Now these premises had been made over to the Municipality thirty-five years ago and the Government wanted to take possession within 12 hours. The President of the Municipality was not allowed to consult the body. There cannot be any doubt about the illegitimacy of the Government's action. But, I am not surprised at the action of the Government. It hardly does anything these days which is legitimate.

The Government should have approached the civil courts for taking possession of these premises, but it chose to use force leaving the Municipality no alternative but to bow before its orders. Having accepted the principle of non-cooperation, the Municipality was not in a position to approach the courts for a stay order. The only purpose the Government had in mind while forcibly occupying these premises was to harm the non-cooperation movement. But, it is clear that if the people of Nadiad do not send their children to schools which the Government wants to open in these premises, it would not gain by such possession.

46

Vallabhbhai Urges People to Give up Everything Foreign and be Fearless

Navjivan, 30 March 1921

I am grateful to you for the love and enthusiasm with which you have welcomed me here today. I know that there is nothing special in me and I am as full of faults as any human being is. I know it fully well that all of us have joined the Great Struggle which has been launched under the leadership of our celestial Commander-in-Chief as soldiers. That is why we are being honoured like this. Bhai Mohanlal while introducing me told you that I was at one time like an English man. He is right. I used to spend all my spare time in recreation. At that time, I believed that the best way to behave in this unfortunate country was to follow in the footsteps of the foreigners. The type of education which I received told me that the people of this country are low and without any merit and the only good people are our rulers who would raise us. I was also told that the people of this country are fit to be the slaves of others. Almost every child in this country is fed on this type of poisonous propaganda. From my childhood, I pined to see the country 7,000 miles away from where our rulers come. I belong to an ordinary family. My father spent all his life in temples and his end came in a temple. He did not have the wherewithal to gratify my desire. I was told that if

I had 10 to 15 thousand rupees, I could go to England but there was nobody who could give me that kind of money. A friend of mine told me that if I tried I could get that amount as loan from the Eeder State. Immersed in such dreams, my friend and I went there and came back empty handed. Finally, it was decided that I must earn that money so that I could travel to England. Later on I studied law and became a lawyer. I thought that I would be able to earn enough to earn the travel expenses. I corresponded with a company which arranges travel to England but a letter from that company fell into my brother's hand. He told me: "I am your elder brother and I should go first. You may get an opportunity after I return, but if you go first, I would never have any chance of going abroad." And my brother went to England after 15 days.

I was faced with some family problems after he had gone. I went to England after the return of my brother three years later. After I returned, we two brothers decided that if we wanted independence, we would have to turn into ascetics and serve the country without any thought of self. We decided, therefore, that one should serve the country and the other look after the family. My brother then left his roaring practice and engaged himself in the service of the country. The looking after of the family fell on my shoulders. The good work was for him and the inferior enterprise was for me. But I was happy in the thought that I also had a share in the good work that he was doing. While working as a lawyer, the idea that honour can come only from aping the rulers became fixed in my mind.

These were the circumstances in which I was involved. Our political life was full of filth at that time. Those who worked for the people were hypocrites. I had a friend at the club where I played cards. He told me that if I have to serve the people, I must leave Ahmedabad. I have left the trade of a lawyer after a bitter experience.

Truth entered our political life when Mahatma Gandhi came here. During the Kheda Satyagraha, he wanted a person who could leave his profession and remain in Nadiad and look after the work of the Satyagraha. I undertook that responsibility. My nearness to Gandhiji convinced me that India had been following a reverse direction, and that it can arise only by following the Mahatma's path.

With God's grace, a huge change is taking place today. India reached the nadir when people forgot their duty. Those who are human beings are not afraid of other humans. The people of India are afraid not only of the Britishers but of those who wear the western dress. Even though they are not as sinful as the latter.

Our Pitiable State

We must think about the state in which we find ourselves and the reasons for it. There was a time when India was so prosperous that people from other countries were attracted towards it. When we were at the pinnacle of progress, our rulers were uncivilized barbarians. Englishmen came here for trade and became our rulers because we were divided. They set one Indian to fight another.

Let us see who is ruling us. We pay crores of rupees by way of income-tax and land revenue, but where does the money go? How is it utilized? If we have to get hundred rupees from somebody, we may have to travel 50 miles, but we do not bother when crores of rupees of Indian money is taken away by the foreigners. There was a time when the Kshatriyas defended our faith and our religion. India today is like a widow. Some people have arms which they use for robbing others but the rest of the people are unarmed and defenceless. Crores of rupees are looted but nobody raises his voice against it.

A view has come to prevail that the Government protects us, that it is a godly empire where the lion and the lamb co-exist. It is said that this state of affairs came about with the foreign rulers. Those who believe in this want to make out as if there was total anarchy before the Britishers came here.

Even today, our Muslim brothers continue to believe that since the Hindus are in a majority, they, the Muslims, would be able to defend their rights so long as the British Government continues to rule India. But those very Muslims have started believing that they can defend their faith only if the Hindus are their friends. All types of hypocrisies have been unmasked by our struggle.

The Government has spread their tentacles throughout India. If we have to defend the honour of our women and India, we must have a government of our own. We do not want to establish our hegemony on any other country, but just as the Frenchmen rule France and Germans rule Germany, we want that Indians should rule India. As things stand today, no Indian, Hindu or Muslim, can expect any respect in any other country.

Get Rid of the Old Ideas

That is why our leaders came together and decided that we must have our own rule in India. After considering the question for a long time, the way appeared to us. It is this that we must get rid of the old ideas. We must do away with all our delusions. We suffer from four kinds of misconceptions:

1. *Education of our children.* The Government takes our children to school. It does not use any force but we have never considered what happens to the child's mentality in those schools. What is the purpose behind the education that is imparted in the Government schools? It is that they should produce people who would perpetuate a state of affairs in which one Englishman rules over three lakh Indians. The Government needs teachers, patwaris, peons, police inspectors, tehsildars and other functionaries. Most Indians are tempted by the prospects of their children getting these jobs. But when atrocities are committed on us, it is through the medium of such functionaries. The Tehsildars and the police inspectors behave in an arbitrary manner. The foreigners have alienated our children from us and have made them the tool of their government. Our leaders have now decided to stop our children from going to government schools. The Britishers cannot import Patwaris from England. That is why we want to stop our men from becoming Patwaris. Those who are in service would be requested to leave it.

Most of them are so set in their ways that they would not listen to our advice. You know that the Congress has decided that the lawyers should leave the profession of law but very few have followed that advice. When we decide to ask people to leave government service, those set in their ways will not listen to us. It is necessary, therefore, that we must have the schools under our control and impart an education which will not encourage the students to commit atrocities but to serve the people. A village is not great because of the number of lawyers and doctors it has produced but by the number of people who serve the people. India today needs such sincere servants.

2. *Government courts.* If we are able to achieve, what I have told you we should, this Government would automatically fall. The Government does not call us to the courts at the point of the gun. It is our delusion which forces us to go there. Let us find a couple of people in each village who can give justice to the people.

3. *Our assemblies.* Prominent Indians are members of the assemblies but they cannot have their way. Even then they do not come out. The government claim that they are ruling the country with the consent of the people and tells the world that they are ruling India with the consent of Indians. As a proof of their claim, they point towards the assemblies. That is why we have boycotted the assemblies. By doing this, we have told the world that the Indians who are members of the Assemblies are not our representatives. The Central Assembly is a farce. The Duke had come to India to inaugurate the assemblies but wherever he went, the people observed strikes.

4. *Foreign textiles.* Before the Britishers came here, we were self-sufficient in textiles, but ever since then textiles worth Rs 60 crores are imported every year. Cotton is taken away from here, made into cloth seven thousand miles away and is sent back for which we pay Rs 60 crores every year. If we become beggars in the process, we should not be surprised. The Britishers do not force us to use that imported cloth but we have ourselves fallen in love with it. If our mothers cannot wear khadi clothes, what kind of strength would they be able to give to their children? Start *charkhas* in the schools, teach the children to spin and let the *charkha* enter every home. Faith in religion is not confined to going to temples or feeding the birds and ants. There are millions of people who do not have any clothes to wear. Our first duty, therefore, is to see that every home has a *charkha.* The day we are able to achieve it, the Government would turn into wax because these Englishmen came here for trade. If the trade flags, so would the government. There should not be a single shop in a village selling imported textiles, nor a tailor or a washerman who would want to touch foreign clothes. We should not accept foreign cloth even to cover our loins. Only then we would get rid of the impression that imported textiles are worthwhile.

KEEP PEACE

We must also exercise self-control. These are troubled times. Questions are asked in the British Parliament as to why Mahatma Gandhi is not banished from India. But the Mahatma is such a celestial personality that nobody can harm him. If people are arrested, we must maintain peace. The only way to defeat this government is not to create any disturbances. In a month or two when the leaders are arrested, please keep peace and do not give expression to your anger. If we use force, the result would be the same as we saw the last time in Biramgam and Ahmedabad. That would set us back. Our struggle is based on peace. The people should maintain unity and not to quarrel amongst themselves.

Remove Your Faults

Let us remove all our faults. We must tell the people of the Dharala caste not to rob the people or consume liquor. We find that the custom in this state is that even if there is no temple in a large village, a liquor shop has to be there. This also is a delusion which we must get rid of. There is a movement on throughout the country against liquor. In Ahmedabad before every liquor shop there are volunteers from 10 in the morning to 8 in the night who request the customers to stop drinking liquor. If the castes in your village are organised, we can achieve this. Let a rule be made that anybody who consumes liquor will be declared an outcaste.

Thievery and robberies can also be dealt with similarly. This used to be the practice among the *sadhus* at one time. But today even the *sadhus* wear foreign clothes. Some of them are even found dealing in shares and stocks.

All these things can be curbed if you do not send your children to government schools. It is the education imparted in those schools which has made the modern generation what it is. We do not have that kind of freedom which people of Kabul or Arabia enjoy. They, the citizens of those countries, permit the foreigners to stay there only if they are friends. The Indians, on the other hand, believe that happiness is possible only if there is foreign rule. That is why we must teach our children to spin cotton. Things would change within a year. Students in England were engaged in the war effort when that country was at war with Germany.

Get Rid of Your Fear

We must never lose sight of the fact that a man dies only once. Everybody is mortal and cannot carry anything with him when he dies. Why, then, are you afraid of death? You forget that it is God who gave us this life. Be pure and remove your faults. Then you would not be afraid of anybody. The moment you are rid of your fears, you are free. As the people lose their fear, the government is afraid. When people lose their sense of fear, the country would become free. The government are afraid because they are ruling against the wishes of the people. If we make others afraid, it is a sin. If fear you must, fear only God. When you are rid of your fears and are free, your religion would be safe. A man shackled by slavery cannot defend his faith.

[1]Sardar Patel's speech on the present situation and Non-Cooperation made in a public meeting on 29th March 1921 at Mohasa.

47

"Independence If not Granted will have to be Achieved"—Vallabhbhai

Navjivan, 10 April 1921

Two years ago on 16th April in this week we became conscious that Hindustan is living and not dead. The wonderful awakening of the people on that day, the Englishmen living in this country were disillusioned, they were shocked. They lost their temper, they could not understand the nature of the awakening, and they could not bear it. They tried to destroy it. We also did not properly assess our strength, and being conscious of our strength, they intoxicated us. We, for a moment, forgot that we are to silently suffer the attack on us of Satanic arms, missed our way, we got angry, and for a moment were tempted to use its arms. We committed crimes, and we did penance for it also. In this week we have to pray God that again we might not commit such mistake, so that we can get full advantage of our wonderful power, and achieve our independence within a stipulated period.

The use of Satanic power on us, because of our momentary mistake, awakened us from deep slumber. We freed from our dream world. For a moment we had forgotten our cultural maxim that State power cannot survive against the saintly power of the saints. Our memory was revived.

In the beginning we were in a semi-conscious state. When we regained full consciousness, we did not demand that enemies or wrongdoers should be punished, but we simply demanded that, and we requested the Emperor to recall as early as possible the Viceroy who manoeuvered the massacre.

At last the Viceroy has left. Instead of listening to the outcry of the people and recalling him, he was allowed to stay here for full term of his office. The future historians will say whether Government has gained, or lost prestige, by this inaction. Whatever it might be, we on our part have long before refused to recognise him as our Viceroy, and since then he has lost the power of doing anything good or bad to us.

New Viceroy has come. Let him come. So many Viceroys have come and gone. But now it is not easy to say as to how many will come. Now Hindustan is not a child of the former times which can be threatened by angry looks, which can be lured by offering toys. There is no reason to believe that Viceroy has more powers than that some of them were bullies. Some were trying to please us by sweet words. Some were so smart that they adopted both types of tactics, but none of them were able to do any good to us. Our welfare is in our own hands. It depends on our capacity of self-sacrifice.

It is said that new Viceroy has come to do Justice. He was a big Judge. So we are asked to have faith in him. The Chairman of the Rowlatt Committee was also a Judge. He had not come here with the intention of doing injustice to us. Yet we saw what kind of justice he has done. The Chairman of the Hunter Committee Lord Hunter was also a well-known judge. He and Tej Bahadur Sapru came to

India from England in the same steamer. Sapru had asked us to have faith in the Viceroy. He had also come here, with a claim to do justice, and we have seen the kind of justice he has done!

Is it necessary to appoint a competent Judge to say that the promises given by the Prime Ministers should be fulfilled? Were there the necessity of a reputed Judge to give a decision that the officer who massacred thousands of innocent persons should be denied emoluments from our treasury? Were the necessity of an eminent Judge in this twentieth century to tell that the people of one country cannot enslave the people of another country? Yet they must get an opportunity of answering such simple questions, and we must give them such opportunity. But to hinge our hopes on their decisions is like, not seeing though eyes are kept open. The man who gives justice should be impartial and independent. Even Gods also are unable to give justice when they have an interest. So if we want justice we have not to demand, but snatch it from them. Independence is not granted, it has to be achieved. If we have enough strength we will achieve it within the stipulated period. May God grant us that strength.

48

Vallabhbhai Deplores Differences between Brahmins and Non-Brahmins

Bombay Chronicle, 18 May 1921

Satara District Conference was held on 16th instant under the presidency of V.J. Patel. Mr. Patel in his presidential address reviewed the demand made by the Congress at its sessions at Calcutta and Nagpur and regretted that the Malegaon tragedy had retarded the realisation of their goal. After resolutions on Khilafat and Non-Cooperation were passed, Mr. Patel concluding the proceedings exhorted the people of the district to join the Congress in large numbers and liberally subscribe to the Tilak Swaraj Fund and deplored the differences between the Brahmin and Non-Bhahmin in the district.

49

Vallabhbhai Decries Western Culture and Emphasises India's Spirit and Culture

Navjivan, 5 June 1921

Some are propagandists of the western way of life; they see in the spinning-wheel a sign that the country is going back a hundred and fifty years; but they fail to realize that western advancement is really the cause of the unsettled state of world today. It has led to differences between the Government and the governed, and through the help of new and more destructive weapons of war, it has destroyed big kingdoms and countries. That type of advancement is today being copied all over the world. India alone prefers to stand out against it and in the process to save not only itself but the world. Moreover, would India be able to adopt wholly these western thoughts and developments? India will always be behind in such a race. Its spirit and culture runs totally counter to it. An India which believes in the strength of the soul cannot be attracted by a shallow demoniacal culture.

We hear of the establishment of Leagues of peace everywhere. I had hoped that Gujarat would be spared this hypocrisy, but I was wrong. If these organizations are being established with the help or at the instance of officials, there is more likelihood of their causing unrest than of their bringing peace. I do not know what the object of the organizers is. Were they, until today, supporters of unrest? The organizers must know that they themselves have little influence with the people. I leave it to them to determine whether they will achieve their object through such bodies or whether they will not lose their little influence with people by becoming tools in the hands of the Government. Do they not know that the remarkable peace which today prevails in the country is not because of the Government's military power but due entirely to the non-violent non-cooperation movement? The so-called peace associations were set up as soon as the non-co-operators started their campaigns. The claim of these associations that law and order is being maintained because of their efforts is comparable to the claim of the dog walking beneath the bullock cart that it was he and not the bullocks which pulled the cart?

50

Vattabhbhai Insists on Changing the System than Appointing a Few Indians on High Posts

Navjivan, 5 June 1921

What difference will it make if we merely replace some foreign officers by Indians? How are we likely to benefit by the appointment of an Indian as a Governor, instead of a Briton? Are there not among the British Governors also, men of noble character and great ability? Although a murderous assault was made on Lord Hardinge in Chandni Chowk,[1] he did not want any retaliatory or repressive action to be taken. Fortunately, such great men are not as rare as one imagines. Even so merely by throwing a few drops of Ganga water into the sewerage, one can scarcely hope to purify it. There must be a radical change of outlook in the administration. The Government of India must be run for the people of India. What indeed do we stand to gain by entering the trap of the reforms, so long as the Government is run in the interests of the foreigners, and only such concessions are granted to us as are acceptable to the British? What guarantee is there that what happened in the Punjab will not recur?

[1]A busy bazar in Delhi.

51

Gandhiji Showers Praises on Vallabhbhai for his Speech (Extract)

Young India, 8 June 1921 and Navjivan, 12 June 1921

Gujarat has held its Provincial Conference and its Khilafat Conference at the historic town of Broach. The Conferences met on the banks of the beautiful Narmada. It had also a *khaddar* and *charkha* exhibition. The great variety of *charkha* showed that India's inventive genius was being profitably utilized. Let not the reader, however, imagine that there was among these specimens a *charkha* with more spindles, yielding a correspondingly larger outturn of yarn. Addresses of the Chairman of the Reception Committee and the President of the Conference were both brief and to the point. The Chairman, Mr. Haribhai Amin, took no more than fifteen minutes to read his simple address. The President, Mr. Vallabhbhai Patel, took no more than thirty minutes to read the whole of his address. I commend the latter to the reader for its simplicity, terseness, relevancy and courtesy. It has not one bitter word for the opponents of non-cooperation. Its criticism of the Government is most restrained. The major part of it deals with the constructive part of non-cooperation.

But the importance of the Conference lies in the resolution allocating to Gujarat its portion of the Bezwada programme. It calls upon Gujarat to furnish more than three times its quota of subscription to the Tilak Swaraj Fund, i.e., ten lakhs, its almost exact quota of members, i.e.,- three lakhs, and one lakh of charkhas, i.e., a little less than double its quota. I do not say it will be a proud record if it is fulfilled. It will not be bad, if it is accomplished before the 30th June. The ten lakhs of rupees have been further allocated to the respective districts so as to systematize the collection. The Congress membership in Gujarat stands at 40,514. The Fund stands at Rs 1,40,149 of which Rs 35,000 have been forwarded to the All-India Congress Committee. The total number of spinning-wheels is 20,058. . . .

The decorations at the Conference were in simple style and only swadeshi materials had been used in putting them up. Seating arrangements for all were on the ground, the President and a few others sitting on a cushioned mattress. The buntings were mostly of khadi. A swaraj flag was fluttering at the entrance to the *pandal.* People refrained from talking noisily and there was no pressure on space. Seating arrangements for women must be counted very good. The speech by the Chairman of the Reception Committee was short and couched in excellent Gujarati. He took only 15 minutes to read it out. The President's speech, too, was short, simple and framed in courteous language. It breathed as much courage as courtesy. We often assume that bluntness and fiery language are inseparable from courage and fighting spirit. Shri Vallabhbhai Patel has proved that pure strength can go with utmost civility. It took him exactly 30 minutes to read out his speech. The brevity of the two speeches saved the people much time, imposed no strain on anyone and made it possible for a great deal of work to be done in two days. The idea of morning and evening sessions saved the people from heat. This idea of holding our meetings in the early morning needs to be popularized among us. In summer, especially, all meetings should be held in the early morning. For an ailing man like me, they provided a chair. We should give up this practice and, in place of the chair, introduce the old-style *bajath*.[1] One solitary chair in the midst of others squatting on the ground or on the dais presents an unbecoming sight. We must convince people that a chair is not necessary for showing respect to a man. At one meeting, the provision of chairs led to an embarrassing situation. Only two chairs were provided, one to enable me to speak sitting and the other for the President. Then came a gentleman, a stranger, a little after the meeting had already started. Though all others sat squatting, the gentleman felt that he would be inviting loss of dignity if he did the same. I looked in the situation. I did not think it would be proper to explain to him that no loss of dignity was involved in the matter. Immediately, therefore, I vacated the chair for him and I myself sat on the President's table. Had only a *bajath* been provided for me, the embarrassing situation would not have arisen. The incident was of no consequence in itself, but it holds a useful lesson.

[1]Low square table.

52

Gandhiji to Vallabhbhai Favouring Civil Disobedience

Bapu Ke Patra Sardar Vallabhbhai Ke Nam[1]

BOMBAY

Friday, 8th July 1921

DEAR VALLABHBHAI,

I would be reaching on Monday morning and would return the same evening. I have written to Indulal[2] about what the political community should do. Please go through that letter. I am sure that we would take a decision in favour of civil disobedience. The only way is to completely boycott the Councils.

Please inform Mavalankar[3] and other friends.

Bandematram,

Yours,

MOHANDAS

[1]In Gujarati, Vol. II, Edited by Maniben Patel, Navjivan Publishing House, Ahmedabad, 1952, p. 3.

[2]Indulal Yagnik, Secretary of the Gujarat Provincial Congress Committee, later left the Congress.

[3]Ganesh Vasudev Mavalankar, famous lawyer of Ahmedabad and Secretary of the Gujarat Provincial Congress Committee from 1921-22, was the Speaker of the Bombay Assembly when the Congress joined the assemblies, later became Speaker of Lok Sabha.

53

Gandhiji to Vallabhbhai Advising Complete Hartal and Boycott of Prince of Wales[1]

Bapu Ke Patra[1]

SYLHET

Tuesday, 30 August 1921

DEAR VALLABHBHAI,

I received your letter. I am sending you a copy of the telegram which I sent today. If we have the strength, I would say that so long as he is in Ahmedabad, the city should be on strike and arrangements should be made for the necessities for the poor to be made available to them. The martial law might be imposed as a result of this action of ours. But we should take that in our stride and die, if need be. But, it appears to me that we would not be able to do it, because we have not yet acquired the strength for it. We should do, however, whatever is possible and tell him that we can cut off our relations with the English. Let the municipality be as free from British control as it can be. Nobody should greet an Englishman. School students should not arise when he goes to visit the schools. If we have the strength we can sit in a *dharna* at the government offices and prevent the people from going there. If we show our dislike in a civilised manner we would find many ways. We should show our feelings in such manner. I think that we should announce our boycott from today and teach the people to be peaceful but firm. We must have the strength to see that he does not assert his powers as the Prince of Wales[2] in Ahmedabad.

What more can I say from here. The only thing I would say is that we should not start anything which we cannot finish. Nor should we run away from a fight. If our insistence on a boycott can lead to violence, please disregard my instructions, by postponing action on them.

It is good that you have accepted the Presidentship of the Reception Committee.[3] Such honour cannot lead to any untoward things when the honour is accepted with humility and a spirit of service.

Bandematram,

Yours,

MOHANDAS

[1]In Gujarati, Vol. II.

[2]The Prince of Wales. The letter contains instructions about his boycott. The Prince of Wales had come to India in November and the Congress had decided to boycott him. There were riots in Bombay when he reached the Bombay harbour. Gandhiji had gone on a fast to show disapproval of the violence committed during the riots. The Prince was boycotted in every large city he visited. At many places the police used lathi-charge against the people.

[3]Of the Congress session scheduled to be held at Ahmedabad.

54

Jamnadas to Vallabhbhai regarding Boycott of Prince of Wales' Visit

Bapu Ke Patra[1]

SYLHET (ASSAM)
30 August 1921

DEAR VALLABHBHAI,

I have sent you the following telegram today:

> "Event coming, have Gujarat's hartal, labourers joining after leave,[2] Wednesday, Thursday Chittagong, Saturday Barisal, Sunday and after Calcutta."

I reached here yesterday from Silchar by special train. I will be leaving at 4 p.m. this afternoon for Chittagong. People this side of the country appear to be without any training. There is a total lack of workers. I have yet to tour the area where there is hartal.[3] I cannot be sure of when I would be reaching Calcutta, but hope that by the evening of the 4th I shall be there.

Some of the Marwari traders have signed the pledge[4] but only the future will tell us how many of them would follow it.

You also must have heard that the Government appear to be thinking of arresting the Ali Brothers.[5]

Yours,
JAMNADAS[6]

[1] In Gujarati, *Bapu Ke Patra Sardar Vallabhbhai Ke Nam,* edited by Maniben, Vol. II.

[2] The advice was to have a one day hartal throughout Gujarat on the day the Prince of Wales went there.

[3] The workers of the tea plantations in Assam had started leaving their jobs because of low wages paid to them. The white owners of the plantations tried to stop the workers from going away. Trouble had been created because of this. The hartal referred to above was the one the plantation workers had gone on.

[4] For boycotting foreign textiles.

[5] Maulana Shaukat Ali and Maulana Mohammed Ali.

[6] Jamnadas Gandhi, nephew of Mahatma Gandhi who was with him in Phonix in South Africa.

55

Gandhiji to Vallabhbhai Advising Postponement of Boycott for a Month

Bapu Ke Patra[1]

MAUNWAR
148, Rassa Road, Calcutta
5 *September, 1921*

DEAR VALLABHBHAI,

I received your letter. I would write about the spectators[2] in the *Young India*.[3]

I am pining to get back, but cannot get away because of pressure of work. Rajagopalacharya[4] has wired from Madras that I should start for that city only on receipt of his telegram. Till the 12th I shall be busy here.

The Swadeshi work in Bengal has failed to pick up momentum. The *charkhas* are being used, but no appreciable yarn has been produced nor any attention paid to *khadi*.

It appears to me that if we could postpone the violation of law for a month, it would be better. *Dharnas* should be undertaken under the agreement at Delhi. When we violate the law let us do it by staking everything we have. Once I have discussed the issue with my companions, I would have a clear idea as to what should be done. For the present we should concentrate our attention on boycott of foreign cloth and production of *khadi*.

Your letter leads me to believe that there is no trouble at the Vidyapeeth.

Take care of your health. We have to do a lot by December. The face of the country would certainly change; whether it wears the face of a lion or of a jackal is in the hands of God.

The address of the Viceroy has further disillusioned me. If the Prince of Wales is not coming for political reasons what is the purpose of his visit? And whose money is he spending on his visit? But that is something we would have to consider later.

Bandematram,

Yours,
MOHANDAS

[1]In Gujarati, *Bapu Ke Patra Sardar Vallabhbhai Ke Nam*, Vol. II.

[2]The visitors to the Congress Session, *Young India*, dated 21st September, 1921.

[3]English weekly published by Gandhiji.

[4]Chakravarty Rajagopalacharya, Congress Leader in Madras, Chief Minister of the Province after the Congress formed governments in the provinces.

Gandhiji to Vallabhbhai regarding His Fast for Hindu-Muslim Unity

Bapu Ke Patra[1]

B.V. 3
16 September 1924

DEAR VALLABHBHAI,

You would have come to know of my decision before you receive this letter. You are a lion-hearted one and should not be nervous. Do what you are engaged in with greater vigour and do not let anybody be afraid. I would like to complete my fast[2] here. Maniben may become nervous because of this, but please tell her that there is nothing to be afraid of. I am not writing to her separately.

Yours,
BAPU

[1]In Gujarati. Vol. II.
[2]Fast undertaken for Hindu-Muslim unity for 21 days.

Gandhiji Advising Vallabhbhai Not to Employ Dahyabhai in Birla Mill

Bapu Ke Patra[1]

26 September 1925

DEAR VALLABHBHAI,

I shall be reaching Bombay on the 20th of next month. You are, I presume, coming to Kutch on the 21st and should be in Bombay on the 20th. Devadhar[2] has sent me a telegram about Maniben, which I have sent to her. I do not think that we should post Dahyabhai[3] in the Mill. If he is with the Birlas,[4] the most he would do is in the Mill. We shall talk about it in detail when we meet. I am discussing it with Jamnalal.[5]

With blessings,

Yours,
BAPU

P.S. I will not get an opportunity to write anything more.

[1]In Gujarati, Vol. II.
[2]Devadhar of the Bharat Sevak Samaj who looked after the Sevasadan in Pune.
[3]The Congress had adopted *Khadi* and because of the non-cooperation movement, it did not appear proper that Dahyabhai should work in a textile mill.
[4]Ghanshyamdas Birla. well-known industrialist. A devotee of Gandhiji and President of the Harijan Sevak Sangh when it was established. At that time he was a member of the Central Assembly.
[5]Jamnalal Bajaj, prominent among Gandhiji's followers in the Central Provinces Assembly. He was President of the Charkha Sangh and Congress Treasurer from 1921 to 1942.

56

Vallabhbhai Defends Ali Brothers' Stand [1]

Prajabandhu, 25 September 1921

This is a solemn occasion and we must celebrate it in a solemn manner. This is the second time that we have gathered together for this great task. Our procession went through the cities peacefully, which is a matter of pride for us. Even though Indians in general and our Muslim brothers in particular have been deeply hurt by the arrest of Maulana Mohammad Ali and Shaukat Ali, they have kept their feelings in check and have remained peaceful. At two places, we confronted troops as the procession was coming here, but nothing untoward happened. They must have returned to where they came from. We did not knowingly or unwittingly do anything to cause them any trouble and remained peaceful as always. If we continue to be peaceful, these soldiers would prove to be toy soldiers and would rust because of disuse. Complete peace is necessary if we want to achieve Swaraj. Ali brothers have been arrested today and other friends may be arrested tomorrow. Even Mahatma Gandhi may be arrested but still we must remain peaceful. We must learn to maintain peace to take the place of the arrested leaders and to carry on their non-violent struggle.

Opposition Party

You must also remember that there are groups who raise their voice against our non-violent movement. The Congress called upon the lawyers to cease practising in the courts. This has not been accepted by the opponents of the Congress. The Congress told the people not to take recourse to the government courts for resolving their disputes. Even this was not liked by our opponents. When we gave a call for weakening the government and to avoid making use of the costly system of education foisted on us by the government and asked the people not to go to the government schools and colleges, our opponents did not like it. Similar opposition was showed to our call for prohibition. There are a large number of Parsis in Ahmedabad but there was not a single one amongst them who could close the liquor shops and help the vendors to take to another occupation. All these matters have been taken into consideration by us. The first demand which we made of the people has been accepted by them. We have been able to collect Rs 1 crore. The people have faith in their leaders. The type of sacrifices the common people can make for achieving Swaraj cannot be made by others. People must now realise that Swaraj cannot be achieved by the mere contribution of Rs one crore, it will not help solve the Khilafat issue, nor would the people of Punjab get justice. Achieving Swaraj is not an every day matter. We will have to make the kind of sacrifices for Swaraj which are not made every day.

Make Sacrifices

Sacrifices are made in many ways. Gandhiji showed us the path of non-violent non-cooperation after considerable thought and after taking into account the conditions prevalent in the country. If our opponents do not like any of our programmes, I ask them: Do you like the way of bombs and guns? Even a small child knows that this country does not have the strength to take up arms. The people of Bengal used bombs on the basis of their experience in the West. It is not wrong to say that the blood of our youngmen boils and they are eager to make sacrifices. But we have seen that if force is used we would have to take the consequences. The use of force does not lead anywhere; on the contrary, we are thrown behind. It will take us years to be able to take up arms against the British. I have my doubts whether they would permit us to become proficient in the use of arms even after years of preparations. I do not believe that they would permit us to be prepared for such a confrontation. The question now is what is the way which we should adopt. Do we continue to groan under the heel of our oppressors? The people are not prepared for this and want independence. It is for that purpose that we have adopted the way of non-violence, non-cooperation. For that we will have to make sacrifices but those sacrifices are of a different kind. The Englishmen know how to make sacrifices and we should not shy away from learning this from them. The people have not demanded anything unusual or asked the Englishmen to make any sacrifice. The only demand we have made is that we should break the shackles of slavery. Only then we will be free. It is for that purpose that we have launched a movement to burn foreign clothes. This movement has had its impact, which is clear to all. We had not yet started burning foreign clothes, but had only decided that we would do it. The very announcement of our decision sent shock waves in Lancashire and now a deputation is preparing to come to India. Let it come; we have to be firm in our resolve to carry on this campaign and have to boycott foreign textiles. If the 33 crores Indians make a firm resolve, Swaraj will not be far away. Probably we would not have to wait even till December. Whether Swaraj comes early or late would depend on the people making sacrifices and maintaining discipline. If a day comes when we are firmly united, do you think that a mere one lakh Englishmen would be able to continue their rule in India? The Englishmen are a clever race and would realise that Indians can no longer continue as slaves.

Government Propaganda

When our movement began, the government thought it prudent to say that the civil disobedience movement was a fit of temporary madness. They had said that the movement would peter out. They had announced in the Assembly that so long as the movement remained non-violent, they would not try to curb it. This promise, however, was not kept for long. The Ali brothers were arrested. Before that the Government had become very vigilant. Minor leaders are being punished with imprisonment. Finally, they decided to arrest the Ali brothers. Thinking that their speeches might create a wrong impression, the Ali brothers listened to Gandhiji's advice and clarified their stand. That clarification was taken by the government as an apology and they started a propaganda that since they had apologised, they would not be prosecuted. Ali brothers are not men who would make an apology for fear of punishment. They replied to the government allegations and challenged it to do what it could. They said that they issued the clarification not because they were afraid of the government but because it was likely to lead to misunderstandings. They said that they wanted to make it clear that they continue to believe in non-violent non-cooperation. When the government found that its hold over the country was likely to slacken if the movement continued they arrested the Ali brothers last Thursday at the dead of night. The people have recognised the government for what it is and whatever the authorities might do, the high regard in which the Ali brothers are held by the people will continue undiminished. The Ali brothers have been charged with spreading disaffection among the armed forces. Let it be said that a true Muslim does not disregard his faith, nor can he advise others to do so. The government's statement issued after the arrest of Ali brothers claims that it tried to save the honour and the loyalty of the armed forces by arresting the Ali brothers. It is not that the people do not know how far this claim is correct. The people also know that the *fatwa* of the Ulemas has also been proscribed.

The government are trying to get the support of the people. They have asked the Indian members of the Assembly, who support it, to try to sway public opinion in favour of the government. It is not that the government party has not started implementing that advice. The meeting of the League of peace and order has been held behind closed doors today. Only those invited to the meeting could take part in it. That appears to be the way in which the League wants to function. Probably the government thinks that this is how public opinion can be created. I cannot say whether 50 or more people attended that meeting but you can be sure that the news of meeting would be getting two columns in the newspapers. The government, however, knows what kind of collaborators it has. It takes as much work as it can from them. It is a moot question how much faith the government's collaborators have in it.

Burning the Third Time

We should consider what is our duty regardless of what the government does. It was because of this consideration that the people were asked by the government to accept foreign clothes. There is not much of sacrifice involved in giving up wearing foreign clothes. If even that much sacrifice cannot be made then the only way is that people should be ready to fill the jails. The time at our disposal is short and by December we must give account of what we can do. During this period, everybody should take a pledge to wear swadeshi only. If there are still some people who have not accepted swadeshi, they should be ready to do so and get rid of the shackles of slavery on the occasion of Gandhiji's birthday when foreign clothes would be burnt the third time. I have just now received news that the Congress Working Committee is meeting on the 6th of the next month. We have to see that the members of the Working Committee form a good opinion about us. I am sure that the people who contributed Rs 1 crore to our fund would also give an appropriate answer with regard to the adoption of swadeshi.

[1]The speech was made by him before a large gathering burning and boycotting foreign clothes.

57

Vallabhbhai's Motion for Appointment of Gore as Municipal Engineer Carried

Ahmedabad Municipal Records G.R. 11/1921-22
25 September 1921

Motion dated 25.9.1921 from Municipal Councillor Mr. Vallabhbhai J. Patel—

As a competent hand is not available at present to the municipality for the post of the Municipal Engineer from outside, Government in the P. W.D. be requested to lend the services of Mr. Y.N. Gore, L.C.E., Assistant Engineer who is now on two years furlough and who is acquainted with the local conditions especially as regards water works for the improvement of which a large scheme is pending, on the scheduled salary and allowances plus pension contribution. The President be authorised to communicate direct with the Secretary to the Government of Bombay, P.W.D.

Mr. Vallabhbhai proposed seconded by Mr. Nathubhai that as a competent hand is not available at present to the Municipality for the post of the Municipal Engineer from outside, Government in the P.W.D. be requested to lend the services of Mr. Y.N. Gore, L.C.E., Assistant Engineer who is now on two years furlough and who is acquainted with the local conditions especially as regards water works for the improvement of which a large scheme is pending on a scheduled salary and allowances plus pension contribution. The President be authorised to communicate direct with the Secretary to Government of Bombay, P.W.D.

Mr. Kalidas put an amendment seconded by Mr. Lala that applications be invited from qualified persons for the post of the Municipal Engineer on the scheduled pay.

Mr. Vallabhbhai withdrew his motion with the consent of his seconder and put another motion as under seconded by Mr. Nathubhai—

As a competent hand is not available at present to the Municipality for the post of the Municipal Engineer from outside, Government in the P.W.D. be requested to lend for a period of five years the services of Mr. Y.N. Gore, L.C.E., Assistant Engineer who is now on two years furlough and who is acquainted with the local conditions especially as regards water works for the improvement of which a large scheme is pending on a scheduled salary and allowances plus pension contribution. The President be authorised to communicate direct with the Secretary to the Government of Bombay, P.W.D.

Mr. Phirozshaw put an amendment seconded by K.S. Dr. Mansuri that Government in P.W.D. be requested to lend the services of Mr. Y.N. Gore, L.C.E.,

Assistant Engineer who is now on two years furlough and who is acquainted with the local conditions on the scheduled salary and allowances plus pension contribution.

The President be authorised to communicate direct with the Secretary to the Government of Bombay, P.W.D. The President is also requested to inform the Government particularly that Government will not to be at liberty to withdraw the services of Mr. Gore within five years on any circumstances. As the Municipality is without an Engineer since a long time, at the same time applications should be invited for the post in the meanwhile. The President is requested to ascertain from Mr. Gore whether he is willing to agree that he will not withdraw from Municipal Service within five years.

Votes were taken between the amendment of Mr. Phirozshaw and the proposal of Mr. Vallabhbhai. Mr. Phirozshaw's proposal was lost.

58

Vallabhbhai and Other Leaders Call Upon Indians not to Serve British Government[1]

4 October 1921 (Modern Review, November 1921)

On October 4, Gandhi convened a meeting of leaders in Bombay to issue a manifesto, defying the Government to do their worst:

"In view of the prosecution of the Ali brothers and others for the reasons stated in the Government of Bombay communique dated 15th September 1921, we the undersigned, speaking in our individual capacity, desire to state that it is the inherent right of every one to express his opinion without restraint about the propriety of citizens offering their services to or remaining in the employ of the Government, whether in the civil or the military department. We, the undersigned, state it as our opinion that it is contrary to national dignity for any Indian to serve as a civilian, and more especially as a soldier, under a system of government, which has brought about India's economic, moral and political degradation and which has used the soldiery and the police for repressing national aspirations, as for instance, at the time of the Rowlatt Act agitation, and which has used the soldiery for crushing the liberty of the Arabs, the Egyptians, the Turks and other nations who have done no harm to India. We are also of the opinion that it is the duty of every Indian soldier and civilian to sever his connection with the Government and find some other means of livelihood."

Some of those fifty leaders who signed the manifesto with Gandhi were: Abul Kalam Azad, Ajmal Khan, Lajpat Rai, Motilal Nehru, Mrs. Naidu, Abbas Tayabji, N.C. Kelkar, V.J. Patel, Vallabhbhai Patel, M.R. Jayakar, Jawaharlal Nehru, Gangadharrao Deshpande, Umar Sobani, Jamnalal Bajaj, M.S. Aney, Dr. Ansari, Abdul Bari, C. Rajagopalachari, Rajendra Prasad, Hasrat Mohani, Yakub Hasan and Dr. Moonje.

[1]Tendulkar, D.G., *Mahatma: Life of Mohandas Karamchand Gandhi.*

59

Vallabhbhai's Proposals for not Submitting any Recommendations to Commissioner in Future

Ahmedabad Municipality Records, G.R.III/1921-22
21 October 1921

No. M.U.N.A.S.R.I. 30 dated 21st October 1921 from the Collector of Ahmedabad forwarding No. M.N.A.-VI-I (168) from the Commissioner N.D. stating that the Municipality's proposals for the revision of the grade of Superintendent of the Schools cannot be sanctioned in view of illegal and unconstitutional proceedings of the Municipality.

Mr. Vallabhbhai proposed seconded by Mr. Thakore that as the Commissioner Northern Division, has now by his letter No. M.U.N.A.-VI-I (168) dated 28th October 1921, expressed his unwillingness to sanction any proposal connected with the educational schedule of the Municipality this Board resolves that no such proposals should henceforward be submitted to him.

Mr. Mulchand raised a point of order if Mr. Vallabhbhai's proposal is in order.

The President ruled that as the suggested course is opposed to provisions of Section 46 of the Act it is not in order.

Mr. Vallabhbhai proposed seconded by Dr. Kanuga that the papers be referred to the Schools Committee for report.

Mr. Chahewala put an amendment seconded by Dr. Dolatram that the Commissioner N.D.'s memo be noted. The Commissioner N.D. having refused to sanction the proposed increased salary for the post of the Superintendent of Municipal Schools and Secretary of the Schools Committee, the present pay of the post as previously sanctioned should be paid, no alteration can be made in the schedule and no increased salary should be paid.

Mr. Pestanshah put an amendment seconded by Mr. Goverdhanbhai that Memo of the Commissioner N.D. be noted. Since the Commissioner N.D. has withheld his sanction to the revised salary of the Superintendent of Municipal Schools and Secretary of the Schools Committee he should continue to draw the schedule salary, viz. Rs 150-10-200 till the necessary sanction is obtained.

Mr. Thakore put an amendment seconded by Mr. Kalidas that the papers be referred to the Schools Committee and in the meanwhile the Superintendent of Schools may be permitted to draw the maximum pay of sanctioned schedule.

R.S. Harilal put an amendment seconded by Sheth Maneklal that the Commissioner N.D. should be requested to submit the proposal for the approval of the Governor-in-Council.

Mr. Krishnalal put an amendment seconded by Mr. Saheba that this Board regrets the tone of the Commissioner's reply because it is arbitrary and based on misconceived notions of law and it challenges the final power of the rate-payers. The President should, therefore, return the papers to the Commissioner stating that the Municipality refuses to consider his reply.

Mr. Phirozshah put an amendment seconded by Mr. Rao that papers be sent to the Schools Committee with a request to make suggestions for the considerations of this Board. The Superintendent of Municipal Schools and Secretary of Schools Committee should be allowed in the meantime the salary which he at present draws:

Mr. Phirozshah raised a point of order whether Mr. Chahewala is in order in referring to Mr. Phirozshah's election to the Managing Committee at Mr. Vallabhbhai's suggestion being the cause of Mr. Phirozshah's supporting Mr. Vallabhbhai on the present question.

The President ruled that this is not a point of order. This is a question of propriety. The President himself thinks that such allusions ought not to be made.

Mr. Vallabhbhai moved closure seconded by Mr. Kalidas and it was lost.

Mr. Abdulkadar moved closure seconded by Mr. Vallabhbhai and it was carried.

Votes were then taken between the amendment of R.S. Harilal and the proposal of Mr. Vallabhbhai. . . . Mr. Vallabhbhai's proposal was carried.

60

Vallabhbhai Happy over Preparedness of People of Bardoli Taluka for Civil Disobedience[1]

Bombay Chronicle, 22 November 1921

The inhabitants of the Bardoli Taluka hold themselves in readiness for the forthcoming campaign of civil disobedience, and as an earnest of their grim determination a procession was organised at Khojpardi on November 11th when the depressed classes mixed freely with other sections of inhabitants resolutely casting out all antiquated notions about untouchability. At Poida, too, at a meeting held two days previously, the inhabitants vowed to wear Khadi for all time and signified their willingness to practise civil disobedience and to refuse to pay taxes. The Leooa [Leva] Patidars of Badthal have adjured *pugrees* till the attainment of Swaraj and decided to use Khadi in marriages and funerals. In order to make assurance doubly sure, Mr. Vallabhbhai J. Patel, Barrister-at-Law, accompanied by Principal Gidwani of the Gujarat National University, Dr. Kanuga and Mr. Luxmidas Purushottam paid a visit to Bardoli on November 11th and addressed at Surat an audience of six thousand men and women on their return from the place with Mr. Syed Ahmed Edroos.

Mr. Vallabhbhai remarked on the threefold object of convening the present meeting, namely, to deliberate how to achieve Swaraj by the end of December in accordance with the Congress resolution, to decide on their course of conduct in respect of the Prince's arrival on November 17th, and to devise means how best to help the Surat Municipal Board in the new situation that has arisen as a result of the Government Resolution inciting the rate-payers against the Municipality. They have deliberately excluded big cities, for Swaraj for the obvious reason that with their exquisitely laid out gardens, pestiferous gutters were inextricably bound up, and it was a matter of deep regret that Surat had not yet altogether emancipated itself from the seductive amenities of material civilisation. Swadeshi was the soul of Swaraj, and they could hope to unfurl the Swaraj Flag only if they made a clean sweep of the antediluvian concept of untouchability. His visit to Bardoli convinced him of its "thorough-preparedness" although he would defer his verdict about Surat till the decision of the ensuing meeting of the Executive Council of the Congress to be held at Surat on November 22nd, was known.

NO ILL-WILL TOWARDS THE PRINCE

Proceeding, Mr. Patel observed that they bore no ill-will to the prince and if they resolved on observing a complete "hartal" on the day of his arrival in India, it was mainly because they protested against the way in which the visit was sought to be exploited. They were not in any way affected by what the toadies and Rao Bahadurs said or did. Regarding the step taken by the Government in respect of the non-cooperating Municipalities of Nadiad, Ahmedabad, and Surat, they might rest assured of the dismal failure of it all provided their determination was unshaken at all hazards, and they refused to be hoodwinked by the attempt made to sow dissensions between the Municipalities and the rate-payers. He was quite at a loss to understand why the Government trembled to translate the threat of suspending the Municipalities concerned into act.

[1]Speech was delivered on 18 November at Surat.

61

Vallabhbhai Opposes Gandhiji's Move for Postponement of Satyagraha

Home Deptt. (Sp.) F. No. 584/1921-22, Bombay Archives
23 November 1921

Bombay Commissioner of Police, dated 23/11/21

A meeting of the Working Committee of the All India Congress Commitee was held last evening in Gandhi's house. This meeting was to be held at Surat on the 17th instant but as C.R. Das, Lala Lajpatrai, Pandit Motilal Nehru, etc. were in Bombay. Gandhi decided to hold it in Bombay. The following were present at the meeting:

M.K. Gandhi
Motilal Nehru
Lala Lajpatrai
C.R. Das

Konda Venkatappaiya
Mrs. Sarladevi Chowdhari
N.C. Kelkar
Vallabhbhai J. Patel
Vithaldas J. Patel, and two others.

Gandhi proposed that civil disobedience should be postponed. Vallabhbhai Patel, N.C. Kelkar, Konda Venkatappaiya and V.J. Patel were against postponement and argued that Gandhi had no authority to make an announcement in the public papers postponing civil disobedience without consulting the Working Committee. The meeting adjourned without coming to a decision and a further discussion is to go on today and a manifesto will be issued later on.

It is expected that Gandhi with the support of C.R. Das and Nehru will carry the day.

62

Vallabhbhai's Soul Stirring Address as Chairman, Reception Committee 36th Session Indian National Congress at Ahmedabad[1]

Navjivan, 28 December 1921

No session of the Congress has been held in the circumstances in which we find ourselves today. Instead of being sorry because our dear and respected workers are not amongst us, we are extremely happy. I do not call them leaders because we have learnt in this year which is ending that leadership lies in the service of the people. We accept that great and learned Muslims and Hindus are languishing in government jails today. It is because they have accepted the responsibility of serving the people and they are undergoing pain for the sake of the people. They are experiencing the happiness for which we are pining. This government which farcically claims to be based on the principle of law and order but which, as is becoming clear day by day, is founded on coercion had been coming in the way of that happiness.

Swaraj is Nearer

We had hoped that we would gather together to celebrate the establishment of Swaraj and had, therefore, decided to welcome you as if we had already become free. But, alas, that auspicious day has not yet dawned. The merciful God is testing us and has given us the opportunity to make sacrifices. There is nothing but imprisonment, physical attacks, body searches, searches of our offices and breaking open the locks. But all these things are the harbingers of the coming Swaraj. That is why we never made any changes in the entertainment programmes, songs and other frills to welcome you because we thought that we would be consoling our Muslim brothers and assuage the pain of the wounds which the Punjabis have suffered.

But we will not ask you to judge our capacity to welcome you from the arrangements we have made for your comforts. The reception committee is cognizant of its shortcomings but it hopes that you would be magnanimous enough to overlook them.

You have established another benchmark to test us which we have gladly accepted. We will be tested on the basis of whether we have done any constructive work in the matter of non-cooperation and how far we have followed the principle of Ahimsa which is the very life of that programme. A government which does not believe in the consent of the people but runs on coercion, we have disassociated ourselves from all its organisations. It means only this that we want to give up violence under any circumstances. I can truly claim that we have accepted Ahimsa in all its shades. We have tried to overcome our weaknesses honestly and in a definite manner. The proof, if any proof is needed, is Hindu-Muslim unity. So far we had lack of confidence and thought that the two were natural enemies but now we love each other and are living like friends. I can proudly claim that our relationship is not merely of friendship but of fruitful cooperation so that we can take the nation forward. Similarly, we have established cordial relations with Parsis, Christians and other citizens of the country.

Tolerance is the Life of Non-violence

We have been following our programmes with enthusiasm. Even so, we tried to maintain friendly relations with those who differ with us. We have seen that tolerance is the very life of Ahimsa. I am sorry to have to say that we could not do anything of which we could be proud in the matter of giving up government honours like Knighthood and of the lawyers stopping to practice in the courts. If we look at the number of people who voted in favour of the boycott of the assemblies, we can say that the idea received a very wide support. In the matter of education, we have been able to achieve considerable successes. Some prominent schools and high schools have cut off their relations with the government and they have not come to any harm. In most of the large national schools, the number of students has been increasing. We have established national universities and colleges and many educational institutions recognised by the universities are being run here. In the recognised and non-recognised national schools, the total number of boys and girls receiving education is 31,000.

Two years ago, you would hardly have found a *charkha* in our province. The number of *charkhas* today is not less than 1,10,000. We have produced so far 2 lakh pounds of *khadi*. All these pandals have been made with the help of *khadi* produced in Khadi Nagar. It is a proof of what we have been able to do in the matter of *swadeshi*.

We have started *dharnas* at all the liquor shops to see that there is total prohibition. The results of our *dharnas* have been encouraging. We have carefully selected the volunteers for these *dharnas*. They have passed the test and some of them had to undergo belabouring by those who buy liquor and those who sell it.

Untouchability is Psychological

Our most notable success has been in the matter of removing untouchability. Our brothers from these castes freely come to our meetings and we have accepted the principle of giving them free admission to our national schools. The steering committee of the university had to wage a difficult struggle in the interests of the removal of untouchability. But we have not been able to make much progress in the matter of persuading the children of the untouchables to join these schools and to tell them that they are not in any way inferior to the caste Hindus. That is why even though it is not our purpose to increase the number of schools for untouchable children, we would have to run these schools for some time. But we cannot estimate the extent to which untouchability has been removed from the number of schools open for the children of the untouchables or from the number of such children who attend the national schools. Untouchability is mainly psychological and I am happy to say that even though much remains to be done, we have been able to bring about a visible change.

But I know that we have not passed through the difficult days through which Bengal, Punjab, United Provinces and other provinces have passed. I hope that our commitment to Ahimsa, of which I have proudly spoken, is not the non-violence of the weak but the result of voluntary acceptance.

The government by taking over the national schools forcibly from the Surat and the Nadiad municipalities has given us an opportunity to show our strength. Ahmedabad has also to solve this problem. This problem can be solved only through civil disobedience. The Bardoli and Anand districts are preparing for collective violation of law or civil disobedience. I am merely expressing the wish of the Congress when I pray to God that He gives us the strength to prove our mettle and enable us to stand proudly with the other provinces. At the same time, I want to assure you that we will not take any step without due consideration. We will not do anything in the defence of national self-respect and rights which does not behove peace-loving people.

I now request Hakim Ajmal Khan Sahib to take the Chair as the acting President. Though Deshbandhu Chitranjan Das is not present amongst us, his pure, patriotic and sacrificing presence can be felt. He has sent his inspiring speech exhorting us to do our duty. The Government of Bengal has created this situation. The Muslim League had also to appoint an Acting President and we have decided to follow in its footsteps. In the absence of the Muslim League President Maulana Mohammed Ali, an Acting President had to be elected and the Congress Working Committee selected Hakim Ajmal Khan Sahib in the place of Deshbandhu Chitranjan Das. Hakim Sahib is a great gentleman and represents Hindu-Muslim unity. If the Muslims trust and love him, so do the Hindus.

Hakim Sahib, I request you to take the Chair. It is my good fortune that I have got this opportunity to make this request to you.

[1]The speech was made by Sardar Patel as the chairman of the Reception Committee at the 36th session of the Indian National Congress in Ahmedabad in December 1921.

63

Vallabhbhai Congratulates People of Bardoli Taluka on Taking Part in Non-Cooperation Movement

Home Deptt. (Sp.) F. No. 584 (6)/1921-22
Bombay Archives, 29 January 1922

A Conference of the Bardoli taluka non-cooperators was convened by the local leaders at Bardoli. A copy of the printed notice convening the Conference is submitted. A pandal was specially erected for the purpose in the compound of the ginning factory of Sheth Zaverchand near the Railway Station. The following local and outside non-cooperating leaders were present at the Conference:

(1) Mohandas Karamchand Gandhi. (2) Vithalbhai Javerbhai Patel. (3) Vallabhbhai J. Patel. (4) Abbas Tyabji. (5) Shankerlal Ghelabhai Banker. (6) Kavi Nanalal Dalputram (7) Ramdas Mohanlal Gandhi (8) M.K. Azad of Chhindwada. (9) Syed Ahmad Edrus. (10) Kunvarji Mithelbhai. (11) Kalyanji Vithalbhai Mehta. (12) Dayalji Nanoobhai. (13) Mohanlal Kedarnath Dixit. (14) Vaman Sitaram Mukadam of Godhra.

The posters in Gujarati of the following effect were noticed in the pandal. (1) It is contrary to religion to help the organization of a sinful Government. (2) It is sinful to pay land revenue and taxes to that Government which is not just. (3) If you wish to obtain redress of the Punjab and the Khilafat and to attain complete swaraj, you should not pay land revenue dues and taxes to the Government. (4) Good Government will not serve the purpose of swaraj. (5) It is not possible to attain swaraj without self-sacrifice.

For admission to the pandal, 8 annas tickets for men and 4 annas tickets for women were issued.

Mr. Gandhi and other leaders arrived at the Pandal at about 3 p.m. when the work of the Conference was started. In the beginning Gujarati songs were sung by one Ishwarlal of Varad.

Mr. Abbas Tyabji congratulated the audience upon having passed the resolution which he said was the result of the strenuous exertions they had made in the Taluka which had passed the test in Guzerat (Gujarat) and he and his men were left behind. Individual civil disobedience had however been started for the last 4-6 days in his charge. He advised the audience to work together. There (in his charge) 20-25 brothers in each village had remained firm, and in some villages 61 brothers. They had taken vows, and attachments of their properties had commenced, but their result was opposite of what the Government believed, because in that village where there were only 5 brothers (who had taken the vows) originally the number rose to 17 when the attachment took place. As Government had started repression, many brothers would take the vow. He concluded by wishing success to the audience in the fight they were going to engage in.

Mr M.K. Azad of Chhindwada wanted to address the meeting but no one would hear him. He however started addressing the meeting and was given two minutes. He said that he was a native of Chhindwada where the Ali brothers were kept. Mahatma Gandhi was now telling the bureaucracy that he alone would break their force. He was then taken down the platform with great difficulty. Whilst being led down the platform he said that swaraj would not be obtained in that way.

Vallabhbhai J. Patel said that for the last 3 months he was of the opinion that if there was any Taluka which was a proper place for this fight, it was Bardoli. He congratulated the audience for having justified his opinion that day but the time of their true test had arrived. He urged the audience to produce from that day not only in the Bardoli Taluka but in the whole District such an atmosphere as would facilitate their fight, "If the Bardoli Taluka undertakes a great fight, the others, Olpad etc., cannot sit quiet. Calmness of course must be completely observed by the whole of Guzerat (Gujarat), but our battle can become easier only when the other talukas take interest in the fight in which the Bardoli Taluka may have been completely involved. I congratulate you upon the great work which you have done today. May God grant you sufficient strength.

Vithalbhai J. Patel (President)—I want to address you a few words before we part. There is no doubt that the success of the whole of India lies in your adherence to the resolution which you have proclaimed to the world to-day. If you hesitate in the least, you would be considered to have deceived the world and God. I leave it to you to consider in what light Bardoli will be known in history for ever. The simple meaning of this resolution is that it is better to die than to endure the condition of slavery. It has been decided by this resolution that many a man and woman who has supported this resolution should give their property and lives for the country to make it independent. I leave it to you, brothers and sisters, to consider which of the two courses is better,— either die or to obtain liberation from slavery of the Government which has kept in confinement for 1-1/2 months without justice and without any cause, C.R. Das, who may be called our Lloyd George and whom we had elected to be our President of the Ahmedabad Congress, the Government which keeps in jail men like Lala Lajpatrai, Motilal Nehru and the Ali brothers. May God grant you strength.

64

CAMP BARDOLI
11 February 1922

From—Thos : N. Lobo, Inspector of Police, Surat.
To—The Collector and District Magistrate, Surat.

SIR,

I beg to submit that in connection with the Working Committee, convened by Mr. M.K. Gandhi today at Bardoli, the following principal persons (given below) came to Bardoli.

2. An informal meeting of about 75 persons was held in the Ashram under the presidentship of Gandhi and discussions were allowed as to whether the movement of Civil Disobedience and non-payment of taxes should be allowed or postponed. The feeling of the Mohamedans was towards the immediate adoption of the movement but Pandit Malavia, Jaikar and Natrajan and also Kelkar spoke in favour of the postponement of the movement. Swami Satya Deo, Mr. Nurmawala were upset but were calmed down by Gandhi. No votes were taken during this meeting which lasted for three hours from 12 to 15 o'clock. Mr. Gandhi wanted to know the mentality of the people.

3. After this meeting was over, the meeting of the Working Committee of five persons was held under the presidentship of Gandhi. Mr. Pandit Malavia was also present by the permission of Gandhi as a spectator and he helped the Committee in the discussions. The five persons were Gandhi, Chhotani, Kelkar, Vithalbhai Patel, and Jamnalal Bajaj. Discussions were held as regards the period of the postponement of the movement of Civil Disobedience and it was decided that the question should be settled by the All India Congress Committee, which wil be held at a place and time convenient to Hakim Azmalkhan who is at present arranging Hartal at Delhi with the help of Dr. Ansari, at the Prince's visit there.

4. When the postponement view was known, to the local as well as outside leaders, they appeared disheartened. Some of the leaders, namely, Messrs Jaikar, Natrajan, Satya Deo, left Bardoli by this evening train, and other leaders including Pandit Malavia, Kelkar, Chhotani, S.R. Bomanji, Vithalbhai and Vallabhbhai Patel, Gangabai, Anusiabai are likely to stay, for one day more. The details and the working of the resolution of the Working Committee will be framed tonight. Mr. Gandhi is disheartened on account of the Gorakhpur outrages, which he has fully believed to be the work of the N.C.Os and he was impressed by Pandit Malavia to suspend Civil Disobedience chiefly in view of this. But Gandhi seems to stick to all other items of the N.C.O. Indications of a split between the Hindu and Mohamedan local leaders of Surat are apparent owing to the precipitous

resolutions arrived at for the postponement of the Civil Disobedience by the Working Committee.

I beg to remain, Sir,
Your most obedient servant
LOBO
Inspector of Police, Surat

1. Pandit M.M. Malavia
2. M.R. Jaikar
3. (K.D.) Natrajan
4. N.C. Kelkar
5. D.V. Gokhale
6. Vallabhbhai J. Patel
7. Vithalbhai J. Patel
8. Anusia Sarabhai
9. Mr. M.K. Gandhi
10. Prof. Anedmal Teckchand Eidwani
11. Mia Mohamed Chhotani
12. S.R. Bomanji
13. Swami Satya Deo
14. Barrister Muazamali
15. Padbadhri, Prof. National School, Bombay
16. R.N. Mandlick
17. Imam Saheb Bavazir of Ahemadebad

65

Vallabhbhai's Address as Chairman, Reception Committee 36th Session—Police Report

Home Department, Political, 1922

In the midst of the cries of "Bandematram" Mr. Vallabhbhai J. Patel, Chairman of the Reception Committee of the Congress, delivered the following speech in Gujarati—

Hakimjisaheb, brother and sister delegates, ladies and gentlemen, just as this National Congress is being held by the Grace of God under His auspices, so was it never held before. Today, how many of our beloved and revered workers have been separated from us? On account of their separation, whereas in our hearts there should be a shadow of grief, it appears that our hearts are full of ecstasy. I will not call those workers "leaders", because during these past 12 months we have shown this the "leadership" is involved in service. It is our belief that howsoever large in numbers our great and educated Mussalman or Hindu brothers have gone to jail, enjoying their well-earned rest, the reason of that is that they have rendered us a service, have suffered troubles ("kasta"), for our sake, and have earned those certificates (desert) for which we have been yearning and which have up to this time been kept by the Government with themselves—the Government which make too much of the plea of law and order, but really speaking, stands on the basis of brute force ("pashubal"), such as is becoming clear day by day. We had hoped that we would be celebrating the great event of establishing *Swaraj,* and, in that behalf, had endeavoured to make preparations for a suitable welcome to be offered to such a consummation. Nevertheless, if today we have not met here together for that solemn function, the most merciful Providence has (however) sent us (the assumption of responsibility of) trouble—suffering, so that we might be tested and befitted to receive that invaluable reward (of *Swaraj*). And these things, namely, imprisonment after imprisonment, assaults, arbitrary searches, the breaking of locks of, and the opening of, our offices and schools,—such happenings are the sure precursors of *Swaraj,* and (also) the assuaging of wounds of our Mussalman and Punjabi brothers. In this belief, we, in respect of every kind of decoration or musical and other gatherings or in regard to any kind of programme which denote our joy, have made no kind of abatement or reduction. But we do not ask you to decide whether we are fit or not for the privilege of inviting you (here) by (merely) looking at the ampleness (or otherwise) of our arrangements for your board, lodging, etc. I know it very well that you will not pay attention to whatever may be the defects in our service to you and the Reception Committee has confidence that you, brothers, will not pay attention to those deficiencies out of your generosity. But what responsibility you laid on us and which we gladly accepted is this that we should complete a constructive programme of non-co-operation, and along with it also its main and soulful principle of non-violence. This Government, so far from manufacturing independent public opinion, conjure up brute force ('pashubal'), and (thus) want to protect themselves. That we are keeping ourselves from their institutions is a sign of this that, under the present circumstances, we are standing away from violence. I claim to say this with truthfulness that we have made effort to become peaceful (non-violent) in thought, in speech, and in action. Having removed from within us our weaknesses, we have seen to it that we do procure the purity of heart with a true conscience and earnestness. The most direct evidence of this is (in) the Hindu-Moslem Unity. Up to this time we never had faith in each other, and we used to take each other (Hindus and Musalmans) to be the natural enemies of each other, but now we have commenced to love each other and have been living on terms of complete intimacy. I feel pride to say this that our friendship is not merely a negative one. On the contrary, we, putting our hands in each other's hands, have done a positive kind of work in the direction of fruition of our political ideal. On similar terms of friendship have we been living with Parsis, Christians and other countrymen, being engaged in doing our work with earnestness according to our programme, we have kept up our relations well with those who differ from our principles. We have recognised this fact that forbearance is the essence of non-violence. I feel sorry that in the matter of discarding titles or giving up the profession by vakils I cannot place before you a picture that would fill me with pride. (But) Yes, the boycott of councils did take place to a degree that was in proportion to the discretion of voters. Of course, in regard to the boycott of educational institutions, all the work that ought to have been done has been done. Some of the best schools and High Schools have cut off their relations with the Government and of these not one is in a bad condition. In most of the national institutions the number of pupils has increased. Here there is one National College and a National University. Many of the National Schools have been affiliated to it (the latter). The number of boys and girls is 31,000 in the National Schools that are or are not affiliated to the Gujarat University. Two years ago, in Gujarat, hardly a single *Charkha* was in use, but today at least 1,10,000 *Charkhas* have done their work. During this time even Khadi has not been produced in a quantity which is less than two lakhs of pounds. In the matter of *Swadeshi* propaganda, we have allotted about five lakhs of rupees. In my opinion, what khadi has been used here (for the Congress Mandap), for other different Mandaps, and for the Khadinagar, is a direct proof of the endeavours we have made in spreading *Swadeshism.* In connection with Temperance, we had been doing picketting work to a large extent, and its result also is very encouraging. We have taken great care to select pickets. They had to do their work under very great difficult circumstances. And some had even to get assaulted at the hands of drunkards and grog-shopkeepers. In the matter of untouchability, our Province has, perhaps, done more work than has been done elsewhere. In our meetings, our "submerged" brothers have been attending without let or hindrance. For their admission in National schools, the idea has been accepted as a matter of theory at least, but (even) for this, the Senate (of the National University) had had to fight toughly. However, incessant efforts have not been made in the direction of:—

(1) Calling the children of these (submerged) brothers (to schools),

(2) Getting them admitted in schools, and

(3) Making them feel that "We are in no sense inferior to other students."

Yet it is not our (final) ideal that separate schools be opened for these boys, but for some time at least, we will have to lean on the side of opening such separate schools. Nevertheless the measures of removal of their curse (accursed condition) is not to be judged (merely) from the fact of the number of their (special) schools or the number of the boys attending National schools. Untouchability is a question of conscience, and I feel pleasure in stating this that, although we have not done much work in this direction, still there has been a change in the (old) feeling of the people about the submerged classes. I am aware of the fact that we, the Gujaratis, have not passed the test of fire of troubled-sufferings, in which fire Bengal, the Punjab, the United Provinces, and other Provinces have been tested. I have been hoping that the non-violence of which I have spoken with pride is not the non-violence born of our weakness but one born of our self-imposed self-restraint. By the forceful possession effected by Government of our Municipal schools in Surat and Nadiad, the Government have given us an opportunity (of going through the fire). The same question is facing Ahmedabad, and it cannot be solved until one goes to the extreme and adopts Civil Disobedience. Bardoli and Anand—these two Tahsils (Districts)—have made preparations with great enthusiasm for mass civil disobedience. I again pray in this National Congress that God may give us such strength that we may suffer troubles and yet pass the test, and stand shoulder to shoulder with the brothers of other Provinces. Along with this, further, I beg to assure you that we will do nothing without proper consideration, nor will we do anything that a peaceful or peace-loving man ought not to do in the name of protecting the national honour and in the name of vindication of the national rights. Now I would ask Hakim Ajmalkhan Saheb that he should take up the duties of the acting President. Today, although Deshbandhu Chittaranjan Das's person is not present here, still his sacred, patriotic and self-sacrificing soul is here. He has sent his speech, which is soul-inspiring and spiritually tuned. The Government of Bengal have created this situation for us. In respect to it we have followed the precedent set by the Muslim League brothers, because they too, in the absence of their (elected) President—Maulana Mahomed Ali— have had to improvise an acting President. I know that Hakimji Ajmalkhan Saheb, who has been elected by the All-India Congress Committee to do the work in the place of Deshbandhu Chittaranjan Das, is a great man of our country, a noble-born man of the country and a man standing on the highest pedestal in the country, because Hakimji is a living example of the Hindu-Moslem Unity. He is as much an object of trust and love to Hindus as he is to the Mussalman brothers and others (Loud cheers).

66

Vallabhbhai Refutes Lord Reading's Observation that Independence could be Got either as Gift or by Sword. "Civil Disobedience was the Third Way," He Asserts

Bombay Chronicle, 30 December 1921

The second and the last day of the Congress opened on Wednesday (at Ahmedabad) with a resolution on Civil Disobedience which was moved by Mahatma Gandhi in a powerful speech. It was seconded by Mr. V.J. Patel and supported by many speakers including Mrs. Sarojini Naidu who eloquently claimed to represent the spirit of free India. Among the four resolutions put from the chair and declared passed unanimously, the first pleaded for the assistance of all those who have no faith in non-cooperation in carrying out various non-controversial items of the movement, the second declaring that the Moplah disturbance which the Congress deplored was not due to the non-cooperation or the Khilafat movement, the third congratulating Ghazi Mustafa Kemal Pasha and the Turks and the fourth deploring the Bombay occurrences of the 17th of November and assuring all communities of the determination of the Congress to guard their rights. A resolution congratulating Babu Gurudatsingji was also passed.

Maulana Hasrat Mohani took his failure to get the resolution regarding the change of the creed of the Congress passed quite in good grace. Mahatma Gandhi made a powerful plea for the retention of the creed which was passed at Nagpur asking whether the creeds for which people die are such simple things as clothes which man can put on and put off at will. His defence was mainly centred round the argument that the Nagpur creed was most comprehensive, covering the "weakest and the strongest among us."

Mahatma Gandhi explained at length, at a meeting of the subjects committee, why he was unable to accept the proposal of a Round Table Conference. The essential condition, said the Mahatma, was a change of heart on the part of the bureaucracy which was lacking.

* * *

Mr. V.J. Patel, seconding the resolution moved by Mahatma Gandhi, said not only did he fully support the resolution, but he agreed with every word that had fallen from the lips of the Mahatma. Never was there such a crisis in the destiny of India under the British as now. Thirty crores of Indians had fallen under British slavery. Lord Reading, who had come to India to give him pure justice, had told them that swaraj could only be obtained in two ways; one by means of sword and the other, by way of gift or *bakshish.* If India wanted Swaraj they were told that they must win it by sword or from the British people as a gift. There was no other way. The resolution only asked for what they had demanded both at Nagpur and Calcutta. He would tell the Government that there was a third way to Swaraj and that was Civil Disobedience and the time had come for them to put it into force. He hoped every Indian heart would be glad to know that it was so. Every one of them, man and woman, must either go to jail or die, or get Swaraj. If they had not the courage to go to jail or die, he asked them to vote against the resolution. If they thought that without Civil Disobedience, without going to jail, without making themselves ready for death, they could get Swaraj, then they must vote against the resolution. When they voted for the resolution they either consented to go to jail or die. If they were unable to win Swaraj it was better they should disappear from the face of the earth only if they agreed with these things, then let them vote for the resolution. Indians wanted to die and not kill others. They were ready to be killed.

Warning to Government

He would tell the Government one word in this connection. Let the Government tell them what they wished to do in this connection. Indians wanted liberty and full liberty as was mentioned in the proclamation. The only difference between the people and Government was this: that Government never kept their promises. They always broke them. Therefore Indians would not put their faith in any such promises. If Government were honest then let them give Indians Swaraj and keep their promises. Indians wanted Swaraj now and immediately. He warned the Government against naked repression. If they put all their leaders into jail there would be nobody to control the violence. If they put down the Congress, there would be secret societies as in Bengal. Therefore, he warned Government against repression. To Moderates he would appeal not to non-cooperate with the Congress but to non-cooperate with a Government which had arrested their countrymen.

[1]Speech was delivered on December 20 at Ahmedabad.

67

Gandhiji Considers Vithalbhai Appropriate for Council Work

Bapu Ke Patra[1]

Friday[2]

DEAR VALLABHBHAI,

I had a detailed discussion with Gidwanibhai.[3] He is unhappy. There are some complaints against Kaka[4] and others in the Ashram. Please call all of them and settle the dispute, if any. I cannot understand how Kaka would be making difficulties. He did not talk about it this time, but it would be better if the whole discontent is removed.

Please decide about Ansuyaben's[5] grant. Please call on her and whatever amount is due to her, give her a cheque for that.

Please tell Maniben and Dahyabhai[6] that the whole thing has been thrashed out with Vithalbhai.[7]1 admit that Vithalbhai now understands the importance of the *charkha.* It appears to me that his true field of action is the Council. He cannot get involved with the people and serve them. It is not that he does not want to serve them, but he has not imbibed the spirit of service of the people. His ability to go to the Council and work there has been developed. I think that separate types of qualities are needed for these two functions. I have not, however, heard anybody criticising Vithalbhai in Bombay.

Yours,
MOHANDAS

[1] *Bapu ke Patra Sardar Vallabhbhai Ke Nam* edited by Maniben Patel, published by Navjivan Publishing House, Ahmedabad, Vol. II, 1952.

[2] It appears that the letter had been written in 1921.

[3] Asoodmal Tekchand Gidwani, Acharya of the Gujarat Vidyapith from 1920-1923.

[4] Dattatraya Balkrishna Kalelkar.

[5] Anusuyaben Sarabhai, President of the Workers Union in Ahmedabad. The grant appears to be for the schools run by the Union.

[6] Vallabhbhai's son.

[7] Elder brother of Sardar Patel.

68

Vallabhbhai Urges Students to Contribute Liberally for Founding National University

Navjivan, Bhadrapad 27 Samvat 1978 (1921)

National education is the life sustaining element of the life of a nation. It is a part of the constructive programme of the Congress. Our opponents also accept the shortcomings and limitations of the prevalent system of education are accepted by everybody. There are no two opinions about the necessity of national education. It is a very powerful means of accelerating the pace of Mahatmaji's constructive programme. The village in which there is national education institution, the natural life is throbbing. Gujarat has taken long strides in that direction.

In only one year's tender life of Gujarat Vidyapith, innumerable primary and secondary schools and colleges have sprung up under its auspices. Thousands of students studying in those schools and colleges are spreading the highest ideals of Swadeshi and Swaraj in thousands of Gujarati families. What more can we expect from an institution which is one year old?

The students studying in national schools and colleges should not forget to contribute for the celebration of national week. There is no necessity to ask mother to take care of the child. Thirty-seven thousand students are studying in natural institutions, out of them if twenty or twenty-five thousand can without displeasing their parents, can request them and bring rupee each, and thus help in the celebration of Mahatmaji's birthday. Those who can afford to contribute more may contribute more.

Out of this money foundation of university is to be laid. So, the sacred memory of having contributed in it will be cherished throughout life. Nobody should get even a jail, by displeasing his parents, but should get as much as possible, they can find willingly.

The teachers of natural schools should not forget their duty to make students conscious of their duty, and arrange for some help from every school.

Gujarat Vidyapith is not solely an institution of Gujarat but an institution which serves the entire country. It desires the help and sympathy of the student world of whole of India.

Those students who have not been able to leave Government schools and college do not have less love for Gandhiji. They should miss this opportunity to show their love.

All the students who receive natural education, and those students who have a liking for that education should perform their duty in this age of action, and give a fitting reply to the government which has imprisoned Mahatma Gandhi—who has sacrified his everything for the country—for sedition. . . may God give them enough strength and good sense.

69

Vallabhbhai's Disclosure of Misconduct of President Ahmedabad Municipality

Ahmedabad Municipality Records G.R. IV/1921-22
7 January 1922

Questions put by Mr. Vallabhbhai J. Patel, Municipal Councillor on 7-1-22 and the replies by the President of Ahmedabad Municipality on 16th January 1922.

Q. 1. Is it a fact that on the night of the 6th January 1922 immediately after the resolution on the question of the withdrawal of Rs 72,000 from the Municipal Account by order of the Commissioner N.D. was passed by the General Board an informal conference was held at the Collector's Bungalow between him and certain members and the Chief Officer or any other officers of the Municipality? If so, who were the officers and members who attended the conference?

Ans. There were no such conference at the Collector's Bungalow.

Q. 2. Is it a fact that a copy of the resolution was supplied to the Collector that very night? If so, who supplied this copy?

Ans. Yes, It was supplied to the Collector under President's signature that very night as per Collector's verbal orders given to the Chief Officer under section 173 of the Act.

Q. 3. Is it a fact that the Collector in that conference decided to suspend a portion of the resolution of this General Board and order of the suspension was received by some officer of the Municipality that very night? If so, who was the Officer, who received that order? And when and at what place the order was received? And by whom was it delivered?

Ans. As there was no conference, no answer is needed to the first part of the question. The order from the Collector was delivered to the President at his residence late at night by the Chief Officer who was asked to do so. It was sent to the Municipal Office on the 7th at noon by the President.

Q. 4. Is it a fact that the question of finding out a way to prevent the Schools Committee or the Municipality from making payment of salaries due to Municipal teachers was discussed in that meeting?

Ans. No.

Q. 5. It is requested that the Chief Officer's statement on the subject be placed on the table.

Ans. The Chief Officer's statement is placed on the table.

V. J. PATEL
Municipal Councillor

RAMANBHAI M. NILKANTHA
President

70

Vallabhbhai Asks Congressmen to Concentrate on Boycott and Stop Talking about Council Entry

Navjivan, 14 January 1922

The faith of the people was put to test in Gaya Congress. All the efforts to make changes in the programme of the Congress failed. The important change was about withdrawing the boycott of the legislatures. Deshbandhu Das, President of the Congress, advocated for this change. Great leaders like Pandit Motilalji and Hakimji tried their level best. But even then majority of delegates flatly refused to lift the boycott, or make it mild. Not only that but they recommended that make it more strong.

In the consultative committee a resolution regarding boycott of British goods which was carried out with a thin majority that was also not accepted by Congress delegates.

Thus Congress has given a strong proof of its faith in the present programme. But mere faith is not sufficient. Faith without strength is of no use. For successful termination of any great work faith and strength both are necessary. Congress gave a proof of the faith of people but side by side it has desired that people should give ample evidence of their strength. In fulfilling that desire people's strength will be put to test. If the faith of people is not void of thinking, if it is not blind faith, then in spite of great difficulties, and there being differences of opinion amongst the leaders, people will respond most favourably to the demand of the Congress.

Congress has demanded that preparations should be made on a large scale for launching individual civil disobedience movement. It has also demanded that until the end of October, Congress institutions are to be made strong, 25 lacs of rupees and 50 thousand volunteers are to be recruited, and thus give a proof that the country is ready for individual civil disobedience. If that preparation is made then the great sacrifice of dedication can be started. It is the duty of those who have faith in the Congress programme to help in the full implementation of the Congress resolution.

On the question of Council entry there will be hot discussions. Leaders have decided to mould public opinion, and attract people towards them. In such an atmosphere if both the sides get busy discussing this issue only, or use their intelligence and strength in mutual attack then it will be unfortunate for the country.

Those who are not for Council entry should desist from discussing that issue, because that issue has been more than necessary discussions on that. We have spent priceless power and talent in discussing that issue. Now let that be left to those persons who have interest in it, and others should attend to their work. The best way to stop discussions regarding Council entry is sound work. As we will be getting more and more proof of our implementation of Congress resolution, discussion about that problem will get weaker and weaker.

71

Vallabhbhai Appeals to People to Refrain from Taking Liquor

Navjivan, 2 February 1922

BROTHERS,

Yesterday prior to the auction of wine shops you were warned. Still because of the backing of the force of the State you disregarded our warning, and therefore as there was no other remedy we had to picket your shops. Last year there was some basis in your argument that warning was not given in time. Now auction for the new year will be done by the end of next month, that is why I beg to warn you in time, that if last year's mistake is repeated by you, and if you take the monopoly for the new year, then you shall have to suffer the consequences.

I think that picketing had desired effect on the shopkeepers as well as on the Government. You might not be unaware that Ahmedabad Municipality has decided to close wine shops in its municipal limit. You must have enough experience by now as to how difficult it is to run the business, which hurt the sentiments of the people. Due to some circumstances the picketing has been discontinued, but do not think that it has been given up for ever. You must not be unaware of the awakening amongst people and specially of the women. I most humbly request you to respect the sentiments of the people, give up the sinful business, and receive the blessings of thousands of poor families.

I assure you that this movement has not been started with the intention of causing damage to you or to prevent Government from getting income from wine business. Because of this religious activity thousands of dealers in foreign cloth have been passing through hard times. Their business is not as abominable as yours, yet they do not seek government's help. If you think that you will be able to run this business by sending picketers to jail then you are living in false hope. Government has not so many prisons and it cannot afford to spend the income from wine after the prisons. This can be easily understood. Give up the hope of making huge profits from meagre amount of auction. I hope you will pay proper attention to my request.

72

CONFIDENTIAL

Home Secretary to Government of Bombay regarding Preparation for Civil Disobedience in Kaira, Nadiad and Anand Talukas

Home Department, (Political) File N.A.I.,
2 February 1922

Demi-official no. S.D.-366, dated Bombay, the 2nd February 1922.

From— The Hon'ble Mr. J. Crerar, C.I.E. I.C.S., Secretary to the Government of Bombay, Home (Special) Department,

To— The Hon'ble Mr. S.P.O' Donnell, C.I.E., I.C.S., Secretary to the Government of India, Home Department.

I am desired to submit my report for the fortnight ending the 31st January 1922.

2. *Political*—The situation still continues fluid. A public meeting of four thousand attended by Gandhi was held in the headquarters town on the 29th at which a resolution for the non-payment of taxes and preparedness to face the

consequences was passed. The decision was considered by the All-India Congress Working Committee at a meeting which was held on the 31st at Surat. It has since been reported in the *Bombay Chronicle* that the Working Committee congratulated the Bardoli Conference on their conclusions. The actual initiation of civil disobedience now appears to depend on the issue of further specific orders by Gandhi, and it is believed that he will give notice to His Excellency the Viceroy in the form of an ultimatum. Gandhi himself does not seem overconfident as is evidenced by his article in *Navjivan* of the 22nd January entitled "Where is Swaraj" and also from a hint thrown out by him at the Bardoli meeting that personally he thought another fortnight's preparation at least necessary. The general tenour of the proceedings at the meeting seem to indicate some indecision or difference of opinion among the leaders, but action may be precipitated by the more extreme sections. The non-cooperators claim that 25 villages in the taluka have decided in favour of non-payment of taxes. As a set off against Bardoli, the situation in the Anand Taluka, the second taluka selected by Gandhi himself as the most likely field for initiating Civil Disobedience, is good, so far as revenue collections are concerned. The latest reports show that, except in two villages, the land revenue is coming in satisfactorily. The local Samiti is reported to have decided not to recommend the Taluka for the initiation of mass Civil Disobedience. Reports continue favourable also in respect of the other talukas in the Kaira District. In the Nadiad taluka, of which headquarters was considered a non-cooperation stronghold, only two villages showing signs of defaulting.

It has been decided to supersede for one year under the Bombay District Municipal Act the Municipalities of Ahmedabad and Surat on the grounds that they have persistently made default in the performance of obligatory duties and have exceeded and abused their powers. The Commissioner, Northern Division, has accordingly been instructed to make all necessary preliminary arrangements for the appointment of persons to discharge the powers and duties of these Municipalities in the manner prescribed by the Act. The formal orders of Government will issue when the preliminary arrangements are complete. On the 27th the Poona City Municipality passed by a large majority a resolution to spend Rs 2,000 for a crusade of preaching against the use of liquor and other intoxicants in the city limits at the hands of approved lecturers and writers. No mention appears to have been made of the picketing of liquor shops which is at present prohibited in the Poona city.

Elsewhere in the Presidency the response to the appeal for volunteers continues languid. Vigorous propaganda in the city of Bombay to secure the minimum of ten thousand laid down has so far only secured 184 enrolments, 131 of whom including most of the leading lights, Chotani, S.R. Bomanji, Umar Sobhani, Banker and others, have only signed as "reservists"

In Mahomedan circles intensity of feeling in regard to the Turkish question continues. It has been exacerbated by the facilities which the British Government is reported to be giving the Greeks for floating a loan of 25 million pounds sterling in Britain. At a meeting of the Working Committee of the Central Khilafat Committee held at Bombay on the 17th January feeling ran very high when the subject was under consideration. A resolution was finally passed pointing out how time and again Government had been warned that any help given to Greece, direct or indirect, financial or otherwise, would be taken by the Mahomedans of India as a breach of neutrality, that Government do not care a straw about their threats, and that if the Mussalmans repudiated loyalty to Government the sole responsibility would rest on Government. It was decided to send the resolution to Gandhi and to inform him that the loyalty of Muslims to Government would cease from the day the loan was floated in England and, if their Ulemas so advised, they would abandon the non-violent movement. It is also rumoured that the British Government intend taking over control or purchasing the Hedjaz Railway either directly or by private enterprise. Much capital may be made out of this. It is highly desirable that the rumour if incorrect, as is presumably the case, should be promptly contradicted. From the telegraphic correspondence noticed in the censorship it would appear that non-cooperation leaders are anxious to placate Hindu feeling in respect of the forcible conversions in Malabar, etc., and that endeavours are being made to procure necessary *Fatwas* from the leading *Ulemas* on the subject. In view, however, of the debates at the Central Khilafat Committee Conference and the Moslem League sessions at Ahmedabad on the subject, it is very doubtful if now at the eleventh hour such a declaration will have the desired effect.

General Forecast—The situation is still one of unstable equilibrium. It seems probable that Gandhi will continue to temporise in the hope of some development which he can take as a text for opening his campaign. He may be forced into action by the more extreme of his following and the fact that the date for land revenue collections in Bardoli is at hand (February 5th).

3. *Press*—The representative Conference of political leaders held in Bombay monopolised a good deal of the attention of the Press. The resolutions passed by the Conference met with the approbation of the Extremist papers and were extolled as proofs positive of Mr. Gandhi's eagerness to arrive at a settlement and all of them seem hopeful to look forward to the holding of the Round Table Conference for the solution of the present troubles in India. Moderate papers like the *Dnyan Prakash,* the *Praja Mitra and Parsi* and the *Jam-e-Jamshed,* however, considered Mr. Gandhi's terms so very uncompromising as to preclude the possibility of Lord Reading convening a Round Table Conference.

The manifesto issued by the Khilafat leaders enumerating the Moslem demands with regard to Turkey and criticising the new terms proposed to be offered to Turkey was received with mixed feelings by the papers. The *Bombay Samachar* endorsed the demands and expressed the hope that England will not lose this last opportunity of establishing peace in the world by conceding the Moslem demands. The *Gujarati,* on the other hand, remarked that the manifesto showed that the Moslem demands were slowly growing and that the spirit of Pan-Islamism was abroad. The *Praja Mitra and Parsi* declared that the Indian Khilafatists in their demands went even further than the Kemalists.

73

Vallabhbhai Expresses Satisfaction over Removal of Untouchability in Taluka

Navjivan, 3 February 1922

Out of a total population of 87,000, roughly 30,000 are Patidars, 45,000 Dublas and other Raniparaj, 3,000 Mussalmans, 3,000 Anavil Brahmins, 2,000 Baniyas and about the same number of "untouchables". The Baniyas and the Brahmins are neither in favour of the struggle nor against it. 75 per cent of the Patidars are whole-heartedly in favour of the struggle and are prepared to make whatever sacrifices they are called upon to make. No attempt has yet been made to win over the Dubla and Raniparaj, but their relationship with Patidars is such that they will do whatever the latter ask them to do. There appears to exist complete unity among Hindus, Muslims and other communities. The progress that the Taluka has made towards the removal of untouchability is satisfactory. A large number of upper class people accompanied me when I visited "untouchable" homes and localities in villages, and they did so without any hesitation. Not enough work has yet been done for the admission of "untouchable" children in the national schools, but what has been done is sufficient to justify going ahead with the decisions to launch the Civil Disobedience Movement. Liquor and toddy shops are far too numerous for so small a Taluka but in the main only the Dubla and Raniparaj are addicted to drink. If the Patidars take the matter into their hands, they will be able to achieve effective control over liquor and toddy shops. There is very little crime in the Taluka and the people are generally not in the habit of going to law courts. The vast majority of disputes are settled privately. There is no reason to apprehend a breach of peace; order and non-violence will be maintained.

74

Vallabhbhai Exhorts People to Wear "Khadi" and Boycott British Goods

Navjivan, 14 February 1922

A parrot which is kept in a cage for years does not like to come out even if the cage is kept open. Slaves even if they find out a way to free themselves from the bondage they hesitate to go to that way. Long time slavery generates a fascination for a state of slavery. Our condition is also the same. After 150 years of slavery we awoke from deep slumber three years before during the national week; we became conscious of our slavery, and we tried to find a way to break the bonds of slavery.

Mahatma Gandhi showed us the way: "Swaraj by spinning, wear *khadi* and have your Swaraj". In the beginning we laughed at it. But with the passage of time we were convinced of its potentiality and then we became conscious of our shortcomings. At that moment we loved to hear the talks about *swadeshi.*

But we who had lost their identity, being fascinated by the lure of slavery, could not give up our dress material and style of wearing cloth. In order to free us from the hallucination, Gandhi gave up wearing all garments except a waist garment (*langot*) and showed us that nice garments do not beautify a person, but a man shines only by his nice righteous behaviour. Yet we have not been able to free ourselves from the lure of foreign cloth.

Today in Gujarat production *of khadi* is very high, but *khadi* produced in Gujarat is not consumed in Gujarat, which is proof of our weakness. Lancashire and Manchester are nervous, because of whatever little we have done. Labourers there are without work, and because of the anger of the capitalists there today Gandhiji is in prison. They believe that by imprisoning Gandhiji *Swadeshi* movement will either die out or it will not spread, while going to jail. Gandhiji has concentrated on *khadi,* and whosoever met him has been advised to wear *khadi.* We have to put into practice.

Uptill now we have been simply talking. Cloth merchants of Bombay met together, talked and dispersed. In Ahmedabad foreign cloth dealers are quarrelling amongst themselves and still they are not able to decide anything. Women are not fully *swadeshi* minded. It is said that in marriage season *khadi* cannot be used. So our condition is like a parrot in the cage. We found out the way to freedom, but we have not freed ourselves from the lure of slavery, till then we shall have to rot in slavery.

We are pained to know that Mahatma Gandhi is suffering in jail. But we are not ready to give him peace of mind by giving up fine cloth and use *khadi.* On coming 18th one month of his imprisonment will be complete. In these days of national week, if we do not do anything more at least we decide that before that day we completely give up foreign cloth, and man, woman, and child, everybody, wears only *khadi.*

Workers in all the provinces except Gujarat are practising penance in jail. Gujarat is saved. By offering meagre sacrifice Gujarat has received highest honour. We had not the occasion to be put to test in Bardoli. But Bardoli earned a name in the world. Mahatma Gandhi has by his penance kept the prestige of Gujarat in tact. Those Gujaratis whether they might be residing in Gujarat or Kathiawar, in Bombay or in foreign lands—if they do not take to wearing *khadi* they should be ashamed of themselves. 18th is a day of prayers. If we pray on that day for his release without wearing *khadi* then it will be an act which would hurt him, and not for his release.

75

SECRET

Secretary Bombay Government on Preparations by Gandhiji and Vallabhbhai for Bardoli Satyagraha (Extracts)

Home Political, 18 February 1922

Demi-official no. S.D.-596, dated Bombay, the 18th February 1922.
From—The Hon'ble Mr. J. Crerar, C.I.E., I.C.S., Secretary to the Government of Bombay, Home (Special) Department,
To—The Hon'ble Mr. S.P.O' Donnell, C.I.E., I.C.S., Secretary to the Government of India, Home Department.

I am desired to submit my report for the fortnight ending the 16th February 1922.

2. *Political*—Having obtained the approval of the All-India Congress Working Committee, as reported in my last fortnightly letter, to the initiation of mass civil disobedience in the Bardoli taluka of the Surat District, Gandhi immediately set about initiating an intensive campaign in the taluka which was divided for the purpose into fourteen areas, each area under a leader with helpers, Gandhi himself visiting villages where special efforts appeared to be required. House-to-house visitations were conducted and meetings held, where social boycott, the withdrawal of services from friends of Government and refusal to work or supply transport to Government officers were threatened and in some cases actually put into force. Gandhi, in conjunction with V.J. Patel, issued printed leaflets calling on Patels to resign and forward their resignations to him, which he would in due course forward to Government and, it is reported, that 22 Patels did so. Gandhi also started the issue of a daily leaflet or *patrika* in Gujarati instructing the people in what they should do. The press paragraph summarises opinion on his manifesto and the Government of India's communique. On the receipt of news regarding the Chauri Chaura tragedy, Gandhi immediately came to Bombay at Malaviya's invitation to discuss the situation. It is reported that Malaviya urged on Gandhi the immediate necessity of abandoning civil disobedience, or at least postponing it for six months, one of the arguments used being the likelihood of an early settlement of the Turkish trouble, and the consequential loss to him of Moslem support. Gandhi appears to have questioned Chotani on this point, but got no definite assurance from him to the contrary. Gandhi is reported to have said that he fully recognised the danger of civil disobedience and to have expressed his willingness to postpone it, but could not do so without the sanction of the Working Committee. He left with Malaviya on the night of the 10th for Bardoli, where a special meeting of the Working Committee took place on the 11th and 12th. There are many indications that the moral effect of the Chauri Chaura outrage was not the sole motive for the suspension of the campaign. Further examination of conditions in the Bardoli taluka had probably made Gandhi apprehensive of

failure even in his selected area, and he had received many urgent messages from leaders in various parts of India vehemently opposing the projected action.

The resolutions passed have received wide publicity in the Press. Civil disobedience in Bardoli and elsewhere was called off and people were advised to pay all dues to Government and volunteer organizations were requested to stop all activities specially designed to court arrest and imprisonment, save normal Congress activities including voluntary *hartals* and *bonafide* picketing for the "peaceful" purpose of warning visitors to liquor shops against the evils of drinking. These resolutions are to have effect only pending the meeting to be specially convened of the All-India Congress Committee, and thereafter subject to confirmation by it. The new programme of work as laid down at the meeting follows closely the lines laid down by the Calcutta, Nagpur and Bezwada resolutions, subject to any revision if necessary by the All-India Congress Committee. From telegrams seen in the censorship, it appears that the Bengal leaders are in doubt whether Bengal will follow the Bardoli lead, and they have wired Gandhi asking for the special meeting of the Congress to be held in Calcutta, but Ajmal Khan, the President, has also wired fixing the date of the meeting for the 24th instant at Delhi. The postponement is reported to have seriously depressed Gandhi's immediate following and judging from newspaper comments the Deccan Nationalists will probably oppose the postponement of mass civil disobedience for more than a very short period with a view to starting it at Ahmedabad and Surat at an early date in connection with the suspension of the local municipalities.

3. *Press*—The question of starting a campaign of civil disobedience in Bardoli monopolised a good deal of the attention of the Press. Mr. Gandhi in his *Young India* eulogised the patience shown by Government towards the Bardoli campaign thus:— "They have not interfered with any of the activities of the people. They have permitted them to make all preparations. I have watched their conduct with wonder and admiration." Mr. Gandhi's "ultimatum" to the Viceroy was welcomed by the extremist papers, and they expressed hope that it would induce Lord Reading to call a Round Table Conference. The *Kesari,* however, was not hopeful in the matter and asked Indians to concentrate their attention upon Bardoli. The moderate papers considered Mr. Gandhi's demands as unreasonable. The *Indian Social Reformer* was shocked by its "pragmatic" tone which, in its opinion, accentuated the general confusion of issues. The communique issued by the Government of India in reply to Mr. Gandhi's ultimatum was thought by the *Bombay Chronicle* to make it clear that "Government have not the will to peace and that they were determined to pit repression against non-co-operation to the bitter end. The *Sind Observer* remarked that Government were not likely to take fright at the threat held out by Mr. Gandhi and that they were strong enough to control the situation. The Extremist Press characterised the communique as disappointing and endorsed Mr. Gandhi's rejoinder. The Moderate papers, however, upheld the contention of the Government communique and

criticised Mr. Gandhi's rejoinder and pointed out that the responsibility for resorting to civil disobedience would now rest solely on Mr. Gandhi and that he could have no justification in telling the people that it was forced upon the people by Government. As the date fixed for starting civil disobedience approached, Extremist papers like the *Bombay Samachar* and the *Sanj Vartman* seem to have been filled with misgivings as to its disastrous consequences and joined the Moderates in warning the Working Committee of the dangers involved in civil disobedience and asked them to postpone it in view of the disturbances at Chauri Chaura. The decision of the Working Committee to postpone civil disobedience in Bardoli caused a feeling of relief among the Moderate papers and even some of the Extremist papers characterised the step as "proper and farsighted". The *Indu Prakash,* however, blamed Mr. Gandhi for retracing his steps and the *Kesari* considered it an error of judgment on his part not to have launched civil disobedience after making so much fuss about it.

Mr. Churchill's pronouncement at the East African dinner in London gave rise to considerable commotion in the Press. The speech was characterised as "thoughtless and foolish" by the *Praja Mitra and Parsi* and the *Jam-e-Jamshed* feared that it would add fuel to the fire of existing discontent in India. The *Mahratta* was of the opinion that Mr. Churchill's pronouncement would not be the last word on the Kenya question and remarked: "Had India been free there would have been heard the retaliatory prohibition to all British whites in India, if not the booming of guns at the gates of Nairobi."

The release and subsequent arrest of Lala Lajpatrai was criticised with considerable warmth and the papers were of the opinion that the "farce" of release should not have been enacted if the Lala was to have been re-arrested so soon.

Forecast—It is probable that there will be a severe contest at the meeting of the All-India Congress Committee between the advocates of direct action and Gandhi's personal followers. If Gandhi's views prevail, a definite schism is likely. The Maharashtra party under Kelkar have never been enthusiastic about Gandhi's leadership and policy and may openly secede. Independent action by the Khilafat party is also likely. A favourable turn in the negotiations for a Turkish settlement would be highly opportune at this juncture and might have far-reaching results.

76

Government Taking over of Municipalities in Gujarat Condemned

Navjivan, 19 February 1922

The Government have suspended the Municipalities of Ahmedabad and Surat, but those who know the mentality of the Government will not be surprised. Many people had forcecast the suspension some time ago. But whether the government decision is legal or illegal is a matter of debate and that is why we must go into the real facts of the matter.

The Ahmedabad Municipality not only refused government assistance in the matter of education but also declared itself free from government control. For a long time afterwards, the Government's behaviour towards the Municipality was such as to give the impression that the government had no objection to the Municipality declaring itself independent of government control. But ever since the government issued orders that since the teachers in the Municipal schools were government employees and should, therefore, be withdrawn and that Municipal teachers trained in the government training college should be recalled and the Municipal schools should be de-recognised and their names struck off the government register and also that students of Municipal schools should not be given admission in government schools, the government have lost the right of control over education. This thing has become amply clear.

But immediately afterwards, the government somersaulted and took certain steps against the Municipality, which were all illegal. It tried to take over the Municipal schools under Section 178 of the Municipal Act, tried to take over the bank accounts of the Municipality and also broken open the locks of the schools, made over by the Municipality to the local Education Board. There is no legal defence for these actions. Under these circumstances, the only recourse open to the government to sweep its illegalities under the carpet and to get out of the difficulties, it had created for itself, was the suspension of the municipalities.

When the question of cooperation is raised, nobody goes into the merits of the case and it is believed that those who believe in non-cooperation are the guilty party. The dispute in the Ahmedabad Municipality was not between cooperation and non-cooperation, but between blind cooperation and self-respect. (That is why Rao Sahib Harilal has refused to stay in the committee appointed by the government.) When the government objected to it, we listened to the advice of all the members of the Ahmedabad Municipality, who believe in non-cooperation, including the Vice-President of the Bombay Assembly, Rao Sahib Harilal, who is also a member of the Ahmedabad Municipality. At our advice, the Ahmedabad Municipality passed a resolution that it should frame rules for Municipalities who do not seek aid for their schools from the government so that those Municipalities are free of government control. A copy of the resolution was sent to the government who wanted to know from the Municipality as to what kind of rules it wanted. But before the Municipality could consider the government communication orders for the suspension of the Municipality were published in the Gazette.

Under Section 178 of the Municipal Act, the orders of the Commissioner to take away the management of the schools from the School Committee were illegal because the Commissioner has no powers under the law to do so. Similarly, the government had no right to withdraw funds from the bank accounts of the Municipality. Rao Sahib Harilal moved a resolution in the Ahmedabad Municipality asking the government to rescind the orders they had issued. The reply received from the government stated that the resolution of the Municipality would be placed before the Governor-in-Council. It appears that it became impossible for the Government to give a valid reply. It, therefore, suspended the Municipality instead of replying to the municipal resolution. After the Montague-Chelmsford reforms on local self-government were published, the Government of India issued a resolution in May 1918. Under the policy announced in that resolution, the Bombay Government order suspending the municipalities is totally illegal. The government resolution had accepted the principle that the local self institutions should be permitted to function and that even if they make mistakes, they should be given an opportunity to correct them and that the government offices should not interfere in the functioning of the local self-government institutions. The resolution states:

> But, as has been stated in the Preamble of the Resolution, the general principle which the Government of India believes in is that except in cases where there is grave public disorder, even if the local self-government institutions make any mistakes, they should be permitted to do so and should be left free to learn from those mistakes. There should not be any interference either from within or from without in their functioning. Except for some rare exceptions, the Government of India does not intend that its officers should have any valid ground for interference in the work of these institutions. The Government of India hope that the above principle will be kept in mind while exercising the wide powers available to the authorities under the law. And before the powers bestowed by laws are utilized to take any stringent action, the Provincial Government would issue orders for holding of fresh elections after the municipal or other local self institutions are dissolved. It would, thus, avoid direct action to punish a municipality.

The local authorities have violated this resolution of the Government of India in respect of Municipalities like the one in Ahmedabad which were considered to be efficient. The interference in the working of the municipal institutions has been further confirmed by the orders of suspension issued by the Bombay Government. The Government of India resolution quoted above has made it clear that before a provincial government takes such a stringent action as the suspension of municipalities, it should order elections to the municipalities so dissolved. It also stated that this action should be taken only if it becomes inevitable without interfering with the law. The resolution further states:

> Most notices under this resolution can be implemented without waiting for a change in the law. Action should be taken without delay, where it is possible to do so.

The Bombay government could have followed the Government of India resolution without making any change in the Municipal Act because the new elections were due. The date of the elections had already been announced and the representatives of the mill owners had already been elected. Even so all these legal requirements were forgotten and the Bombay Government clearly disregarded the Government of India resolution by suspending the Municipality.

What could be a better proof of the failure of the Reforms when municipalities can be suspended in this manner when the local self department is under an elected minister. Only God knows whether the minister has any idea of the above resolution of the Government of India which sets forth the policy on local-self government. Ever since he has became the Minister, this is probably the first notable action that has been taken by him. Before he was appointed, the previous assembly had tried to make ineffective the reforms with regard to local-self government. One Mr. Martin, an officer, had been appointed to make amendments in the law concerning local self-government, to recommend improvements and to prepare a draft of the new law. He had prepared a draft before the honourable minister took over the department. That is why the government cannot consider the question of making improvements in the law. Some time ago, the Bombay government had appointed an Inquiry Committee to go into the ways and means of increasing the income of the local self institutions. The recommendations of the Committee and Mr. Martin's draft are still pending with the minister. That is why I say that so long as this honourable minister and the Assembly are there, it would be futile to hope that the local-self institutions would be free. It is clear that if these institutions try to become independent, the honourable minister and the Assembly would see to it that the attempt fails. This is what is termed as "Reforms" by the Government. There is a party amongst us who believes in this and who has been trying to prove that the Reforms have been successful. Could there be any thing more regretful?

77

Vallabhbhai Lauds Pranjivandas of Rangoon for his Liberal Donation to Vidyapith

Navjivan, 24 February, 1922

An illustrious son of Gujarat Dr. Pranjivandas Mehta who is a resident of Rangoon was moved by the agony of Gujarat and emptied the treasury on his generous heart. He alone donated one-fourth of the amount wanted for the Vidyapith. Let God give good sense to the rich people of Gujarat and Bombay to learn to imitate this extremely generous person who resides in a distant land.

After a week we will be celebrating Second October. Yet five lacs of rupees are to be collected. Money is flickery. It is with us today and leave us tomorrow. But second October of 1922, and Mahatmaji's 54th birthday won't come again.

One week's time is not short. Much more can be done in a week. It is said that in a week so many people will be ruined and many people will earn lacs of rupees. For Bombay which is rich and generous city one week's time is not short to get a small sum of five lacs of rupees.

We have full faith in Bombay. Bombay will give us as much as we want. But Gujarat must understand its responsibility. All men and women should wear only khadi on that day to celebrate Mahatma Gandhi's birthday. Let there be voluntary stoppage of work on that day and people should take out *khadi* processions, hold public meetings, and pray God to give long life to Gandhiji and ask Him to give us the power of getting Gandhiji released.

78

Vallabhbhai Urges People of Gujarat to Prove Worthy of Gandhiji's Trust

Navjivan, 11 March 1922

At last the government has imprisoned the greatest leader of India, who in the history of the world experimented a new technique for achievement of independence and protection of the ethical standards. Since last two years Gandhiji had not full meals, nor has he a peaceful sleep. His soul which was terribly in agony, because of the insult to Punjab, injustice to Khilafat, and the pains of the chains of slavery, was clamouring for peace. The person who is worshipped in whole of India, because of the lustre of his ethical personality, after many centuries the attention of the whole world is attracted towards India, by whose momentary touch, the lives of thousands have completely transformed. For such a divine person in this rule how can any other place than prison can give him peace?

Many persons who did not understand the significance of Bardoli resolution, had doubts about his style of working. In political matters, for the sake of convenience of the fighters, religion and ethics cannot be conveniently used, that was his unshakable stand. Many people who did not understand the significance of his ethical stand, his attitude to consider himself morally responsible for the bad behaviour of any section of the people in any part, found fault in his behaviour, but now they must have seen that Gandhiji has an X-ray eye which an ordinary politician does not possess.

He postponed civil disobedience activities, and made herculean efforts to concentrate on constructive programme, to spread the atmosphere of pure peace, at that very moment Government thought it wise to arrest him, so what other auspicious occasion can there be for him and for the people.

British lion has been offered many beasts of prey. But it is for the first time that it has the fortune to get such a hunt. But it is not easy for it to digest such a hunt. In April 1919 once before it had stretched its paw for this prey, but it had to leave it at that very moment. But this time we have tested the lion to our hearts' content. Its eyes are red with anger. Since many days it has been terribly shaking its mane. But *rishis* and sages of India have by the power of their penance had turned ferocious lions into mild lambs. Similarly this lion also is going to be transformed into a goat by the power of penance of this great man. There is no doubt about it.

He was greatly pleased by seeing that in Ahmedabad there is lasting peace. Compared to our madness in April 1919, this peace established as a result of proper understanding speaks volumes of our progress and training. It is a matter of great joy. If whole of India learns to maintain such a peace. Government shall have to release our each and every prisoner.

Great responsibility lies on the head of Gujarat. Gujarat is now put on test. Gandhiji has shown in clear words, what he expects us to do. The real way of showing our feelings for him is not to shout his *jai* or to rush for his *darshan* but to engage ourselves in making his four-point people's programme successful.

If whole of the country takes time to understand, but Gujarat, where he has directly spent his life energy, should understand his crystal clear words coming from his heart, and should prove its capacity to assimilate those words and put into action.

79

"Hindu-Muslim Unity My Life-long Aim"—Vallabhbhai

Bombay Chronicle, 13 March 1922

The following interview was granted by Mr. V.J. Patel, the General Secretary, the All-India Congress Committee, to a representative of the *Bombay Chronicle* in regard to the situation arising out of the arrest of Mahatma Gandhi at Ahmedabad.

Questioned as to what was the programme now before the country, Mr. V.J. Patel said, "We should continue and consolidate the constructive work of the Congress:

(1) Swadeshi should be developed by the spread of hand-spun khadi, by introducing more looms for weaving hand-spun yarn and by making the spinning wheel more universal.

(2) The untouchables should be taught cleanliness, they should by gentle persuasion be weaned from besh-eating and especially carrion. Every untouchable child should be accounted for and induced to come to National Schools.

(3) Friendship between different classes should be cultivated by each understanding and sharing the difficulty of the other.

(4) Non-violence should be inculcated as the virtue of the strong.

(5) Panchayats should be organised and the people should be weaned from the law-courts.

(6) National Schools should be properly organised.

(7) Drink-evil should be completely eradicated by practising among those who are addicted to the vice and by peaceful picketing, if necessary. Ladies should be enlisted as special volunteers for the purpose of visiting families where the vice is prevalent.

(8) Workers cannot rest till every adult male and female in the country has been registered in the Congress ledger.

(9) Collection of the 'Tilak Swaraj Fund' for this year should be immediately

undertaken and all Congressmen and sympathisers should be approached by the workers to induce them to contribute one per cent of their income towards the Fund."

Representative: Mr. Patel, will you make your point clear with regard to picketing of liquor-shop, foreign cloth shops, etc.

Mr. Patel: "No picketing in respect of foreign-cloth shops, liquor-shop or law courts should be resorted to unless absolute non-violence can be insured."

Questioned as to the effect of Mahatma Gandhi's arrest on his followers, Mr. Patel said, "I believe, people will now see their way to concentrate more on Mass Civil Disobedience."

Questioned as to the desirability of carrying on the Civil Disobedience Movement, Mr. Patel said, "No, in my opinion the two lists of volunteers sanctioned by the Working Committee in pursuance of the Congress resolutions should continue. But care must be taken that no one who does not conform strictly to the requirements of the Congress should be enrolled. At the same time the existing lists of Volunteers in all Provinces should be purged of the names of those who should not have been there. The All-India Congress Committee at Delhi has directed the suspension of the Mass Civil Disobedience.

But in regard to Individual Civil Disobedience (both offensive and defensive) the Committee gives full powers to each Province to deal with the question as it likes.

I have no hesitation in saying that Individual Civil Disobedience of an aggressive character should not be for the time being undertaken by any Province. I am equally clear that the Individual Civil Disobedience of a defensive character should be undertaken only where it is absolutely necessary at any rate for the present. In any case, side by side with the working out of the constructive programme must be strictly followed until the adoption of any new programme by the All-India Congress Committee.

Lying and absolutely groundless statements are circulated by a so-called 'Information Bureau' of Calcutta as to my doings at Ahmedabad last December. I never spoke a word against Mahatma Gandhi nor against the Hindus generally. Hindu-Muslim unity has been my life-long aim and I shall be the last person to say or do anything which may imperil it in the least. This is my cherished object."

80

Vallabhbhai Holds People Responsible for Failure to Achieve Swaraj

Navjivan, 26 March 1922

In March 1921, Gandhiji was sentenced to six years' imprisonment. Sardar Patel made an appeal to the people on the occasion which is as follows:

The friend of the Indian people, Mahatma Gandhi, has gone to jail, but that should not create any despondency amongst us. He has left us an invaluable legacy which we must utilize to good effect.

Before December he tried his level best to bring in Swaraj but the people did not pay the price for it. People who were in government positions stuck to them. People continue to go to the courts in search of justice. The students have not got rid of their attachment to degrees. We went into the assemblies and some of us came out, but even they have not stopped feeling sorry on having left them. Those who sell liquor continue to do so and people are still consuming liquor. Those who deal in imported textiles continue to sell them. The people are not prepared to burn foreign clothes or to boycott them. It is still a mark of distinction to wear fine imported clothes at times of marriages and other functions. The women love to wear fine saris. Only a few are content with the white cap. The mill owners want to increase their profits by using imported yarn and if the mill made cloth is still popular in spite of the swadeshi movement, they increase the prices and thus their profits. The capitalists want to enhance their capital. Nobody is prepared to leave the luxuries of life. Most of the people feel that Swaraj can come if they shout "Long Live Mahatma Gandhi" and contribute a few rupees to the national movement. Gandhiji has said time and again that this is not the way to achieve Swaraj.

Even so whatever a wakening has come among the people is surprising. It is admitted on all hands that we have achieved in a year which could have been possible in a century. Then, why should we lose hope? The prestige of the government on which it was founded has been shaken and the government knows it well. That is why it is determined to take strong measures to terrorise the people and to re-establish its prestige.

Even so are the people afraid? This is one condition which is necessary for the achievement of Swaraj. We did not get Swaraj before December, but if there is an assurance that we have taken to the path of Swaraj, there is nothing on which we should become despondent. It is for us to continue to follow this path and to reach our goal, namely, Swaraj. If we are unable to achieve the goal, it would only be our indolence and lack of strength. Nobody else would be to blame.

If Gandhiji has gone to jail, it does not matter. He would continue to w6rk for us even in jail. But he has told us time and again and in plain language as to what we have to do. If you look through the *Navjivan* file, you would come to know that it is a sacred book which preaches non-cooperation. Nobody can add another word to it.

Some people ask: "Now that Gandhiji is in jail, what would his companions do? There is no person as strong or as full of character as Gandhiji was who could complete his task". They are right. Gandhiji's companions have lost their way. There is a world of difference between him and his companions. The weaknesses and the shortcomings of his companions are countless and it is because of them that Gandhiji had to go to jail. His companions do not speak the language of love, lack self-discipline and tolerance. But in spite of those shortcomings, there is one good thing in them and that is they are aware of those shortcomings.

Just as a mason or a draftsman cannot claim to have the qualities of the Engineer but still finds it easy to follow the plans and to build the house, similarly if

Gandhiji's followers have understood the plans he prepared for the edifice of Swaraj, they should not find it difficult to contribute to its building.

There is no end to their difficulties. There is nobody who can hide their weaknesses now. Still the people's love for Gandhi, their grief over his incarceration and the spirit of Swaraj are the biggest stock-in-trade which his followers have. If they work day and night while they remember the principle of Ahimsa, the love that Gandhiji gave to the people and his dedication to the idea of Swaraj and implement the comprehensive programme for Swaraj given to them by Gandhiji, they should be able to overcome their weaknesses. I have no doubt that they would be able to add to the good name of Gandhi and show their dedication to his principles.

81

Vallabhbhai Showers Praises on Raja Gopaldas for giving up his State in National Cause

Navjivan, 30 March 1922

The Patidar community considers the gifted land more dear than its life. "When we loose the land, where is the security of life" is common proverb prevalent amongst the people of the community. Several Patidars have laid down lives for a piece of land, some have even been executed for it. The main sustaining food for the government courts is land dispute. Gopaldasbhai who is the most precious jewel of Patidar community—which is prepared to loose everything for the sake of land—has spurned the land gift of the government which earned for him an income of more than thirty thousand a year, for a religious cause.

Gopaldasbhai is Darbar (small ruler) of Dhasa village in Kathiawar and Talukdar of Raisankli. He had the good fortune of studying in college of princes, but his training is not ended. It is put to test now when there is a possibility of the people being terrorised by attachment process of the government.

Gopaldasbhai has left his kingdom, has come to Gujarat, and moves in the villages on foot, eating stale bread, and serving the people. We will find many such people in this *Kaliyug* (age of Satan) who will say that he had acted foolishly. It is no wonder that, in this age when people sidetrack religion and acquire wealth by unethical means, a person who has his lawful right over the land, leaves it for ethical reason, is considered as fool. But wealth above everything are numbered. I am sure that this sacrifice of Gopaldas will be written in golden letters in the history of Gujarat, and his sacrifice will inspire hundreds and thousands of young men and women. I am proud to acknowledge that in this crusade I have had the good fortune of having him as my companion.

82

CONFIDENTIAL

Secretary Bombay (Home) to Home Secretary, Government of India on Political Situation (Extract)

Home Political
D.O. No. S.D.-1018

MAHABALESHWAR
4 April 1922

MY DEAR O'DONNELL

I am desired to submit my report for the fortnight ending the 31st March 1922.

Political.—There has been a lull in political agitation in the Presidency during the past fortnight, owing to a general lack of cohesion between the various sections of the non-cooperation party and between it and the Khilafat party and the absence of any immediate objective appealing strongly to the popular imagination. The opening stages in the proceedings of the Legislative Assembly raised expectations in non-cooperation circles of a conflict between the Assembly and the Government of India, and Mr. Montagu's resignation, taken with Lord Curzon's speech in the House of Lords on the subject, excited hopes that the proposals for the modification of the treaty of Sevres would afford material for inflaming Moslem opinion. These expectations were disappointed and the moderate pary have gained a considerable access of prestige. It is clear, however, that the appointment of Sir Henry Wheeler as Governor of the province of Bihar and Orissa instead of an Indian, or the appointment as an alternative of another Indian Member of the Executive Council of the Governor General has caused disappointment in Moderate circles who are inclined to view this as a decided setback to their influence. The extremist press are making as much capital out of it as they can undoubtedly the delay in making the announcement had helped to confirm expectations in Indian circles and it is naturally being concluded that Mr. Montagu's recommendation, an Indian Governor, has been set aside by his successor in favour of a European civilian.

The only fresh development anticipated is a general decision by the Deccan party of their future policy at the Maharashtra Provincial Congress Conference, which is to be held at Pen in the Kolaba district about the end of this month. K.P. Khadilkar, one of the bitterest extremists and one who was never very enamoured of Mr. Gandhi's halting methods, is to preside. For the rest, both the Congress and Central Khilafat Committees have decided to follow Gandhi's last injunction and confine their activities to enlisting members, collecting funds, pushing Khaddar and generally preparing the ground for a definite step forward, a mandate for which is expected to be given at a special joint session of both

Vallabhbhai's favourite Gujarat Club, Ahmedabad

Elder brother, Vithalbhai

With his mentor Gandhi: turning point in life

Vallabhbhai's favourite comrade Shankarlal Dwarka Das Parikh who took part in Kheda Satyagraha

As a Satyagrahi in Kheda Non-Cooperation Movement

A group of Kheda Satyagrahis

Khushalbhai M. Patel

With Gandhiji, Mrs Sarojini Naidu and other at
Congress session, 1921 at Ahmedabad

As a leader of Nagpur Flag Agitation

With his barrister friends and also Satyagrahis at Borsad

parties to be held some time in June. The Central Khilafat Committee are to vary the programme somewhat by propaganda in France and England in favour of an Arabia independent of all European control and have decided to appoint, if necessary, a deputation to exchange views with the Turkish delegation and to represent to them the Indian Muslims' view—unfortunately for them one which the Turks themselves are not anxious to support just now.

News of the conviction of M.K. Gandhi was received quietly throughout the Presidency, but the sentence of six years' simple imprisonment was generally considered to be too severe. How little feeling is evinced over the conviction, at least in commercial circles, can be seen from the lack of support which was given to a resolution proposed at a meeting of the Bombay Piece Goods Merchants' Association held in Bombay on the 30th to the effect that no member of the Association should deal, directly, or indirectly, in foreign goods until Gandhi's release or pending a further resolution: any member acting in contravention to be fined Rs 100 per package. The motion found no seconder, at least none till after waiting the usual time the President had declared it lost.

At the recent Municipal elections in Poona, 35 so-called "Extremists" were elected out of a total of 43. It is not, however, expected that they will be a very happy family, a good many of them being 'non-cooperators' in name only. N.C. Kelkar will probably be elected as President.

Reports received from time to time show that fair and satisfactory prices are being received for the sale of liquor shops in the Presidency.

Press.—Mr. Gandhi's arrest and conviction absorbed a great deal of attention of the Indian Press. The Moderates continued to blame Government for arresting Mr. Gandhi when he was losing his influence with the country. The *Servant of India* observed, "Neither as a deliberate provocation nor as a measure of fancied self-defence is the arrest of Mr. Gandhi at this juncture anything but idiotic." The Extremists regarded Mr. Gandhi's arrest as a sudden change in the policy of Government. Mr. Gandhi himself in his *Young India,* however, made the following acknowledgment: "I myself cannot see how Government can avoid to arrest me if they want a permanent abandonment of civil disobedience whether individual or mass." The *Kesari* expressed the opinion that the arrest was due to pressure from England which in its opinion was seriously affected by the boycott movement. The sentence of six years' simple imprisonment was stigmatised as "inhuman, cruel, unkind and arbitrary" by the *Indu Prakash.* The *Dnyan Prakash* also considered the sentence as "severe beyond expectations" and opined that Mr. Gandhi's conviction on the strength of his own admission was not legally sound. The *Kaiser-i-Hind* however considered the sentence as justifiable on the admission made by Mr. Gandhi in his statement before the court.

The resignation of Mr. Montagu offered the papers an opportunity for the first time to sing his praises and to recognize the "valuable services" rendered by him to India. The *Bombay Chronicle* remarked: "To the best of his powers Mr. Montagu has done his duty to God and man" and the *Mahratta* added

"Mr. Montagu's resignation has indeed deprived India of one of her greatest friends." The *Jam-e-Jamshed* bemoaned the resignation as a "great misfortune" for India. The appointment of Lord Peel to succeed Mr. Montagu was disapproved on all hands.

The Government of India's despatch to the Secretary of State regarding the Turkish Peace Treaty was considered as satisfactory on the whole and calculated to show respect for Moslem feelings if acted upon by the Near East Conference.

Yours sincerely,
J. CRERAR

83

Vallabhbhai Calls on People to follow Gandhiji's Programme[1]

Bombay Chronicle, 21 April 1922

Mr. V.J. Patel arrived here (Chhindwara) from Bombay yesterday morning. In the evening a public meeting was held, attended by more than seven thousand men and women in the Gandhi Chowk, Seth Jamnalalji presiding. Mr. Patel and Mrs. Naidu addressed the meeting, emphasising on the significance of the Gandhi Day, the Mahatma's message, *Khadi* and the constructive programme of Bardoli. Mr. Patel protested against the tendency appearing in some quarters to make alterations in the Congress programme and to deviate from the path chalked out by the Mahatma so soon after his conviction. He said that that would be the greatest ungratefulness to those twenty-five thousands who were suffering on account of that programme. Those sufferers were the only right persons to ask for any changes. The Mahatma, said Mr. Patel, would not have gone to jail if the people had honestly and completely followed his injunctions. They were responsible for the incarceration of the greatest man in the world today. They had a right to change the programme, only after having fully tried and found it wanting.

[1]Speech was delivered on April 20 at Chhindwara.

84

Vallabhbhai for Revival of Non-Cooperation Movement[1]

Bombay Chronicle, 24 April 1922

Some members of the Congress Working Committee now in Calcutta addressed a largely attending public meeting, last night, on the present situation.

Mr. V.J. Patel, in the course of a speech, said when Mr. Gandhi and twenty-five thousand Indians were in jail they were not justified in talking of the formation of a New League of Co-operators and Non-Cooperators, nor in calling a special session of the Congress for that purpose. He also condemned the suggestion, made in certain quarters, of capturing the legislative councils while leaders and workers were in jail. He asked the audience to carry on the work as chalked out by the Congress under the advice of Mr. Gandhi.

Continuing, he said that by the Bardoli resolutions they had not given a go-by to Civil Disobedience. He would like to tell the Government and the people that the time was not far distant when the programme of Civil Disobedience would be revived.

[1]Speech was delivered on April 22 in Calcutta.

85

Gujarat under Leadership of Vallabhbhai follows Gandhi's Principles of Non-Cooperation

Navjivan, 4 May 1922

The resolutions passed at the Sixth Gujarat Provincial Congress Council held at Anand, were in brief, as follows:

1. Truth, non-violence, sacrifices and the capacity to bear pain is the only way in which the country can make progress. All men, women and children should, therefore, follow these principles sincerely.

2. The people of the country deserve our thanks for having kept the peace even after the arrest of leaders, big and small. Peaceful non-cooperation is the best way to achieve our triple goal.

3. This Conference expresses its full confidence in the Delhi-Bardoli decision. Gujarat should not exercise its right to engage in civil disobedience so long as it is not able to complete its constructive work.

4. The Council has full faith in the boycott of the assemblies and believes that the interest of the people demands that we should boycott the assemblies.

5. *Khadi* has not been made as popular in Gujarat as it should have been. Men and women of the province should, therefore, make all efforts to see that all citizens wear clothes made of *khadi* manufactured in Gujarat.

6. All committees and national institutions should try their level best to put an end to untouchability.

7. The Council exhorts the people of Ahmedabad and Surat to decide, after a careful consideration of the circumstances prevailing in their cities, not to pay taxes to the municipalities.

8. It is not yet needed that we keep a vigil on the schools being run with government aid, but the people should voluntarily boycott them and open national institutes. The members of this Council should go from door to door

and make the people understand the importance of a national system of education. National schools must teach the students how to spin and weave.

86

Vallabhbhai on Futility of Reforms[1]

Bombay Chronicle, 9 May 1922

Mr. V.J. Patel, General Secretary, Indian National Congress, addressed a public meeting here (Ahmedabad) last night, on the present situation. In the course of his speech he said that the supreme duty of every Indian was to loyally and vigorously, carry out the constructive programme of the Congress. For some time, he heard there was a general depression in the country, but his observation during his recent tours in Bengal, U.P., C.P., the Punjab, and Rajputana, showed that the feeling was not one of depression, but of disappointment caused by the suspension of Mass Civil Disobedience This feeling only showed clearly, that the country was prepared to put in greater sacrifices and undergo greater sufferings. He showed the utter hollowness of the Reforms and supreme importance of the reformed Councils.

Referring to the Budget, he showed how all available monies were relentlessly reserved for the "Reserved Subjects" and how the so-called nation-building subjects were made to starve for want of funds.

Referring to the repeal of some of the repressive laws, he said that what if some of these laws were repealed so long as Sections 107 and 144 of the Criminal Procedure Code were there to be misapplied by Government for killing national movements. He humorously said he would not be surprised if, on some occasion, this resourceful Government requisitioned Section 144 for prohibiting a citizen from taking his daily food say for a week in the interests of peace, order, and good Government.

In short, he showed the absolute futility of the Reforms and how the Indian Ministers had hopelessly failed to show any appreciable progress in the subjects "transferred" to them.

[1]Speech delivered at Ahmedabad on 8 May 1922.

87

Congress Working Committee's Resolutions with Vallabhbhai as General Secretary

Jayakar Collection, National Archives of India, 12 May 1922

Resolutions passed by the Working Committee which met on the 12th, 13th and 15th May 1922 at the offices of the All India Congress Committee, Arya

Bhavan, Sandhurst Road, Bombay, Hakim Ajmal Khan Sahib presiding.

1. That the minutes of the last meeting of the Committee held on the 20th, 21 st and 22nd April 1922 at Calcutta be confirmed.

2. Resolved that the Presidents of the Central Khilafat Committee and Jamaitul-Ulema be requested to call meetings of their respective Working Committees on the day and at the place of the next meeting of this Committee in order to enable the three bodies to confer together, if necessary.

That the next meeting of the Working Committee be held at Lucknow on the 5th June 1922.

3. That copies of the draft rules regarding the distribution of departments be circulated to all the members and considered at the next meeting of this Committee.

4. With reference to the President's telegram dated the 2nd April, resolved that the Provincial Congress Committee, Punjab, be asked if in view of the Committee of Inquiry appointed to investigate cases of repression in the Punjab, any further action by this Committee is necessary.

5. Read papers in connection with Nagpur Provincial Congress Committee and Wardha Taluk Congress Committee elections and Dr. Moonje's wires and resolved,

(*a*) That the Provincial Congress Committee be asked to explain why they have postponed the annual elections, and

(*b*) That Mr. Prakasam be deputed to proceed to Nagpur and Wardha to investigate and dispose of the question before the 25th May, his decision being final.

6. Resolved that the Treasurer's Audited Statement of Accounts of the All India Tilak Memorial Swaraj Fund up to the 30th April 1922 be passed.

7. Resolved that the General Secretary be requested to take steps to convene the next meeting of the All India Congress Committee on Wednesday the 7th June at Lucknow.

8. Resolved

(*a*) That a Committee consisting of Hakim Ajmal Khan Sahib, Dr. Ansari, Mr. S. Srinivasa Iyengar and Principal Gidwani be appointed to prepare a scheme for organizing and financing national education in the country and for that purpose to raise funds, prepare a budget and submit the proposals at the next meeting of this Committee.

(*b*) That all applications for grants or loans for national education received so far and to be received in future be referred to the foregoing committee for their opinion.

9. With reference to Bengal Provincial Congress Committee's application for the remission of 25 per cent of Tilak Swaraj Fund collections due to the All India Congress Committee, resolved that the application be rejected.

10. Resolved that Rs 17,381 be recommended to be paid to the Antyaja Karyalaya, Ahmedabad, in addition to Rs 5,000 already recommended by this Committee.

11. Resolved that the Punjab Provincial Congress Committee's application for Rs 1,25,000 for Shahadara depressed classes settlement cannot be considered unless the Working Committee is satisfied that sufficient funds are raised locally to start the scheme and the scheme so started is in working order.

12. Resolved that Rs 5,000 be earmarked for the Ahmednagar depressed classes home and that the amount be recommended to be paid when the Working Committee is satisfied that the home is started by local efforts and is in working order.

13. On the application of Mr. S. Srinivasa Iyengar resolved that Rs 10,000 be earmarked for depressed classes work in Madras and that the amount be recommended to be paid when the application is sent to this Committee through the Provincial Congress Committee and on this Committee being satisfied that at least an equal amount is raised by local efforts.

14. Resolved that Mr. G.P. Blizard's claim for £ 68-13-8 be allowed as recommended by Mr. Kelkar.

15. (*a*) Resolved that the application of Dr. Nur Mohammed of Kabul dated 5 February 1922, for affiliation of the Kabul Committee be placed for consideration at the next session of the Congress, provided in the meantime every member of the organization signs the Congress creed and accepts the "Non-violent Non-cooperation" Resolution of the Congress.

(*b*) Resolved further that his request for permission to raise loan cannot be granted.

16. With reference to Mr. Tyabji's inquiry regarding Rs 18,00,000 recommended for Khaddar work in Gujarat, resolved that Mr. Tyabji be informed that this Committee has received no complaint on that account from the Gujarat Provincial Congress Committee.

17. Resolved that Mr. Patel's report regarding Ajmer elections be confirmed.

18. That the resignation of Mr. Kashive, member, All India Congress Committee, forwarded by the UPPCC be recorded.

19. With reference to Mr. Dixit's letter dated 3 May 1922 inquiring whether non-cooperators can make legal defence in a civil suit, resolved that the attention of Mr. Dixit be drawn to this Committee's resolution No. 10 dated 14 June 1922 on the subject of non-cooperators and law courts.

20. That the following Khaddar Scheme be adopted by the Committee:

The Working Committee resolves that in pursuance of the constructive programme now before the country, special efforts should be made by every province to stimulate the production and consumption of hand-spun and hand-woven Khaddar on a sound organized basis.

With a view to help the provinces by way of loans, and technical advice and to make available to each province the experience of other parts and to collect and disseminate useful information, the Working Committee resolves to entrust Seth Jamnalal Bajaj with the organization of a special department for which the Committee sanctions Rs 17 lakhs.

The Department shall consist of three divisions:

1. Technical instruction
2. Production
3. Sale.

Technical instruction will be provided for at the Sabarmati Ashram under the direction of Mr. Maganlal Gandhi. Every Province will be invited to send two or three students each to this institute for a six months course, to be trained in all the processes of Khadi production. Students trained in this institute will be engaged for the organization of Khadi Centres or similar training institutes in their respective Provinces.

The Department of Production will aim at the coordination of interprovincial work and the standardization of yarn or cloth. The department will not ordinarily interfere with the administration of local organizations. Mr. Lakhmidas Purshottam will direct the department with the help of a staff of travelling inspectors.

The Sales department will open Khadi Stores in some select places where Provincial Congress Committees are unable to provide adequate facilities for consumers. Mr. Vithaldas Jerajani will be in charge of this department.

Seth Jamnalal Bajaj will be responsible for the coordination of the departments and general propaganda work. He will be solely responsible for the administration of finances.

All applications for loans shall be forwarded by the Provinces to Seth Jamnalal who will submit them to the Working Committee for disposal with his own recommendations, provided that in case of emergency Seth Jamnalal may grant loans not exceeding Rs 5,000 in anticipation of the Working Committee's sanction.

In deciding applications for loans the Working Committee shall keep in view both the requirements of Provinces and the extent of their investments in Khadi in order to stimulate local effort and help deserving cases.

Budget	*Rs*
Technical Instruction	25,000
Sales Department	2,00,000
Production Department Office	20,000
Propaganda, Information Bureau	1,00,000
Loans to Provinces	13,55,000

21. In supersession of its resolution No. 22 dated 6 November 1921 recommending a grant of Rs 18 lakhs to Gujarat for Khaddar work and in so far as it has not been carried out hitherto, and in view of the fact that large funds are immediately necessary to finance the Provinces in terms of the resolution regarding the Khaddar Scheme adopted by this Committee on the 13th May 1922, the Committee resolves

(*a*) That the whole amount now in the hands of the Trustees, Bombay Tilak Swaraj Fund, excepting the amount earmarked by the donors for any specific purpose should be transferred by the Trustees to Seth Jamnalal Bajaj.

(*b*) That the amount of Rs 6,00,000 reserved by the Provincial Congress Committee, Bombay, for its expenses should also be transferred to Seth Jamnalal Bajaj for the same purpose, after deducting such amount as may be considered reasonable and necessary for carrying on the normal activities of the Provincial Congress Committee for the current year, and to that end the Working Committee requests that the Bombay Provincial Congress Committee will take into consideration the urgency and importance of prosecuting the Khaddar programme and take steps to modify its resolution reserving Rs 6,00,000 for their expenses and thus enable the Trustees to transfer the amount to Seth Jamnalal Bajaj at an early date.

That a copy of this resolution be sent to the Bombay Provincial Congress Committee, the Trustees, Bombay Tilak Swaraj Fund and Seth Jamnalal Bajaj for necessary action, a report of which should be submitted to the All India Congress Committee office before the 28th May 1922.

22. Resolved that all applications for grants or loans for Khaddar work received upto now or to be received hereafter be referred to Seth Jamnalal Bajaj for consideration and report.

23. Read and considered correspondence between Pt. Jawaharlal Nehru on behalf of UP Provincial Congress Committee and the General Secretary regarding the claim of the All India Congress Committee to the full 25 per cent contribution from the UP total collections; resolved

(*a*) That Seth Jamnalal Bajaj and Mr. Patel be authorized to go into the whole matter and determine the amount due to the All India funds from UP Provincial Congress Committee.

(*b*) That in the meantime the General Secretary should remit without delay Rs 25,000 to the Allahabad Bank to the credit of the Nationalist Journals Ltd. through the UP Provincial Congress Committee and that the said amount should be treated not as a grant to be paid to the UP Provincial Congress Committee as per resolution No. 19 passed by this Committee at Calcutta on the 20th April 1922 but should be treated as a loan to the Provincial Congress Committee, and

(*c*) That the amount that may be found due by Messrs Jamnalal Bajaj and Patel from the UP Provincial Congress Committee shall be recovered from that Committee and the General Secretary shall make no further grant or loan till that amount is recovered.

24. Read and considered the application of Mr. T. Prakasam for Rs 7,000 for depressed classes work in Andhra. Resolved that the Trustees, Tilak Swaraj Fund, Bombay, be requested to pay the amount to Mr. Prakasam, President, Andhra Provincial Congress Committee, 2/27 Broadway, Madras.

25. That the application of Madyapana Partibandhak Mandal, Poona, for

Rs 25,000 for anti-drink campaign be rejected.

26. Resolved that in supersession of Resolution No. 8 passed by this Committee on the 5th October 1921, Mr. C. Rajagopalachariar be appointed to investigate and decide the Andhra-Utkal dispute, his decision being final.

V.J. PATEL
General Secretary

88

"Truth and Non-Violence to be Sheet-Anchor of Our Movement"—Vallabhbhai[1]

Bombay Chronicle, 27 May 1922

As soon as the conference met at 10.30 in the morning the first resolution was moved by Mr. Vallabhbhai Patel and seconded by Mrs. Sarojini Naidu. This resolution asserted that Mahatma Gandhi, the father of the Gujarat Political Conference, had, by following the principles of Non-violence and Truth, taught the Indians the secret of soul-force and advancement, and thus made India famous throughout the world. This Conference was firmly of opinion that their highest duty lay in strictly following Truth and Non-violence and that should be done in thought, word, and deed, by every man and woman in India.

Mr. Vallabhbhai Patel, proposing this, said the first part of this resolution firmly asserted that Mahatma Gandhi had rivetted the attention of the world to it by his (the Mahatma's) work and never before was that done. It was hitherto believed that might was right, but Mahatma Gandhi had taught the world that their greatness consisted in suffering for others and that only right was might. By his marvellous work India had become known throughout the world. He was the only real Christian and yet he was in prison. The Conference was held for the country to ascertain, how far Gujarat had assimilated the Mahatma's principles and how far they were prepared to follow them, particularly at the time when doubts were raised in many parts of the country about their ability. Gujarat fully believed in Non-violence and the day they gave up that great principle their fight was lost. Non-violence spelt greater bravery than violence. Anybody could be violent with a revolver in his hand, but very few could be non-violent.

[1]Gujarat Political Conference held at Anand on 26 May 1922.

89

Vallabhbhai Advises Teachers Not to Court Arrest[1]

Bombay Chronicle, 14 June 1922

After the graduates were given their diplomas, Mr. Vallabhbhai Patel said that he was asked by the Senate to perform the Convocation ceremony, in the unavoidable absence of Hakim Ajmal Khan, who was to do it in the place of their Chancellor, Mr. Gandhi. He was not fit to bless them but they had the blessings of their Chancellor for ever. They should therefore ever strive to carry out his ideals of service and self-sacrifices. Within a short time, they might be expected to follow the students and teachers in other parts of the country who were going to jail. Government could not tolerate the educational progress of Gujarat and if all their teachers are imprisoned, they should fill their post with courage and love. Mr. Vallabhbhai, however, advised the teachers and Senators not to court imprisonment.

[1]Speech delivered at first convocation of Gujarat Vidyapith on 12 June 1922.

90

Vallabhbhai on Government's Failure to take over Control of Education by Suspending Ahmedabad Municipality

Navjivan, 25 June 1922

The Sardar wrote an article in the *Navjivan* entitled *Hamara Hisaab* which clarified his position.

The Ahmedabad Municipality was suspended four months ago. The Government, through this suspension, had intended to take over control of education. Being in the habit of listening to only pleasant things, it is hardly likely to come to grips with reality. The suspension of the municipalities would put paid to our agitation, that lack of funds would lead to closure of the schools, that parents would be afraid to send their children to new government schools, that the teachers are powerless to do anything and would not leave the schools they are serving in to go to new schools—such was the talk which led the Government to suspend the Surat and Ahmedabad municipalities. But all the calculations of the Government proved to be wrong. The Public Education Board is running 43 schools in Ahmedabad, 13 of them for girls and 8 teaching through the Urdu medium. The various communities have donated the use of spacious buildings for running these schools. Two hundred and seventy teachers are working in these schools; 65 of them are trained teachers. One hundred and sixty of the teachers left their jobs in municipal schools to join the schools under the Public

Education Board. The number of students in these schools has jumped to 8400 this week, out of whom Muslim students number 904. The number of girls in the girls schools has gone up to 2107. The number of students in most of the schools is increasing constantly.

A sum of about Rs 30,000 has been spent so far and the monthly expenditure comes to Rs 10,000. Contributions to the Public Education Board have amounted to Rs 1,25,000 out of which a payment of Rs 50,000 has been received.

The number of schools being run under the control of the committee appointed by the Government is 57 to which two new schools have been added. The number of teachers is 250 and that of students less than 2,000. The number of students in the municipal schools before the municipalities were suspended was never less than 10,500 and the number of students would now be less than 1,700. Some of the schools are empty and in others the number of students is not more than that of the teachers. Even so, the number of schools has been added to the number which could cater to 10,000 students. And even with the 57 new schools the total number of student is not more than 1,700.

91

Vallabhbhai against Picketing of Shops[1]

Bombay Chronicle, 27 June 1922

The annual general meeting of the voters of Deskroi Taluka Samiti was held here (Ahmedabad) last evening in the Premabhai Hall, under the presidentship of Sjt. Vallabhbhai Patel.

Mr. Patel was then unanimously elected president of the Deskroi Taluka Samiti, in spite of his express desire to be relieved from the responsibility of that office, in view of the fact that he had to work as president of the Provincial District and Taluka Committees.

After the elections were over, Mr. Patel spoke impressively on the present situation and the duty of Gujarat. He appealed to all those present to vigorously carry out the constructive programme, so that Gujarat could give a proper account of itself before the bar of the country. The Civil Disobedience Enquiry Commission was about to visit Gujarat and he therefore called upon all workers whether elected on different committees or not to put on a greater effort, so that the roving commission may carry the impression that Gujarat knew and did its duty well.

He said that he was asked by someone to start picketing of cloth and liquor shops, but he emphatically discountenances picketing in the present circumstances since, experience in other provinces clearly showed that it did more harm than good to the cause. He cited the instance of one cloth merchant in Agra who approached the Collector there with the request to prosecute picketers and an offer of Rs 5,000 to enable Government to send picketers to jail. Finally he appealed to all to help him to steer the movement successfully.

[1]Speech delivered on 26 June 1922 at Ahmedabad.

92

Vallabhbhai Urges Gujaratis to Carry on Bardoli Programme

Navjivan, 23 July 1922

Members of the Committee appointed to inquire and decide whether to make change in Bardoli programme, and if it decided to make changes, then what kind of changes are necessary—travelled in several parts of the country and inquired. They came here also. Upto 15th August they would tour remaining part of the country, inquire there, and it will present its report to the AICC session which is to be held at Calcutta. By that time Deshbandhu Chitaranjan Das will leave opposition camp. The AICC will deliberate on all aspects of the question, if it thinks proper it will not hesitate to make changes in the schedule of the battle.

But what are we expected to do till the decision is taken ? Are we to sit with folded hands till the changes to our liking are made? In the battle-field when the commanders meet together and hold consultations regarding the strategy or its schedule, the soldiers engaged in battle do not put their arms aside. True soldiers, till they receive next orders, act according to their previous order, and die during his duty but will not leave his place. If we wish to be victorious, till we receive next order we should use all our energy, out mind, and our time for implementing the Bardoli programme. If we do not do that, we will not be able to get our desired changes in the schedule of the battle.

We cannot get more sincere, and righteous adviser than Pandit Motilalji. He has given us the same advice. Many find constructive work uninteresting. Everybody is charmed with civil disobedience. Panditji has advised us that till there is a change in our schedule, everybody should do that work enthusiastically with dexterity.

"If it is thought proper to make changes in the present programme, I will be the first man to advise you for it. But if it is thought that it is not proper to make the changes, we will definitely give such an opinion. Therefore all of you try to complete your work according to our present programme." This is his clear cut advice. Therefore in the hope that there will be change in programme, which will be convenient to us, our speed should not be less, but it should be more. On the completion of our present programme rests the early implementation of civil disobedience programme.

After Mahatmaji was arrested, naturally, our work slowed down. Marriage season gave it a fillip, so we worked at snail's speed. Last year Congress had enrolled 1,74,500 Congress members. This year only 60,000 members are enrolled. Last year we had collected about 16 lacs in Swaraj Fund. This year we have been able to collect only 4 lacs uptil now. This is the situation when our responsibility has increased, we have done very good work in the direction of national education and members of the Committee are highly pleased with our work. But if we want our work to shine, we must be more energetic, must attain the capacity to finish the work.

Foundation of Gujarat Vidyapith was laid with the pious hands of Mahatmaji. Its Chancellor has demanded ten lac rupees from Gujarat. One article by Gandhiji in *Navjivan,* and money from Gujarat, Kathiawad, Africa and other places would have poured in Gujarat for this sacred work. Now at the time of his imprisonment will generous Gujaratis allow this tree which he planted to wither? Some religious and generous persons had given financial help for upliftment of untouchables. That money has been used for opening *ashrams* and schools for untouchables, and higher Hindus have dedicated their lives to those institutions. Gujarat is duty bound to see that this work is done with more vigour and enthusiasm.

Khadi has been given a prominent place in constructive work. Today Mahatmaji and Shankerlal though they are practising penance in Yervada jail they are busy spinning on *charkha.* Mahadev in Lucknow jail is also busy with spinning wheel. If Gujarat will not understand its significance then which other part of the country will understand? Panditji chided us in very mild words and said "In Gujarat *khadi* is being used more than in other provinces. But we had hoped that in Gujarat after the imprisonment of Gandhiji, nobody will be using any other cloth than *khadi,* but instead we see here many persons wearing foreign cloth". We deserve this rebuke. Really speaking we deserve much more rebuke. Five months have elapsed since Gandhiji is imprisoned yet there is not heartache, thousands and lacs of Gujaratis while wearing foreign cloth. Before hoping for change of heart of the foreigners we should change the heart of our brethren.

From this it will be clear that we have to work a lot in direction of constructive programme. Before the meeting of AICC in Calcutta, all the workers are requested to concentrate in speedily completing this work. Gujarat is in no way backward in comparison with other provinces, but we should show such a splendid work that our delegates can boldly say to the AICC that we are prepared for any kind of proper change.

93

Vallabhbhai to Mathuradas on Collection of Funds for Gujarat Vidyapith

Sardar Shrino Anyo Patro[1]

24 July 1922

BHAI MATHURADAS,

Received your letter and cheque.

Manilal[2] is not at fault. At the time when the collection of funds amounting to ten lacs[3] was announced, some amount was expected, out of which some donors have relented, and the rest which was estimate of collections from markets should be collected anyhow. So Manilal has to finish the remaining half finished task. In a month or two, when the account is published by that time, if ten lac rupees are not collected and we are not in a position to publish the accounts then we will lose our credibility. Vidyapith will be desparately in need of money, but at present we are not collecting more than ten lacs.

Yet Manilal needs your help. Thinking that ten lacs have already been collected, if it becomes difficult to collect expected amount from Bombay, then we shall have to collect the amount anyhow from other sources.

The Inquiry Committee about civil disobedience has wasted its energy. It appears that it has increased our difficulties. Panditji,[4] Hakimji,[5] and Vithalbhai[6] and Das[7] have joined hands. It seems that with the exception of Dr. Ansari,[8] Rajgopalachari,[9] and Kasturi Ayanger[10] all are in favour of entering the legislature. From the writings of *Independent* of Allahabad, it appears that they have come to the conclusion that pleaders should be allowed to practise and we should not boycott Government schools. Please be vigilant in the election of Congress delegates.

VALLABHBHAI'S
Bande Matram

[1]In Gujarati, Vol. V, edited by G.M. Nardurkar.
[2]Manilal Kothari, constructive worker and nationalist leader of Kathiawad and Gujarat Provincial Congress Committee.
[3]For Gujarat Vidyapith.
[4]Motilal Nehru.
[5]Hakim Ajmal Khan.
[6]Elder brother of Vallabhbhai, later on President, Central Assembly.
[7]Deshbandhu Chittaranjan Das, one of the top ranking leaders of Indian National Congress. Founder of Swaraj Party.
[8]A leader of Indian National Congress.
[9]C. Rajgopalachari, eminent leader of Congress. Thrice elected as Chief Minister of Madras. Governor of West Bengal, first and last Governor-General of India, writer and thinker.
[10]Non-cooperation leader of the South.

94

Vallabhbhai Criticizes Government for not giving Substantial Funds to Municipalities

Navjivan, 13 August 1922

Two years have elapsed since the reforms were implemented. Present legislative assembly has only now one budget to be presented before it. One can easily have a glimpse of the plight of the local self-government institutions, if we have a cursory glance at the history of the working of local self-government during these two years. The local self-government is in charge of the ministers who are elected by the people. During the working of this department two of the biggest municipalities of the presidency have been suspended. These two municipalities tried to handle the education department in their own way bearing the expenses, which government did not like. The third Nadiad municipality as it is going that way is about to be suspended. As these three municipalities are fighting with the government, naturally people's attention is drawn towards them. But nobody looks at the miserable conditions of those municipalities which are helping the government, and cooperating with it.

Nearly seventy-five per cent municipalities are dying. Everywhere the expenditure is more than income. There is no scope for enhancing the taxes. The education portfolio is in the hands of a clever minister. It does not appear that while deciding the pay scales of the teacher, he had thought whether municipalities will be able to bear the burden. Municipalities are not able to bear the burden. Municipalities have not the power either to appoint a teacher, to transfer or to suspend him; only the power to pay the teachers is given. In such conditions most of the municipalities are on the verge of bankruptcy.

Since some months Borsad municipality is not paying its teachers. Hence the teachers have gone on *hartal.* Students are roaming about. Honourable minister who thought about the plight of the education of the children of Ahmedabad, Surat and Nadiad is unable to do anything for the children of Borsad municipality which is a government municipality. Collector also is helpless because the money of the municipality is not deposited in any bank or government treasury. In municipality's treasury only six annas are there. The officers of the education department had to leave criticising the financial conditions of national schools and were forced to go to Borsad. Teachers were persuaded to give up agitation. Teachers showed their empty stomach. They were persuaded to have confidence in the assurances of government and requested to resume duties. But teachers flatly told them that their empty stomachs will not be full by simple assurances. So officers had to return empty-handed.

The teachers of Dolera municipality have not got their salary since last eight months and so it is thought to suspend the municipality, because of lack of funds, Mahua municipality had to be closed. Bharuch municipality which is considered as sound municipality is not in a position to pay its teachers, then one can imagine the pathetic condition of smaller municipalities.

Before the implementation of reforms, as the government was responsible for the financial condition of municipality, it directly or indirectly gave financial help. But after the implementation of reforms, government was relieved of that responsibility, and so that help is stopped gradually. Recently a government's decision has been published, by which it has decided to discontinue the financial help given to the municipalities, which amounted to one-third of the salary of chief executive of the municipality. In pre-reform period the central government scheme of sharing half of the expenses of the municipalities which undertook to start drainage and water works schemes. This help has not been given at present to any municipality. In Ahmedabad the Committee appointed by government prepared such a plan and sent it to the government, asking for financial assistance as per rules which the government flatly refused.

In the next session of legislative assembly Local Board Bill is to be presented. It is difficult to understand as to how it will benefit the people. To start institutions which have no money, or to make some changes in those institutions is cheating the people. The financial condition of local boards is worst than the municipalities. A committee was appointed to inquire as to what ways and means can be adopted by the government to improve their condition, and the committee has submitted the report before the reforms were implemented. But the honourable minister has not touched that report. Formerly road tax was collected on the roads of local board, but poor farmers were unnecessarily harassed. Government put the pressure on local boards and the tax was withdrawn. Again that tax is being collected during post-reform period.

Howsoever good the institutions might be, and howsoever honest and competent the persons running the institutions might be, but if there is no money to run the institutions, then the institutions instead of serving the people would be a burden on the heads of the people and be harmful. It does not seem possible that financial condition of local self-government bodies will improve. Government, by transferring such expensive department to the elected representatives of the people, has shirked its responsibility. A huge amount of the money has been usurped by it for the reserved subjects. Yet if we just look at the administration of such subject pennywise and pound foolish policy is being followed. An order has been issued to use *babool* thorns, in stead of pins because the large amount is being spent for pins. From this order one can imagine as to what extent the government can help the local self-government institutions.

Alleging that Ahmedabad, Surat and Nadiad municipalities have broken rule No. 3 of the education department, the government frowned at them, but today seventy-five per cent of the municipalities are breaking the rule number two, because there is not enough money to observe the rule. But government is silent, and unable to take any action, nor it is giving any help to see that rule is observed, because the government has not enough money to run the institutions which are under reserved subjects. So how can it help the institutions in the transferred subjects. Under such circumstances government should implement the reforms by suspending many of the municipalities or turn a blind eye to the breaking of rules.

95

Vallabhbhai on Plight of Municipalities

Navjivan, 13 August 1922

About an article entitled "The plight of local self-government" which appeared in *Navjivan* on the 13 August 1922, Sardar Patel wrote:

Seventy-five per cent of the municipalities are on the brink of disaster. Everywhere the expenditure has gone beyond their income. There is no room for further taxation. The Education Department is under a capable minister who has fixed the pay scales of teachers but, it appears, that no attention was paid to the fact whether the municipalities would be able to pay those scales. The municipalities would not be able to bear this burden and the Government is not in a position to help them. . . . Even so, when two large municipalities tried to take over education on their own responsibility, the Government could not tolerate it. . . . The Ahmedabad, Surat and Nadiad Municipal Committees violated Rule No. 3 of the Education Department (regarding examinations and inspection by the inspectors) and they became the targets of Government's wrath. Seventy-five per cent of the municipalities are violating Rule No. 2 (about the payment of salaries to the teachers), because they do not have any funds to pay those salaries. The Government cannot harm them, nor can it help them to follow the rule because when the Government does not have sufficient funds to run the departments under it how can it help the departments responsible to the people?

96

Vallabhbhai Urges People of Nadiad to Boycott Government Schools and instead Join Nadiad Schools

Navjivan, 20 August 1922

Some days ago Government had withdrawn from the deposit of the municipality three thousand rupees for the expenditure of the municipal schools run by the government against the wishes of the Municipality and demanded another eleven thousand rupees. As Municipality had no more money, meeting the expenses of running the schools became an acute problem for the Government. Government solved the problem by an order issued on 8 August 1922, and gave notice to the Municipality to return the schools to the Municipality from 1 September 1922, and according to section 58 of the Municipal Act consider it responsible for primary education. As a result Nadjad Municipality has passed this resolution on 17 February 1922:

Because of the desire of tax-payers, in October 1920 the board decided to free municipal schools from the control of Education Department, and for making arrangements for imparting national education decided not to accept Government grant. This decision which gave financial relief to the Government, and the purpose of which was to train the people in the working of pure local self-government should have been welcomed by the Government.

In the beginning it did not appear that the attitude of the Government was to smash this experiment. It pretended that it was though not sympathetic was averse to this experiment. In the beginning Collector drew the attention to the economic condition of the Municipality. Municipality informed him that it would arrange for the necessary funds. Then the Education Department inquired whether the Municipality wants to retain municipal teachers. Municipality relieved those teachers who wanted to return to the government service, and made arrangement for other teachers in their place. Government with the help of the teachers relieved by the Municipality opened separate schools in the city in competition with municipal schools. Collector who was misguided by the relieved teachers thought that if the possession of municipal school buildings is taken by the government, and if arrangements are made to run government schools in those buildings, the municipal school will close down. So Collector setting aside the legal aspect of the problem broken open the locks of the school buildings, forcibly took possession of the school buildings. Though Government forcibly took possession of the building its purpose was not served. Government schools were empty. After some months Government returned the buildings to the Municipality and government schools were shifted elsewhere. Thus for one year competition to measure the strength of public opinion, went on between the Government and the Municipality. In that venture Government was defeated and it changed its policy. It gave up sophisticated method and adopted bullying attitude. In December 1921 Government warned the Municipality, and informed it that it had made a mistake by not accepting the control of Education Department, and so it must rectify the mistake by 17 December 1921. Municipality felt that Government anyhow wants to smash the national schools, and because of the conflict between the Government and the people, the students' education was suffering. Municipal Board gave the possession of schools to local national education committee and decided to give 2500 rupees per month from municipal funds. Government did not like this decision. Collector ordered retaining the operation of that decision, and by the order of Commissioner, the possession of all the municipal schools was given to Education Department, and got Rs 9000 per month sanctioned for running the government schools from the municipal funds. As both these orders were illegal Municipal Board retained its original decision, gave the possession of schools and entrusted their administration to education committee. From that time onwards the schools are run by education committee. Municipality declined to give nine thousand rupees which government wanted. Therefore from the deposit which the Municipality had in government treasury first instalment of Rupees 3000 was given to the officer of the Education Department without informing the Municipality about it. This action was an insult to the Municipality. Eleven elected members of the Municipality resigned to express their displeasure, and to give additional proof of the public opinion After that in the beginning of 1922, again by-election was held. It gave a clear indication of people's opinion, and all the eleven members who were for people's education were elected uncontested. In 1922, again general municipal election was held. In that election 20 people's representatives were to be elected. Out of those 19 candidates who were committed to national education were elected. As soon as new members took charge of the administration they saw that though in the schools run by Government the number of students was less, and in some schools there were no students at all, large amount is spent in paying teachers and building rent. In order to stop this wasteful expenditure, and to regularise the spendings, Municipality wrote to the Officer of the Education Department and to the Commissioner, but they did not pay any attention. So Municipality declined to give the money for that item, then once again out of Rupees 9000 that were in subtreasury, Rupees 3000 were withdrawn.

In the schools run by the education committee there are 2300 students, while in the schools run by the Government with municipal finance, the number of students is 391, according to information supplied by the Education Department to the Municipality. All the expenses of the education committee schools were incurred without any financial help from the Municipality, while the money required for the schools run by the government are withdrawn by the government from municipal deposits in the treasury. Thus the money collected as taxes from the people by members of the Municipality, which is used by the government according to its sweet will. Municipality resolved to give Rupees 900 to education committee to teach children of the people. Government filed a civil suit in the civil court and got a stay order on the implementation of the resolution of the previous Municipality to give Rupees 2500 per month, and the resolution of the present municipality to give Rupees 900 per month to the education committee, and thus stopped the help given by the Municipality to the education committee. Besides that Government filed another suit against the eleven members who voted for the resolution as they were personally responsible for the expenditure after municipality schools from March 1921 to December 1921, and requested the court to ask the respondents to pay the amount. These eleven members while performing their duty, spend the money properly according to the wishes of the people Yet they were dragged to the court, so one out of eleven members applied to the Municipality, that it should pay for their defence, so Municipality sanctioned rupees five hundred for his defence. The Collector has reversed that decision.

At last the Government has just now issued an order that the municipal schools which are run by the Government should be returned to the Municipality, and henceforward according to the section 58 of the Municipal Act the government will hold Municipality responsible for performing its duty regarding primary education and the Education Department should hand over the schools, and their administration to the Municipality from 1st September. We do not say that Government is not honest in issuing this order. The government's order is not such that it can be believed that government intends to give a free hand to the Municipalities. In such circumstances it is difficult to understand the purpose of giving back to the Municipality the schools and its administration after harassing the Municipality for a long period. Till there was balance in municipal treasury money were spent lavishly; teachers were paid even though they did not teach; it did not care to see whether the children are properly taught or not. Now when there is no money in municipal treasury, and when the teachers have not been paid for the last two months, then putting the burden of this unnecessary expenses on the head of the municipality, we suspect that the Government wanted to create difficulty for the Municipality and to declare it unfit. Whatever might be the intention of the government, but until an unrestricted power is given to the Municipality regarding running of the schools, Municipality is unable to manage the affairs of these, or any other schools. When it was decided to return the schools to the municipality, pro-government teachers became nervous. But this Municipality does not wish to imitate the government which harassed the Municipality by harassing pro-government teachers. Above-mentioned chain of incidents go to prove that the Municipality is not the local self-government institution, but an institution to make the people dependent. From the experience it can be definitely proved that these institutions are meant to make the elected members an instrument for making the people dependent and the members of the Municipality who have been elected by the people are not willing to be used as tools. Let us find out such persons who are willing to be such instrument and put them in charge to run the institution. We are sure that in such a big city Government will easily find out such people. But the Government will never get an honest person, who wants to serve the people. We members who have been elected by the people have not entered the Municipality for getting power or honour. We will get enough opportunity to make use of our energy by joining other institutions and will get ample opportunity to serve the people. So we regret to announce that before even one year has not elapsed since our election we leave the Municipality. We are sure that within a short time government will understand that it has erred!

After the resolution was passed, out of 20 elected members eighteen resigned immediately.

Dholka Municipality was served the notice by the Government and informed that its financial condition is very bad, and if there is no improvement, and if it does not enhance its income it will be suspended.

Farmers of Gujarat awake! For you also local self-government minister is preparing a gift of reform. He is going to present new local board bill in the next session of legislative assembly. He desires to impose hundred per cent hike of local fund tax. Your welfare cannot be done by such a meagre amount so you will be given legal power to tax yourselves. If after getting this power your condition does not improve, you must also hope to receive a notice like Dholka Municipality.

97

President Nadiad Municipality Refuses to Take over Govt. Schools

Navjivan, 22 August 1922

In Nadiad a new drama of local self-government has been enacted. The schools which were opened in competition of municipal schools, for the education of co-operators, were decided to be returned back to the municipality. In this decision the seventeen elected members of the municipality smelt a rat and so they resigned. The President of the Municipality refused to take over the charge of Government schools. New elections were held and the children of the cooperators joined the national schools. Government school leaders have no work, nobody is there to give them work and they being government servants they had to be paid.

By-elections were held, and out of seventeen seats no candidate could be found for nine seats. Eight seats were filled, and in that one seat was filled by an ex-peon of the municipality and seven by the untouchables for which there was no contest.

For nine vacant seats fresh elections were not held, in the regime of the elected minister, nine co-operators were found out, and they were nominated, and the seats were filled. From the experience of suspending Surat and Ahmedabad municipalities, government had become wise and so it was afraid of suspending it, and so it found out a new way out. . . .

The President of the Municipality does not accept the right of the government to fill in the nine vacant seats, and refuses to conduct municipal affairs through them. He has written to the government that these seats should be filled by election only. In the meanwhile some taxpayers had filed a civil suit against municipality and these nine persons, and asked the court to order their membership null and void, and asked the court a temporary stay order against them. Court has issued such a stay order. So at present municipal work is in the state of standstill.

Thus every day new local self-government force is enacted and government and reforms are being exposed.

98

Vallabhbhai's Call to Gujaratis to Collect Funds and Wear Khadi to Celebrate Gandhiji's Birth Anniversary

Navjivan, 27 August 1922

Gujarat Provincial Congress Committee has decided to celebrate Mahatma Gandhi's birthday on 2-10-22. On that day everybody is expected not to attend to his or her work and concentrate on prayer. On that day nobody can wear anything but *khadi.* Ladies of Gujarat should begin purchasing saris and other cloth from today for wearing on that occasion. Processions should be taken out in every village; meetings should be held, and all men and women should join and contribute his or her mite.

Besides this it has been decided to undertake a special work on that auspicious day, and that is to collect funds for Vidyapith. The work has already been started.

We have prepared a scheme for the collection of funds. According to the scheme we want to get volunteers from Gujarat, Kutch, and Kathiawar. Each volunteer has to take the responsibility of depositing at least one thousand rupees in the Provincial Committee office by 2-10-22. Provincial Committee is enrolling the volunteers who are prepared to take such responsibility. They are being supplied with receipt books. Thus the responsibility is divided, so that in a short time we can reach every corner.

Separate management has also been made to give another type of receipt books for those volunteers who collect a smaller amount.

Gujarat has got the opportunity of being free after paying some amount. Government runs the administration by raising the taxes which we have to pay anyhow. If we do not pay Government forcibly collects the taxes. We have no voice in the administration which runs from our tax.

Congress administration can be run because of goodwill of the people. Its sway over the people will be known only from the donation they give to the institutions run by it.

Ten thousand readers of *Navjivan* can easily pay ten rupees each. If everybody considering his or her religious duty sends the amount to *Navjivan* office, one lac rupees can be easily collected.

People have genuine love for the Congress. People are ready to pay. We require a scheme and ability to reach everybody. The workers of the PCC and members of the Programme Implementation Committee should do everything for successful implementation of the scheme.

I have confidence that large number of volunteers will come forward, and collect the money befitting Gujarat.

The public declaration of the funds collected will be made at a public meeting which will be held at Ahmedabad on 2.10.22.

99

Vallabhbhai Exhorts Gujaratis to Collect More Funds for Vidyapith

Navjivan, 31 August 1922

Remember, second October is approaching near, only one month is left. Last year Gujarat had collected ten lacs of rupees within a month. He has established Vidyapith. The tree he has planted—when he is practising penance for us in jail—if we allow it to whither, how can we show our face when he is released? We have got this nice opportunity, to earn a glory of righteousness of imparting education, and show our love for Mahatma Gandhi. Such opportunity we get only once a while in life.

Gujarat has spent much after Vidyapith. There are books worth 40 thousand rupees in archaeological department, and in the college there are books worth 35 thousand rupees. We have no space to keep these costly books and students do not get opportunity to take the advantage.

In the college 250 students are studying. There are countless secondary schools and high schools affiliated to it. Thirty seven thousand students are studying in these schools. If such institution withers because of want of funds then it will be great loss to Gujarat. Vidyapith from its very beginning has not adopted the policy to collect huge amount of money and to run the institutions from the interest on it. Its capital is its work and people's satisfaction.

In Gujarat and Kathiawar there are hundreds of villages, that if there is one true and hard working volunteer in every village, then from each village minimum one thousand rupees can be collected within a month. Gujarat has not got the opportunity of enlisting volunteers to fill the jails. That burden Mahatmaji has lifted on his shoulders. If Gujarat does not supply volunteers for a work in which there is no risk, then Gujarat will lose its prestige.

Rich men love money more than poor people. Usually they do charity from either out of the interest they get from the investment, or from the profit and this they consider as practical way of living. We do not depend on such millionaires. Time has not yet come to turn the religious sense of the rich people towards Swaraj institutions, otherwise only Ahmedabad can, if it so desires, will not allow Vidyapith to suffer. We depend on common and poor people of Gujarat who run their household anyhow with difficulty. Their love for Gandhiji is genuine, and they have faith in his work. Let such faithful and devoted Gujaratis search their bodies and pockets. Let them give what they can afford from their pockets, and celebrate Mahatma Gandhi's birthday by removing foreign cloth from their body.

100

Vallabhbhai Appeals to Gujaratis to Keep Flag Aloft

Navjivan, 3 September 1922

Preparations should be made in each village of Gujarat for celebration of Mahatmaji's birthday. Gujaratis! whether you reside in Gujarat or outside; you are cooperators or non-cooperators; whether you are government servants or not. Whether you are men or women, child or aged person; poor or rich, all of you have equal place and equal love in Mahatmaji's heart. You cannot wear any other cloth than *khadi* on his birthday. Gujarat can celebrate his birthday only if it becomes *khadi* minded.

After Gandhiji's birthday, there will be Diwali festival. But for Gujarat it is an occasion of grief. In this year if we celebrate Diwali by wearing costly clothes of various colours; eat sweets, and have exploded crackers, then it will be a mockery of his penance and sacrifice. Gujarat has to pass those days in agony.

Gujaratis spend lakhs of rupees in fireworks only. This year if we save that amount and donate to Gujarat Vidyapith, then the work undertaken by Gujarat can be completed and Mahatmaji's birthday can be celebrated nicely

There are Mahatmaji's devotees in every village of Gujarat. Out of them if a true devotee from every village collects some donation, and sends it, then also Gujarat's work will be applauded.

Congress again and again asks for donations. Appeals were made for Swaraj Fund; fund for primary education, and other small donations also. Thus how many times people are to contribute? It is true. But what we eat today will not be useful tomorrow. Even if we eat in the morning, in the evening we are hungry. The seeds sown last year will not yield crops this year. If we want fresh crops this year we have to sow new seeds. So until we get Swaraj we have to procure necessary funds for maintaining Swaraj institutions. If the giver is reluctant those who ask for donations should not be disappointed. If he does not give today, he will give tomorrow. We have no other course open but to tolerate silently if the donor says some unpleasant things.

The accounts of Gujarat Provincial Congress Committee are as clear as daylight. It is published every month. Anybody can come to the Committee's office and inspect it. The Committee if it has gained public confidence in its management, why should Gujarat not give money for necessity for running the institutions? Readers of *Navjivan* are requested to send their contributions to *Navjivan* office.

In the public meeting to be held on the banks of Sabarmati river in the capital of Gujarat, there will be a review of the work, which Gujarat has undertaken. Everybody is requested to send his or her contribution and keep Gujarat's honour intact.

101

Bombay Government Report on Vallabhbhai's Role in Flag Satyagraha

Confidential Home Department (Special) Notes F.No. 355-19(A)/1923

Bombay Archives, 14 September 1922

1. At pages 3 to 5 ante will be found quoted the resolution passed by the various Congress Committees at meetings held in the Bombay Presy in regard to the Nagpur National Flag Satyagraha. The statements also indicate the leaders of the Bombay Presy present on each occasion.

2. We have received no information from our officers that any batch of volunteers have actually started from Gujarat. As a matter of fact in only one district, Kaira, have volunteers actually been enrolled for Nagpur—70 in all (File No. 355/19A).

3. The telegram is rather ambiguous. It is not clear whether the intention is to prosecute Bombay leaders in respect of incitements or active encouragement given in the Bombay Presy, e.g. pages 3 to 5 ante. On the other hand and rather more likely, the intention would appear to be to prosecute those of our leaders who actively incited or encouraged breaches of the law while on a visit at Nagpur. We know that Vallabhbhai J. Patel and G.B. Deshpande were at Nagpur on 30th and 31st May, and that they attended public meetings and spoke at them in support of the campaign. Vallabhbhai J. Patel in fact said he would send 200 volunteers from Gujarat. The prosecution of these by C.P. Government, as such action would hardly react in this Presy. The difficulty would be to arrest and transfer them. . . the route of their journey. If, however, the C.P. intend to

rope in all Bombay leaders for inciting and encouraging while in the Bombay Presy. . . .

102

Vallabhbhai Urges Gujaratis and Maharashtrians to Donate Liberally

Navjivan, 22 September 1922

Day by day second October is approaching nearer and nearer. Thinking that there are yet twenty-one days left, nobody should delay either in sending his contribution to Vidyapith fund or collection. Those who ill-spend their youth repent in their old age.

Our devotion is put to a mild test. It is not a much disgrace if a person fails in a hard test. For him the very fact that he has prepared himself for a hard test is enough to retain his grace. But, failing in a mild test is most shameful. If a student studying in seventh class, appears in the examination of third class, he must top the list of successful candidates. If he fails he must drown himself. If he passes in lower grade, then he can save his reputation only by leaving the school.

In this fight we are students of seventh class. We were well equipped to start a civil disobedience movement in Bardoli. For us to collect ten lacs of rupees from Gujarat is just like appearing in the examination of the third class.

Test is very light. But because it is light we must pass in it, and that also we should be the toppers.

Even in the smallest village, there should be an arrangement of collection of contributions. Readers of *Navjivan* can send their and their friends' contribution to Navjivan Office.

I have come to Bombay with high hope. On every occasion Bombay had a lion's share in contributions. Last year Bombay had taken on its head the burden of collection of Tilak Swaraj Fund for Mahatmaji. I hope that in the absence of Gandhiji, Bombay will take the responsibility of running his activities. Bombay has given liberal donations during last fifty or sixty years for educational activities. Now when there is need of money for national education, I am confident that Bombay will not lag behind to extend its helping hand.

103

Vallabhbhai asks Maniben to Collect her Share of One Thousand Rupees

Sardar Shrino Patro-3

BOMBAY
11 October 1922

DEAR DAUGHTER MANIBEN AND SON DAHYABHAI,

I am entangled here.[1] I expected that the work will last for some days, but the circumstances arc such that I have to stay here for a longer time. There is no other go.

What happened to your responsibility of collecting donation of one thousand rupees?[2] How much have you collected?

Nanduben[3] also is here. From tomorrow she is going to collect donations from Lawyers of Police court.

If there is any work please tell Bhai Mavalankar[4] or Pandit,[5] or his doctorsaheb.[6]

Take care of your health.

Bapu's blessings

[1]To collect donations for Gujarat Vidyapith. Sardarshri had collected rupees ten lacs upto 2nd October 1922.

[2] Maniben also had taken the responsibility of collecting Rs 1,000.

[3]Vijayagauri Kanuga, wife of Dr. Balvantrai Kanuga. friend of Sardar.

[4]G.V Mavalankar, one of the dearest colleagues of Sardar. First Speaker of Lok Sabha.

5Neighbour of Sardar.

[6]Dr. Balvantrai Kanuga.

104

Vallabhbhai Castigates Government for not Supplying Adequate Water

Navjivan, 15 October 1922

As water works of Ahmedabad Municipality is not able to supply enough water to the city, engineering department of Bombay city was entrusted with the work of restructuring it. By the sanction of the Government Engineering Department prepared a plan, and work of implementation of the plan was started. Municipality expressed doubt about the success of the scheme. But no attention was paid to it. The work on that scheme lasted for about ten years during which the city faced serious water problem. At last the work of the scheme was completed. 14 lacs of rupees of Government and Municipality were wasted. The result, as Municipality had foreseen, was negative. Water supply did not increase. *Status quo* was maintained, and water scarcity remained as it was.

In this scheme, an additional machine was to be installed. In 1914-15 Bombay government had taken a decision that as soon as the work of scheme is complete a new engine as per requirement of the Municipality should be installed after consulting the Municipality and without caring to know whether the machine will be of a right type, the Engineering Department of the Government imported a machine from England at a cost of three lacs of rupees. Municipality knew about it when the money was demanded from it. As the machine was of no use, Municipality refused to take the machine. As it was not useful to any other Municipality, Government at last made arrangement in the budget to grant three lacs of rupees to the Municipality being the cost of the machine. Then the Municipality was suspended, and the Legislative Assembly put cuts in the budget, so the amount mentioned in the budget was deleted, and the amount was again demanded from the committee appointed by the government to run the municipal administration. Committee after consulting its engineer replied that as the engine was of no use, and as according to Government's own decision, the machine was imported without consulting the Municipality, Municipality was not responsible for the payment, and so it refused to take the machine. So, the engine remained with the government. The year was ending. As the government budget was cut there was shortage of funds. Every department was short of funds, and so the situation was like hungry cat eating its own cubs.

Seventy thousand rupees grant of department of education which was sanctioned to be given to the Committee, that grant was stopped, and order was issued that grant will be given only if the Committee pays the cost of machine. So it was decided not to give the yearly grant of education department till the amount was recovered.

Suspended Municipality declined to accept the grant for education. Government fraudulently usurped the grant leaving aside members of Cooperative Committee. Thus the members of committee were put in an embarrassing position.

Only this can be the result of blind cooperation.

105

Vallabhbhai Exhorts Gujaratis to Fight to the Finish

Navjivan, 16 October 1922

I shall prove to the Committee appointed for the task of enrolling volunteers that I have persuaded every member of my family, whom I am in a position to influence, to give up the use of foreign cloth.

Gujarat has money. It has organizing ability. It has moderation. But it cannot be gainsaid there is a dearth of volunteer workers in Gujarat. Every Gujarati, who has love for his country, must dedicate one of his sons for the work of the country. All patriotic young men of Gujarat and Kathiawad should pledge themselves to the service of their country until such time as Gandhiji is released. If you wish to keep up the prestige of Gujarat, give up idleness; otherwise as time passes, it will be said that while the world recognized the greatness of Gandhiji, it was only Gujarat which failed to do so.

Would you rather that the workers of Gujarat give up all their other work for the service of Gujarat in order to picket your shops? Will you not close your business in foreign cloth so long as Gandhiji is in jail? If you will take the first step it is possible that the whole country will follow in your footsteps and Gandhiji may well be freed from the jail much earlier.

106

"Reforms in Local Self-Government Illusory"—Vallabhbhai

Navjivan, 22 October 1922

"Seventeen elected representatives of the people tendered their resignations.... Bye-elections to fill the vacancies were announced. There were no candidates for nine of the seventeen seats. The other eight seats were filled with one former peon of the Municipality and two Harijans winning unopposed.

Nine of the seats were filled by the government with nine of its collaborators who were nominated. It happened when a popular minister is in charge of the department. The Government had learnt a lesson from the dismissal of the Ahmedabad and Surat Municipalities and afraid of repeating the mistake they took to this new expedient. Some of the nine nominated members are conservatives and favour untouchability. It is in this manner that the non-cooperation movement leads to a fight for removing untouchability.

The President of the Municipality disagrees with the Government contention that it had the right to make the nominations to these posts. He refuses to let such nominees work for the Municipality and has written to the Government that the vacancies be filled through an election. Simultaneously a taxpayer has filed a suit contending the membership of the nominated members and the court has granted an interim stay which has led to the Municipality becoming defunct temporarily.

This is how something or the other happens in the Local Self-Government Department and the claim of the Government to having made reforms is being exposed everyday.

107

Vallabhbhai Showers Praises on Akalis for Non-Violence

Navjivan, 19 November 1922

Brave Akalis who are pillars of the British Empire have taken the path of an ideal of self-sacrifice and non-violence. On their chest are seen the medals which they have received as a mark of appreciation of their services to the empire, on different battle-fields, where they were seriously wounded while fighting with the enemies. Such robust and brave Akalis though had Kirpan tied to their waist, silently watched the lathi charge on them by the police, who were ordered by the Government which they had loyally served. The government has now realised that attacking with arms can be successful only on cowards, and so it has stopped beating and decided to defend the prisons.

Punjab government has to build new prisons. More than 5000 Akalis have already gone to jail. On one side a batch of one hundred Akalis is arrested, and on the other hand recruitment of sepoys who want to go to jails is going on.

Akalis wear only *khadi.* In this crusade Akali women are showing great courage and enthusiasm. A hospital has been opened to treat Akalis who have been beaten by police. Akali sisters have taken up the duty of nursing them. They have also undertaken the work of cooking and serving as well as looking after the patients, who are there in recruitment camp. In this work also one can see military training, and perfection. Akali sisters also wear only *khadi.*

Religious sacrifice which is performed in Punjab is such that even gods from heaven would like to come and watch. While the country is peaceful, Akalis have performed the great sacrifice, the honour of which Bardoli could not get, and that too when Mahatma Gandhi is in jail. They have silenced those who were ridiculing non-violence and saying that *satyagraha* is dead.

Gujarat's faith in *Ahimsa* (non-violence) is not in any way less than that of the Akalis. Gujarat is the birth-place of that concept. Gujarat is the centre of Jain community, and so it is but natural that there non-violence is an article of faith. But has Gujarat the courage, valour, forbearance, capacity to suffer, unity, spirit of sacrifice, and training which Akalis possess? Have Gujarati Jains that religious fervour, which Akalis have? As a reply to this query it is said to cover the prestige of Gujarat "If Chauri Chaura had not intervened, Bardoli would have set an example" but how long such a false assertion survive? Foreign cloth trade is mostly in the hands of Jains who are worshippers of non-violence. Can we hide that fact from the world? Even though Punjab becomes *khadi* minded, in Gandhiji's Gujarat the fascination of foreign cloth is still evident, and how can we hide that fact? "Whatever is there in our house we will wear, and will not buy new foreign cloth" is Gujarati's excuse for wearing cloth, and though eight months have elapsed to Gandhiji's imprisonment, the foreign cloth from

Gujarati's house is not exhausted and *khadi* has not found a place. What is the reason ? What is the reason that not a single foreign cloth shop is closed?

Gujarat's duty does not end simply by saying that Gujarat is firm in council boycott, and there are no two opinions in the matter. It is not a matter of surprise that Gujarat which knows Gandhiji full well could not talk of entering legislature. But Gujarat's responsibility does not end there.

You Gujaratis who are mad after Gandhiji and who loudly shout his *jai* (victory) in his presence, awake. If you want to maintain Gujarat's dignity, leave lethargy. Otherwise in near future history will blame Gujarat for not knowing Gandhiji whom whole world has known. Youths from Gujarat and Kathiawar who have a genuine love for the country should take a vow to give their full time for national service till Gandhiji is released from jail. Gujarat has faith in Gandhiji's programme, has money, organising power, has modesty, but there is a dearth of workers and volunteers. Every patriotic Gujarati should offer one son to serve the nation.

Gujarat Provincial Congress Committee has at present asked for 2500 volunteers only. From 1-12-22 we will start picketing foreign cloth shops. If for this work we are not able to recruit 2500 volunteers from Gujarat then Gujarat's patriotism and Gujarat's love for Gandhiji will be exposed.

For this work anybody from Gujarat, Kathiawar or Kutch will be recruited. Camps will be opened at convenient places and lodging and boarding arrangements will be made for those who come from outside. Those who want to recruit themselves as volunteers should write to Gujarat Provincial Committee and get the pledge forms. Fill the same and send to committee office.

108

"Gandhiji is a Beacon Light for the Whole World"—Vallabhbhai

Navjivan, 22 November 1922

Who does not sympathize with a person who is prepared to undergo all pain? When a person is prepared to go through every kind of trouble and pain for the achievement of a noble ideal, it gives rise to a feeling of awe and reverence in the minds of the people. When we think of Mahatma Gandhi, our thoughts turn to our own lives. The Mahatma is like a beacon which lights the way and warns us of the dangers ahead. He is an effulgent personality because of his experience of the world around him, his capacity to bear pain and to make all kinds of sacrifices. And he lights up the world around him. It is idle to think of the responsibility he shoulders. Does a peacock ever find its finery burdensome? If we are able to understand the reason why the Mahatma is able to bear the pain inflicted on him, we would be able to understand the message which his life gives to those around him. His life is an open book, which teaches us in golden words: "Divest your life of all unnecessary finery and you would realise the true spiritual life". The ideal of such a life is very important. All that you need for the realisation of that ideal is self-control. Self-indulgence leads to a fall; self-abnegation means self-realisation. Those who think that this means a withdrawal from life are wrong. The self-control that the Mahatma talks about does not lead to inaction, but action in which you do not expect any rewards. A spiritual life does not bother about the physical and material losses. When a man recognises and realises his soul, his body becomes a slave to his spirit. He gives up his immoral ways. This is the process through which bodily pain is converted into the victory of the soul.

109

Vallabhbhai Deprecates Use of Foreign Cloth

Navjivan, 26 November 1922

Foreign cloth business has ruined our country. It has made people irreligious and servile. The big leaders of the country are making herculean efforts to make people understand their religious duty of using *swadeshi* goods. Thousands of persons who have dedicated their life for service of land are suffering various kinds of difficulties in jail. Since eight months Mahatma Gandhi is in jail. While going to jail he has given us the message of *swadeshi.* Your love and devotion for Gandhi is not less. You are also not less patriotic. Yet the people, who have been slaves for a long time, find it difficult to observe the vow of *swadeshi.* Similarly, you also find it difficult to leave the foreign goods business. But the popular feeling has now taken a turn, and day by day it is changing and people are trying hard to shun their weaknesses.

Though love for *swadeshi* is expanding, yet *swadeshi* work has not got momentum as yet. One of the reasons for it is trading in foreign cloth.

Will you like the workers of Gujarat to leave their national service in other fields of Gujarat and picket your shops?

Will you not have courage to stop sale of foreign cloth till Mahatmaji is in jail? It is possible that if you make a beginning the whole nation will follow you and Mahatmaji will be released from jail soon.

110

Vallabhbhai on Rules to be Observed by Swadeshi Volunteers

Navjivan, 3 December 1922

1. Wherever the volunteer is appointed, he should be under the Chief Commander of that place, and act according to his instructions.

2. A volunteer, keeping himself as much away as possible from the cloth shop, persuade the buyers not to buy foreign cloth, and should not enter within ten feet of the boundary or the shop platform against the wishes of the shopkeeper.

3. Should take the precaution that while persuading buyers not to buy foreign cloth, people do not assemble. If a crowd is gathered, the volunteer should request the crowd to disperse. If the crowd do not disperse, the main office should be informed about it.

4. As far as possible, volunteers should generate the goodwill and sympathy of the houseowners of the places near the foreign cloth shops and secure their permission to stand or sit on the verandah outside their house and from there try to persuade the buyers not to buy foreign cloth. This will eliminate the people flocking on the roads.

5. It is desirable that instead of requesting the buyers near the shops, volunteers should occupy the roads leading to the shops and persuade buyers from there only.

6. Nobody who buys foreign cloth from the shops and comes out should be talked to nor they should be advised or explained not to buy foreign cloth.

7. While explaining to the buyers of foreign cloth, utmost courtesy and politeness should be observed. Harsh or unpleasant words should not be used.

8. Volunteers should be courteous while explaining the significance of boycott of foreign cloth, their body should not be touched.

9. If police wants to arrest any volunteer, he should be allowed to do so without any resistance, and other volunteers should immediately inform about it to the main office.

10. If police asks the name of the volunteer, it should be given without any murmur, and one need not enter into discussion with the police who asks the name, and immediately main office should be informed about it.

11. If others engage themselves in vandalism, volunteers should maintain peace, and even if they are beaten they should suffer it calmly. In spite of all sorts of instigation and teasing, volunteers should not show any temper, or hit anybody.

111

Vallabhbhai against Hurling Abuses on Officials

Navjivan, 3 December 1922

"Judging from what I have learnt about them", said Vallabhbhai, in the course of the last few days since this campaign started, "I can assure you that the various epithets which we have been using when referring to them—scoundrels, dishonest fellow, thieves—are all epithets which could more appropriately be applied to us rather than to them. We did not have any business commitments. All we had to do was to set fire to the foreign clothes we might have in our houses worth a hundred or two hundred rupees. We had at the most to withdraw from Government Schools one or two of our boys. We might have had to contribute some money for running the National Schools in which our children are now studying. But did we do any of these things? For the merchants, on the other hand, it is a question of giving up their sole or main source of livelihood. We do not examine our own actions and are only too anxious to ask others to render account. It is our duty today to encourage the merchants in the good start they have made and not to say anything which would render their task more difficult and make them despair. If during this intervening period we all change over to the use of Indian cloth, why would they want to import any more foreign cloth?"

112

Vallabhbhai Foresees Decline in Public Enthusiasm after Entering Legislatures

Navjivan, 12 December 1922

I am not a leader; I am a soldier. I am the son of a peasant and do not believe that we can gain independence by merely talking. We shall not be able to fight the Government on its own ground. Once we enter the Legislatures, the people will lose their enthusiasm for independence and the Congress will lose the confidence of the people. It will indeed be ruinous to the Congress. It is only when the Congress announced its policy of non-cooperation that it began to be supported by agriculturists, labourers and women. That is so because it is only such activity which gives scope for participating in the national struggle and for making sacrifices. The Government knew well before the reforms the nature of the people with whom it had to deal. The reforms were drawn up with reference to their strong and their weak points. Even if you conducted your campaign for a hundred years, through the Legislatures, you will not get independence.

113

Vallabhbhai Criticises His Brother's Plea to Enter Councils

Navjivan, 12 December 1922

Patelsaheb (Vithalbhai) who is a supporter of entry into the Legislature went to England to give evidence and knows, therefore, the persons who have drafted the Constitution. They designed the Legislatures bearing in mind that people like him would enter the legislatures, and so they provided safeguards against possible subversive activities and thus made the legislatures practically ineffective. Therefore the fortress of the enemy is not located in the legislatures. It lies elsewhere and so long as that remains uncaptured, this Government can continue to function even for a hundred years without a legislature.

114

Vallabhbhai Commends Village Traders and Volunteers on Boycott of Foreign Cloth in Gujarat

Navjivan, 17 December 1922

We have not fully understood that the main reason of our slavery is the business of foreign cloth, otherwise eight months after Mahatmaji, who gave us the doctrine of pure Swadeshi—going to jail, situation would not have deteriorated to such an extent that foreign cloth shops had to be picketed. After Mahatmaji was imprisoned, Gujarat brought foreign cloth worth lacs of rupees and betrayed him, and committed the sin of making powerful the hands of Government. After Mahatmaji's imprisonment had the cloth dealers of India taken a vow not to import foreign cloth till Mahatmaji was in jail he would not have been in jail today. But till now cloth dealers do not understand. If Gujarat merchants do not understand these things, how can others understand?

But only cloth dealers need not to be blamed. Merchants are also surcharged with as much of emotion as common people. They also understand that foreign cloth causes downfall of our country. But their religious instinct slips with the intrusion of instinct of selfishness. Dealers have self-interest. For years they have engaged in one field of business and so they have been slaves of their weaknesses, and so it is difficult for them to extricate themselves. But people have self-interest in Swadeshi, they do not lose anything by using Swadeshi. They have understood importance of Swadeshi, yet they are tempted to buy foreign cloth. Except those who are very poor, most of the people under spell leave aside religious instinct without any hesitation. Mill owners and members of their family do not get satisfaction by using cloth made in the mills. Mill workers either do not like mill cloth or they cannot afford it. And for those who are extremely poor, they like to buy the cloth that is cheap.

Picketing is going on since last fortnight. It appears from experience that volunteers who are men of character are able to impress upon dealers as well as common people. Seller and purchaser both feel ashamed but their weaknesses come on the surface. Dealers have not the courage to stop altogether dealing in foreign cloth, yet they are willing to make honest efforts in that direction. Love for Swadeshi amongst the people is increasing day by day. Yet it is difficult for them to be out of lure of fine cloth. Therefore, from one side we shall have to make efforts for stopping the import of foreign cloth and from the other side we shall have to give boost to Swadeshi movement.

Cloth merchants of Chikli and Sayan have taken a vow not to buy foreign cloth. The merchants of Karadi village of Jalalpur Taluka have taken a pledge that they will stop foreign cloth trade after 31st December and besides that they have also taken a pledge either to burn the stock of foreign cloth which they have in their possession or give away to district committee. The merchants of Amod have also taken a pledge to stop selling foreign cloth till the Congress permits them to sell. Thus small dealers have started refraining themselves from the sale of foreign cloth but big merchants are hesitant to show that much courage. All the cloth dealers of Surat city have resolved not to sell any kind of foreign cloth for a year. Most of the cloth dealers of Nadiad have also resolved similarly.

But cloth dealers of Ahmedabad are yet hesitant to go to that extent. One association has resolved not to import foreign cloth for six months, another for eight months and third for nine months. We have asked these associations to extend the time limit of one year like the merchants of Surat and Nadiad. If they do not extend the time limit then the Congress Committee will do what it deems proper. Yet two merchant associations of Ahmedabad have not taken any action. From those association shops which have stopped importing foreign cloth the picketing has been lifted. It has been strictly arranged through the association to see that the cloth merchants act in accordance with the pledge. We have proofs that pledge takers are sincere and honest. Some traders of silk cloth called the meeting of the association, sat upto 3 a.m. and passed a resolution, and that very evening some merchants had gone to Bombay to purchase cloth who were telegraphically informed before they reached Bombay, and thus prevented from buying cloth; otherwise cloth worth four or five lac rupees would have reached Ahmedabad. It is a matter of satisfaction that the traders of Gujarat take special care to see that they keep their word.

The effect of the resolution of boycott by the civil disobedience committee on the merchants is clearly visible. On the basis of that resolution they were insisting for import of cloth from the cloth manufacturers in countries like China, Japan and other non-European countries.

In picketing programme some ladies from Gujarat are doing commendable work. If all the cloth dealers of Gujarat stop importing foreign cloth for one year, volunteers during that period engaged in picketing can be spared to explain the significance of Swadeshi to the persons who go to Hindu temples, and Jain temples for *darshan* wearing foreign clothes and thus give impetus to *swadeshi* programme. On one side volunteers will propagate *swadeshi* and on the other side if the dealers sell only *swadeshi* cloth, then we will be able to stop foreign cloth trade from Gujarat.

115

Vallabhbhai on Gandhiji's Attempts to Win over Dacoits and Save People[1]

Times of India, 22 December 1922

In the beginning, Shri Patel gave a detailed account of the brutal atrocities committed by Babar Deva, and expressed his opinion that Babar Deva has been able to commit such inhuman acts, because the Government has failed to arrest him. He refuted the charge that people do not help the police, and charged the government that whenever people went to the police officers with a complaint, and asked for police protection, the officials rudely told them, "Go to Gandhi". He also charged the government with supplying guns to another dacoit Ali, getting Babar arrested, as Government had failed to arrest him. As a result with those guns Ali murdered several innocent people. He also told people that for the last seven years Government has not been able to arrest him. So, we infer that in the two Talukas either the police is not there to protect people or police has joined hands with dacoits. He also said that before Gandhiji was prosecuted he had the intention of winning Babar Deva by love. After the imprisonment of Gandhiji, he himself had sent one of his colleagues to see the dacoits. That man with Gandhi cap went to the dacoits, sat there fearlessly, encircled by dacoits, and chided them for the murders and atrocities committed by them. He also persuaded them to give up the sinful way. But dacoits expressed their inability, and said that if they change their way of life and come out of their hideouts, immediately police would arrest them. Patel told the audience that had the Government declared that the dacoits would not be arrested, by now Borsad and Anand talukas would have been free from the menace of dacoits. He also denounced the policy of the Government to station additional police there at people's cost and he gave a clear warning to the Government that people were not willing to pay the fine, and they are ready to fight to the last with the weapons of *satyagraha.* He also said that the Government had given guns to Ali, who had murdered many people with those guns for which government was guilty.

At the end of his speech Patel appealed to the people of Bombay to help the people who were oppressed by the tax as well as drought.

[1]On 21 December 1923 in a meeting held under the auspices of Bombay Provincial Congress Committee at Marwari Vidyalaya Hall, Vallabhbhai Patel had given this lecture on the Borsad Satyagraha. K.P. Khadilkar presided over the meeting.

116

Vallabhbhai against Council Entry

Bombay Police Secret Abstract of Intelligence, 1923

BOMBAY
4 January 1923

Under the auspices of the Mandvi District Congress Committee a public meeting was held on January 4th at the Cutchi Dasa Oswal Mahajan Wadi, Khadak, when Vallabhbhai Jhaverbhai Patel of Ahmedabad and Dr. Chandulal Manilal Desai of Broach spoke on the subject of the "Gaya Congress" before an audience of about 400 persons.

V.J. Patel said he very much regretted the waste of time at Gaya disputing about Council-entry. The country should stick to Gandhi's programme and not be misled into side issues. Progress was apparent from the fact that even renowned leaders like C.R. Das had failed to win over people to Council-entry. The people were no longer like sheep but thought for themselves.

He hoped Bombay would do great things in responding to the call of Rs 25 lakhs and fifty thousand volunteers within five months.

117

Vallabhbhai Congratulates People and Governor Leslie Wilson on Victory of Borsad Satyagraha[1]

Navjivan, 13 January 1923

The Borsad Satyagraha is over. Truth, *ahimsa* and sacrifice have again won. It is a matter of gratification that we won this struggle because our fight was for justice. This victory is unique because this time both the parties have won. The government have openly and with courage accepted their mistakes. The government have won because they gave up their custom of sticking to a wrong stand for the sake of their prestige and save themselves from the crime of further troubling the innocent and oppressed people. They have also accepted the truth and if we do not congratulate the new Governor, Sir Leslie Wilson, for showing this moral courage, we would not be doing our duty.

Our victory consists not only in this that the government has decided to return the fines realized from the people and their attached properties and also to bear the expenses of the special police themselves, but in the fact that the government have withdrawn the allegations made against us. Our real victory lies in the fact that we have realised the greatness which the government have shown. The government is generally afraid of admitting its errors. The government considers that giving in to the people who are fighting injustice with moral strength is a danger to the Empire. This is the first occasion when the government has without hesitation publicly accepted its error and has bowed before the Satyagrahis thereby admitting that their struggle was "valid". We think that instead of words, our future conduct should reassure the government that we would not misuse its generosity.

There is a grace and sweetness in the end of this Satyagraha. The people, and equally the local authorities and government employees have the responsibility to maintain this atmosphere of sweetness and grace. When the government employees behaved with harshness in the attachment proceedings, bitterness created against them was natural. Some Patels and other functionaries have had to resign, some properties have been destroyed and false complaints have been made against some employees. We hope that now that the Satyagraha is over, both the parties would overlook the shortcomings of each other and behave in a cultured and liberal manner. We had ourselves criticised bitterly the police while the Satyagraha was on but that did not give us any pleasure. We have no animus against the police department or any police officer. The goal of the police is the same as is ours but our methods are as alike as chalk and cheese. Both the police and we want that the people should live happily. The government used their methods on Thakur day community for many years but it had a contrary effect. We do not deny that the purpose of the government was good but the results were contrary to expectations. The government knows it well. What is needed is that we should reassure this community. Many people have lost their lives in an attempt to catch murderers and dacoits; but we have not heard the government speak one word of sympathy towards their families nor have they sent one letter of condolence to them. This has pained us. We had to mention this because the last part of the government communique forced us to mention it.

We congratulate the people of Borsad Tehsil who underwent all the troubles peacefully and with a sense of discipline. The volunteers deserve our thanks because they have served the people of Borsad Tehsil with dedication, zeal and courage. We are grateful to those men and newspapers who have directly or indirectly helped us.

With God's grace, the Borsad Satyagraha has ended in victory. We are happy to say that we are grateful to God for this victory of truth and non-violence.

[1]Just after the victorious culmination of the Nagpur Flag Satyagraha, Vallabhbhai was approached by the villagers of the Borsad Taluka for redress of their grievances. They were the victims of the ravages of the dacoits who carried their loot and plunder with the connivance of the police. Instead of taking action against their own officers, the Government levied punitive tax of two and half rupees on every adult person in the taluka on the ground that they were harbouring the dacoits. After satisfying himself with the veracity of the facts, Vallabhbhai asked the villagers to refuse to pay the punitive tax. However, he took a pledge from the villagers that they would remain patient even if their property is attached. . . Meanwhile, Sir Leslie Wilson took over as Governor of Bombay. He found substance in Vallabhbhai's allegations, and had the punitive tax withdrawn. The struggle too was, therefore, called off. The Borsad Satyagraha was of short duration. It lasted only five weeks but was a unique example of Vallabhbhai's meticulous organisation and inspiring leadership which earned him the title of "King of Borsad" from Gandhiji.

118

Vallabhbhai to Mathuradas regarding Swaraj Party

Sardar Shrino Anyo Patro

14 January 1923

BROTHER MATHURADAS,

Excuse me for not replying your letter because I am down with fever since last four days. Today I feel somewhat better, but side by side there is severe toothache. For that I shall have to seek medical help for some days.

Congress has passed the resolution.[1] So now it is of no avail to change it, and to waste time in getting the resolution changed is harmful to the country. That is what I think.

Bhai Jaykar[2] and Natrajan[3] believe that this disruption is injurious for the nation. They are right. It is painful that the leaders started a separate party,[4] opposing the Congress resolution. Its remedy is not deleting Congress resolution but explaining the leaders. I don't think that at present anybody will succeed in explaining them. I think they are in angry mood. Time will dilute their anger.

I will come there on 28th. At that time we will meet Jaykar and Natrajan. Bhai Jaykar was in Gaya till the end. He is in know of everything.

You must have read that Das Babu has said that the resolution of the Congress does not reflect the voice of the nation.

VALLABHBHAI'S
Bande Matram

[1]In Gaya session of the Congress, Congress programme of non-cooperation was endorsed. But the leaders who advocated council entry did not approve that resolution was passed by a majority.

[2]M.R. Jaykar, moderate leader, a leading lawyer of the country, and expert in constitutional matters.

[3]Editor, *Social Reformer.*

[4]Swaraj Party.

119

Vallabhbhai on Viceroy's Arbitrary Decision to Enhance Salt Tax

Navjivan, 14 January 1923

There is a possibility that it may not be necessary to take stringent steps to enforce the Congress Resolution regarding the boycott of Legislatures. The Government itself has made our task easy. The Government's decision to enhance the salt tax has made it clear that the Legislatures are altogether futile. The proposal was rejected by a majority vote not once but twice. Nevertheless the Viceroy ignored the majority and certified the proposal. It was but natural to hope that now at least the Members of the Legislatures would be disillusioned enough to want to quit the Legislatures. What more can we do in the Legislatures than thus to defeat the Government by our majority? That has been done several times in the present session and yet whenever the Government thought it fit, it has ignored the majority view. In the circumstances one would have thought that not much argument was necessary to convince the voters of the futility of the Legislatures. Anyhow, there does not seem to be any reason to fear the growth of bitterness or disunity among the two sections of the Congress.

120

Vallabhbhai Asks People to be Prepared for Individual Civil Disobedience

Navjivan, 14 January 1923

[While Gandhiji was in jail, the Congress had passed a resolution that the country be prepared for individual civil disobedience. The following article was written by the Sardar on that subject.]

The faith of the people has been tested at the time of the Gaya Congress. All attempts to change the Congress programme met with failure. The most notable of the change sought to be made was the giving up of the boycott of the assemblies. The Congress President Deshbandhu Chittaranjan Das had supported it (the proposal to give up the boycott). Leaders like Motilal Nehru and Hakim Sahib tried their might, but in spite of that the delegates refused either to give up the boycott or to make it milder. Not only that, the Gaya Congress recommended that the boycott of the assemblies should be further strengthened.

The resolution on the boycott of British goods had been passed with a slender majority in the Subjects Committee; it was rejected by the delegates.

This is how a proof is now available that the people of the country support the Congress programme. But faith alone will not be of much use, because unless it is supported by strength, faith is ineffective. You need both faith and strength if you want to succeed in any great task. The Congress had given proof of the faith the people have in it and has called upon them to give proof of their strength. The people are now on test because if they give proof of their strength they would have succeeded. If the faith they have is not thoughtless, if it is not blind, the people would be able to show their strength in spite of all difficulties and the differences among the leaders.

The Congress has demanded that preparations be made quickly to start individual civil disobedience. It has asked the people to contribute a sum of Rs 25 lakhs to the Congress Fund and to raise a corps of 50,000 volunteers by the end of April next through the strengthening of the Congress organisations. That would be the proof that the country is ready to launch the individual civil disobedience movement. If we are able to make those preparations, we would start a new era of sacrifices. Those who have faith in the Congress programme as it stands today they must find it their duty to implement successfully this resolution.

The subject of our entry into the assemblies would continue to be a matter of debate. It may become intensified. The leaders have decided to create public opinion in their favour. But if both the opponents and the proponents of entry into the assemblies use all their time and strength to undo the work of each other, it would be India's misfortune.

Those who have no faith in the assemblies should withdraw from the controversy. The subject has taken more time to discuss than it should have; invaluable strength and intelligence has been spent on the controversy. Those who want to go to the assemblies may be left to their own devices; the rest of us should do their duty. The best way to put an end to this controversy is to do solid work. As the Congress programme is implemented, the controversy on this question will quieten and then cease altogether.

121

Vallabhbhai Urges People of Gujarat to Stop Payment of Revenue to Government

Bombay Police Secret Abstract of Intelligence

NADIAD
19 February 1923

Audience 700. President Vallabhbhai J. Patel delivered an eulogy in Gandhi's honour and referred to the signal services he had rendered to the whole of India in general and to Gujarat and the Patidar community in particular. Gujarat alone, he said, is able to bring about the Mahatma's release in a single day if it so desires. It however does not do so and contend itself by paying for the upkeep of Gandhi's jailors. Eleven months, the speaker continued, had been idled away. It was now time for the country to act. It was impossible to contend against Government with words alone. What was now wanted was that not a pie of revenue should be paid to Government. The ryots of Kaira successfully resisted Government by refusing to pay their land revenue when their crops were bad. But this was after all an insignificant grievance. The country nowdays was labouring under a host of grievances.

The speaker then referred to the Nadiad derailment case and stated that it was no credit to have derailed a train. Those who were responsible should now come forward as volunteers and court imprisonment. The Patidar community alone should furnish 3,000 volunteers. It was the duty of each household in the district to contribute one volunteer. The speaker concluded by impressing on his audience that this was the time to go to jail and not to seek service or enter on commerce.

122

Vallabhbhai Urges People to Take up Congress Programmes to Celebrate Anniversary of Gandhiji's Arrest

Navjivan, 25 February 1923

18th March is approaching. One year of Mahatmaji's imprisonment will be complete. Congress has issued an appeal to observe peaceful strike in whole of India on that day. Gujarat Provincial Congress Committee has instructed people to fast and pray on that day.

We have not to observe strike in order to impress the government. This government is not going to be impressed by any outward demonstration. We have no idea of our weaknesses, but the government has. Had we fulfilled what Gandhiji wanted us to fulfil we should have achieved Swaraj within a year. Even if we had followed the path he had shown us, even after his imprisonment, then he would not have been in jail. The support of the government is not its strength, but our weakness. We forget this. That is the reason why all the people of our country should leave their daily routine, and concentrate their mind on finding out their weaknesses, and pray to God to free them from their weaknesses and decide to go ahead on the path of Swaraj with faith and determination. This is the idea behind the request to observe the strike on that day.

Key to Swaraj rests in *swadeshi.* Mahatmaji had given only one message while going to jail. It was, produce and wear *khadi,* then swaraj will come to your door-step. It is true that consumption of *khadi* has increased in Gujarat. But Gujarat has not become *khadi* minded so far. On 18th *khadi* processions are to be taken out in every village. On that day if Gujarat becomes *khadi* minded only then Gujarat will be fit to observe that day. Those who have not yet been wearing *khadi,* let them buy *khadi* from today, and prepare themselves for joining the celebrations of that day.

Gandhiji had deep feeling for the untouchables. He could not bear the pangs of untouchability. He tried his level best to remove that stigma. We being tempted by the idea of achieving Swaraj in a year allowed untouchables to join our meetings, get togethers, and schools, but did not allow them entry in our hearts. That is why after Mahatmaji's imprisonment, and hope of attaining Swaraj being razed to the ground, our sin became manifest. If we want to celebrate that day, we should take a true decision to remove untouchability, and prepare to serve the untouchables according to our capacity. In Gujarat an institution has been founded for the service of untouchables. Ten to twelve youths have joined the institution on the condition that for three years they will do nothing but engage themselves in the service of the untouchables. Gujarat Provincial Congress

Committee has decided to spend at least 25,000 rupees for the service of untouchables through this institution. Those who celebrate 18th March, who rightly understand Mahatmaji's agony, should join this institution and serve the untouchables or help the institution by collecting funds required for the work of the institution.

Every man and woman of eighteen years and above should enrol himself or herself as member of the Congress before 18th March. From every village and every locality volunteers should go to their district committees, get enrolment receipt books, and enrol thousands as Congress members. Those who join the processions and meetings on 18th March should be members of the Congress only then the processions and meetings will be meaningful, otherwise on festive occasions many types of entertainment programmes are arranged; fairs are held, people assemble, and some people gamble, some sit in the wheels, some drink heavily, some quarrel and abuse each other. Thus everybody engages himself or herself in gimmicks and while away the time. But the festival of 18th March should be celebrated seriously. Everybody's goal should be to attain swaraj. Those who are not keen to attain swaraj cannot understand the significance of this day. Those who are keen to attain swaraj should be Congress members, and those who want to enrol themselves as members should do so prior to that day.

Mahatmaji had started collecting funds for implementing Congress programme, till we attain swaraj, and the auspicious name of late Lokmanya was given to that fund, which was named as Tilak Swaraj Fund. This year, Congress has decided to collect 25 lacs of rupees. Gujarat Provincial Congress Committee having considered its needs, and other circumstances, has resolved to collect five lac rupees. Every Gujarati should send his or her contribution for this fund before 18th March, and celebrate this befitting Gujarat.

Volunteers of every village should get the receipt books and certificates from the office of Provincial Congress Committee, and collect the funds from their villages before 18th. Gujaratis who live outside Gujarat should remember Gujarat on this day should contribute to this fund, as much as possible, and celebrate the day befitting Gujarat.

In religious places like Dakor, thousands of pilgrims being guided by their devotion, go to the temple of Ranchhodji, have a glimpse of the Lord and get purified. But in the habitants of Dakor instead of devotion, selfishness gets inflated. They only wait for the festive day. The reason is that they want to exploit the devolution of the pilgrims and fleece them.

Late Lokmanya was there in Sabarmati Jail. Mahatmaji has made that place auspicious by being there. Swami Anand and Dayaljibhao are in that jail. Kaka Saheb has gone there yesterday. Thousands of patriots have made that place sacred. Everyday somebody enters its gate, and somebody comes out of it. There is such a sacred place in Gujarat. If Gujaratis give send off to those who go there, and welcome those who come out of it, then they will be benumbed like the residents of the temple town. Congress has demanded three thousand Gujaratis to go to such a temple. Will Gujarat be able to comply with that demand?

May God give Gujarat that much strength and intelligence.

123

Vallabhbhai's Report on AICC Meeting outlining Compromise Formula for Council Entry

Young India, 8 March 1923

The new party met at Allahabad on February 20th and appointed a special committee with authority to agree on their behalf to such terms of settlement as they might approve after discussion with the Working Committee which was to meet at Allahabad on February 26th. Four sets of proposals were considered during the conversation at Allahabad between the Working Committee and the new party's special committee. Two of them implied suspension of the resolution regarding the boycott of the council elections without reference to any fresh Congress sessions. Of the other two one was Maulana's proposal as modified and added to by Deshbandhu Das and the other was the following:

(1) Suspension of council propaganda on both sides till the 30th April.

(2) Both parties to be at liberty to work the remaining items of their respective programmes in the interval without interfering with each other.

(3) Each party to adopt such course after the 30th April as it may be advised.

(4) No special Congress.

The new party, however, made all the four proposals subject to the following condition:

"Every proposal subject to the condition that there is no dissolution of the existing councils in any province before the expiry of the full term for which they have been constituted."

The Working Committee decided against accepting any of the two proposals that involved a reversal of the resolution regarding council boycott without reference to Congress. It decided to accept either of the other two sets of proposals but modified the terms drafted by Deshbandhu Das in some particulars and by substituting for the special election machinery proposed by him a clause that the All India Congress Committee should provide at its meeting in any satisfactory machinery for disposal of disputes regarding election of delegates to the special Congress in a fair and impartial manner.

To the other alternative proposal the Working Committee added terms to secure cooperation in collection of funds and enlistment of workers.

The two sets of proposals either of which the Working Committee agreed to accept were as follows:

Azad-Das Draft as amended by the Working Committee

No. I

(1) Both parties while adhering to their respective opinion agree to suspend their differences and jointly work the programme as laid down at Gaya.
(2) There should be no propaganda by either party concerning council election till the end of April.
(3) The All-India Congress Committee will meet before the end of May and if in view of the situation at the time it decides to undertake Individual Civil Disobedience on a large scale both parties will join in such Civil Disobedience and there will be no special session of the Congress.
(4) If, however, the All-India Congress Committee declares against such Civil Disobedience both the parties will thereafter be free to educate public opinion according to their views.
(5) If the All-India Congress Committee to be convened before 31st May declares against such Civil Disobedience a special session of the Congress should meet about the end of June.
(6) The All-India Congress Committee meeting in May will provide satisfactory machinery for the disposal of disputes regarding the election of delegates in a fair and impartical manner.
(7) The decision of the Special Session will be loyally carried out by all parties and there will be no separate organisations for taking action contrary to that decision.

No. II

(1) Suspension of council propaganda on both sides till the 30th April.
(2) Both parties to be at liberty to work the remaining items of their respective programmes in the interval without interfering with each other.
(3) Majority party will cooperate with the minority party in appealing for the raising of such funds and enlisting such workers as may be necessary for the constructive programme and also in working the constructive programme and other common matters.
(4) Majority party will be at liberty to carry on their propaganda in accordance with the Gaya programme about money and volunteers.
(5) Each party to adopt such course after the 30th April as it may be advised.

The Working Committee left these two proposals with Committee of the new party for the latter to decide whichever they might accept after consultation among themselves. The latter intimated their acceptance of the terms of Scheme No. II which were accordingly placed before the All-India Congress Committee at its meeting of Feb. 21st and confirmed.

It will be seen from the terms thus finally adopted that unless the Government advances the date of the council election there will be no controversial propaganda, that the collection of money and enlistment of workers by the majority party will be supported by the cooperation of the minority, and that the majority party's efforts at launching a campaign of Individual Civil Disobedience will not be opposed by the minority party. It is hoped that all workers will observe the letter and spirit of the compromise and help to secure the letter and spirit and atmosphere of peace and cooperation; and taking full advantage of it, strengthen the Congress organisation throughout the country. The collections for the Tilak Swaraj Fund and enrolment of workers and volunteers should be pushed on with vigour and all Congress Committees should resume their activities by which alone real faith and lasting enthusiasm can be restored.

RAJENDRA PRASAD
VALLABHBHAI PATEL
General Secretaries, INC

124

Vallabhbhai asks Maniben to Borrow Money from Congress Office to Pay Landlord

Sardar Shrino Patro[1]

CALCUTTA
15 *March 1923*

MY DEAR DAUGHTER MANIBEN,

I reached here on 12th morning.[2] I am staying here till eighteenth. Thereafter I will go to Zaria for two days or three days. Then I am going to Rangoon. I will be there for 10 to 15 days. From there I will return to Ahmedabad.

If you want money or anything else get it from the office.[3] Don't suffer hardship. If the landlord comes for rent, then get it paid from the office.

Take care of your health.

Bapu's blessings

[1]In Gujarati, Vol. III.

[2]At that time Sardar was collecting funds for Swaraj Kosh or Gujarat Vidyapith and therefore he had to travel for a longer period.

[3]Office of the Gujarat Provincial Congress Committee.

125

Vallabhbhai to Maniben regarding His Brief Encounter with Gandhiji

Sardar Shrino Patro[1]

POONA
16 April 1923

DEAR DAUGHTER MANIBEN,

As soon as I came to Bombay, I was informed that a working committee meeting has been convened at Poona on 17th. Then I came here today. Devadasbhai was going to meet Gandhiji today.[2] I went with him. So, my coming here turned a blessing. I was standing at the gate outside. As soon as interview with Devdas was over Bapu came out. So I had a good fortune to have his "darshan" (glimpse). I did not get the chance to speak to him, but seeing him also was a good fortune. He said with a smile "Today I achieved something which is not very easy to achieve."

Bhai Shankarlal[3] is going to be released tomorrow. I will start for Ahmedabad from Bombay by a mail train day after tomorrow evening and reach Ahmedabad on 19th morning. I have hurriedly written after returning from jail. If Mahadevbhai[4] comes then give him this letter to read. But the contents are not to be given to the press.

Dahyabhai[5] saw me yesterday in Bombay. I will bring him if possible.

Bapu's blessings

[1]In Gujarati, Vol. III.
[2]In Yervada jail.
[3]Shankarlal Banker. He was also sentenced with Gandhiji for sedition.
[4]Mahadevbhai Desai.
[5]Dahyabhai Patel, Sardar's son. He was one and a half years younger than Maniben.

126

Vallabhbhai on Congress Anxiety to Win Swaraj Early

Bombay Police Secret Abstract of Intelligence, 1923

AHMEDABAD
21 April 1923

Vallabhbhai J. Patel opened his speech in Gujarati and there was a certain amount of disorder as the audience insisted on his speaking either in Hindi or

Marathi, when order was restored, Patel continued in Hindi and asked his audience to give their opinion by show of hands as to (1) whether they were in favour of the Gaya resolutions, (2) whether they were against the resolutions, (3) whether they were willing to register their names as Congress members, (4) whether they had registered their names as Congress members, (5) whether they were willing to subscribe to the Tilak Swaraj Fund, and (6) whether they had subscribed. Much to Patel's disappointment, voting for and against the Congress resolutions was fairly even divided and he expressed his disappointment. The show of hands of those who had registered their names as Congress members and of those who had already subscribed to the Tilak Swaraj Fund was very meagre, and Patel appealed to the audience to register their names as members and volunteers early as the policy of the Congress was lowering the prestige of Government and thus bringing Swaraj nearer.

127

Vallabhbhai Finds People of Burma not Interested in Throwing their Lot with India

Bombay Police Secret Abstract of Intelligence

AHMED ABAD
21 April 1923

Vallabhbhai J. Patel returned here from Burma on April 19th. I had a talk with him on April 21st. He said that the principal object of his visit to Burma was to ascertain at first-hand whether the Burmans desired to throw in their lot with India and become a member of an Indian Commonwealth. He found that they wanted to be completely independent of India. He considered the Burmans to be much inferior to Indians in intellectual capacity. The Indians in Burma took practically no interest in politics.

Talking of decision to start the civil disobedience from May 1st, he stated that he was entirely opposed to it as he knew that the country was not prepared for it. He was content with the constructive programme, but there was a universal demand for something more exciting, some more aggressive policy. When Kalelkar was sent to jail in February 1st, it was with the greatest difficulty he prevented Yajnik and others from publishing the offending articles so as to invite imprisonment. When he returned from Burma after Yajnik's imprisonment he found that many of the younger political workers in Ahmedabad were determined on going to jail. They argued that if they remained out it would show weakness. He argued that to throw up the sponge in that manner was not only futile but proof of weakness. He told them that as long as they accepted his leadership they must carry out the constructive programme otherwise they should get someone else to take his place. (There is a rumour in the bazar that the political workers are hurriedly making for the jail so as to escape the bullets that will be flying next month when civil disobedience is started. I mentioned this to him.)

With regard to the next municipal elections in Ahmedabad, he expected that his party would win a majority of the seats. He expected that there would be some trouble about the schools unless Government changed their policy and gave them control over the education of their children. Notwithstanding the Reforms and then at that Education was a transferred subject under an Indian Minister, an enlightened and advanced Municipality like the Ahmedabad Municipality had not the power to sack even a pattawala or to transfer a teacher. Many of them were men who had sacrificed their careers and everything they possessed in the social service of their country, and they were embittered by the humiliating manner in which they had been treated. They had no objection to the school being inspected by Government Inspectors in an advisory capacity. The duty of these Inspectors should be to see that the teaching was carried out in an efficient and proper manner. The Municipality should have the power to modify the curriculum where they thought necessary.

The Nadiad Municipality, he said, had not been suspended as the Governor objected to the suspension of municipalities. The breaking of locks and attachment of property for failure to pay the municipal taxes cannot go on year after year.

128

Vallabhbhai on Dismissal of Government Case in District[1] Court

Navjivan, 22 April 1923

. . . The Government are in the habit of behaving immorally in the name of law and order and that is what they have done in this case. The 19 members who had started a campaign to remove government control from education are the ones who were accused of "wrongly spending money" on education and a case was filed to recover the sums. The Municipality is legally bound to spend appropriate sums on primary education, but the Government had the temerity to file a suit for the recovery of that money from the members of the Municipal Committee—that too in a province where reforms have been brought about and the department of local self-government is in the hands of a popular minister. What more proof is needed of the travesty of local self-government?

In Ahmedabad the Government lost. The court not only rejected the Government case but also awarded costs to the respondents. This surprised many people. One can understand the sense of astonishment because people who are in the habit of tolerating injustice would be surprised when they find justice. But such occasional instances of justice can deceive the people. There was no attempt to seek justice in this case. Only the Government can have the audacity to demand that an injustice be done, because it has the power. The Government pleader prayed to the court that the case be decided as early as possible. The Government are not going to gain anything out of it. Even so, from the interest that they are taking in the case it leads one to believe that they are bent upon influencing the decision of the court and making the best of their position. The Justice Department is in the hands of the Government whose chief officer gets thousands of rupees by way of salary.

There is hardly a court in the land where the Government's law officer does not operate, and who does not draw a handsome salary from the treasury. Even so, the Government had the temerity to make the type of claim it did. Is it not misapplication of Government money that the Government were ordered to pay the costs of the case to the respondents. Will it be the appropriate use of money when the lawyer of the Government is paid for conducting the case in the way he did? It is only this group of traders which can misuse public moneys which should have been utilised for purposes of education and lay a claim to being a government. Had the Department of Local Self-Government been under the charge of a popular minister, its officers would not have had the guts to behave in the manner in which they did.

The taxpayers of Ahmedabad find that the money collected from them is being mismanaged. They have the right to sue the Government for this mismanagement, but none of them comes forward to do it. The Government knew fully well that the people's representatives had spent the funds with the consent of the people and had launched a campaign against the Government. Even so, when the Government claims to act in the interest of the taxpayers, it knows that it was making a false claim and one knows why they acted in this manner.

In spite of the strictures passed by the District Judge and the disapproval of the people, the Government went in appeal to the High Court where it was dismissed.

[1]The District Judge gave his decision on the 14th April 1923. The Sardar wrote an article in the *Navjivan* dated the 22nd April 1923 about this case.

129

Vallabhbhai Deplores Government Action against Members of Municipalities of Ahmedabad, Surat and Nadiad

Navjivan, 22 April 1923

As a result of the fight of the municipalities of Ahmedabad, Surat, and Nadiad with the government, Government has filed suits in district courts against the members of the municipality, considering them as personally responsible for the money spent for education, when they were in charge of administration of that department. Out of three suits a judgement of the suits filed against the members of Ahmedabad municipality was delivered last week.

Yet, the judgments of the suits filed in Surat and Nadiad are not announced. In Ahmedabad suit 19 members were made defendants and amount of Rs 1,68,000 was claimed from them. Municipality had spent this amount after (for) primary education. The rules and standard which were observed, in spending after the education, prior to the quarrel with the government, were not altered after the quarrel, but were kept intact. Arrangement was also exactly the same. No changes were made in the curriculum or standards, or styles of running the schools. Every pie was spent after getting proper sanction of the government, only the difference was that municipality had rejected the right of government to hold examination of the education department or its right to inspect the schools, and as against that municipality had given up the government grant of one lakh rupees. Because of this government has taken recourse to all the stringent steps suggested in the Municipal Act, and used the most stringent remedy of suspension of the municipality. In spite of that the government was defeated. People with the help of their dismissed representatives ran independent schools. Government did not regain control on education, and that the government was not able to tolerate. At last government did an immoral act which it habitually does, in the name of maintenance of law and order. A suit was filed against those 19 members, who had started struggle for the removal of government control over education department to recover the amount illegally spent after education. The government has the audacity to file suit for recovery against the members of the municipality, which is duty bound by law to spend after education and that also in a civilised state—when local self-government department is transferred to elected representatives of the people—is an ample proof of the hypocrisy prevalent in the name of local self-government.

In Ahmedabad the government was defeated. Court dismissed the claim of the government and ordered the government to pay the legal cost to the defendants. Some are surprised by the court's decision. It is but natural that people who are habituated to injustice are surprised when they have an inkling of justice. But people are deluded by such rare instances of justice. Really speaking there was no effort to get justice in this instance. Only government can dare to demand such an open injustice, because it has the warmth of power. Government pleader had applied to the court to conduct the proceedings as soon as possible. If the judgement had been delivered earlier government would not have got anything. But this is usual method of impressing the court that government takes unusual keen interest, and to take as much advantage of the situation as possible. Government has with it department of justice. The highest officer of the department is paid thousands of rupees as salary. Government pleader also gets fat salary. In this government there is no court where government pleader is not there. In spite of having such legal help how did government dare to file a suit? Will the money spent in this law suit, and the money to be paid as cost to the defendants, will be considered as money well spent or ill spent? The huge amount that the government pleader will get for fighting this unjust suit will be considered as money well spent? Only in this government one can expect such hypocrisy, where gangs of respectable persons who make good use of money, file a suit to get it declared that those who spend their own money for education of their own children are squandering money. Had the local self-government not been in charge of the minister, such audacity would not have been there.

No taxpayer in Ahmedabad thinks that their money had been squandered, or improperly spent. Taxpayers have a right to file a suit, but nobody has filed a suit. The representatives had spent the money with the consent of the people and they had started a struggle against the government. Government has definite information about it. Yet why did the government pretend that it had filed a suit in the interest of the taxpayers? It is not a secret.

Government anyhow wants that agitation for national education should be curbed. This suit was filed with the intention to threaten, and to harass those who were in forefront in the movement for national education. Its defeat in the suit does not mean that it will sit with folded hands. It will try other means. For us it has devised a new weapon of compulsory education. Shortly a time will come when we shall have to fight against it. This fight has started on such an auspicious moment that uptill now on every occasion we have defeated the government, and we will defeat it many more times, because truth and justice are on our side.

130

Vallabhbhai Unhappy over Events in Gujarat and Other Provinces[1]

Navjivan, 22 April 1923

I had been touring outside Gujarat for the past six to seven weeks. I was with the Congress delegation which toured Calcutta, Bombay, Jharia and Rangoon and Mandalay in Burma. I find that a great change has taken place in Gujarat during this period that I was out of the province. I do not see signs of any new awakening among the people of Gujarat, but find that the Congress workers in the province are impatient to fill the jails. The Mahatma has been in jail for the past 13 months and there is hardly any unfortunate Indian who has been feeling easy during this period. Some persons had become very impatient after the arrest of Kakasaheb. Some persons brought a resolution before the Congress saying that the articles on the basis of which Kakasaheb has been arrested should be published. They were somehow or the other dissuaded from the enterprise. But Indulal was later on arrested. It appears now that most of the workers in Gujarat are itching for battle with the authorities.

Last week the Political Conference was held at Amod in Broach and I have gone into the views of Mahadevbhai which he expressed in his Presidential address to the Council. I also went into the resolution passed there which calls for

Individual Civil Disobedience by the workers. I also found that there were notices from persons that they wanted to violate the Salt Act individually. All these things bear witness to the pain which the workers of Gujarat are feeling and it grieves me. But I find that the feeling of unease and anger which informs the workers of the Congress in Gujarat is not evident among the people of the province. Whatever the reason might be—the people may not be liking what we want to do or there is something lacking in our way of working—one thing is clear. It is that we have failed to produce a leader in Gujarat who can take the place of Kakasaheb. The place vacated by the arrest of Indubhai is also vacant. It is our duty to see that there are workers who can take the place of those who are so eager to fill the jails in the province.

When I heard that the resolution for launching a civil disobedience movement was passed unanimously at the Amod Conference it warmed the cockles of my heart. I took it that three thousand workers of the Congress which Gujarat has produced were ready to jump into the fray. But, if those who raised their hands in support of the resolution Gujarat would have done its duty. But when I found that the volunteers prepared by Indubhai before he was arrested did not come forward, I was astonished. All the delegates from Bombay had voted in favour of the resolution passed at the Gaya Congress, but who is working to see that it is implemented?

Some of us might argue that once the struggle is launched, money and volunteers would automatically come forward. It appears to be that such a thing would be thoughtless because the hope of volunteers coming forward might not be realised.

We would continue to flounder so long as we do not understand that the independence of the country depends on the constructive work which we started in Bardoli. The time set apart for making preparations for launching a civil disobedience movement under the programme adopted at the Gaya Congress is yet to run out. To think that it cannot be done before that time is over and to launch the movement without adequate preparations would be a thoughtless act. The volunteers who are working in the field of education, *khadi* and the organisations of the Harijans have also taken the oath to work for the Congress. They are also itching to go to jail. But I think that they have not thought out the consequence of acting in haste. I am not happy at the prospect one single constructive worker going to jail. It would be extremely harmful to Gujarat. Those who are engaged in constructive work and want to go to jail should either produce their replacements or work with such vigour that the Government are forced to arrest them. Jail is for rootless persons like me who do not believe in constructive work. After April there would be no obstacle to the volunteers to court arrest. But even that has to be done in an organised manner.

No worker in Gujarat would leave his place. I would request all the workers that they should not try to court arrest so long as the Provincial Congress Committee does not permit them.

[1]When the Sardar had gone out of Gujarat to collect funds for the Gujarat Vidyapith, the Broach District Political Council passed a resolution in favour of the Civil Disobedience Movement. Sardar gave the above warning to the workers of the Movement in Gujarat.

131

Vallabhbhai Refutes C.R. Das's Criticism of Gandhiji for Not Accepting Lord Reading's Offer

Navjivan, 22 April 1923

What is the point of saying eight months after his release from jail that Gandhiji had committed a blunder by not accepting Lord Reading's offer? Why did he not say so earlier? Ever since he came out of jail, Deshbandhu has been attacking those holding views with which he is not in agreement, in the hope, presumably, of securing a general acceptance of his own views. For a short time after his release, he kept quiet on the subject of entry into Legislatures and discoursed in public only on religious and philosophical matters. Some thought that perhaps he might retire into solitude like Aurobindo Ghosh. At an opportune moment, however, he has taken charge of the movement which had been set afoot by Vithalbhai and others who were members of the Civil Disobedience Committee set up by the Lucknow Conference. At the All-India Congress Committee at Calcutta, the issue was debated but a frontal clash between the opposing parties was avoided. At the Gaya Congress, however, he joined issue with all his strength. When, however, the majority did not accept his view, he attacked the resolution of the Congress from the Presidential Chair and resigned from the Presidentship. He organized a party against the Congress and resumed his attack on the Congress policy. Finding, however, that the public was not sufficiently responsive, he accepted at Allahabad recommendation for a truce for two months. Finally on winning over the All-India Congress Committee, he has now at last regained courage and begun a frontal attack from Madras. Had he ventured to charge Mahatmaji in this bitter manner eight months ago, would anyone have listened to him? But that would not have been Deshbandhu's way.

132

Vallabhbhai on Struggle for Self-Government in Surat and Nadiad[1]

Navjivan, 22 April 1923

News has been received that a new chapter in the struggle for local self-government in Surat and Nadiad has started with a bang in Gujarat. A year has passed since the taxpayers in both the cities stopped paying taxes. In Surat many water taps were cut, yet people did not relent, so the officers of the revenue department were entrusted the work to collect the taxes by confiscating the property. There the confiscation work is in progress, since some time. In Nadiad the President of the Municipality was *Mamlatdar.* But he was not so hard hearted to torture people and confiscate their belongings he was transferred. New *Mamlatdar's* regime has begun. Besides that after having sanctioned the expenses of Rs 300 per month, the three officers of the revenue department have started the confiscation work in right earnest. The rule of law and good order prevails there with all its irritants, while confiscation is done no *Panchnama* is made and no independent witnesses are called, not only that even no receipt is given for the goods which are confiscated. *Mamlatdar* himself is taking out ornaments from the bodies. That guy is aspiring for deputy-collectorship. Armed police has been posted on police gates. Bandits cover their faces with black cloth at night and in speedily and disorderly manner do their work out of fear. Thus in broad daylight work is carried on in a disorderly manner. See the plight of slaves. The confiscators are ours, *Mamlatdar* is also ours. The buyers of confiscated goods are also ours, those who have usurped the seats which have fallen vacant due to resignations of our men are also ours, and poor men whose goods are confiscated are also ours. Those who are making us play this game are all throughout absent. The people of Nadiad are firm and if they remain firm, we will be victorious. Besides refusing to pay the taxes we must have to undertake the work of cleansing and lighting our streets, our victory will be earlier.

Notice to Borsad Municipality

Government shows its strength more in cities than in villages. When the village people become more conscious about their power, then we will be emancipated. The government which was fighting with Ahmedabad, Surat and Nadiad has been defeated by a small Municipality of Borsad. Government issued a small press note on 18th April in which it charged the municipality of mismanagement and disregard of Government orders. Then the Municipality is informed that if the people do not want the Municipality then Government shall have to close it. But before doing so it gives one more opportunity to the municipalities to improve, and put things in order and if it is not done by the coming 1st of September then there will be no other course left open for the government than to close the Municipality. If the people of Borsad have realised the bogusness of local self-government, then instead of waiting for the 1st September immediately they should pass a resolution and send it to the Government, stating Government should without any hesitation suspend the municipalities, so that people may get the opportunity to manage their own affairs. The institution in which there is no freedom to keep their streets clean and to teach their own children, what good such institution can do the people?

The Mismanagement stated by the Government in Press Note:

"1. The main source of income of municipality is tax collection. The annual tax is Rs 15,000 out of which this year only Rs 5,000 have been collected. The remaining ten thousand are not being collected. If the whole amount had been collected even then there would have been a deficit of Rs 2,700.

2. The Collector suggested to impose Municipal tax which was totally rejected by the Municipality.

3. Government had given a grant of Rs 5,171 to be utilised for a special purpose, which was used for other purpose and the grant money has not been returned.

4. Municipal servants are not getting their salaries regularly and teachers have to resort to strike for being paid the salary fixed by the government.

5. Mrs. Gandhi[2] and some Gopaldas of Vaso, were honoured in public function, and Rs 64 were spent on it. Though the Collector overruled the decision, but the Municipality disregarded the order of the Collector and spent the amount".

The Government has not liked that "some Gopaldas of Vaso" should be honoured, but once upon a time Government had claimed to be the friend of Gopaldas, and now as if it does not know him, he has been referred as "one Gopaldas of Vaso" in its press note. When Collectors, Commissioners and Governors were honoured, Government liked it, when in the corporation hall of Bombay a dinner function is held for Governor, Government likes it, but when those who are revered by the entire population are honoured, that Government objects on legal ground.

What is the use if such a municipality is retained in Borsad? If all the municipalities of Gujarat are suspended one by one then soon we will be able to attain true local self-government.

[1]Later, on the advice of Sardar Patel, the people started the movement for non-payment of taxes to the Municipality. The people of Surat also decided not to pay any taxes. The movement gathered momentum in both the cities in April 1923. The Sardar wrote in the *Navjivan* of 22nd April 1923, the article entitled "Local Self-Govemment in Gurajat."

[2]Kasturba Gandhi.

133

Vallabhbhai to Fight for Control of Education after Municipal Elections

Bombay Police Secret Abstract of Intelligence

AHMEDABAD
28 April 1923

The District Magistrate writes: "The recent trials of Yajnik and M.M. Bhat have aroused no enthusiasm whatever, and the non-cooperation party badly needs a new rallying cry else it will die, so far as Ahmedabad is concerned, of sheer boredom. I think that the confusion now prevailing in the minds of the non-cooperation leaders is very well shown by the different attitudes taken up about the need for going to jail 'as a sacrifice'. V.J. Patel has been expostulating with the young men and urging that it is futile and merely a proof of weakness; and it is significant that at a meeting on 16th April convened to congratulate Bhat on his impending imprisonment. Bhat said that he did not want to go to jail as by going to jail nothing was gained, but he said that he would go to jail as he was not prepared to withdraw what he had written. If these views are becoming more popular, and I think they are, the days of the 'jail martyrs' will be numbered. But it is difficult to see what the next move will be. Personally I think that so far as Ahmedabad is concerned it will centre round education when the new Municipality comes into office in February 1924 unless the Council elections have raised other issues. V. J. Patel says that the non-cooperators will get a majority of seats and will raise the same difficulty as before about the control of education by Government. I fear V.J. Patel is right in his views. I consider that the non-cooperators will be able to obstruct the new Municipality over education and will try to raise difficulties in the same way as before. The result of the recent suit against the 19 Councillors for recovery of monies 'misapplied on education' was against Government and was to the effect that the money was not 'misapplied' although the action of the Councillors was not legal. V.J. Patel's demand is that the Municipality shall have power to modify educational curricula as they think necessary but he had no objection to schools being inspected by Government inspectors in an advisory capacity. I think all this points to a non-cooperative attempt to capture the seats at the next elections in order to force this matter to the front. I know of no means of combating the claim except by measures which accentuate differences and lead to the embitterment of feelings. But I do think that unless something is done to clarify and defuse the situation the non-cooperation party will seize on the control of educational policy of Government in municipal schools as the best slogan for Ahmedabad. But the application of a campaign like this could be only local unless other issues were raised when feelings are roused.

The reports from the districts show that all is quiet. No trouble is anticipated in this district over opposition to the salt tax and it is not expected that efforts will be made to manufacture salt here.

134

Vallabhbhai not in Favour of Launching Civil Disobedience Movement before CWC takes Decision

Navjivan, 29 April 1923

The subject of civil disobedience is being discussed in Gujarat after my article appeared in the last issue. Some have liked my views and some have not. It is desirable that both the supporters and opponents of the Civil Disobedience Movement discuss the question. I think that we should wait till the session of the

Congress scheduled to be held in May next in Bombay or launch the movement earlier if the Bombay government force us as the Central Provinces Government had forced the volunteers in Jabalpur and Nagpur.

The Congress had passed the resolution that we should make preparations to launch the Civil Disobedience Movement. Another resolution had said that we should collect a sum of Rs 25 lakhs in the country and prepare at least 25 thousand volunteers in the provinces. The time during which this had to be done is now over. The Congress has asked the provinces to indicate as to how much work they have done in this direction. In some provinces, it has become impossible to implement this resolution. In the Gaya Congress, it were the delegates from Punjab who were the most vociferous supporters of the civil disobedience idea. But I find that the Congress organisations in that province are totally inactive. In the United Provinces also, the resolution has not been acted upon. It is not possible to implement it in Delhi either. It appears to me that in Bombay too, the workers are not eager to implement the resolution. In North India, the Hindus and the Muslims are sick of their fight against the Government. That is why the Government is instigating communal disturbances and the two communities are at each other's throats. Some people believe that the propagation of the principle of *Ahimsa* by Gandhiji has emasculated the Indians. Some leaders felt that the peace in the country was not something good and that an atmosphere of hatred had to be created. Now they must be happy because the Hindus and Muslims have given the go-bye to *Ahimsa* and are murdering and robbing each other. They think that that type of conduct is a badge of manhood. The newspapers on both sides are contributing to the perpetuation of this hatred and moneyed people of both the communities are helping with money. An attempt is being made to poison the atmosphere in the whole country. Under these circumstances, if the provinces where some preparations have been made, the civil disobedience movement could be launched, but that would not be proper. I think that we must give an opportunity to the Congress Working Committee to take a final decision in the matter after it has discussed the situation and made an assessment of the preparations made in each province to launch the movement. It would be better if we did not start the movement in every province, where full preparations have not been made but to take up arms in those areas where the government have given us sufficient reason and to help in that province. Our struggle would be more effective if Gujarat is prepared to send its volunteers to Nagpur or Jabalpur if need be and also help with money. Other provinces should also be prepared to help such struggles. Even if we want the Provincial Congress Committees to launch individual civil disobedience, it should be done after due consideration. When we start the movement, we should care to see that a situation is not created whereby no constructive workers remain out of jail. People tell me that they are no longer able to stay out of jails. I want to tell them that some of them must remain out and we should make arrangements to see that they are able to stay out of jail peacefully.

We must tell the volunteers about the goal of civil disobedience and about its consequences. We must understand that if the civil disobedience movement is unable to create any impact on the government in the present circumstances, we would not be able to achieve anything. A spirit of sacrifice and undergoing pain has been awoken among the people and we must take to civil disobedience in a disciplined manner so that that feeling is not destroyed. Whatever we do creates hopes in the minds of the volunteers and the people of the country. We must tell them the true facts so that they do not feel disappointed when the movement fails to create the impact expected of it. The civil disobedience idea would be useful only if we can continue our constructive work and that work is not interrupted because some workers have courted arrest. It is wrong to believe, as some people do, that staying out of jail does not achieve anything and that they must court arrest. If we honestly want to serve the people, the people would not let us go. We would have to change our methods of working. Our struggle is a long one. We must not be under the impression that mere zeal would produce the expected results in a hurry. If the workers' zeal is dampened, it becomes a big burden on them. That is why I say that a decision should be taken only after we have considered all aspects of the matter. On the 15th May, the Gujarat Provincial Congress Committee is meeting in Broach. All the matters pertaining to the movement would be considered at the meeting. Those who have signed the Congress pledge should, in the meantime, deeply ponder over this question.

135

Vallabhbhai Foresees Merger of No-Changers and Changers in Near Future

Navjivan, 29 April 1923

Tomorrow the time limit of the compromise between two groups of the Congress at Allahabad will be over. From tomorrow both the groups will be engaged in publicly propagating their views. From the very nature of compromise it appeared that permanent compromise was not possible. Difference of opinion is very wide. If one of the groups leaves its honest belief and merges in the other group, then only permanent unity could be a reality. But such an unity will be ultimately harmful. Country will be benefited if both the groups stick to their honest belief and propagate their views. It will train the people. Both the groups are highly patriotic and so if they feel that the welfare of the nation lies in abandoning one's identity and surrendering to the other group, they won't hesitate to do so. Many members of both the groups are pained because they had to part from the other group, and in future also they will be unhappy. Both the groups are going to merge in the end because their goal is the same though their ways might be different.

Some people have fear that when both the groups will start propagating their views there will be a fighting mood, emitting poison against the adversary, and there will be deep abyss between them, as a result prestige of the country shall be down. I think that such fear is unfounded. In Gaya session of the Congress though there was sharp difference of opinion, there was not dearth of tolerance or large-heartedness. As a result of three years' struggle people are well trained. The members belonging to the moderate group did not resign from the legislature till the end, yet I do not see any venom or a feeling of disgust towards them at least in Gujarat. Of course their prestige was lost, but because the prestige of legislature suffered, and so naturally they as members of legislature lost the prestige. But there is no reason to believe that people had any personal grievance against them. Therefore in propagating the boycott of legislatures, or taking steps for its implementation there is no reason to believe that if one group favours legislative entry will incur wrath of the people. There is no place for fear when there are differences of opinion between father and son, brother and brother, friend and friend. Yet, I have no doubt that both the groups will take necessary precautions to see that the propagation of their views produce adverse effect.

There is a possibility that we will not have the occasion to take stringent steps to implement the boycott resolution of the Congress. Government has made our task easy. The steps that government took in enhancing salt tax has enlightened the people's mind about the futility of legislatures. The members of legislatures have voted against it, and defeated the government thrice. Yet the Viceroy spurned the majority opinion. Now everybody desires that members of legislature should resign. Then instead of leaving the legislature after entering there, why not leave in the beginning? What else can we do except defeating the government after entering the legislatures by a majority vote? The present legislature defeated the government many a time. Yet when the government thought it proper, it has not cared for the majority view. Under such circumstances there is hardly any need to start a movement to explain to the people about the futility of legislatures. Therefore there is no possibility of poison being emitted, or any heart-burning will be there.

Yet it is advisable for workers and newspapers should be cautious and be on guard. Nobody should indulge in character assassination, and while discussing the issue there should be restraint on the language. It is the special duty of the boycott group that even if the opposite group commits any mistake, it had to be cool-hearted, and not to imitate the mistake committed by them.

136

Vallabhbhai Criticises Bombay Chronicle for its Report

Sardar Shrino Patro[1]

7 May 1923

DEAR MATHURADAS,

Mahadevbhai is in Nagpur these days and I am sure he must have met you before he left. I am in sick-bed and may continue to be ill for some more days.

The *Chronicle*[2] really crossed the limits. Even our opponents[3] did not make such shameless allegations. Who is behind all this?

What of the future? All are coming to Bombay.[4] Have you made arrangements for their stay? Has Rajendrababu[5] written to you?

Bande Matram,

Yours,
VALLABHBHAI

[1]In Gujarati, Vol V.
[2] A nationalist daily of Bombay.
[3]The Swaraj Party leaders.
[4]For the session of the Congress Working Committee.
[5]One of the chosen companions of Gandhiji, a senior leader of the Indian National Congress and constructive worker, Dr. Rajendra Prasad. He was thrice elected President of the Congress, was the President of the Constituent Assembly and the first President of independent India.

137

Vallabhbhai Advises Maniben to meet Gandhiji in Yervada Jail

Sardar Shrino Patro[1]

AHMEDABAD
12 May 1923

DEAR DAUGHTER MANIBEN,

My health is now improved, and there is no cause for anxiety. Today Mahadevbhai must have come to Bombay. He will see you.

You need not come here now. Bapuji has been permitted to see five persons in Yervada Jail.[2] Your name is included amongst those five persons. Within a week you will be going there. Respected Kasturba is also going. I shall inform you beforehand when she comes to Bombay. So, you go with her to Poona. See Bapuji and return with Ba. Then if you feel that it is not necessary to stay in Bombay then come with Ba to Ahmedabad. I am also coming to Bombay on 23.5.1923.1 might come there one day earlier.

Hope you are in good health.

Bapu's blessings

[1]In Gujarati, Vol. V.
[2] At that time Mahatma Gandhi was serving his sentence for "sedition" in Yervada Jail.

138

Motilal Nehru Defends Swarajya Party against Vallabhbhai's Views

Maratha, 13 May 1923

Pandit Motilal Nehru, the General Secretary of the Swarajya Party, has addressed a letter from Allahabad dated 1st May 1923, to the Members of the AICC and of Provincial Committees on the present situation as follows:

The compromise of the 28th February last between the two wings of the Congress ceases to have effect from today. There has been carried on an intensive propaganda in the interval by the No-Change Party to complete their preparations for Civil Disobedience according to their own conception. Leading members of that party have travelled far and near and carried the campaign to the furthermost limits of India and Burma. They have set an example of unceasing, unremitting toil which members of the Swarajya Party will do well to follow. I have nothing but admiration for their single-minded devotion to what they conceived to be their duty, and I hope it will not be taken amiss when I say that I am sincerely sorry that they have not met with the success they deserved. What we, who do not agree with them, were waiting to see was how the mechanical process of collecting money and registering volunteers would create the requisite mental and spiritual atmosphere needed for Civil Disobedience of the right sort. Unfortunately the day we were looking forward to has not arrived. Our friends have failed to get the men and money they counted upon and the unique experiment has not been tried for want of adequate material within the stipulated time. Disappointing as the result of this great endeavour to achieve its aim has been, it is impossible to suppress a feeling of keener disappointment at the thought of what might have been, if only the time, energy and money spent had been employed in a united effort to prepare the country to capture the Councils. Can there be any reasonable doubt that all the Councils in the country would today have been at the feet of the Congress to be dealt with, as the Congress pleased? Has not the result of the recent Municipal elections in the UP achieved by a minimum of joint effort a lesson of its own to teach?

Turning to the work of the Swarajya Party during this period we find that prominent members have given their time and attention whole-heartedly to the general Congress work, studiously keeping the Party entirely in the background. Mr. C.R. Das and I have spent most of the time in the Punjab and Hakim Ajmal Khan has, despite his falling health, not only rendered valuable services to the Aligarh National University, but has never failed to answer the call of the Punjab in its hour of need. The compromise only suspended Council propaganda and reserved to both parties, full "liberty to work the remaining items of their respective programmes in the interval without interfering with each other." It was however felt that nothing should be done to embarrass the other party in the work they had laid out for themselves, and all party propaganda was severely eschewed. This had the unfortunate effect of cooling down the enthusiasm of our organizers, the great majority of whom failed to carry out the very specific instructions given to them to establish provincial and district committees and complete the necessary spade work before the 30th April.

I regret to have to say that so far from doing any practical good to either party the compromise of the 28th February has materially prejudiced both. The idea has taken root among Congressmen and the general public that some similar or more permanent arrangement between the two parties will be effected. The terms of likely compromises have from time to time been discussed among both responsible and irresponsible people, the effect of which in my opinion has been disastrous to the whole movement. The expectation of an early coalition in the minds of the workers and the public has induced habits of sloth and given rise to an inclination to wait and see how things will take their final shape. As I have said elsewhere the constant talk of compromise has relieved the people of the necessity of thinking for themselves. They have left all the thinking to the leaders and are occupying themselves with the innocent pastime of breaking each other's heads.

The fact that a basis for a fresh understanding between the parties was arrived at in Delhi the other day has already been announced in the press and is public property. It is my duty, involving in my opinion no breach of confidence, to relieve the public mind of the suspense caused by the announcement. Mr. C. Rajagopalachariar has now wired from Ahmedabad to Mr. C.R. Das that the proposed understanding was unacceptable to Mr. Vallabhbhai Patel and Seth Jamnalal Bajaj, and the compromise has failed.

There are however certain Congressmen who are still building hopes of an amicable settlement at the meeting of the All-India Committee notified for the 25th May at Bombay. I earnestly beseech them to waste no more time in the pursuit of a phantasm. It is now abundantly clear that the only possible compromise between the two parties must permit entry into the Councils either by the withdrawal or suspension of the boycott. The alternative offered at Gaya has been tried and has failed. I can conceive of no arrangement acceptable to the Swarajya Party which ignores this obvious fact, and confidently assert that whatever happens the Party will not desist from contesting the forthcoming elections. This being so what is the clear duty of every member of the party? I go further and ask what is the clear duty of every true Congressman? Is this the time to wait and look on while the Moderates and hangers-on of the bureaucracy are putting forth strenuous effort to give the country another three years of Government by mock parliaments?

I have no desire to enter into a discussion of the merits and demerits of capturing the Councils. The question has been discussed threadbare and we have now seen the failure of the only possible alternative suggested. It will however not be out of place here to give you the impression I gathered in the Punjab. I have no doubt in my own mind that the Punjab Council is to a very great extent responsible for the communal differences which have arisen in that Province. You have only to glance through the reports of the interpellations and debates to see how that council has day after day and month after month been busily feeding the fire of communal disputes for the last three years. Are you going to let the flame envelop the other Provinces as well by leaving them to tender mercies of the existing type of the Council or for another term? Indications are not wanting that several districts in the UP have already been more or less affected by the happenings in the Punjab. I should have thought that collective individual Civil Disobedience was quite out of the question at a time when the whole of large Province was rent with communal disputes culminating in bloodshed. Chauri-Chaura was but a sudden outburst of mob frenzy in a small out of the way village. The causes of the Punjab trouble lie deep and are showing themselves in a sustained and determined hostility between two great communities numbering millions.

I am addressing this letter to all members of the All-India Committee and of the Provincial Committees of various Provinces as I take them to be the selected representatives of the Congress in the country. I divide them into the following groups:

1. Those who have already joined the Swarajya Party.
2. Those who were ready to be in the Party but were kept back by the compromise of the 28th February last.
3. Those who did not believe in the Gaya resolution on civil disobedience but were desirous of giving the majority who supported it a fair chance of carrying it out.
4. Those who were against dividing the Congress under any circumstances quite apart from their own personal inclinations.
5. Those who did believe in the Gaya resolution but have now seen that it would not work.
6. The waverers.
7. The diehards or those who will not countenance any change in the original N.O.O. programme whatever the circumstances may be and however much the public may be disinclined to follow it.

I have nothing to say to the last group as it is impossible to expect them to see things as I do. To the other groups I have a word to say.

I put it to those in the first three and the sixth groups whether it is not past high time to be up and doing? Have you not by this time seen enough to dispel all your doubts and misgivings ? Our friends are evidently anxious to keep their word and bring about some sort of Civil Disobedience as soon as possible. You have seen the Jubbulpore incident in connection with the National flag and are no doubt aware of a similar venture being contemplated at Nagpur. I confess I do not appreciate either the appropriateness or the utility of these undertakings. The net result will in my opinion be the temporary loss of the valuable services of some of the most ardent workers. Another idea has struck some of our friends in the South. They are going to disobey the Finance Act imposing the enhanced salt tax, but it is not stated how it is to be done. To an ordinary man of affairs, it seems that the tax not being a direct one the only way to withhold it is either to engage in the illicit manufacture of salt on the extensive sea board of India or else to smuggle it into our bazars. Do you take any of these proposals seriously? If not, what else do you expect in the way of immediate Civil Disobedience? I have not heard or read of any other suggestion and the anxious enquiries I have made on the subject have only met with evasive answers from the leading exponents of the doctrine.

Those of you whom I have classed in groups 4 and 5 will pardon me if I say that I do not understand your position. You think that the prestige of the Congress will suffer by a division among its ranks. But the division is there already and will not be removed by your backing the wrong party. And may I ask in all seriousness whether the prestige of the Congress is likely to be enhanced by the sort of civil disobedience I have just referred to? Some of you are very nervous about the results of the Council elections if they are not run by and in the name of the Congress. You instance the success of the Municipal elections in the UP as showing the great weight which the name of the Congress carries with the multitude and draw from it the illogical inference that the name of the Swarajya Party will not carry any weight if the elections are opposed in the name of the Congress. Need I remind you that the conveyance of every proposition is not true, and that the influence of the Swarajya Party with the masses has not yet been tried? I cannot conceive how people who had the bitter taste of the last Council Government can for a moment hesitate to throw in their lot with the party which approaches them with the election cry "mend or end the Councils". Can you imagine for a moment that the UP agriculturist will be persuaded by the siren voice of the moderate or the somber accents of the no-changer to grant a fresh lease of life to a Council which, by passing the Tenancy Act, has delivered him to the tender mercies of the Talukedar and the Zamindar? If you can, allow me to say that you do not know what is passing in his mind. Take it from me who have been listening to his grievances during the last two years that he is a highly practical person and is no longer to be led away from hard facts by any inducement. Besides, are we not as much of the Congress as the no-changers? Assuming without admitting that we will not succeed in taking a very large number of voters to the polls can you doubt that at least ten times the number which attended at the last election will gladly support us. I assure you that your nervousness is wholly unjustified and beseech you to save the Congress even at this eleventh hour. Allow another month to pass by and you will again be in the grip of the very Councils which have faithfully carried out the behests of the bureaucracy and helplessly looked on while autocracy ruled that land.

I have addressed this letter to you all as I believe that the real diehards are but few, and that the great bulk of the Gaya majority is composed of the other groups I have mentioned. Do not continue to delude yourselves with the hope of a common understanding either at the next meeting of the All-India Committee or at any other time in the near future. As at present advised Mr. Das, Hakim Ajmal Khan and I do not intend going to Bombay for the All-India Congress Committee meeting. We do not think our joining this meeting will serve any useful purpose. I beg you to throw off the spell, think for yourselves and come to a final decision without running further risks.

139

"Council Entry would be Suicidal for Non-Cooperation Movement"— Vallabhbhai

Bombay Police Secret Abstract of Intelligence

AHMEDABAD
18 May 1923

On May 18th a public meeting was held in Manek Chowk to celebrate the 14th Gandhi day. About 700 persons were present. Vallabhbhai J. Patel said that the non-cooperation movement had convinced every Indian that there could be no happiness without "Swaraj". The certification of the salt tax had produced a greater effect on the people than thousands of speeches. Referring to the pro-Council agitation he said that they could not understand how by capturing the Councils, the people would be victorious in their fight against Government. They might get some concessions, but they would not get "Swaraj". Government ruled over them owing to their weakness and by going to the Councils they would become doubly weak. They had already informed the Government that they would have no connection with it. They were sitting quietly now because they had no strength, but when they acquired sufficient strength, they would rise up against Government. The Council party argued that they should be allowed to go to the Councils as people were doing nothing, but he assured them that if they took the lead in going to jail, he would supply 2,000 men to follow them. Compromise was impossible. They would not interfere with them if they went to the Councils, but they would not give them their votes. There were many sub-divisions in the Council party and nobody knew what they would do after they entered the Councils. Dissensions were caused by the campaign for entry into the Councils. The agitation had a very depressing effect on the country and he was certain that if they entered the Councils the whole non-cooperation movement would die. Gandhi had advised them to boycott the Councils, and till his return from jail he could not advise people to do otherwise. He would have a referendum in Gujarat. He did not wish to create ill feelings by delivering speeches.

140

Vithalbhai Explains His Differences with Vallabhbhai on Council Entry

Bombay Police Secret Abstract of Intelligence

AHMEDABAD
19 May 1923

Vithalbhai J. Patel arrived on the morning of May 15th and stayed with his brother Vallabhbhai. In the afternoon a private meeting of the supporters of the Swaraj party was held in the Sansar Sudhara Hall. Nineteen persons were present. Vithalbhai explained that as the country was not prepared for civil disobedience and as by working the constructive programme alone, they were making no progress towards Swaraj, it was, therefore proposed that the Councils should be captured. They would there put the demands of the Congress before the Government and though by entering the Councils, they would not obtain Swaraj, yet they would be able to remove the obstacles to Swaraj. He advised them to work without creating bitterness between the pro-Council and the anti-Council parties. He said that by constant conflict with Government inside the Councils, the people would be prepared for civil disobedience.

Sixteen persons were declared members of the Swaraj party. Professor Jethalal C. Swaminarayen was elected president and Harilal Dalsukhram Saheba, secretary of the Ahmedabad Branch.

The same night Vithalbhai J. Patel addressed a public meeting in Manek Chowk at which about 1,000 persons were present. Manilal Harivallabhdas Bhagat presided. Vithalbhai J. Patel said that they had reached a critical period in the history of the country. Government was imposing new taxes year after year and the people had to pay them. Gandhi had been in jail for the past 14 months and they were unable to secure his release. Some of the leaders advised that they should carry out the constructive programme, others said that they should start civil disobedience and go to jail, and others said that they should send selected persons to the Councils in addition to carrying on the constructive programme. He was a believer in the constructive programme, but they all knew that little progress had been made in carrying it out. They did not want to wait for another 50 years, till untouchability had been removed and the whole of India wore *khaddar.* They wanted Swaraj which was their birth-right at once. This was their own country. Nobody had a right to ask whether they were fit or unfit for Swaraj. He was convinced that Government would yield only when mass civil disobedience was started simultaneously in every part of the country, and when people stopped the payment of taxes. The country was not prepared for such civil disobedience at present. They had to find some way of paralysing Government and putting it in such a position that it must yield to their demands. If they depended upon their constructive programme alone, they would have to wait till doomsday. There were two forces working against them at present. One was Government and the other the Council manned by the moderates. They could remove the latter force by capturing the Councils. They must now use their common sense. They must consider whether Vallabhbhai was right or Vithalbhai was right. If they allowed the moderates to go to the Councils again their movement would be crushed within the next three years. He was certain that if Vallabhbhai or Mavalankar were in the Council their Municipality would not have been suspended. He did not see any harm in going to the Councils.The Prantic Samiti should select men for the Council and thus displace the moderates. After that he would advise the boycott of British goods. The Government would be perplexed and might suspend the Councils and carry on the administration under martial law. They would then go to the taxpayers and conduct a campaign for the non-payment of taxes.

The District Magistrate remarks: "The split in the ranks of the non-cooperators over the question of entry into the Councils has become wider. The two V.J. Patels have been delivering exactly opposite advice to those who are against Government. What is a poor non-cooperator to do in the circumstances? All the same the apathy which surrounds the moderate party is itself, as a danger nothing whatever has been done to consolidate opinion in favour of the Councils by those who believe in them. It only requires some new battle-cry by the malcontents, such a one will rouse emotion and sentiment, to enable them to win many of the seats here. But they have first of all to make up their mind what they mean to do and at present they seem to be unable to do that. The election rolls were published during the week. The publications had excited no interest whatever. In view of the.fact that the Ahmedabad city roll in its present condition is very full of mistakes I consider that the lack of interest taken in the publication is a sign of complete apathy."

141

Vallabhbhai against Council Entry

Bombay Chronicle, 21 May 1923

Addressing a public meeting at Ahmedabad last night on the occasion of Gandhi Day, Mr. Vallabhbhai Patel said that the country was progressing only in some direction while in others there was no progress. People were learning the lessons of fearlessness, discipline and non-violence as was evidenced by the peaceful strike of 5,000 millhands of Ahmedabad, the Akali Movement and volunteers of Nagpur. They were not giving up Hindu-Muslim distrust and dissensions nor using *khadi*. Meanwhile there was raised the question of Council entry by persons who were placed at the helm of affairs by Mr. Gandhi. Council entry, according to Patel, would undermine the progress they had achieved. People, he said, would be awakened not by entering Councils but by working outside them. There was no unanimity among the advocates of Council entry.

142

Vallabhbhai Opposes Council Entry and Advocates Civil Disobedience

Bombay Police Secret Abstract of Intelligence

BROACH
26 May 1923

During the week the Gujarat Provincial Congress Committee met in Broach on April 20th. Vallabhbhai Jhaverbhai Patel, Professor Assudamal Teckchand Gidwani, Imamsaheb Ba Vazir, G.V. Mavalankar of Ahmedabad, Gopaldas Ambaidas Desai, Mohanlal Kameshwar Pandya, Kalyanji Vithalbhai Mehta, Pragji Khandubhai Desai and Mahadev Haribhai Desai were the more important members who attended. The total number of the Provincial Congress Committee members, I am told, is about 120 out of which only about half attended. Waman Sitaram Mukadam of Godhra (who, I know, is a pro-councilite) and Abbas Tyabji were conspicuous by their absence. Vallabhbhai J. Patel presided and in fact did most of the talking. The whole thing had been cut and dried at the earlier meeting of the Executive Committee on May 17th at Ahmedabad and was gone through without any obstruction worth the name. The resolutions passed were as follows:

1. That mass and aggressive civil disobedience should be postponed in view of the present unfavourable circumstances of the country. However individual defensive civil disobedience will be open at all times to meet any Government obstruction to the constructive programme.

2. That the national flag struggle in progress at Nagpur should be supported and Gujarat should contribute its quota by sending a contingent of Gujarat volunteers to continue the fight.

3. That necessary steps should be taken to carry on the boycott of Councils propaganda.

4. That greater attention should be concentrated within select areas for the completion of the constructive programme.

The chief interest centred round resolutions No. I and III. Pragji Khandubhai Desai moved an amendment in favour of starting civil disobedience in some form or other on the oft-repeated ground that there could be no salvation for the country without suffering but he agreed to withdraw it on the pressure of his other colleagues as Vallabhbhai J. Patel was anxious to score an unanimous opposition to the resolution passed with such great unanimity at the last Amod Conference. His chief grounds of appeal were—Firstly that the constructive programme was still incomplete and therefore they were not justified in taking up their last and the most effective weapon immediately. Secondly that the country being unprepared for civil disobedience the leading workers would have to go forward for the fight and if they went to jail, as they must, all non-cooperation work would automatically stop. This resolution was therefore passed unanimously. Mahadev Haribhai Desai, Professor A.T. Gidwani and Dr. Chandulal Manilal Desai, who were loudest for civil disobedience at Amod, were apparently won over by striking a compromise in the shape of resolution No. II to continue the civil disobedience at Nagpur with the assistance of the Gujarat contingent.

As regards resolution No. III (Boycott of Councils) Dr. Chandulal M. Desai had privately given expression to certain views in favour of the Das programme before this meeting came off. In the course of discussion he said that he was not keen on obstructing a trial of the pro-Council programme and should offer no effective opposition to those who cared to go to the Councils. This was however strongly opposed by Vallabhbhai J. Patel who insisted on effective boycott of Councils if non-cooperators as such cared to exist. As a result of voting, Dr. Chandulal, Krishnalal Narsilal Desai of Ahmedabad and Kalidas Jeshkaran of Ahmedabad and one other from Bardoli (whose name could not be ascertained but probably a schoolmaster) remained neutral and G.K. Mavalankar of Ahmedabad opposed.

Twenty-eight new Congress members were enrolled during the week.

143

Vallabhbhai Advises Pro-Councillors to Court Arrest[1]

Bombay Chronicle, 2 June 1923

At a public meeting held last night at Nagpur, Mr. Vallabhbhai Patel assured the Nagpur people that he would send from Gujarat 200 volunteers as a first instalment to join the fight for the Swaraj Flag. Referring to the proceedings of the All-India Congress Committee he endorsed the views expressed by Babu Hardayal relating to contesting the council election and stated that unless the pro-Councillors carry the Swaraj Flag and court arrest once or twice before the election, they could not approach the electorate to beg for vote.

[1]Speech was delivered at Nagpur on June 1.

144

Vallabhbhai to Send 200 Volunteers for Nagpur Flag Satyagraha

Bombay Chronicle, 2 June 1923

At a public meeting held last night, Mr. Vallabhbhai Patel assured the Nagpur people that he would send from Gujarat two hundred volunteers as a first instalment to join the fight for the Swaraj Flag. Referring to the proceedings of the All-India Congress Committee, he endorsed the views expressed by Babu Hardayal Nag relating to contesting the Council election and stated that unless the pro-councillors carry the Swaraj Flag and court arrest once or twice before the election they could not approach the electorate to beg for vote.

145

Chief Secretary Central Provinces to Secretary, Home Department regarding Satyagrahis arriving from Gujarat

Home Department (Political) Records File No. 280, NAI, 9 June 1923

Telegram P., from the Chief Secretary to the Government of Central Provinces, to the Secretary to the Government of India, Home Department no. C.-879-II, dated Pachmarhi, the 9th June 1923.

Clear the Line—More volunteers than were anticipated have been attracted by civil disobedience at Nagpur and over 400 arrests have been reported. In the hope that support from outside the province would not be forthcoming local Government has hitherto refrained from starting criminal cases under section 120-B of the Indian Penal Code against Congress leaders. But it seems clear now that the disobedience has the support of the All-India Congress Committee and that volunteers will arrive from other provinces, principally from Gujarat. Another difficulty (it) is that prohibitory order under section 144 Criminal Procedure Code expires on July 1st and there is legal difficulty about its extension or issue of new order. Local Government have therefore decided to arrest Congress leaders concerned at Nagpur and to institute criminal prosecution under 120 Indian Penal Code for which it is believed that the evidence available will secure conviction. This step may affect political situation in other parts of India and increase the amount of help for Nagpur civil disobedience from different provinces, and the local Government therefore enquires whether the Government of India desire to give any advice before this step is taken.

Telegram from the Secretary to the Government of India, Home Department, to the Chief Secretary to the Government of Bombay, no. 1387-D., dated the 10th June 1923.

Clear the Line—Telegram received from Central Provinces stating that owing to number of volunteers arriving from other provinces, principally from Gujarat, they contemplate taking steps against Congress leaders under section 120-B., Indian Penal Code. This may ultimately involve prosecution of certain leaders in Bombay as well as those in the Central Provinces. Government of India would be greatly obliged if Government of Bombay would wire immediately their views if such action would prove embarrassing.

146

Vallabhbhai to Mathuradas Expressing Disagreement with Jawaharlal on Arrest of only 6 Volunteers Daily

Sardar Shrino Patro[1]

AHMEDABAD
24 June 1923

DEAR MATHURADAS,

I am receiving many suggestions, but who is there to implement them? It had been decided to hold the meeting of the Working Committee on the 28th at Nagpur, but now it looks that a decision has been taken to hold it on the 6th July 1923.

Everybody in Nagpur has been arrested.[2] There is nobody left to look after the work in the city.[3] Those who had accompanied the volunteers from Gujarat have taken over today. Gujarati women had gone as volunteers and have taken over the kitchen duties. There is nobody from outside there. I am sending two good workers to look after the office work. Four women volunteers are being sent to help in the kitchen. The two workers who are due to go there would be posing as reporters, failing which they might also be arrested. A party of 50 workers from Broach would come to Ahmedabad after stopping for some time in some cities of Gujarat and would reach Surat on the 28th. I would be leaving for Nagpur either on the 29th or the 30th morning.

Work is going on apace in Nagpur. There is no hurdle in the way of taking out a procession with flags. But that would not help us in any manner. There are internecine troubles and nothing might be done.[4] Provinces where there are no disputes can get things done. Peace could be maintained while taking out processions.[5]

What is the reason why only six volunteers have been sent? Jawaharlal has issued a circular to that effect and I do not like it. We can shake up the country only if volunteers are arrested on way to Nagpur or hundreds of people in Nagpur are arrested. We can take advantage of the arrest of Jamnalal Bajaj only if we launch a powerful movement. I propose to send as many as I can from Gujarat.

I shall go (to Nagpur) only when I am feeling better.
Vande Matram,

Yours,
VALLABHBHAI

[1]In Gujarati, Vol. V.
[2]On the 17th June 1923, police encircled the vounteers' camp and arrested 250 of them including their leaders.
[3]Jamnalal Bajaj had taken over the command of the procession with flags. After his arrest, Sardar Patel took over the command.
[4]Congressmen had divided themselves, into two groups viz. who wanted a change, in other words getting into the legislative bodies and those who supported the non-cooperation movement. The Nagpur Provincial Committee was dominated by the Swarajists.
[5]The suggestion was that six volunteers should get themselves arrested everyday.

147

Vallabhbhai Not in Favour of Constructive Workers Courting Arrest

Navjivan, 24 June 1923

The programme at Gaya is the programme for Civil Disobedience. We have not had time to complete our preparations. To be in a hurry to start it before we are ready is suicidal. I realize that many who are constructive workers have also signed on as volunteers. They are anxious to go to jail but I am not ready to let a single person who is engaged in constructive work, go to jail. The prison is for people like myself, or for those who have no confidence in constructive work; even then they should not court imprisonment until the Provincial Committee has given them permission.

Civil Disobedience would be useful only if our constructive work continues. We must continue our constructive work, and only if by some of us going to jail, we are able to increase the tempo of that work, could we regard Civil Disobedience as useful. It is a mistake to think that because we cannot do anything outside, we help matters by going to jail.

148

Vallabhbhai Criticises Swarajists for Ignoring Resolutions of Working Committee for their Own Ends[1]

Navjivan, 24 June 1923

In Madras, Das Babu spoiled the whole thing because of his hurry. He made serious charges against Mahatma Gandhi. A public meeting was held in Mandvi on the occasion of last birthday of Gandhiji at which a leader of the Swaraj Party

Shri Vithalbhai Patel made forceful objections and said: "When one thousand Dasses cannot be equal to the little finger of Mahatma Gandhi, he has no right to say that Gandhiji was wrong. What is the good of saying eight months after release from jail that Gandhiji was wrong in rejecting the compromise offered by the Viceroy?" A follower of Das Babu like Shri Vithalbhai is unable to understand the reason, at which I am surprised. The meaning of the whole thing is very clear. Ever since Das Babu has come out of jail, he has been trying to persuade the people to follow him and has been criticising them. For some time after release from jail, he did not say a word about the question of the boycott of the assemblies. Some people thought that he might follow in the footsteps of Shri Aurobindo Ghosh and might take *sanyas.* But when the time came, he supported the rumours spread by some members of the Civil Disobedience Committee like Shri Vithalbhai and his friends. He tried his level best at the Calcutta session of the Working Committee and tried to create an atmosphere of uncertainty on this question. In the Gaya Congress too, he persisted in his attempts and when the people refused to give up the boycott, he questioned the very existence of the Congress as the President of the organisation. He submitted his resignation and went away while the Working Committee meeting was still going on. He raised a faction to oppose the Congress and when he came to Bombay he started attacking the Congress Resolution. When he found that his views were not acceptable to the people, he exercised some caution, went to Allahabad and for a couple of months kept quiet. When in the last Working Committee meeting, he came out on top, he regained his courage to attack the people again. He went to Madras and made serious charges against Gandhiji. Who was ready to listen to such things after eight months? It is generally supposed that the people are poor and that there is nobody to lead them. He thought that what he says would be quietly pocketed by the people, that no other leader would be available and there would not be any alternative before them except to believe in what he was saying. If a leader who has been in jail for eight months is attacked because of something he did or decided in the past, the purpose of such attacks becomes clear. It appears to be against the principle of the Swarajists to consider whether the means they adopt for their ends are pure or not. The difficulty is that the people of Gujarat will not take to such things kindly and will not tolerate that such charges are made against Gandhiji. That is why the leader of the Swaraj Dal in Gujarat, Vithalbhai, can face greater difficulties. That is why he has raised these two objections that what good would it do to Das Babu if he raised this matter and how would the Swaraj party benefit. This is the reason behind the statement of Shri Vithalbhai Patel.

Vithalbhai Patel says that he finds that the image of the Congress is being tarnished. He says in order to maintain the prestige of the Congress, we must accept and respect the resolution of the Working Committee. It appears to me that hypocrisy is now getting the pride of place in the Congress. Those who have thrown the honour of the Congress into the dust are shedding crocodile tears. They accepted only those resolutions which suited them but showed open disrespect for those resolutions which could come in the way of the fulfilment of their desire. They rebelled against the Congress by organising a new party. Are these the ways to defend the honour of the Congress? When the President of the Congress became the leader of the Gang of rebels and said that the Congress did not voice the feelings of the people but of a mere two per cent of the population, did he not see that the leaders of the Swaraj Party have not done anything except object to every part of the Congress programme merely for the purpose of serving their own selfish interests. Does the Swaraj Party care for the prestige of the Congress? Their real purpose is to force Congressmen to pass resolutions which they like and they want to sell the prestige of the party for the purpose of getting into the assembly. I do not see anything except cowardice in their attempt to honour only those resolutions which are passed with the support of the rebels because that means that the Congress resolutions are not implemented and the people's opinion is being trampled upon. If we listen to the views of these obstinate people under compulsion, the people will never rise. These people showed disrespect towards the Congress and are not prepared to accept its decisions taken at a special meeting. If we look at it from the point of view of morality and justice, the resolutions passed at the Bombay session of the Congress Committee are not such that they should be respected. Not only that, implementing or accepting those resolutions would be against pragmatism. They are a handful of obstinate persons even if they happen to be the great leaders of this country. They are being permitted to have their way. Those who give up their own decisions and also ask others to follow suit merely to appease such people are totally oblivious of the great harm that would come to India. If we want to save whatever is left of the prestige of the Congress, all the committees should oppose such persons. The only reply to rebellion is another revolt.

Mr. Patel says that "now even the workers and the leaders are divided and that there is no hope of capturing the assemblies. If the President of the Gujarat Provincial Committee learns to honour the resolution of the Working Committee, the prestige of the Congress can be enhanced. Even Mahatma Gandhi respected the decisions of the Working Committee". He is right. The parties have not risen today. If there is factionalism, it is the Swaraj Party which is responsible for it. Even today, we can restore the prestige of the Congress but for that these people must disband the Swaraj Party and give up hopes of capturing the assemblies. The day the Gujarat Provincial Congress Committee is assured that we can work honourably in the assemblies, it will not hesitate to decide to enter them. Gujarat knows Gandhiji better than it knows Mr. Patel. His party has utilized the name of Gandhiji but Gujarat has honestly tried to follow in the footsteps of the Mahatma. Gandhiji, the world and even God will pardon Gujarat for its weakness. But Gujarat would never be guilty of treachery. Gandhiji respected the resolutions of the Working Committee but Mr. Patel need not remind Gujarat of this fact. Gujarat knows that when Gandhiji was out of jail, the whole country hung on his every word. The leaders today do not respect the Congress resolution and are asking others to accept only that resolution which they like. The Working Committee in its meeting at Bombay had passed two resolutions. The Swaraj Party insists that only one of those resolutions should be respected. It is that committee which decided to help the Nagpur Satyagraha. In that there was no difference of opinion as there was on the question of entry into the assemblies. The Swaraj Party has yet to express its approval and respect for a resolution unanimously adopted at that meeting. If after the arrest of the Congress treasurer Shri Jamnalal Bajaj, who is a pillar of the Congress, we give secondary importance to the unanimous resolution and give the pride of place to the resolution on the assembly, how can the prestige of the Congress be enhanced?

[1]Vithalbhai started a campaign to persuade Congressmen to give up the boycott of the Assemblies. In reply, the Sardar wrote this article.

149

Vallabhbhai to Mathuradas on Nagpur Flag Satyagraha

AHMEDABAD
24 June 1923

DEAR MATHURADASBHAI,

Received your letter.

Many suggestions are made, but who is there to implement? It was decided to hold a meeting of the Working Committee at Nagpur on 28th. It appears that has been postponed to 6.7.1923.

All are arrested in Nagpur.[1] There is nobody[2] to look after the affairs there? The persons who had gone to give send off to Gujarati volunteers have looked after uptill now. Gujarati ladies had gone as volunteers. They managed the kitchen. Now there is nobody from outside there. I am sending two nice workers from here to look after office work there, and sending four persons to manage the kitchen. The two persons who are going will be sent there as reporters, because there is a possibility of their being arrested. A batch of fifty volunteers from Broach have come to Ahmedabad. They will move about in all important cities of Gujarat for some days and afterward staying at Surat on 28th, they will start for Nagpur on morning of 29th or 30th.

Nagpur work is getting more and more interesting. There is no difficulty in taking out flag processions. But it won't serve our purpose where there are mutual bickerings no work can be done?[3] Good work can be done in the provinces where there are no quarrels. Even though we take out processions we can maintain peace.

What is the reason behind sending six volunteers?[4] Jawahar had made that suggestion. I do not like it. The emotions of the people of the country can only be aroused if hundreds of people are continuously arrested at Nagpur or on the way to Nagpur. If we want to take advantage of Jamnalalji's arrest then our movement should be more vigorous. I am thinking of sending as many people from Gujarat as possible.

I will leave as soon as my health improves. That's all.

VALLABHBHAI'S
Bandematram

[1]On 17th June about 250 volunteers with their leaders were arrested after their camp was cordoned by the police.

[2]Jamnalal Bajaj had taken the leadership of Nagpur Flag Satyagraha. After his arrest Sardarshri had conducted the struggle.

[3]At that time Congress leaders had been divided into two camps, changers and no-changers, i.e. those who favoured council entry and those who were for boycott of councils.

[4]It was suggested that daily six volunteers should take part in satyagraha.

150

Vallabhbhai Feels Frustrated on Gandhiji's Advice to Suspend Satyagraha If Mohammed Ali Wishes

Navjivan, 24 June 1923

We carried on this fight until now to the limit of our strength and ability and kept the flag of non-cooperation flying. We are, however, all soldiers. There is no leader among us but there is one person among us who has an acute brain and who thinks clearly. The message which he has sent from his sick-bed has just arrived. He says: "I advise you to place the entire responsibility on Maulana Mohammed Ali. Do not do anything that does not please him. If he is very keen upon a settlement, well, accept it. I have a feeling that the country has to pass through bitter experiences. It is useless to discuss and to argue. There is no point in our preventing people from doing what they want. We have done what we could. We have lost many colleagues. We must not lose Maulana Mohammad Ali." I accept this advice.

I have thought a great deal and I see that I can help Maulana best by withdrawing my opposition. He says that I must consider the position of one who comes back after an absence of two years. He must have realized by now the difficulties of those who had remained outside during these two years. I know that by the stand I am now taking hundreds of young men will be disappointed. I am not sure that this resolution will not deal a death-blow to non-cooperation. Today we look upon each other with suspicion and without love. There is an attempt to reestablish affection. It was a painful task during all this period to oppose great leaders of this country. At the same time it is equally difficult today to give up that opposition. Nevertheless, I request all those who are in favour of 'no change' that they should willingly accept our present position. I place the entire responsibility on Maulana Mohammad Ali. Jamnalalji and Gangadharrao

Deshpande, who have been my colleagues in opposition, hold the same view as myself. If I may sum up our attitude in a sentence, we do neither support this resolution nor oppose it.

151

Vallabhbhai Urges Gujarat to Join Nagpur Flag Satyagraha[1]

Bombay Police Secret Abstract of Intelligence, 1923

AHMEDABAD
30 June 1923

Forty-four volunteers from Broach under the leadership of Dr Chandulal M. Desai arrived at Ahmedabad in the afternoon of June 28th and were taken in procession through the city to the river-bed. About 450 persons took part in the procession and large crowds of spectators lined the streets. They were presented with flowers at various places. On the arrival of the procession at the river-bed, a public meeting was held at which Vallabhbhai J. Patel presided.

He said that they had assembled there to congratulate the Broach volunteers who were going to Nagpur to take part in the National Flag Satyagraha movement. Broach had set a good example to Gujarat, and a time was coming in the near future when every young man in Ahmedabad above the age of 18 would have to go to Nagpur. He was proud to say that, in spite of Hindu-Moslem disunion in some parts of the country, half of the Broach volunteers were Hindus and the other half Mohammedans. . . .

Vallabhbhai Patel, in bringing the meeting to a close, said that he, Balwantrai P. Thakore, Jiwanlal Hariprasad Diwan and Dr. Kanuga were prepared to go to jail on behalf of the national flag. He saw no enthusiasm in Ahmedabad. They were all enjoying themselves in wedding processions and caste dinners. For the past three months he has been incurring debts in order to carry on the national schools. He was going to appeal to the young men of Gujarat; he wanted to create a desire in the youths of Gujarat to go to jail. How could they stay out of jail when Jamnalal Bajaj, the fifth son of Gandhiji, was in jail?

[1]The flying of the National Flag on Municipal Buildings and public places was prohibited by the Government. In April 1923 a meeting of Congress workers in Nagpur Municipality was held when National Flag was hoisted in place of the Union Jack. It was resented by local authorities and Jamnalal Bajaj, a prominent Congress Leader of Wardha, was arrested while leading a procession of Congress volunteers carrying the National Flag. Vallabhbhai was entrusted with the direction of the Flag Satyagraha at Nagpur. In response to Vallabhbhai's appeal, hundreds of volunteers from all over India began to pour into Nagpur and took out processions with the National Flag. In spite of brutal beatings, the volunteers remained non-violent and courted arrest. The jails became overcrowded, the Government saw the persistence of the Satyagrahis and eventually released them. A triumphant procession was taken through the Civil Lines, the Government abstained from taking any action.

152

Vallabhbhai Calls upon Gujaratis to Volunteer for Participating in Nagpur Flag Satyagraha

Navjivan, 1 July 1923

Oh! you residents of Gujarat! Have you heard the mysterious sound of drum beats from the holy warfield of Nagpur?

Remember, the flag that was hoisted on the pandal of the Congress session, held on the banks of Sabarmati in presence of Mahatma Gandhi, is being dishonoured at Nagpur. The foreign power ruling us having seen our lethargy and diffidence, has become shameless and it seems it is determined to pull down the national emblem which has been accepted by India.

Now the battle is not of Nagpur alone. All-India Congress Committee has resolved to turn the holy land of Nagpur into a battlefield of India's religious struggle. On Gandhiji's last birthday the soldiers from different parts of the country dedicated their lives in this great sacrificial fire. Gujarat also creditably contributed in it. Heartless, and power drunk Government servants considered those innocent and brave soldiers as vagabonds, and jobless creatures of lower strata, have added insult to injury. Do your hearts bleed because of the insult? Do you feel that you have been branded by iron rods?

One rarely gets such pure, and nice golden opportunity to sacrifice. Every country has sacrificed thousands and lacs of lives for their flag.

No country has got most precious object like flag without sacrifice. Today we are fighting for retention of our flag. Government has also made tremendous preparations to fight against us, which indicates the great importance of our fight.

When the very existence of non-cooperation is doubted when non-cooperation has become an object of mockery, we cannot lose this opportunity to show the purest form of non-cooperation. This is a fight of self-defence. Our object is not to insult anybody, anybody's life or property or anybody's flag. We have not the least intention of troubling the foreigners who are rootless vagabonds, who have come here to earn their bread by snatching the bread of hungry people. But we are determined to extricate ourselves from their claws.

A time has come when Gujarat is put to test. Uptill now we had not got the opportunities to give tremendous sacrifices. I desire that when such most precious occasion is knocking our doors, Gujarat which is in agony because it is separted from Gandhiji, will welcome this God-send occasion and show its mettle. Recruitment work has started. Get yourself recruited as satyagraha soldiers, sign the pledge, and march towards Nagpur when ordered.

153

Vallabhbhai to Maniben asking Her to Serve Kasturba

Sardar Shrino Patro[1]

AHMEDABAD
3 July 1923

DEAR DAUGHTER MANIBEN,

Your letters are received regularly. Received one letter from Ramdasbhai[2] also. There is not yet total improvement of my health.[3] But I don't want to get operated for the present. There is a possibility that by regular washing for some days it might be cured.

I am starting by evening train tomorrow. Tomorrow I will go to Bombay. I will stay there for a day and next day I will start for Nagpur. I will be able to reach Nagpur on seventh.[4]

Mahadevbhai was to come with me. But same day he received by wire the sad news of his father's demise. So, today he will go to his village by night train.

Dahyabhai is enjoying.

You and Ramdasbhai go and serve Ba[5] extremely well. Thanks all.

Bapu's blessings

[1]In Gujarati, Vol. III.

[2]Mahatmaji's second son, constructive worker.

[3]About his nose trouble. This trouble was there throughout his life.

[4]On 17th June the Central Provinces Government had arrested Jamnalal Bajaj in connection with Nagpur flag satyagraha. Because of this incident a Congress Working Committee meeting was called at Nagpur from 7th to 9th July.

[5]Mahatmaji's wife, Kasturba Gandhi.

154

Vallabhbhai to Mahadev Desai to Collect Money and Recruit Volunteers for Satyagraha

Maniben Collection, 12 July 1923

This is indeed a stimulating struggle. If only the people are united, it would be possible to make the Government yield within a week. But here we have an orchestra in which every player plays whatever tune he likes. All the English newspapers are either opposed to the struggle or are indifferent. The publicmen seem interested only in getting their own point of view accepted. The Government of the day is very determined. In spite of these difficulties, we have to see that the attention of everyone in the country is focussed on Nagpur. The Government have already discovered that the fight is far from over. Workers have started coming in accordance with my programme. On the 3rd there is a meeting of the Executive Council of the C.P. Government and on the 6th the Legislature meets. The Flag question is bound to be considered in the Legislature, but that will not lead to a solution. It will only give the Government an opportunity to express itself strongly against us. But it might enable us to discover the Government's intentions.

In the next issue or two of *Young India,* you must appeal for money. The appeal should be well drafted. Keep on asking also for more volunteers. It does not look as if they are likely to arrest me in the near future. When I first arrived, they had no good reason for arresting me; now that the movement is regaining strength, they might reconsider the matter, but I doubt if they will do any thing until after the Legislature adjourns.

Let Devadas not be wholly tied to his work of the Press. Let him move about a little; he does not yet know Gujarat well and Gujarat must also come to know him.

I hope you and Devdas will be able to find time to look up my children; they should not feel desolate. I cannot understand why Maniben wept. This is not the time to weep. She has plenty of courage. After giving advice to people in C.P. to go to jail, how can we cry?

Please tell Ba to be ready to go to jail. If it is possible, issue an appeal over Ba's signature to the women of Gujarat to come forward to join her, when she leaves for Nagpur on the 18th. The present order expires on the 17th. If the Government extends it, women also must take part in the movement from the 18th; that cannot fail to arouse the country. We must proceed on the assumption that the Government will prolong the order. If it does not how can they continue to keep the volunteers imprisoned?

Remember me to everyone in the Ashram. Give my *pranam* to Ba.

155

Vallabhbhai Appeals for Men and Money to Succeed in Flag Satyagraha in Central Provinces

Navjivan, 12 July 1923

The Congress Working Committee has ordered me to stay in the Central Provinces so long as the satyagraha continues in Nagpur, I am going to Nagpur today. Only God knows how long I would have to stay away from Gujarat. I had not even dreamt that I will get an opportunity to serve another province. I am not worried about Gujarat because Gandhiji's soldiers who are more faithful than I am are here to serve the people. I have no doubt that they would be able to bear the responsibility for Gujarat. What worries me is what I would be able to achieve in the Central Provinces.

The fight in Nagpur is not of the Central Provinces but of the whole country. Every province has welcomed it by sending its volunteers there. The honour of the country would suffer if we are not able to carry on the struggle in a disciplined manner. Every battle needs not only soldiers but money too. The Government does not lack highly paid officers and the low-paid policemen. The Britishers are fighting with other people's money and would not lack for it. We will not face any shortage of volunteers because every province is prepared to send them. These fighters will not have to be paid any salaries. But vast sums would be needed for them when they are in Nagpur. Volunteers coming from Madras would need a sum of Rs 60 per head for rail fare. Some provinces do not have any funds. How can we carry on this major battle without any money?

If we want to send our volunteers in this battle we would need Rs 5 lakhs for rail fare alone. One single Marwari might be able to contribute that amount. When I had toured the country in the company of Jamnalal, many Marwaris had joined the Congress. I have seen that the Marwari community loves Jamnalal very much because he has served them well. Would his sacrifice not melt the heart of the Marwaris? I am sure that if the Marwaris are told of our need for funds for this struggle, they could easily send us the required sum. I have sent Manilal Kothari to give this message of mine to the Marwaris.

But my real hopes are centred on the people of Gujarat. When there was nothing but darkness and despondency throughout the country, it was Jamnalal who had, single-handed, created an atmosphere of sacrifice and had attracted the attention of the whole country. Gujarat gave its sons as sacrificial offering. If we allow the struggle to flag for lack of money we would lose our honour. If the Gujaratis want they can rain money on the Gujarat Provincial Congress Committee. Volunteers who cannot take part in the satyagraha for lack of money would welcome such a thing. I am sure that Gujaratis, wherever they are, would hear this message of mine and would send their contributions to the Secretary of the Gujarat Provincial Congress Committee.

156

Vallabhbhai's Message to His Followers to Work for Peace and Hindu-Muslim Unity during his Absence to Nagpur

Bombay Police Secret Abstract of Intelligence, 1923

AHMEDABAD
21 July 1923

July 18th was observed as Gandhi Day almost throughout the district. At Ahmedabad, the procession was chiefly formed of students of the national school, local leaders and women; they carried flags, and at intervals sang the Bharat Nishan song.

At 7 a.m. a meeting was held in the river-bed. Kalidas Jaskaran Jhaveri proposed Vallabhbai J. Patel to the chair who was supported by B.P. Thakore and Abu Jaffer Nadvi.

V.J. Patel said: "To-day is the sixteenth month of the Mahatma's imprisonment, and we have the opportunity of making sacrifices after a year and a half. I have been to Nagpur and have been permitted to interview the Kaira and Broach prisoners and I learnt from them that the Gujarat volunteers behaved very well, and knew the purpose of the movement. The volunteers were at first arrested near the Zanda Chowk, but are now being arrested at the railway station. This matters very little. I have been directed by the All-India Congress Working Committee to take up the work of the Nagpur movement where I am proceeding shortly. Before leaving, I, however, wish to say a few words, as I am not certain when we shall meet again—Preserve Hindu-Moslem unity; keep on friendly terms with the Parsis; always keep on good terms with the Police and other Government officials as this is very important; be friendly with the Moderates and Swaraj party.

The Gujarat people, he continued, should either go to Nagpur or do constructive work, failing which they should sacrifice a year's income. The Municipal struggle at Surat, Nadiad and Ahmedabad has earned a name which I appeal to you to uphold. The next election takes place in January, and I advise you to send such representatives as will not fear civil suits in lakhs. My last request is that you should do nothing to harm our cause. . . .

V.J. Patel left Ahmedabad for Bombay on July 21st from whence he will proceed to Nagpur to join in the Swaraj flag struggle. There was no *tamasha* on the station at his departure. He announced at the meeting about that he would stay in Nagpur as long as the campaign continued.

157

Vallabhbhai Appeals to Marwaris to Donate Liberally for Success of Satyagraha

Navjivan, 22 July 1923

Readers can read elsewhere in this issue about the appointment of Sardar Vallabhbhai Patel as the director of the Nagpur Satyagraha by the Congress Working Committee. Shri Patel left on Friday for Nagpur, after making the following appeal to the people to help in this Satyagraha:

The fight in Nagpur is not the fight of the people of Central Provinces, but of the people of India as a whole. All parts of the country have accepted the fight as their own by sending their volunteers. The honour of the country demands that the fight is carried on in a disciplined and organised manner. Every war needs soldiers and money. The Government has highly paid officers and has no dearth of low-paid soldiers. When you are fighting a war with other people's money, you can not lack for material resources. We also have plenty of soldiers, but of money there is shortage. It costs Rs 60 to bring one volunteer from other parts of the country to Nagpur but none of the provinces have any money. How can we carry on this fight without money?

If thousands of volunteers are to be sent to Nagpur, we would need a sum of Rs 5 lakhs for rail fare alone. This is not a very large amount; one of the Marwari businessmen might be able to contribute it. I had come in contact with many Marwaris when I toured the country in the company of Jamnalal Bajaj. I was present at the Marwari convention. I found that the Marwaris loved Jamnalal because he has served his community well. Will not his record of service inspire the Marwaris? I am sure that if the Marwaris are told about our need they would easily give us the money. I am sending Manilal Kothari to the Marwaris with this appeal for funds.

158

Vallabhbhai Advises Satyagrahis Released from Jail to Teach Love and Not Hatred

Navjivan, 22 July 1923

We have had today a first-hand account of the hardships which our brothers have had to endure in jail. They are naturally very angry, and it is understandable that they should have described in a somewhat emotional way the hardship and the inhuman treatment they have had to undergo in jail. But we should be careful not to exaggerate. Besides, instead of concerning ourselves with what Government servants should have done or should not have done, let us think of what we have failed to do. Before looking at their faults, let us look at ours. It is our duty to fit ourselves for discharging what we consider to be right. My advice to those who have come out of jail is that they should teach our people the twin lessons of love and of duty. That should be their main task. May God give you strength to fight many more such battles in the interest of truth and duty.

159

Vallabhbhai to Maniben not Expecting Arrest

Sardar Shrino Patro[1]

NAGPUR
23 July 1923

DEAR DAUGHTER AND SON DAHYABHAI,

I came here yesterday[2]. . . . uptill now nobody has touched me. Respected Kaka[3] is coming here tomorrow from Bombay. Shankerlal Parikh[4] is also here. If there is anything worth knowing, then you will know about it.

Do not worry. That's all.

Bapu's blessings

[1]In Gujarati, Vol. III.

[2]After Jamnalalji's arrest the A.I.C.C. Session held at Nagpur, had put Sardar Patel in charge of Flag Satyagraha, and so he had reached Nagpur on 22nd July.

[3]Vithalbhai Patel. He has played a leading role in the negotiations with the Central Provinces Government.

[4]Constructive worker of Kheda.

160

Vallabhbhai's Advice to Participants in Nagpur Flag Satyagraha

Navjivan, 23 July 1923

I have informed all the provinces of the number of volunteers they must send and the dates on which they must arrive. Volunteers should, accordingly, continue coming every day so that at least 50 would be available for arrest at the station.

After four or five days, we shall make such changes in this programme as may be necessary.

161

Gopaldas's Sacrifices Fit to be Written in Letters of Gold[1]

Navjivan, 30 July 1923

The lease-holders of Charotar considered their land dearer than their life. An old proverb says: "If the land is taken over by somebody, what is left?" Many lease-holders have given up their lives and gone to the gallows for the sake of their lands. The main work in the Government courts and offices is to resolve land disputes. It is the most prominent among this class of lease-holders. Bhai Gopaldas, who has gladly washed his hands of his land which gave him an income of more than Rs 30,000 per year because of his commitment to duty.

Gopaldasbhai is the Darbar of Dhasa village of Kathiawad and the Talukedar of Rai Sankli. He was educated in the Princes College. He got many opportunities of mixing with the political agent, the Governor and knew what to wear, how to behave on special occasions. He also hunted with them, aped the Englishmen and was trained in how to behave in the Darbars. But he never got involved in this kind of life because of his culture of an earlier life.

When the Governor of Bombay came to Kathiawad on the last occasion, Gopaldasbhai participated in the struggle for Swaraj in the Kheda district under the leaderhip of the revered Mr. Abbas. It was there that the Political Agent sent him orders to come to Kathiawad to welcome the Governor. But Gopalbhai listened to his commander in the struggle for Swaraj and respectfully disobeyed the order of the Political Agent. At this, both the civil and the criminal powers were taken away from Gopalbhai. The Bombay Government asked him to apologise for his being unable to be present to welcome the Governor and to dissociate himself from the Civil Disobedience Movement. Gopaldasbhai very humbly, but with firmness and courage, refused to apologise and said that it was the religious duty of every Indian to take part in the Civil Disobedience Movement. The result was that on the 17th July 1922, the government started attachment proceedings in Dhasa and Raisankli. At the same time, in that very ground, girls from the village started a *Garba* song which described the incident. The police inspector had notices of attachment affixed to the houses in the village and started telling everybody that he was their *Darbar* from that day.

The people of the area revere Gopaldasbhai as a God. He has won over the hearts of the people with his love. The Police Inspector's conduct angered the people. Fortunately, Gopaldasbhai was there and he pacified the people. The school in the village being under the control of the Agency, the children have stopped going to it. Arrangements are being made to start a private school. After the attachment proceedings, the people of the area have taken a pledge that they would no longer practice untouchability and would wear only Swadeshi clothes.

The Government may have taken over the Taluka but Gopaldasbhai has won over the hearts of the people. It is the people's hearts which the Government can never influence. The matter, however, will not end there. It is possible that the people would be subjected to atrocities by the government. A time is coming when their love for peace would be tested.

Gopaldasbhai has given up his powers, and goes about barefoot in the villages of Gujarat in the service of the people. There will be many people who might say that he has committed a folly. It is not surprising that there would be people who might say that a person who gives up a property from which he was having a large income for the sake of what he considered his duty is a fool. But the age in which physical comforts and money were the only things that mattered is going to be over. I am sure that the sacrifice made by Gopaldasbhai would be written in golden letters in the history of Gujarat. His example would inspire thousands of youngmen. I am proud that I have a companion like him in our battle for justice.

[1]The Government attached the Taluka of Darbar Sahib. The Sardar.wrote an article on this on the 30th July 1922 in *Navjivan.*

162

Vallabhbhai asks Maniben to Borrow Money from Congress Office when Required

Sardar Shrino Patro-3

NAGPUR
31 July 1923

DEAR DAUGHTER MANIBEN AND SON DAHYABHAI,

I had gone to Calcutta for two or three days . . . I returned yesterday. I received your two letters after coming here. . . .

If you want money, office will give you debiting from my account. So when you want you can collect from there. Don't suffer difficulties. Don't worry. Be cheerful.

Bapu's blessings

163

Vallabhbhai Exhorts People to Join Flag Satyagraha (Extracts from Police Report)

Home Department (Political), 1923
File No. 280, 2 August 1923

A meeting was held at the Town Hall last night and was addressed by the two Patels, the audience being about one thousand. Munjee and Cholkar were both present, and the former was proposed for the chair but refused to take it. The speeches made by the two Patels are interesting and may be taken to indicate the lines on which the attack in council will develop. I have therefore thought it better not to boil them down for the purpose of this report but to enclose the police report in original with the copy of this which goes to the Commissioner. Both speeches contain direct incitements to the people of Nagpur to join in the flag movement, and were delivered with an obvious eye on the council. The only point on which it is necessary for me to comment at present is Vithalbhai's assurance, given as a responsible servant of the Congress, that Satyagraha has not the slightest intention of annoying Europeans or hoisting the national flag on Government buildings or insulting the Union Jack. As pointed out by the *Times of India* in a recent leading article, not one of the persons who made the statements attributed to them in the last Government communique has publicly denied that he used the words attributed to him. This belated assurance is therefore only a move in the game. Another point which speakers like Vithalbhai do not seem to appreciate is that whatever rights of this nature a man may consider that he possesses, common decency and good nature will stop him from exercising them if he sees that their exercise annoys other people—however unjustified he may privately consider that annoyance to be. Every man, for instance, has a right to whistle in a public restaurant, but if his fellow diners complain, he cannot be surprised if the manager chucks him out. The meeting was closed with a short speech by Tijare in which he definitely asked that people should come forward and volunteer to celebrate the anniversary of Tilak's death.

164

Vallabhbhai to Maniben regarding His Arrest

Sardar Shrino Patro[1]

NAGPUR
12 August 1923

MY DEAR DAUGHTER MANIBEN AND SON DAHYABHAI,

Received your letters. . . . the conditions here are unsettled,[2] but now it appears that I won't be arrested. Whether the fight will continue or stop will be decided on 18th.[3] Nobody is to be called from Ahmedabad or Gujarat till it is decided. It is difficult to arrange for the boarding and lodging for all, and besides, unnecessary expenses are incurred.

Both of us are well.

Bapu's blessings

[1]In Gujarati, Vol. III.

[2]In this connection it may be mentioned that Central Provinces Legislative Assembly session was held for a week. At that time, Vithalbhai Patel had through the elected members of. the Assembly, got some resolutions passed, condemning the policy of the Government regarding Nagpur Flag Satyagraha. But Governor had made use of his special powers and declared them null and void. In spite of that the Governor of Central Provinces was conducting negotiations through a member of Executive Council with Vithalbhai concerning this matter. This was the political atmosphere when this letter was written.

[3]Sardar had made all arrangements ready for mass Satyagraha on 18th August; women also were going to take part in it, and one batch of women Satyagrahis of Gujarat under the leadership of Kasturba was to go to Nagpur.

165

Vallabhbhai Instructs Congress Workers regarding Celebration of Flag Satyagraha Victory

Congress Office Circular, 18 August 1923

The public statement issued by Shri Vallabhbhai on 16th has been published in the editorial of yesterday's *Navjivan.* Its copies were printed on Friday and distributed amongst the volunteers as well as general public of the city. A copy was also sent to the Police Chief of the place. As stated therein, a procession of five volunteers was to go with flags to Sadar Bazar passing through the roads which were prohibited.

Thereafter it came to our notice that 18th of this month is on Saturday. Saturday is observed as rest day from the beginning of this struggle. So, the procession which was to be taken out on 17th was decided to be taken out on Saturday the 18th and Friday the 17th was declared as rest day, and it was announced that a procession of about hundred volunteers will march on 18th, i.e. 17th auspicious day of imprisonment.

A batch of hundred volunteers was selected. Shri Makhanlal Chaturvedi was appointed as the Commander. In order that the procession may proceed, maintaining the seriousness of the occasion, every volunteer was intimated to observe the following rules of discipline.

Instructions to the Volunteers

1. The Commander will march with a flag in his hand, and other volunteers will wear flag batches.

2. There should not be unnecessary crowds gathered on the roads through which the procession proceeds which might cause inconvenience to the passers-by or people living in vicinity.

3. The persons in charge of management of procession should make such arrangement from the office building to Christian Church that it would be quite evident that we care for the sentiments of the whites living in our country.

4. *Route of the procession.*—As usual the procession will take this route—from Zanda Pul, District Office, pass through Court of the Judicial Commissioner and Secretariat buildings, then march forward to Lai Bungalow, which is in the corner where four roads meet. Then turn to the road on left hand side, then from the front of Commissioner's office, go to the northern side of Telanbedi tank, proceed towards Sadar Bazar. *Time.*—The procession will start at 12 noon from National Flag Satyagraha office, and will reach Sadar Bazar at about 2 p.m.

A public meeting was held in the Town Hall grounds, where there was a huge audience. Pandit Makhanlal Chaturvedi presided.

As Shri Vallabhbhai Patel was invested with the powers, being appointed as a conductor of Nagpur Satyagraha by the Working Committee of Indian National Congress read a public statement in the meeting.

"I had issued a statement on behalf of the Working Committee on the day previous to 17th May, the day on which the prohibitive order of the District Magistrate banning the taking out of procession from the elite locality expired. It has been published in the newspapers. I had announced in that statement that a procession of five volunteers will start from the prohibited area of elite locality. On 17th August simultaneously detailed instructions were published regarding the route of the procession as well as the norms to be observed by the volunteers. I had made it clear that if the procession is not allowed to proceed then the struggle will take a new turn. As soon as the statement regarding the programme of 17th was published the District Superintendent of Police issued an order as per Police Act banning taking out of the procession from 'elite locality'.

"Now it so happened that 18th—sacred Gandhi day—was Saturday. Uptill now Saturday was observed as rest day. But how can a sacred day be observed without sacrifice? So, I made a change in the programme and decided to observe 17th as a rest day, and announced that the procession which was to start and pass through banned routes will start in the same way and taking the same route, and will consist of one hundred volunteers. The copies of this new programme were widely distributed and one copy of the statement was sent to the District Superintendent of Police for information. On 18th, procession under the leadership of Pandit Makhanlal Chaturvedi with National Flag in his hand started from the city with the pomp and dignity and entered the prohibited area. It passed through Railway bridge, Zanda Chowk, High Court, District Court, went in front of office of the Commissioner, then passed through Christian Church and reached Sadar Bazar. It was not stopped at any of those places.

"Thus the dignity of National flag is admitted at last and we have regained our right to take out National Flag procession in a peaceful and orderly manner through the public roads. I consider this as a victory of truth, non-violence and penance. Hence by the grace of God, I am in a position to declare on this auspicious day that Nagpur Satyagraha has victorious end, as it is fought according to the letter and spirit of Gandhiji's advice.

"I am grateful to various provinces which have enthusiastically helped and exhibited strength of national integration. I will be ungrateful if I do not congratulate those brothers and sisters who have suffered and are suffering miseries for the motherland and honour of the national flag, and who have gird up their loins for the struggle. I take this opportunity to publicly thank those who have directly and indirectly helped me in launching this struggle, conducting it, and culminating it to a victorious end."

"Now I officially declare that Nagpur Satyagraha is terminated from this evening. Vande Matram."[1]

[1]Due to indisposition Vallabhbhai after reading this statement did not give a speech. So Rajendra Babu gave a lengthy speech.

166

Correspondence between Secretary of State and Government of India on Negotiations between Patel Brothers and the Government

Home Department (Political) Confidential Records N.A.I., File No. 280, 21 August 1923

Telegram P. . from Secretary of State, to Viceroy (Home Department), no. 3087, dated London, the 21st (received the 22nd) August 1923.

Nagpur flag demonstrations. It is reported in Press telegrams dated 19th and 20th August from Allahabad to *Times* and *Daily Telegraph* that permission was granted to procession through civil station, and brief statements explaining the matter are given. Will you kindly let me have a full account of what was done and reasons for the action of Government.

Telegram from the Chief Secretary to the Government of the Central Provinces, to the Secretary to the Government of India, Home Department, no. 146-A., dated the 23rd August 1923.

Your telegrams of the 21st and 22nd August. Flag agitation. Full information has been sent already by Governor in two demi-official letters addressed to Sir M. Hailey and negotiation for settlement were initiated by the Patel brothers as representatives of Congress Committee with the Home Member. They also asked for an interview with Governor which was granted. As a result of the negotiations a settlement was effected. A declaration was issued by Working Committee that *one* they did not claim the right unrestricted to take processions quietly on public roads. *Two* the processions are not intended to annoy any section of public. *Three,* there is no intention to insult Union Jack. Further the Patel brothers accepted additional conditions that before any procession was permitted there should be an application to the District Superintendent of Police and that processions would strictly abide by conditions laid down by Government as regards (1) the route did not include the strictly residental portion civil station; (2) The time of the procession; (3) The limit of numbers; (4) Orderly conduct with no singing songs or shouting *jai* beyond a fixed point on the route. Further Patel brothers undertook that after this single procession a declaration would be made that Satyagraha ceased and that no further processions would be taken into the prohibited area except one which would be taken under exactly similar conditions if and when prisoners were released. These negotiations were carried out under a promise by both sides that they would not be published. The procession took place August 18th when application was made to District Superintendent of Police and the conditions were strictly observed. The same evening Satyagraha was declared to be ended and no attempt has since been made to bring any procession. We intend to release prisoners after a few days when the second procession will be permitted.

Telegram P., from the Secretary to the Government of India, Home Department, to the Chief Secretary to the Government of the Central Provinces. No. D.-2214-Poll., dated Simla, the 25th August 1923.

Clear the Line.—Flag agitation. Reference your telegram no. 146-A., dated the 23rd instant. We should be glad to know whether release of prisoners formed an integral part of the agreement with the representatives of the Congress Committee, and if so what were the precise terms. In particular whether anything was said which might be construed as promise or as indication of future action. If release of prisoners was not part of the agreement any general release should be deferred pending further communication from the Government of India. In any case, Government of India consider that prisoners, if any, convicted of offences involving violence or guilty of serious prison offences should not be released.

Telegram P., from the Government of the Central Provinces, to the Secretary to the Government of India, Home Department, no. C.-43. dated the 26th August 1923.

Clear the Line.—Flag agitation.

During negotiations Patel brothers pressed for the release of prisoners but were informed that no undertaking could be given and that they must trust in the judgement and good intentions of the Government. Failure to release will be regarded as justifying non-cooperation creed and distrust of British good faith especially as subsequent declaration that Satyagraha had ceased. There has been a discussion between the Home Member and Patel regarding the arrangement for the repatriation of prisoners. Local officers support the release. The retention of prisoners under the security section when civil disobedience has ceased cannot be justified and the District Magistrate in whose discretion this matter lies is in favour of release. Instructions have been issued deferring the release of the prisoners until your further communication is received.

No Satyagraha prisoners have been convicted of crime of violence and local Government has already decided not to release those convicted of prison offences until they have served their sentences under that Act.

The above is with reference to your telegram of the 25th August.

Telegram (Cipher) from the Secretary to the Government of India to the Government of the Central Provinces, no. D.-2227-Poll, dated the 1st September 1923.

Clear the Line.—No Nagpur Flag agitation. Reference correspondence ending your telegram no. C.-43 of 26th August. Government of India recognise serious embarrassment of situation to local Government, dislocation of normal administration involved and possibility that any indiscretion on part of subordinate officers might at any time have gravely aggravated these difficulties and incidentally they desire to express acknowledgement of tact, and judgment shown by local officers during a period of prolonged strain. Nevertheless, while sympathising in their desire to find a solution for situation Government of India regret that the Government of Central Provinces considered it necessary, as they infer from your telegram to the case, to enter into understanding involving release of prisoners. On this point, in view of our endorsement no. 312 of 9th February 1923 and of effect on general political situation of action proposed, Government of India consider that they should have been previously consulted. They also consider that promise to permit second procession on release of prisoners is liable to much misconstruction and will be claimed by Congress Party as a substantial success. On careful consideration, however, of your telegrams of 23rd and 26th August they recognise that they must accept the view of the local Government that any withdrawal or variation at this juncture of terms arranged would be construed as breach of faith and will probably lead to a renewal of agitation on this highly unfavourable issue. They have decided therefore not to advise any modification of the action proposed.

They are, however, of opinion that in order to counteract the misleading reports which have appeared in the press, a full statement of the action taken by the C.P. Government should be published as soon as possible. It has, for instance, been alleged that interview with Patel Brothers took place at instance of His Excellency the Governor and that no application for license for first procession was made. If a written application for a license was made it appears desirable to publish it. It would also be desirable to require written applications for any future procession.

As regards the return of prisoners from other provinces Central Provinces Government might consider expediency of arranging for their transfer to jails in their respective provinces before release with a view to reduce the possibilities of local demonstration. Government of India agree that action in regard to security prisoners must depend on discretion of magistrates in respect of modification of circumstances which originally necessitated security.

167

Government's Confidential Report about Release of Nagpur Flag Satyagraha Prisoners

Home Department (Political) Confidential Report
N.A.I. File No. 280 of 1923
21 August 1923

Telegram from the Central Provinces Government, no. 146-A., dated the 23rd August 1923.

The report may be communicated to the Secretary of State as in the draft submitted for approval. His Excellency should first see. It will be seen that full information has been communicated to Hon'ble Member at Calcutta, demi-officially.

J.M.D.,—24-8-23

The draft is for approval. The Secretary of State asked for the reasons of the Central Provinces Government but no reasons have been given. The reasons are fairly obvious and we may send the telegram without comment. My own feeling is that the Central Provinces Government went too far in the matter of compromise. His Excellency should see.

G.H.W. Davies,—24-8-23.

It is necessary I think to indicate the views of the Government of India on the action taken by the local Government.

We had no intimation of the intention of the Central Provinces Government to negotiate and on this point Sir M. Hailey's telegram of the 3rd July is relevant. We pointed out clearly that the assurances which would alone justify the withdrawal of the order under section 144 of the Criminal Procedure Code must bear directly on specific grounds for Government's action hitherto, *viz.*, vindication of law and maintenance of order. The actual terms of the present agreement go far to satisfy the stipulations in our telegram. In view of this and of the fact that the agreement promises to abate what had become rather a public nuisance than a serious agitation, I think that we should support as far as possible the action taken, though I must confess that I am doubtful of the desirability both of negotiating at all, and, in particular, of the permission to hold a second procession.

An addendum to the draft in the above sense in submitted.

3. I think we should advise the local Government that releases should not include any prisoners convicted of offences involving violence or guilty of any serious prison offence after conviction. We may also inform them of our general approval of the course taken.

J. Crerar,—24-8-23.

His Excellency agrees that the substance of the Central Provinces Government's telegram of 23rd August should be telegraphed at once to the Secretary of State and that it should be stated in the communication that the comments of the Government of India will follow when one point, on which information has been sought from the Central Provinces Government by clear the line telegram, has been elucidated.

2. His Excellency considers that enquiry may be made by the Home Department from the Government of the Central Provinces whether the release of prisoners was part of the agreement with representative of Congress Committee or whether anything was said to them which might be construed as a promise or as an indication of future action. If release of prisoners was not part of the agreement Central Provinces may be asked to defer general release until they have heard again from the Government of India on the point. In any case, they should be asked not to release those guilty of violence or of serious jail offences.

G.F. de Montmorency,—25-8-23.

Telegram from the Government of Central Provinces, No. C.-43, dated the 26th August 1923.

It is clear from the Central Provinces Government's telegram of 26th that though no actual undertaking for the release of prisoners was given, there was a pretty definite understanding to this effect. Otherwise the reference to "distrust of British good faith" and to the procession after the release of prisoners would be meaningless.

Whatever may be said of the decision to negotiate at all, if the understanding regarding release and if the second procession, it seems clear that interference with any material point of the settlement would involve the local Government in a charge of breach of faith and probably lead to an aggravated recrudescence of the agitation. It appears therefore that the "fait accompli" should be accepted. Drafts to the Secretary of State and the Central Provinces Government are submitted.

J. Crerar,—27-8-23.

His Excellency does not approve of the draft *vide* his marginal notes on draft. Will Mr. Crerar kindly ring me up and I will explain further. His Excellency's objections mainly rest in the two newspaper cuttings below received with the Central Provinces telegram of August 23rd.

G.F. de Montmorency,—27-8-23.

In the Central Provinces telegram about the Nagpur flag business there is a sentence about the Home Member of the Central Provinces Government discussing *"repatriation"* of released prisoners with Mr. Pala. His Excellency thought this improper; but as it is a minor point, he does not wish to raise it: but he wishes the Secretary, Home Department, to discuss with him what *repatriation* means.

I explained to His Excellency the system prevailing in most provinces by which when a convict is sentenced, he may be imprisoned in any jail in the province and transferred from one jail to another; but eventually when he is about to be released one *e.g., Mohammad Ali's transfer* of two courses are usually taken, either he is *to the Jhansi Jail* transferred to a jail near his home and his release takes place there or he is given a free warrant on release to his home railway station (*e.g.,* the Sikh prisoners from Amritsar who were confined in the Attock jail).

H.E. observed that there seemed to be something almost Gilberton in a situation where the extremists pay the tickets of persons from S. Madura or Guzerat to come to Nagpur to annoy Government and commit a technical offence and at the end of the sentence or on release from a well deserved punishment in conviction the Government are at pains and expense to repatriate them to their homes.

G.F. de Montmorency,—27-8-23.

Letter from the Government of the C.P., no. 163-1, dated the 1st October 1923.

The Secretary of State has asked for a full report by mail on the whole matter of the Nagpur flag incident with the comments of the Government of India. The report from the C.P. Government has now been received.

2. The flying of the national flag began to assume prominence in the latter half of 1922. There had been earlier demonstrations at Bangalore and Bhagalpur but the present agitation commenced with a resolution of the Jubbulpore Municipality in July 1922 to present an address of welcome to the Civil Disobedience Committee and to hoist the national flag on the Municipal buildings. The local Government and the Government of India thought it wise to ignore this action of the Municipality but subsequently at the instance of the Secretary of State the. Government of India took steps to prevent the flag from being flown on the buildings of Municipality and other local bodies and in their letter no. D.-7341, (Poll. File no. 941 of 1922), dated the 17th August 1922 they issued general instructions on the subject of flying the flag. In March 1923

signs of organised attempts to fly the flag were perceived at Jubbulpore and the persons behind this movement shortly afterwards shifted their ground to Nagpur, where the battle royal was waged. On the 6th June the Congress sitting at Nagpur decided to take up the flag movement as an all-India affair and to extend the agitation to other provinces. Sporadic but unimportant outbursts of flag-flying occurred in Bengal, Bombay and elsewhere and the 18th July was proclaimed as an all-India flag day when the flag was flown in several places in India. The movement did not take on and by the middle of August, it may safely be said, all general interest in it had ceased except so far as regards the struggle at Nagpur and its effects, an account of which is given in the P.U.C.

3. It is not easy to estimate correctly what was the driving force at the back of the movement and what is its exact significance on the political situation. The movement I think originally arose as an expression of national sentiment. The apostles of non-cooperation had for some time been preaching national self-reliance, boycott and Khaddar and it was natural that a desire for an emblem of national significance should spring up. The fact that the adoption of a national flag would be resented by the members of a Satanic Government as an insult to the Union Jack doubtless lent a fillip to the idea, and if as they thought probable, the Government took strong measures to put down the national flag, this incident would afford a fine rallying ground for the party and would furnish a useful battle-cry against Government. They were hampered, however, by the fact that by the creed of their party they were pledged nominally to non-provocative measures and they had to keep in the background the provocative aspect of their programme and as Government steadily refused "to hang men and women for the wearing of the green" or to take repressive measures against casual exhibitions of the flag, their guns were spiked from the start. Their difficulties were intensified because the Swaraj party which was daily growing in strength was bent on obtaining for its own ends an effective position in the Government of the country and was entirely opposed to frittering away its energies on a campaign which, however great a victory it might bring in matters spiritual, would have little effect on practical politics and would bring no real power in the material world. In fact the cleavage within the ranks of the Congress had become so pronounced that the time when the flag agitation at Nagpur reached its height that the Swaraj party were anxious to see the no-change party (who ran the flag movement) defeated in their battle with Government. The governing factors therefore appear to have been that the No-change party were anxious to obtain a victory for non-violent non-cooperation that would exalt their party in the eyes of the Swarajists, that they did not openly desire to clamour for severance of the English connection, that they were precluded by their creed from pressing the provocative aspect of their programme and that the Government refused to take offence where possibly offence was meant. Moreover, there was a large body of loyal Indian opinion that would regard an insult to the Union Jack as an insult to the Crown. The movement accordingly was proclaimed to be a form of Satyagraha or civil disobedience, an attempt to assert the rights of the individual as against the laws enforced by a Satanic Government.

4. On the other hand the position of the Government was not easy. Every Englishman I feel sure, resented that flag movement first and foremost on the ground that it offered an insult to the Union Jack and Government must have shared this sentiment. But the admission that the blow had gone home would only encourage more blows and the agitation if encouraged by repression might easily grow to alarming dimensions. Moreover, the weapons of defence were limited. Flying the national flag, however much it might be reprobated, was not in itself an offence and there was no certain ground for action unless the movement developed into an attack on Government in its functions of maintaining law and order. The Government therefore controlled their injured feelings and ignored the movement as far as possible, until it came into collision with Government on an issue on which it could be safely fought. Before long the tactics adopted by the Nagpur agitators furnished such an issue. In carrying out their programme of flag-processions as a part of civil disobedience, they came within the scope of the preventive sections of the Criminal Procedure Code because they annoyed certain sections of the community and they clashed with the police because they refused to observe the law relating to the conduct of processions in public places. The Government of the C.P. were not slow to seize the opportunity to fight from a strong tactical position. The District Magistrate issued an order under section 144 Criminal Procedure Code on 1st May prohibiting meetings and processions within part of the area of the civil station and again a fresh order under the same section on 18th June extending the prohibited area. The latter order would expire on 18th August and could not be repeated unless there was likelihood of a riot or an affray.

5. It is quite clear from the proceedings of the C.P. Legislative Council that towards the beginning of August pressure was brought on the local Government to compromise and the Council proceedings for 7th-9th August showed that the majority of the Council disapproved of the action taken by the Government. In fact the Hon. Mr. Joshi admitted at a later date that pressure from the Council had forced the Government to release the prisoners. The Government appear to have yielded to this pressure because they were weary of the struggle which was holding up the ordinary administration and because they were in doubt as to their ability to succeed in retaining command of the position without the help of section 144. The daily average number of volunteers coming forward in August showed a considerable increase.

6. The main points of the compromise agreed to by the Government were logical enough from their point of view. They had fought on the grounds of law and order and submission to authority and once the flag party yielded in these matters they saw no point in continuing the struggle. They imposed conditions that turned the procession in "a funeral procession" instead of a triumphal procession. They had to give away something to effect the compromise so they agreed to release the prisoners, an act which was likely to appease popular opinion and which seemed innocuous now that law and order had been vindicated. From

their point of view there could be no strong objection to a second procession on similar terms to the first.

7. The question is what judgment is to be passed on this act of compromise. I have attempted to show that the C.P. Government were driven by circumstances to fight on somewhat narrow issues and those issues they proved victorious. At the time I cannot help feeling that the C.P. Government was rather like a mouse in a cage; they could see no world beyond the walls of their little prison. The Union Jack was undoubtedly flouted because the Swaraj flag was allowed to be carried in procession through the civil station; and it does not really make much difference that the Swarajists declared that they intended no insult and agreed not to carry their procession through what is euphemously described as "the strictly residential portion of the civil station." And the feelings of annoyance of the resident in the Civil Station can hardly have been lessened by the knowledge that their patriotic objections had become of no account to Government, as no longer furnishing a legal ground of action under section 144. The granting of permission to hold the second procession which did not eventually take place was even a worse mistake from this point of view. As regards the release of the prisoners, I think a wholesale release was injudicious. There could not be much harm in releasing those who were confined for not giving security or for disobeying the order under section 144, particularly as the majority of them were mere tools in the hands of unscrupulous persons; but it is more difficult to justify the release of persons who had deliberately organised a criminal conspiracy to defy law and order. It is true that the retention of these men in jail would have marred the effect of the amnesty and would have proved a standing source of embarrassment to the Government, but the dangerous doctrine that men by professing repentance can escape the consequences of their actions is much too prevalent in this country. I do not, however, think that much blame can be attached to the C.P. Government for the action that they took. Their attention was naturally focussed on the early cessation of an irritating and embarrassing struggle, in which on the whole local feeling did not support them, and they saw a way to secure a victory on the issues on which the battle was fought. There can, however, be no question that the flag-flying incident as a whole was of more than merely local interest and they should certainly have consulted the Government of India before deciding to enter into negotiations and, particularly in view of our letter of the 9th February 1923, before releasing the prisoners.

8. The end of the struggle appears to have been hailed as a victory by the "No-Change" newspapers and generally speaking as a defeat by the Anglo-Indian and Swaraj newspapers. The attitude adopted by the Anglo-Indian press was due to their reluctance to attach any importance to a discreditable performance and due to the fact that the issue had been narrowed down to a battle between civil disobedience and law and order. The Swaraj organs were only too glad to seize the opportunity of pouring contempt on their political opponents and attempting to make capital out of their mistakes.

9. It would seem appropriate to address the Secretary of State in a despatch and in commenting the incident we may lay stress on the following points:—

(*a*) The instigators of the movement made an injudicious choice of an instrument of agitation—there was no deep-seated feeling in the country in favour of a national flag.

(*b*) They made an injudicious choice of the time for this agitation—the Swaraj party which was growing in strength and vociferousness was hostile from the start.

(*c*) Partly through the restraint of Government and partly as the result of their creed the agitators were compelled to fight on an unfavourable battle-ground.

(*d*) The C.P. Government adopted sound tactics in fighting on the ground of law and order and localising the struggle as far as possible.

(*e*) The C.P. Government, showed too great anxiety to compromise at any cost. Their hands were forced by local sentiment, by the fact that the expiry of the order under section 144 would weaken their armoury, and by weariness of the struggle which to them appeared to be increasing in intensity. From their point of view the terms of the compromise were not unsatisfactory, but it is impossible to treat the incident as of merely local significance. The wholesale release of the prisoners and the permission to hold a second procession were liable to be represented as admissions of wrong and were likely to have repercussion outside the province. They should have consulted the Government of India before entering into negotiations on these matters.

(*f*) In the light of subsequent happenings it is difficult to say that the action of the C.P. Government has resulted in any untoward effects. Circumstances have prevented the anti-Government press from uniting to hail a victory and politicians are much too busy with preparations for the coming elections to think much about the Nagpur campaign; but organised flag-flying will quite probably occur in the future and it may be doubted whether the hands of Government have been strengthened for dealing with agitation by the results of the struggle at Nagpur.

10. The replies to the four questions specifically addressed to the C.P. Government are:—

(*i*) When negotiations were opened the local Government had reason to believe that the agitation was increasing in force. I question whether their assumption was altogether correct. Locally the number of volunteers may have been increasing, but I think that the country generally was beginning to realise that the agitation was futile and it may be doubted whether funds would have been forthcoming for long to continue the battle.

(*ii*) The local Government admit that they should have consulted the Government of India before releasing the prisoners. As regards the processions they contend that they merely followed the policy approved by the Government of India. Logically this contention is correct as has been pointed out, but the struggle was of more than local interest and I think we should have been consulted.

(*iii*) The local Government claim that their decision to allow the processions was logical and cannot be regarded as a triumph for the flag movement or an admission that their policy was wrong. Here again they seem to be right from their own point of view, but they seem to be wrong when the general significance of the incident is considered. But circumstances have prevented any general claim of victory for the agitators.

(*iv*) The local Government claim that they did not modify their original attitude recently justified in the Legislative Council. I have gone through the debates and this contention seems to be correct, both with regard to the speeches of the Home Member and to the statement made by the H.E. the Governor, which is referred to in para. 8 of the paper under consideration.

G.H.W. Davies,—12-10-23.

It will be necessary for H. E. to read the C.P. letter, and Mr. Davies' note from paras 2-10 gives a useful summary of the various aspects of this incident. I need not recapitulate and proceed to give at once my own conclusions on the matter.

2. From the first the "National Flag" controversy never was,—and by its nature could never have been, a purely local issue. Earlier incidents at Jubbulpore forced it on the attention of the Central Provinces, and those incidents as the C.P. Government were aware, had attracted wide attention both in India and England. When therefore the demonstrations at Nagpur assumed the aspect of a concerted campaign, the C.P. Government rightly took up the challenge. In view of the fact that the exhibition of the Flag was not in itself an offence, their legal position was not an easy one; but they maintained a sound, firm and perfectly consistent policy in regard to flag processions. Their local officers behaved with discretion and restraint, and were successful in preventing any incidents which could give vitality and substance to what was really a factitious agitation. The movement commanded little support, but attracted wide interest outside the province; yet the interest did not extend to general sympathy with the agitators. Moderate opinion was opposed to them; the Swarajist party was lukewarm where it did not openly criticize the expenditure of energy and enthusiasm in so mistaken a cause. So much was this the case that towards the middle of July it appeared likely that the movement would collapse.

3. The apprehension of this failure was indeed so imminent that the extreme Congress party at large decided to come to the assistance of the agitators from the C.P. and Gujerat who had hitherto mainly interested themselves in the movement. But this fact, if it threatened increased embarrassment to the Central Provinces Government, also affected their own position. The issue had never really been local it now became more than ever, and on a wider scale, a contest between the general administration and the forces organized against it. The Central Provinces

Government itself recognized this; the Governor had recently personally consulted the Viceroy and the Government of India and could have been under no mistake as to their attitude towards the new phase of the operations. To all appearances the Governor was prepared to continue to take a firm line against the agitation, in spite of the obvious embarrassment caused to his local officers and the general administration of this province. In his speech to the local Council on the 6th August he said:—

> The Local Government regards this agitation as clearly Civil Disobedience, an attempt to overcome the authority of Government, and is determined that this challenge to lawful authority, this defiance of the law, should be resisted with all the resources at its command. In this policy it confidently hopes for the support of all law-abiding citizens, including the members of this Council.

4. A few days after he had delivered that speech, his Council passed two resolutions calling for the withdrawal of the prohibition orders and the release of the prisoners. In both cases, the majority against Government was narrow; and I hold that in view of the character which this conflict had assumed, a local Government could not allow to a vote of this kind the influence it might have carried in a purely local matter. Indeed the only new feature in the situation at this stage—apart from the wider scope which the agitation was taking under the influence of the Congress—was the fact that the order of the Magistrate was about to expire (it would expire on 17th August) under the ordinary operation of the law. In the debate of the 7th August the Home Member referred to this fact, and stated that the order would not be renewed unless there existed a likelihood of an affray. The legal position is fully stated in paragraph 2 of the Central Provinces letter, and the Home Member was perfectly correct in the attitude he took up on this aspect of the question. But the provisions of 30 (1) and 30 (2) of the Police Act remained, and the local Government was by no means without means of maintaining the policy announced by the Governor. The Police Superintendent could under 30 (1) prescribe the route of processions and under 30 (2) require a license to be taken out if in the opinion of the Magistrate there was danger of a breach of the peace. It is maintained in the C.P. letter that the Magistrate could give no such opinion. Up to the 17th August he was maintaining in force a prohibition order which had validity only if his prohibition was "likely to prevent annoyance to any person lawfully employed or a disturbance of the public tranquillity or a riot or affray." Apparently the C.P. held that the Magistrate could certify to the likelihood of annoyance, but not of a breach of the peace. I am unwilling to suggest that the Magistrate should have stained the point against his convictions; it was unnecessary in the interests of the Government policy that he should do so; for the Superintendent could, and did issue an order under 30 (1) specifying the roads through which a procession could not be taken without his permission. The roads specified were those running through the residential portion of the Civil Station. If that order has been disobeyed, the Magistrate could have renewed his prohibitory order under 144 Cr. P.C. and the Government

position would again have been the same as that occupied by it during the preceding two months.

5. I have analysed the legal aspect of the position because it may perhaps be assumed that the local Government were obliged to abate something of their attitude owing to a deficiency in the legal measures at their disposal. I do not think that this justification can be pleaded; they did not give the procedure under the Police Act a trial. Admittedly they would have been obliged to allow processions over any, except the prohibited roads, even without permission; or would have been obliged to give permission to go over the prohibited roads, if a license were applied for, and proper guarantees given. But this involved an abandonment by the opposition of the claims they had put forward; and it did not seem likely that they would yield to this extent. If they had, the victory of Government would have been complete. Certainly neither we nor any of those who had been supporting the Central Provinces Government in the Press would have had any cause to complain.

6. As I have said, they did not give the new procedure a trial. They accepted an offer of negotiation from the opposition. As His Excellency is aware, they had been warned of the possible dangers of such negotiations; nevertheless, I should not be disposed to complain of their action, if they had gone into the interviews in the proper spirit. Our whole judgement of the question indeed depends on our view of the objective which the Government should have had before it when its members saw the Patels. At the stage at which the matter had reached, ought they to have determined to stand by the order under the Police Act and face the consequences; or were they justified in attempting any kind of compromise? The first action would admittedly have been contrary to the wishes of their Council; it would have prolonged the contest; it would have added to the embarrassment caused by the long conflict in which they had already engaged. Nevertheless, I hold that it was the only course open to them. If the conflict was not being waged on a real issue, and was an open contest between Government and civil disobedience, then I maintain that once having accepted the challenge they should have seen the matter through, any compromise inevitably involved a reflection on the correctness of the attitude they had taken up for the last two months; any accommodation would inevitably strengthen the hands of the party of non-cooperation.

7. As a result of these negotiations, the opposition admittedly made many concessions. They were obliged to agree that they would only take a procession over an agreed route and in an orderly manner: they were obliged also to agree that as the result of the compromise future agitation should cease. It was unfortunate that the local Government should not have insisted on a formal application for permission to take the procession out; for the "intimation" which they admitted in its place did not contain an admission that it was only proposed to take it out over the roads and in the manner already agreed upon. The opposition was consequently able to claim *more suo* that they had not asked for permission, but had only asserted their intention. That was a mistake of detail for which the

local Government has paid somewhat dearly, though it is exactly what might have been expected when admitting the Patels to negotiation. It was unfortunate that they did not obtain a formal agreement that Satyagraha should cease after the procession, for here again the Patels were, in the absence of such an agreement, able to perjure themselves to their friends. From one further somewhat unfortunate concession, namely that there should be a second procession when prisoners were released, they were apparently saved by the disinclination of the opposition to repeat the funeral experience of the first day.

8. These however are comparatively minor matters, not calling for animadversion. It is no discredit to be euchred when one plays cards with the Devil; the mistake lies in sitting down with him at all. But we are bound to look with disfavour on the fact that the local Government first of all deliberately set out to secure a compromise on a matter affecting the Government of India and other local Governments without even intimating to us that they intended to do so; and secondly that in order to secure a compromise they had to agree to release their prisoners. The papers forwarded to us do not contain any statement that the latter condition was explicitly made by the Patels or agreed to by Government: and the telegram sent to us on the 23rd August, in response to our enquiries, avoided reference to it. Their telegram of the 26th, in reply to a definite question on the subject, said that the Patels were informed that "no undertaking could be given on the subject and that they must trust in the judgement and good intentions of Government." But since the local Government held (*vide* the same telegram) that failure to release would be regarded as justifying non-cooperation and distrust (?) of British good faith, we may reasonably hold that the condition was implied in the negotiations; and this is confirmed by the insertion of a definite agreement that a second procession should take place when the prisoners were released. The local Government admits that it overlooked our instructions in coming to a decision to release the prisoners without consulting us. I think myself that their error goes further back.

9. As to the exact effect of the compromise, opinions may differ. The local Government claims that it has done no good to extremists, has been welcomed by moderates and has been treated by Swarajists as a triumph for Government. There is to my mind little doubt that it has done real harm to Government. It certainly strengthened the hands of the extremist party at the Delhi Congress and the Purbandak Committee has quoted it not once but a hundred times as an encouragement to its followers. It may indeed be claimed that it has ended the National Flag demonstrations. For a time, it seems to have done so; and this would have been a distinct gain if it had thereby done anything to damp the ardour or discourage the efforts of non-cooperators. The flag demonstrations were only a gesture in a long campaign of attack on Government; their cessation has not abated the desire, nor reduced the ability of non-cooperation to attack us in other directions.

10. We have not failed to see the difficulties of the local Government nor to appreciate the embarrassment caused to their administration by this campaign.

But I think that our conclusion on the whole affair must be in the sense I have indicated. In almost every contingency I prefer to support a local Government against the criticism of the Secretary of State, even when it is wrong, but the criticisms of the Secretary of State in this case unfortunately coincide with those which we had already formulated ourselves.

W.M.H[ailey],—16-10-23.

I agree with Sir M. Hailey. I am not disposed to view too critically the various minor matters referred to by Sir Malcolm and I am in complete accord with him that these minor matters do not call for animadversion. But the negotiations should never have been commenced without consultation with the Government of India in view of the importance to Central Government of other local Governments of maintaining authority unimpaired to the end. I can understand the desire of C.P. Government to rid themselves of the embarrassing situation but in the circumstances they ought not to have acted on their own judgement and especially after they had consulted Government of India and had agreed upon the cause of action; again in regard to the release of prisoners it would appear that an implied understanding was arrived at by C.P. Government with Patel, and in this they were undoubtedly wrong. My view is substantially the same as that of Sir M. Hailey in treating these as the important questions. It is necessary to emphasise them as there is danger of Provincial Governments taking action based upon local considerations and embarrassments without regard to the effect upon the rest of India.

R[eading],—18-10-23.
W.M.H[ailey],—19-10-23.

Demi-official from the Hon'ble Sir W.M. Hailey, K.C.S.I., C.I.E., Member of Viceroy's Council and In charge Home Department, to Sir G.F. de Montmorency, K.C.V.O., C.I.E., C.B.E., I.C.S. . Private Secretary to H.E. the Viceroy, dated Simla, the 19th October 1923.

His Excellency asked me this morning in connection with the Nagpur Flag case to examine the point whether our telegram to the Central Provinces issued on receipt of their explanation of the circumstances connected with the compromise did not in itself require an answer from the local Government.

I have examined the papers and find that the facts are as follows:—The local Government did not of course inform us of the result of their negotiations. We pressed for news on the 22nd August in view of what we had seen in the Press; on the 23rd they sent us their explanation which we repeated to the Secretary of State and at the same time asked on the 25th for further information whether anything that had been said could be construed as a promise that prisoners would be released. They replied on the 26th and on the first September we sent them our considered views. We regretted that they considered it necessary, as we inferred from their telegram to be the case, to enter into an understanding involving the release of prisoners. On this point, in view of our orders of the 9th February

1923 and of the effect on the general political situation of the action proposed, we stated that we considered that we should have been previously consulted.

On the 6th September they merely informed us that the civil disobedience prisoners had been released; there were no demonstrations and no second flag procession through the prohibited areas. On the 8th they sent us a copy of their published resolution giving a history of the case and referring to the action of various officers concerned in it. They did not answer our telegram of the 1st September which had implied a censure on them for agreeing to the release of prisoners and had pointed out their neglect of the definite instructions of February 1923. It was not until we forwarded to them a copy of the Secretary of State's telegram of the 20th September calling for further information that they acknowledged the incorrectness of their action in this respect. In short they neither acknowledged the receipt nor protested against the tenor of our criticisms until the 1st October when, as I say, they were answering a demand not from us but from the Secretary of State.

A draft Despatch to the Secretary of State is submitted.

J. Crerar,—20-10-23.
W.M.H[ailey],—20-10-23.

168

Vallabhbhai Awaiting Release of Nagpur Flag Satyagrahis

Sardar Shrino Patro-5

NAGPUR
21 August 1923

DEAR DAUGHTER MANIBEN AND SON DAHYABHAI,

Here we have succeeded straightaway. I have been resting since last two days. Within two or three days our men will be released, and I will return bringing them with me. It is not proper to leave them and come alone.

Respected uncle has gone to Bombay on 13th. Now there is no necessity of his coming here, because there is no special work, and I am also returning.

Bapu's blessings

169

Mahadev to Vallabhbhai on Release of Prisoners

Sardar Shrino Patro-4 [1]

AHMEDABAD
27 August 1923

REVERED BROTHER,

There is no news from you. Mavalankar[2] has some difficulties.[3] That is why he has not sent money. But Manilal[4] has sent Rs 4000 from Petlad, and has made arrangements for other 10,000. Here also we have issued an appeal, and it appears that Manilal will be able to collect something.

Can you give me some information about the state of affairs there?[5]

Do you know how much *Kesari*[6] abuses you? and *Gutmati*[7] also, and other your well wishers too.[8] We are not afraid of abuses. Was Bapu not abused?

You shall have to[9] issue a statement which might satisfy everybody, when everything is settled.

"We do not want to leave this place unless all of you are released."[10] This lecture of Vithalbhai which he delivered in Bombay has complicated matters. Then why should we imagine things.

This much for the present.

Mahadev's Pranam

[1]In Gujarati, vol. IV.

[2]Ganesh Vasudev Mavalankar, Sardar's trusted college friend, President of Gandhi Memorial Trust. First Speaker of independent India's Lok Sabha.

[3]To collect contribution for Satyagrahis taking part in Nagpur Satyagraha.

[4]Manilal Kothari. first enthusiastic worker from Saurashtra, Secretary of Gujarat Provincial Congress Committee. He was expert in getting donations from public.

[5]About the compromise regarding Nagpur Flag Satyagraha.

[6]Poona's Marathi periodical.

[7]Bombay's weekly.

[8]Some newspapers has propagated that Sardar had asked for permission from Government for flag march. Pandit Motilal Nehru also had criticised Sardar for this. Systematic answer to this propaganda was given by Sardar at the public meeting (3.9.23) held for celebration of victory of Nagpur Flag Satyagraha.

[9]Prisoners who were arrested at the time of Flag Satyagraha.

[10]Vithalbhai had referred about the negotiations which were going on between him and the Sardar with the Govt. of Madhya Prant. Commissioner of Nagpur was against this compromise. Therefore, the Governor had side-tracked him and continued negotiations. But before the conditions of compromise were implemented, there were differences between Governor and Commissioner and therefore the problem of release of prisoners was kept hanging.

170

Vallabhbhai to Mahadev on Measures to Intensify Nagpur Satyagraha

Sardar Shrino Patro-4

August 1923

DEAR BROTHER MAHADEV,

. . . battle is very fine. If people are united, they can put the government on tenterhooks in a week's time. But at present the pipe playing different tunes. So how can the voice of Nagpur reach the people? All English newspapers are either antagonistic or indifferent. Leaders are harking on their thoughts and there is no objective thinking.

In this province Government is very strict. All the local workers have been arrested. The local Provincial Congress Committee[1] had shown no interest from the very beginning. Under such circumstances we are fighting.

Dasbabu has gone to the opposite camp. The Congress Working Committee meeting was to be held on 28th—the venue was shifted from Bombay to Visagapattam. Date was also changed. Then AICC meeting was also fixed, and it was decided to call all of them there. In spite of these various difficulties, we have to work hard for attracting the attention of everybody towards Nagpur.

Government has come to know that the struggle[2] has again gained momentum. Lots of people come as per arrangement. On 3rd there is a meeting of the Executive Council of Central Provinces Government, and on 6th State Legislative Assembly session begins. This question will surely be discussed in Legislative Assembly, but nothing will emerge out of it. Only Government will get an opportunity to abuse us. Yet we might get the opportunity of knowing the intention of the government. Those who are hoping that the fight will be over, before the Assembly session is held are disappointed. All these are not to be printed.

We have to prepare a batch for next eighteenth. I will write to you afterwards about the number of satyagrahis to be sent (from Gujarat). Chinai (Chimanlal) from Surat is ready. He can be the leader. There are 20-25 soldiers from Surat. We have to try to get others.

We have to appeal for funds in one or two issues.[3] Please get a very fine appeal printed; continue recruiting volunteers. It seems that I won't be arrested at present. Previously they had no solid reasons, but as (Satyagraha) has got momentum, so (Govt.) might think over it. But I believe that no action will be taken till Assembly session is over.

Don't confine Devdas to press only. Let him move outside also. Gujarat has not yet known him. He does not get a chance.

Saw Chandubhai[4] and Pandya[5] in jail. Both have been kept as ordinary prisoners. They have given work in the printing press. They are cheerful, officers love them, and are in good health.

You and Devdas visit home now and then, and see that children[6] do not feel lonely. I do not understand why Maniben cried. Now there should not be any crying. She is very brave. She advised the people of Madhya Prant to go to jail. Then how can she cry? Tell respected Ba[7] to be ready for going to jail. If you can issue an appeal to Gujarat women in Ba's name to come to Nagpur on 18th instant.

Seventeenth is the expiry date of the order.[8] If the order is expanded then from eighteenth, women should begin their sacrifice. It is a fine way of awakening the people. We must believe that Government will extend the term of the order. If it is not extended then with what face can it keep the prisoners in jail?

VALLABHABHAI'S
Vande Matram

[1]Nagpur Provincial Congress Committee.
[2]Nagpur Flag Satyagraha.
[3]Of *Navjivan.*
[4]Dr. Chandulal Desai freedom fighter.
[5]Mohanlal Pandya, well known freedom fighter took part in Kaira, Borsad and Bardoli Satyagraha.
[6]Maniben and Dahyabhai.
[7]Kasturba Gandhi.
[8]Order banning the procession.

171

Vallabhbhai to Maniben regarding Domestic Problems

Sardar Shrino Patro-5

NAGPUR
1 September 1923

DEAR MANIBEN AND DAHYABHAI,

I am sorry that I stayed here for longer time than expected. But in such a gigantic work[1] it is just possible that I have to spend some more days. It appears that my stay will be prolonged for some time more.

I have given all information to Mahadev. He will talk to you in detail. I will try to come as soon as possible.

Don't worry. Employ some other cook. Do not suffer hardship unnecessarily. If you are unable to find one, go to the office[2] and tell Krushnalal,[3] he will find out somebody for you.

I am well.

Bapu's blessings

[1]Madhya Prant Government was delaying the release of the persons arrested during flag satyagraha and therefore Sardar had to stay for a longer period in Nagpur.
[2]Office of Gujarat Provincial Congress Committee.
[3]Accountant of Gujarat Provincial Congress Committee.

172

Vallabhbhai Blames Vithalbhai for Delay in Release of Prisoners

Sardar Shrino Patro-4

NAGPUR
1 September 1923

DEAR BROTHER MAHADEV,

I am fighting a fierce battle. The glory of our victory cannot be understood by those who are not in fight. At present I have sealed my mouth. Government is in a fix. Does not utter a single word.

I am sending a copy of *Pioneer* for your perusal. There people who have read the leader[1] of *Times* are crying. But it is all false. Truth can be told only at the opportune time. But our people are very impatient and they lack faith.

When I published my statement and declared our victory,[2] it was the duty of the Government to speak. But it has become dumbfounded. You see the exasperation of *Pioneer.* I think Vithalbhai's utterance is untimely.[3] What he spoke in Bombay has highly disturbed civil service.

I have entrapped the Commissioner here. Here many civilians are on his side. Here there is one "Civil Service Club". It has become entirely anti-government. They have seen in this matter total defeat of the Government. It appears that they have protested against the release of prisoners. Here their protest is of no avail. But India Government has forcibly taken the matter into its own hand. The whole case has gone there. I am highly amused to see the changing colours of their internecine fight, which is more interesting than our outward fight.

Kesari and *Maratha* are showering abuses on me. Yet I am silent. I am not going to utter a word till our prisoners are released. It is difficult to say how long I will be staying here.

Now let us see what India Government does. If prisoners are not released the prestige and sincerity of the local government will be lost, and if the prisoners are released then civil service people will get angry, I disclose all these secrets to you for your information. Those should not be out from any quarters.

I will tell you when I come there as to how and in which way we won victory. The victory does not depend on release of prisoners. The procession with flag entered the Civil Lines, that was our clear-cut victory. Now I am not worried even if the prisoners are not released. Only Govt. will lose its prestige and for that I have enough material with me. I am waiting for the final decision of the Government.

I am astonished to know that there are people in Gujarat, who believe that prisoners can be released through Legislative State Assembly. Had there not been State the whole matter would have been settled. Please think twice before you tell this to anybody. Nothing should appear in the press till I come there.

Otherwise the whole thing will be spoiled. I think that if Vithalbhai had not untimely spoken in Bombay, I would have left this place with prisoners.

That Commissioner had sent the news that we had applied to the Police Superintendent for permission to take out the procession. I have caught him by the neck. He has been silent by exposing his secret fight. He is the person who has instigated *Pioneer* against the Government.

Thus the prisoners shall have to be in jail for some more days, but there is no end to Government's. Let us see what happens now. Within two or three days some result will come. But there is a tug of war between two[4] Governments. One does not know how much time will elapse. Therefore you all have to keep patience.

VALLABHBHAI'S
Bandematram

[1]Editorial. There was a false statement in it that Sardar had asked for the permission of Police Superintendent to take out a procession.

[2]On 18th August after leading a mammoth flag march Sardar had said in public meeting: "The dignity of our national flag has been at last accepted. We have secured the right to take out a procession with our flag on public roads. I consider it as the victory of truth, non-violence and patience."

[3]Vithalbhai Patel played a leading role in the negotiations with the Government of Madhya Prant. The Governor of M.P. desired that there should not be any discussion in public till the accord is given a final shape. But Vithalbhai in his speech in Bombay had given some indication of the accord.

[4]Between Central and Madhya Prant Governments.

173

Vallabhbhai's Criticism Refuted

Young India, 6 September 1923

Mr. Vallabhbhai's statement was received by wire long after the notes were in type. It is a magnificent document which would do credit to any true disciple of Mahatmaji. The facts leading up to the preliminary triumph have been narrated with remarkable candour and fairness and one can plainly see that Mr. Vallabhbhai must have been pained even to have to make a reference to all sorts of hostile criticism against what is miscalled the Nagpur compromise painful as it may be it was a clear duty. He owed it to the released satyagrahis who went fighting to prison absolutely confident that the flag would be kept flying by those who remained behind. He was bound to make it clear to them, if not to the carping world, that they were out, not because some one had pleaded for mercy or clemency on their behalf, not because the movement was defeated, not because the council had passed a resolution that they should be released but because the honour of the flag was vindicated, and the Government had seen the injustice of keeping them a day longer in jail.

We have no doubt Mr. Vallabhbhai's statement will give a quietus to all the criticism, honest and mischievous, levelled against him. Pandit Jawaharlal has, as we have shown in a note, fully anticipated Mr. Vallabhbhai.

We wish Mr. Vallabhbhai had magnanimously omitted the amusing reference to the Commissioner of Nagpur whom the inadvertent (or shall we say the more honest) "statesman" has unwittingly betrayed. Not that he did not deserve to be exposed, but this great statement was not place for it.

Mr. Vallabhbhai was deputed to Nagpur to carry on a task which was hardly easy or encouraging. He has carried it out nobly and manfully. Those who fought whilst the struggle was on, demonstrated by their manner of fighting that no battle could be fought in a cleaner manner. It was left to Mr. Vallabhbhai to demonstrate that none could be won also in a cleaner manner.

174

Vallabhbhai's Stirring Message at the Triumphant Conclusion of Nagpur Flag Satyagraha

Young India, 6 September 1923

We have pleasure in publishing below the statement read by Mr. Vallabhbhai Patel at a meeting in Nagpur held on the Janmashtmi day to welcome the released satyagrahis:

I take this opportunity of making a final statement with a view to dispel all doubts, to set at rest all the controversies that have been raised by the misleading, mischievous and inaccurate reports circulated by interested persons regarding the happenings of the 18th August which resulted in the successful termination of our struggle. It is well known to all that this struggle had to be commenced when under the guise of regulating processions on public roads the District Magistrate of Nagpur prohibited processions with the national flag beyond the District Court buildings in the civil lines by issuing an order on the 1st of May 1923. This order was regarded, and as later events have conclusively shown rightly regarded, as a challenge and an insult to the national flag and a denial of our elementary right to possess and exhibit the flag and to carry it in a peaceful and orderly procession on public roads. For about a month even a single person, man or woman, attempting to carry a flag into the prohibited area was arrested. The flags of the arrested persons were confiscated. When such open prostitution of law unheard of in any civilised country, that was being perpetrated in the sacred name of law and order was publicly exposed, the Government of Central Provinces had to revise its notions about the legal definition of the term procession. A group of any two persons carrying a national flag continued however to be regarded as a procession right up to the end of the struggle. Another District Magistrate went to the length of publicly advising the people not to interest themselves in the national flag affair as their forefathers had no national flag; and laterly respectable persons coming to Nagpur were arrested on railway stations as vagrants or as persons not able to give satisfactory account if they happened to have a flag with them.

The campaign was thus directed not for the purpose of claiming an unrestricted use of public roads or for insulting the Union Jack, or for annoying any section of the people, but for the vindication of the honour of the national flag and against an attempt of setting up Highlands in the heart of India under the cover of police regulations. After a prolonged struggle of three months and a half the national flag procession of a hundred volunteers entered the prohibited area and passed through a large portion of the civil lines without interruption amidst a surprisingly large demonstration of force all over the route through which the procession passed on the afternoon of the 18th August and this enabled me to publicly announce the victorious termination of the struggle that evening. I do not propose to answer all speculative surmises for the benefit of those of you who have come out now from seclusion and also for others that want to understand how the struggle ended so suddenly and so successfully after the issue of the police order, I desire to explain the situation. For obvious reasons I did not want to disturb the normal course of the struggle till the Government took its decision on the council resolutions. There was no doubt in my mind that an important expression of opinion however strongly expressed if adverse was bound to provoke the official European element of the Civil area and to stiffen the back of the irresponsible uncontrolled Executive. When the movement steered clear of the Council influence, I at once issued my statement on the 16th, clearing the issue of the struggle of all misunderstandings and misrepresentations by once more repeating the position taken by the Nagpur Committee from the beginning and next day arranged the programme of the procession of the 18th specifying the route, time and instructions regarding the conduct of the procession taking into account the special circumstances of tension and high feelings prevailing on that particular occasion and which were further actuated by that wordy warfare on the council floor. The programme of the 18th was apparently so adjusted as to meet the opposite point of view as far as it was possible without giving up anything essential for which the struggle was fought. The result was that the Government thought it better to let the procession pass through without interference. Immediately after the procession passed through the prohibited area and the announcement of the success of the movement was made, the whole country and particularly the Anglo-Indian press was flooded with all sorts of mischievous, misleading and inaccurate reports and the controversy about our interview with His Excellency the Governor of the Central Provinces was also raised in the press. To me, how the interview was brought about, is of little consequence. The general impression that the non-cooperators stand on ceremonies is unfounded. Personally I would not even wait for a formal invitation, if I felt assured of a genuine desire for mutual understanding. But I stand here today to contradict publicly in no uncertain terms all reports and rumours about the compromise or agreement. There is no truth in such reports. We have made no compromise or agreement with the Governor nor have we given any undertaking. The interview took place on the 13th August. It only afforded us an opportunity of placing each other's points of view. Reports have been circulated that an application to the District Superintendent of Police to hold a procession was put in. I would have taken no notice of such reports had it not been for the fact (of which reference is made at a later stage) that a very high placed officer of government is responsible for circulating such mischievous and inaccurate reports in the public press. If I wanted to apply for permission, the struggle could have ended long ago. It was not beyond my knowledge that a large procession passed through the prohibited area on the Turkish peace celebration day presumably with permission obtained from the District Magistrate. Some members of the local council suggested repeatedly to me that they could apply and obtain permission in their name. I knew that a mere verbal request from me to the District Magistrate would have been enough, ordinarily there would be no objection to an application for such permission. The Congress has not prohibited such action. But at that stage of the struggle I felt it was impossible for me to do so without compromising the prestige of the Congress when an application was expected to be obtained at the point of the bayonet. In fact it was the crux of the whole question. All other points were more or less matters of detail. It was easy enough for any one to see that the struggle at that stage was crystallised and was concentrated mainly on one issue, viz. the determination to put down with all the resources of the Government what they called open defiance of lawful authority on one side and an equal determination of the people to maintain their right with all the sufferings and sacrifices that it may involve to offer civil disobedience against arbitrary and unjustifiable use of authority on the other side. In the intimation given to the District Superintendent of Police of my proposed plan of action against his order on the 18th, there was nothing by which it could be interpreted as an application. On the contrary the copy of the programme clearly indicated that it was intended to test the newly issued order. In any case I have no doubt I would have failed in my duty if I had not given intimation of such an unusual change in the programme in all its aspects especially when such a change was made for the first time since the commencement of the struggle. It would have been unfair to take the police by surprise immediately after the District Magistrate retired from the field. To my mind surprise attacks are not permissible in a struggle of this nature. The large concentration of police force in the prohibited area shortly after the intimation was sent and which it is not for me to explain, amply justifies the need of such intimation. If, however, that intimation or the details in the programme regarding the conduct of the procession were considered convenient enough for retiring from an inconvenient battle, I should be happy to think that without sacrificing anything. I also relieved to some extent the embarrassment of the Government and made it possible for them to retire with honour. But I repeat that no application has been put in nor has any permission or license been obtained. I have noticed some controversy going on in the press as to the effect of the resolutions of the council on the struggle. It is not my desire to express any opinion whether the council proceedings have helped or hindered me, as it is likely to be misunderstood. It is enough to say that the police order was issued after the council resolutions and no effect was given to any of them till the end of the struggle; but as soon as the struggle ended all the under-trial prisoners were discharged. Let there be no delusion that a government that claims to know its business best and recognises nothing but force, either moral or physical, can ever understand gratuitous advice even if such advice assumes the dignified name of a Council Resolution. All such attempts afford opportunities for unfair and sometimes even mean attacks on those who are not there to defend themselves. Such resolutions can only serve the purpose of their convenient use at a suitable time for a suitable purpose if the matter is disposed of independently of them. The Government were in honour bound to release all the prisoners in jail after the procession was allowed to pass and I thank the Government of the Central Provinces for acting honourably. I regret to find that seven out of about a thousand prisoners released here have yet been detained for some offences against jail discipline. I trust however that they will also be released soon. Even the little delay that has taken place is I have no doubt due to circumstances beyond the Government's control. I am glad that my brother who followed me here immediately after my arrival and who closely cooperated with me in conducting the struggle almost up to the end agrees with me entirely in this particular case about the futility of those resolutions though I must say, on different grounds. It is well known to all that we stand poles apart in our political convictions. But we both go back from Nagpur more or less confirmed in our individual political convictions.

I welcome you all who have returned from your self-imposed seclusion back again in our midst where you will find ample opportunities for much higher sacrifice in a greater struggle awaiting you. With your return back amongst us today I stand on stronger grounds to reaffirm with greater emphasis what I had said on the last occasion that the Nagpur Flag Satyagraha struggle has ended in the vindication of the honour of our national flag, the restoration of our right to take peaceful and orderly processions on public roads and in the complete triumph of truth, nonviolence and suffering.

But there is nothing to boast of in our achievement. Victory does not lie in what we have achieved not even in what we have suffered but in our readiness to suffer more and more till we achieve our final goal. Believe me when I say that the credit of our struggle is not due to me in the least degree but to all of you who suffered and many others who were ready to suffer for the cause and also to the indefatigable energy and the admirable sense of discipline which the Nagpur Congress Committee has shown throughout the conduct of the struggle.

I cannot close this statement without placing before the public as well as Government one important fact which has come to my knowledge whilst I was trying to trace the source of all the mischievous reports that were circulated in the press about the happening of the 18th. I came across a curious piece of evidence which probably also accounts for the famous four letters appearing in the *Times of India* in the last week of June, after the arrest of Seth Jamnalal Bajaj and his co-workers as also for the general attitude of that journal towards this movement throughout. In the issues of the *Statesman* of August 21st there appears a telegraphic message dated 19th instant from the Commissioner of Nagpur under the headings "Satyagraha to cease", "leaders submit to authority". The report of the correspondent of the *Times of India* of the same date appearing in the issue of the 20th of August under the heading "government authority recognised" happens to be a verbatim copy of the Commissioner's message appearing in the *Statesman.* Reading the two together it is difficult to make out whether the correspondent of the *Times of India* is the Commissioner of Nagpur or the Commissioner of Nagpur is the correspondent of the *Times of India.* It is possible that the inadvertence of the *Statesman* unlike its Bombay contemporary in publishing it as the message from the Commissioner of Nagpur instead of "from its own correspondent", has exposed him. For some time I did not believe that the statement was issued by him. On inquiry I found that he had done so. I have been assured however that the Commissioner on a former occasion also had brought the Government into trouble by his activities in this direction in connection with this very movement, in spite of the orders not to meddle with the affairs of the Government. In such a manner he goes his own way. Whilst I readily acknowledge the genuine desire of the Government for an honourable end of the struggle and whilst I have no doubt that his action is regretted, I feel bound to say that the Government cannot escape the responsibility of his action in the end.

We have to thank God that at a time when personal prejudices, party politics and communal strifes subordinated mutual tolerance, wider political vision and higher common interest and when forces of doubt and despair were getting the upper hand, He blesses us with this humble opportunity of demonstrating the under-currents of solidity, strength and the soundness of heart of the nation and in spite of all misunderstanding of friends and misrepresentations by foes, this neat, clean and courageous display of moral warfare will in future be remembered by nation with pride and will inspire greater faith in the superiority of the weapons of truth, non-violence and suffering, which alone, as Mahatma Gandhi has said, are suited to the condition and the culture of our nation. Bande Matram.

175

Vallabhbhai Criticizes Government for Imposing Taxes on Villagers in Borsad

Navjivan, 9 September 1923

It seems that an outlaw named Babar made his appearance in Golel in 1917. He indulged in petty crimes in the beginning. When the Government fails to detect crime, the man turns into a brute. Babar has been at large all these years, and has committed numerous crimes. Instead of arresting him, the police sent panicky reports against the people and have tried to make out that they are guilty of complicity in his crimes. On these reports the Government imposed punitive police on two villages, Khadana and Jogan, two years ago, and ordered the cost to be realized from a poll-tax on Patanwadias and Dharalas, the communities alleged to be guilty of complicity. But you know how entirely useless the police was. In Jogan itself Babar murdered a man named Shivbhai in broad daylight. The police could have caught him then and there, but they rested content with alleging that people do not give information against the outlaw. In Golel the outlaw assaulted the punitive police. The people saw the District Magistrate and said they could not pay the fine. The *mamlatdar* also reported that it was impossible to realize fine from people who, not being contumacious, were too poor to pay it. This he said in his letter P.O.L.245 dated Borsad 16th February in which he protests against the imposition of any further burden. "No villager," he said, "seems willing for the continuance of the additional police in the villages." The District Superintendent of Police disagreed with this *Mamlatdar*—the man on the spot and insisted that the impost should be continued. His reasons were that Babar and his gang were still at large, that though Babar killed Shivbhai in broad daylight, no evidence was forthcoming: What are the policemen in the village doing? How are the people to furnish evidence, if the police are impotent to do so? The third reason is that Khadana Patanwadias never give information about outlaws, that they on the contrary shelter them and give them food and drink, and so on. One of the reasons is that some of the Khadana Patanwadias would join Babar's gang, were it not for the check imposed by the special police. The funniest part of the affair is that the Collector disagreed, in turn, with this Superintendent of Police, and he reported entirely differently to the Commissioner. His letter too is in my possession. He was against the continuation of the additional police in either of the villages because "the additional police are useless to prevent" Babar's being sheltered in the villages, but he felt that there was a general increase of crime in the whole of Taluka, and "every village is directly or indirectly, more or less responsible for the general breakdown of order," and so he suggested that some additional force may be imposed on the whole Taluka as may be proposed by him after consultation with the D.S.P. It seems that consultation is at the back of the impost. I may also add that the Collector admitted that the people do not give information or shelter the miscreants "from fear or from selfish desire to save themselves immediate trouble." The Commissioner disagreed with the Collector and the Mamlatdar; he felt that the Superintendent had given solid reasons for the continuance of the police in the two villages for another year and issued orders accordingly. That was in June. How all of a sudden in October the Government resolved to impose the police on the whole Taluka passes comprehension. I have not those communications in my possession. But I am sure about my facts. Everyone I have met has told me what has happened. There is a Mussalman outlaw abroad named Ali. When Babar could not be got hold of, the police made friends with this new genius, sought to get rid of an outlaw with the help of an outlaw, and provided him with arms and ammunition. Oh the pity and the shame of it! The Government ceased to rule, making room for the outlaw. Who is going to punish the Government for having leagued with this outlaw? God alone. The Government surely knows what a number of murders and dacoities this Ali has committed, having been armed by the Government itself. No doubt its intention was to catch Babar through Ali, but how are the people to know? I hold the Government responsible for all the misdeeds of that miscreant Ali.

Another thing to be noted is that Ali himself was not an outlaw originally. He had murdered a Borsad Vakil in broad daylight, just a stone's throw from the police station. But the police could not lay hands on him. Surely anyone who can thus see through the impotence of the Government would turn an outlaw when later he is made friends of.

The only reason assigned by the Government for punishing a whole people is that they do not provide information or evidence. Let us see how far this is true. Babar has to his credit 22 murders. Not one of the victims was a rich man. He did not murder them for the mere fun of it. He murdered them as they were informants. If after 22 such informants were murdered, the Government seriously argues that the people do not give information, shall we ask how many policemen were murdered? An informant was crucified to a tree by Babar. How many would Government have to suffer the fate of this informant? An informant's job is no easy job then. A first class magistrate was waylaid by an outlaw on his way from Wasad to Borsad. The outlaw gave a smack on his face, and wrested his rifle from his hands. The poor fellow had to represent that he was an ordinary clerk and not a magistrate, to escape with his life. A Government with such a magistracy has no title to exist, has surely no title to punish a people.

All these things go to show that the Government knows that the people are innocent. But the Government has no money. It still wants to hold its head erect before the princely States in the vicinity. Those States have imposed on their villages additional police to protect them from those very outlaws, but they have not taxed their raiyats. Our Government apes those States in imposing the police but money it tries to find out of the people's pockets. Well, if it wants money, let it beg of us. But why should it cast a slur on our name, why should it asperse our behaviour, treat us as criminals and extort the cost of the police as fine?

Those who can be charged with the utmost complicity in the crimes are exempted, viz. the Government servants. My information is that every petty village officer knows the whereabouts of these outlaws but is afraid of them. We may note that even the new M.L.C. is not exempt from the fine. What a curious commentary on the Government which thought out Reception Committee Chairman good enough to be elected to the Council but not good enough to be exempt from fine!

Let us then make up our minds. Do not for a moment think that you are fighting for the paltry amount of Rs 2-7-0. If you do so, the sooner you pay the fine the better. You are fined because of complicity in crime, because you are suspected of sheltering the outlaws and befriending them. I ask you to fight only if you are convinced that no power on earth has the right thus to malign your character. Let us plainly tell the Government that we are honourable men of character, we shall not sign certificates of our bad behaviour with our own hands. We refuse to pay the fine. You might plunder us if you like, like the outlaws, and realize the fine. Fight the fight then like Mahatmaji's men—his men do not need a stick or a dharia, they need brave backs to receive blows. Be not be tempted into anger, do not be tempted into violence for the tempter will be there. Now then I ask you if you are prepared to fight raise your hands. (Up went all the hands.)

One thing more. Complaints have reached me that the punitive police is oppressing you, that they are plundering your fodder, that they have not even hesitated to molest our sisters. A Government servant told Shri Tyabji yesterday that steps are immediately taken by the Government whenever such complaints come; the people need only put in their complaints. I ask you not to lodge such complaints. The police is imposed to prevent *zoolum* and you have to complain against their own *zoolum*. We shall not recognize this police. Let us have our own Volunteer Corps. I ask you to raise a corps from amongst yourselves. I ask young men to give their names to Darbar Saheb Gopaldas.

I appeal to all such present here, as have ever helped the dacoits in any way, to realize that it is a hateful thing. I ask them to give up that nefarious business. I ask Dharalas amongst you to give up drink. I may warn you that the Government thinks of removing you from the District, and penning you up in a criminal settlement. That will be a sorry plight indeed. I ask you each and all to reform yourselves and let not a whole people suffer for the misdeeds of a few ruffians.

176

Vallabhbhai Refutes Government Contention regarding Congress Applying for Permission for Procession in Nagpur

Navjivan, 9 September 1923

Both Shri Patel and the Home Member very rightly say in their joint statement that neither party would publish an account of any of the interviews. The Chief

Secretary has however freed me from this obligation and if the Government chooses to deny any of the statement I will make hereunder. I propose to publish not only the whole correspondence but also the full account as far as I remember of the interviews.

Firstly, as for the interview with the Governor, Mr Vithalbhai Patel got a letter from the Chief Secretary requesting us to see him and discuss the situation with him. We did so and during our coversation it was suggested that we should interview the Governor. We were not called upon to make any reply to this suggestion, and we made none. Next day Mr Vithalbhai Patel got a letter from the Chief Secretary intimating to us that if we desired to see His Excellency he would be glad to see us at 11 a.m. next day at the residency. We accordingly interviewed His Excellency and discussed the whole situation for nearly three hours. We had never made any oral or written request for an interview.

Secondly, as for permission for procession, the statement suggests that we applied for permission. Nothing of the kind, however, was done. My letter to the District Superintendent of Police speaks for itself.

When Mr Vithalbhai had his first interview with the Home Member before the Council sitting, the Home Member after consulting his other colleagues wrote to Mr Vithalbhai that the Government had no objection to the passing of processions if someone on behalf of the Congress Committee approached the District Magistrate in that behalf.

We at once wrote back to say that we could make no such application to the District Magistrate whose very order had given rise to the Satyagraha movement.

The suggestion in the statement of the Chief Secretary that we applied to the District Superintendent of Police is, therefore, wholly incorrect and grossly misleading.

Thirdly, the statement that we gave an undertaking that the prisoners would not take any further part in the Nagpur Flag agitation except under certain conditions is baseless and appears to have deliberately introduced for obvious reasons.

Fourthly, there was no undertaking given by the Government to us nor by us to the Government on any point.

I would add in conclusion that all negotiations and interviews were conducted throughout by Shri Vithalbhai Patel and lately by both of us when in view of the unequivocal statement amounting to an invitation for negotiations made by the Home Member in his speech in the Council, the Working Committee authorized us both to do so. All these interviews and negotiations were conducted strictly on a basis of mutual trust.

The Chief Secretary has chosen to publish a one-sided and distorted account. We waive our objection to the publication of all (not such of them as they like) letters written by us and now in the possession of the Government Members can have no objection to our publication of their letters in our possession.

177

Vallabhbhai's Speech on Nagpur Satyagraha

Navjivan, 9 September 1923

In advising the volunteers to maintain silence when passing in front of the Christian church as also the houses of Europeans, I was asking them only to act in a manner which was courteous and in keeping with our dignity. I wanted the British to appreciate that it was not our intention to hurt their feelings, in any way. We were opposing only what we considered to be an improper step of the Government.

178

Vallabhbhai on the Historic Victory in Nagpur Flag Satyagraha

Navjivan, 9 September 1923

The following statement was read at the public meeting held at Nagpur on Janmastami day.

On this occasion, I take this opportunity to give my last statement, I see the necessity to make this statement in order to dispel the doubts regarding our struggle, and the incidents of 18th August culminating in our victory. Some utterly selfish people have with a malafide intention have circulated misleading, false, defaming news, which has generated some ill will and so in order to restore the amity and remove the ill feeling I see the necessity of issuing this statement. It is well known to everybody that on 1st May 1923 the District Magistrate of Nagpur, under the pretext of restoring the processions on the public roads, stopped the procession carrying national flag from proceeding from the Civil Court building in Civil lines, then we had to decide to start a struggle. In that order we saw challenge and insult to our national flag. In the order we felt that it was denial of our fundamental right of holding our flag, to unfurl it, and to take out peaceful and well organised processions on public roads. The later events proved that our interpretation was correct, for nearly two months any person who tried to defy the order single handed was arrested. The flags of the arrested persons were confiscated. When in the sacred name of law and order, restrictions were placed which was not heard in any civilized nation, the government was put in an embarrassing position, the Central Provinces government had to change the legal definition of the word procession. Even upto the end of the struggle, any two persons carrying the flag was considered as procession. One District Magistrate went a step further and he publicly advised the people that there was never any national flag during the time of their forefathers. So they should not even look at the national flag for the honour of which a struggle was launched. Afterwards, when respectable persons coming to Nagpur were found to have a national flag with them they were abused as vagabonds, scoundrels and arrested at the railway station. Thus the object of the struggle was not to establish the right to freely move about on the public roads, to insult Union Jack or to tease any section of the people. Real object was to protect the honour of national flag and to protest against the effort to establish an "elite land" in Central India under the guise of people rules. After a long struggle of three and a half months, a procession of one hundred volunteers entered the prohibited area with national flag, and after passing through the main area of civil lines, and the row of soldiers fully equipped with arms standing on both the sides of the road, marched forward in the afternoon of 18th August. Nobody stopped it. On the basis of this fact I declared our victory that evening.

Today I don't want to reply to all the gossips, and the fancies of the vagrant people. But I want to explain to those comrades who have been released from jail and to those inquisitive persons, that even after the prohibitory orders, how this struggle was carried on to its victorious end. The circumstances, under which we fought. I had not the desire to make any big change in the routine of the struggle till the government took a decision on the resolution of legislative assembly. There are open reasons for this. I had not the least doubt in my mind that the opinion which is not supported by action, even though announced at the top of the voice, yet if it is unpalatable it will infuriate the white officer residing in civil lines, and it will strengthen the hand of the irresponsible and uncontrolled execution. As soon as the smoke clouds of legislative assembly were cleared I issued my statement on 16th. In that, I reiterated the real object of Nagpur Committee for launching the struggle, and blow off the misunderstandings and false news which were circulated. Then on the next day, I arranged the programme of taking out the procession on 18th. In the programme the route and timings of the procession and instructions to the volunteers were announced. While deciding the programme, I had in my mind turbulent feeling of the people and the effect of the war of words in the hall of the legislative assembly. All these situations were taken into consideration while formulating the programme. It is observed that the programme for the 18th was so arranged that the point of view of the opposition can be taken care of and at the same time, the objectives for which we had launched the struggle might not be jeopardised. The result was that Government thought it proper to allow the procession to pass without any interference.

After the procession passed through the prohibited area and our victory was announced, whole of the country and especially the Anglo-Indian newspapers came out with false, misleading and slanderous reports, with the object of deceiving the people. In newspapers there was open criticism regarding my meeting with the governor. I give least importance to the circumstances in which our meeting was held. It is generally believed that non-cooperators are mostly confined in external formalities, but that belief is baseless. I myself would not wait for a formal invitation, only if I find that he has a genuine desire for mutual understanding. Yet reports and rumours are circulated about some concessions, and some pact, between us. I hereby publicly deny from this place in strong words, that anything of that sort has taken place. There is absolutely no truth in those reports and rumours. We have neither conceded anything, nor given any undertaking, or binding. We met on 13th October. We simply mutually explained our viewpoints. That's all.

Somebody has circulated rumours that I had applied to the District Superintendent of Police for permitting us to take out a procession. If the person responsible for publishing such deceitful and adverse news had not been a top ranking government officer (his name will be disclosed afterwards), I would not have taken notice of such rumours. If I had desired to take permission the struggle must have ended much earlier. It was not out of my mind that during the celebration of the Turkish peace pact a big procession was taken out and permission was asked from District Magistrate to allow it to pass through prohibited areas, which was granted. Some local members of legislative assembly had again and again suggested to me that they may be permitted to ask for permission in their name. I understood that my oral request to the District Magistrate would be enough. Under ordinary circumstances there cannot be any objection in asking for such permission to take out a procession. Congress also does not object to such an act. But it was impossible for me to ask for permission, when the struggle was heading towards victory. If I apply when the government wants us to apply at the point of bayonet, then Congress would lose its credibility. Truly speaking the struggle was started on that issue. Other issues which were there were of details. Anybody could see that the struggle had taken its roots, and had been concentrated on one issue only. The issue was on one side the firm resolve of the government with all its terrorising machinery to crack down on the public law breaking activities as termed by it, and on the other side, the firm determination of the people to assert that fundamental right to break the law of the autocratic, unjust, and unethical regime, the people fully prepared to suffer and sacrifice for assertion of their right, I had informed the District Superintendent of Police my plan to defy the prohibitory order on 18th. In giving that information there was nothing in it which can be termed as application. On the contrary, in the copy of the programme that was sent to him, it was clearly stated that the objective was to test his prohibitory order whatever it might be but when a big change is made in the programme, and that also for the first time after launching the struggle, and I do not inform him then I would have failed in my duty. I have no doubt about it. To attack the policemen and to take them unawares, when the District Superintendent of Police had left the battlefield, would have been improper. In my opinion, in the struggle of this type there is no place for attack on the adversary when he is not prepared for it. Soon after receiving the information police troops were sent to the prohibited area. It is not my business to give reasons for it, but it is a proof of the fact that there was need of informing the police. Yet if by informing the government, I have given an opportunity to the government to extricate itself from a difficult and intricate situation, then I am happy about it, because without in any way compromising our principle, I have been able to lighten the burden of the government and paved the way for their honourable retreat. I again repeat that I have not applied for permission, and neither any permit has been obtained from the government.

I have been told that there is some dispute about the newspaper reports regarding the effect of the resolutions of legislative assembly on our struggle. I have no desire to pass any judgement as to whether the work done by legislative assembly has helped me or created hurdles in my work because there is likelihood of misunderstanding being created. I will say only that much that the police order was issued after the legislative assembly resolutions were passed. The resolutions were not implemented till the end of the struggle, but as soon as the struggle ended all the undertrial prisoners were released. The government which claims to its job better and which refuses to recognise anything else than moral or physical force, has been given *gratis* advice—even if that advice might have been given a big name of legislative assembly resolutions—but nobody should have any illusion that the advice would be acceptable to the government. All such efforts on the contrary provide occasions to lay baseless and heinous charges against the persons who are not there to defend themselves. If those resolutions serve any purpose, it is if those resolutions are set aside and work is carried on that at proper occasion and for a proper cause those can be used.

It was the religious duty of the government to release all the prisoners after the procession passed through the prohibitory route, and I am thankful to the Government of Central Provinces for performing its duty. I am pained to see that out of one thousand prisoners, seven have not yet been released because they have broken the jail rules. Yet have confidence that they will be released soon. The delay in releasing prisoners is due to the circumstances beyond the control of Central Provinces government. I am happy to tell you that those persons who immediately came after me and who gave me full cooperation in fighting the battle fully concur with me regarding the failure of the resolutions passed by legislative assembly, though I must say that our viewpoints about the failure are different. Everybody knows that in political matters our view-points are poles apart. Yet, I and they are returning from Nagpur with a firm opinion on political matters.

I welcome you all, who have voluntarily courted arrest and now are again in midst of us. Struggle bigger than which have fought and greater sacrifices await you. Last time I told you that Flag Satyagraha has ended, and we have protected the dignity and honour of our national flag. We have again got restored our right to take out peaceful and orderly processions and passing through public roads. Truth and non-violence have triumphed. I have been inspired to say these words, when I see you in midst of us.

But there is nothing to be proud of our achievements. The victory is not in what we have achieved or what we have suffered. Our true victory will be our readiness to suffer more and more till we achieve our goal. It is truth that I do not deserve the credit for our victory, all the credit goes to the persons who have suffered and those who had prepared themselves to suffer in the struggle. Nagpur A.I.C.C. Committee had also shown unique power of management from the beginning to the end of our struggle and so the credit goes to it also.

I cannot finish this statement without referring to one matter. I was trying to find the source of the deceitful, and scandalous news which have been circulated about the incident of 18th. While any search was in progress I found a strange proof. A key to the attitude of *Times of India* towards this struggle from the beginning to the end, and the publication of famous four letters in *Times of India* after the arrest of Seth Jamnalal Bajaj and his colleagues in the first week of June also is found in the proof which I was able to get. In the issue of the 18th August of the *Statesman* of Calcutta, a wire sent by Commissioner of Nagpur on 19th is published. Its caption is "Satyagraha is to be Suspended"; "Leaders had to bow down before power"; the wire of the same date of the correspondent of *Times of India* is published in the issue of 20th under the caption, *"Accepted Government's orders"*. The wire is word by word a copy of the wire published in *Statesman.* Putting those two wires side by side and reading them it is difficult to determine whether the correspondent of *Times of India* is the Commissioner of Nagpur or the Nagpur Commissioner is the correspondent of *Times of India.* It is possible that *Statesman* instead of publishing from our correspondent like *Times of India;* inadvertently published "Wire received from the Commissioner of Nagpur" and thus the Commissioner was exposed. Even after getting this proof for some time, I could not believe that he must have published such a news item. While investigating further I found out that it was true. Yet I was assured that Nagpur Commissioner was not authorised to publish the news which was published in *Statesman.* Side by side I also saw that Central Provinces government has no control over the relations of the Commissioner with newspapers, nor over his activities. Previously also though he was ordered not to interfere in the work of the government by his activities concerning our struggle, he has put the government in an uncomfortable position. Thus he is arbitrary in his activities. I agree that government had a sincere desire to do something to see that the struggle is brought to an honourable end, and I have no doubt that Government is displeased by the activities of the Commissioner yet it is my bounden duty to tell that the government cannot escape from the responsibility of the actions of the Commissioner.

We have to thank Almighty that at a time when the mutual tolerance, political foresight, and the highest good of the country were crushed under the burden of personal likes and prejudices, partisanship, and communal riots, and at a time when the clouds of despondency, and doubts were encircling the country at the time merciful Lord showered mercy on us. He gave us this opportunity to demonstrate that under the apparent quarrels, prejudices, and bitterness, lies undercurrent of the strength, firmness, and unity of the people. In spite of the misunderstanding amongst friends, and all kinds of falsehood of the enemies, our holy war which is based on purity and fearlessness will be proudly remembered by the future generations, and will infuse in the people a sense of confidence regarding the superiority of the weapons of truth, non-violence and self-sacrifice in the holy war. Mahatma Gandhi's sermon is that truth, non-violence, and self-sacrifice are relevant to our nature as well as culture. Vande Matram.

179

Vallabhbhai Refutes Motilal Nehru's Allegation that Satyagraha was Called Off

Navjivan, 9 September 1923

Whatever I had to say about this struggle, I have given in writing. I am not afraid of criticism. If Pandit Motilal Nehru chooses to criticise me, I would only submit that I am a child before him and can hardly comment on the sacrifice he has made for the country or estimate the services he had rendered to the nation. If a greenhorn like me makes a mistake, it is his right as a senior and more experienced person to point it out. But in this campaign, Vithalbhai, my elder brother, was with me from the beginning and I was happy that a person who thought differently was fighting shoulder to shoulder with me. If we have won the battle, the credit goes to those who underwent all the troubles and were prepared to make all sacrifices. But if there was no victory, if a mistake like withdrawing from the struggle had been committed, the responsibility would be mine. I did not call off the struggle because I had no fighters to follow me in battle. Even on the last day I had 148 volunteers. I had to try to keep the number of volunteers down but in spite of that they came and were arrested at the railway station. The Government knew that even if I was arrested, there would be 15,000 volunteers who would come for the Satyagraha.

There was no reason for me, therefore, to call off the struggle. But I continued it only so long it was a battle for truth. Whenever and in whatever shape I see untruth, I tremble with fright. I found that keeping peace before the church was the right thing to do, but to shout *"Jais"* before the residence of the British officers was not. I followed the right course in directing the volunteers accordingly. If that action of mine is wrong in the eyes of some persons I would like to tell them that I would commit such errors throughout my life. We had to show to the Britishers that we did not want to obstruct every good thing that they did, but we opposed every wrong action of the rulers. We won the battle to the extent we followed the principles of truth, non-violence and tolerance. But, if it was our objective to plant the national flag on the government buildings, I must say that we failed to achieve that. When the volunteers carne out of the jails I asked them whether they were happy with the outcome of the struggle. They were and I was contented, but I cannot satisfy everybody.

Those who have a different style of fighting would naturally find my ways wrong. I was with Gandhiji for nine months in the Kheda satyagraha. But the

Mahatma informed the Government about his intention before he undertook something. Had I been in Nagpur before the *satyagraha* was launched, I would have similarly informed the authorities. The Government would have said "No" to such a thing and I have proof that it would have behaved in that manner. On the 6th April when Sunderlalji was stopped from entering Jabalpur, he made an application in writing, but it was rejected. The permission in Nagpur came later. Before that not a single person, not even a woman, could have walked carrying the national flag. When the government found that they would have to permit people to carry the flag they insisted that prior permission be sought. So long as the Government orders were there I fought against them till the last moment. When the magistrate and the police superintendent entered my house, I told them that I would fight their orders by disobeying them. Thousands of volunteers who had been arrested were released, but none of them was told not to do what they did again. And the world knows that they would do it again.

Two youngmen who were like tiger cubs have addressed you today. They know how to grin and bear all the troubles that come in the way and when I went to the jail when they were to be released, I was sorry to see how reduced they were physically. I could not even recognise my friend Bhogilal Lala, so weak he was after his stay in jail. The jail authorities use prisoners instead of oxen in the oil expeller. Each one of them has to work for eight hours in the day, walking a distance of 32 miles each eight hours. And then, the warders beat and belabour them. Our victory lies in the fact that volunteers from Gujarat themselves asked to be put on the oil expellers. Dr. Chandulal asked for solitary confinement. The government men were afraid of the volunteers from Gujarat and impressed both the authorities and the volunteers from other parts of the country with their courage. This in itself is, in my opinion, our victory.

The second thing which points to our victory is the fact that the people showed their courage and grit at a time when everybody had lost hope and it looked as if there is no fight left in them. Volunteers came from all parts of the country, went to jail with smiles on their lips and underwent all the troubles and tribulations. A youngman from Bihar died in the jail. One hour before the end came, he was offered release if he apologised. But he refused and laid down his life in captivity. What better victory could we hope for when we got an opportunity to show to the Britishers the stuff we were made of?

We should be humble in victory. Defeat and victory is in the hands of God. One who is vain about his victory is really a loser. Those who won in Europe really lost because they were vain about their conquest. Drunk with victory they are worse than the losers. Let us be confident that God is with us when we are on the right path and would help us.

Even those who are sent to the Andamans are afraid of the jails in the Central Provinces. Getting the volunteers to apologise being the sole aim of the authorities, they commit every atrocity within the parameters of the Jail Manual to bring them down to knees. Such things have happened in the jails. In spite of that the volunteers from Gujarat have said that they would be prepared to go to jail again and again. That leads me to believe that Gandhiji's movement has taken firm roots in Gujarat.

180

Vallabhbhai Criticizes Chief Secretary C.P. for his Distorted Version of Talks

Bombay Chronicle, 12 September 1923

Mr. Vallabhbhai Patel has issued the following statement showing that the Chief Secretary, C.P. Government, had in his resolution on Nagpur Flag agitation given a distorted account of negotiations. Whilst I was travelling to Delhi my attention was drawn to two statements, one issued by Mr. Vithalbhai Patel in concurrence with the Home Member of the C.P. Government and another by the Chief Secretary of that Government each referring to the various stages of negotiations about the Nagpur struggle. Having read both these statements, I feel bound to explain to the public the real facts as they happened in connection with the so-called negotiation. Unfortunately the whole correspondence that passed between my brother and the Home Member and myself and the Home Member is lying at Ahmedabad and shall publish the whole of it at a later stage, if the C.P. Government challenges any of the statements, I am going to make hereunder. I do not desire to controvert all points referred to in the statement of the Chief Secretary, but will confine myself to two or three more important of them. I may say at once that I have no quarrel with the statement issued by Mr. Vithalbhai Patel in concurrence with the Home Member. If matters had stood there probably I should have said nothing. But I cannot allow the statement of the Chief Secretary to stand uncontradicted. Both Mr. Patel and the Home Member very rightly say in their joint statement that neither party was to publish any account of any of the interview. The Chief Secretary, however, has freed me from this obligation, and if government chooses to deny any of the statements I will make hereunder I propose to publish not only the whole of the correspondence but also the full account as far as I remember of the interviews. That no Government, least of all, the Government of India is expected to admit their mistakes or confess defeats is understandable. But in this case the C.P. Government has gone further and is guilty of a breach of confidence by publishing the accounts of interviews that they promised to treat as confidential and asked us to treat as such. One might conceive the circumstances in which such disclosure may be pardonable. But I least expected that in doing so the facts would be distorted and grossly misrepresented. I am sorry for the C.P. Government about whom I had carried favourable impression.

I repeat that I take no exception to the joint statement but I desire to state my version on two or three points in the statement of the Chief Secretary and would wait to see what the C.P. Government has got to say about it. Firstly, as far the interview with the Governor, Mr. Vithalbhai Patel got a letter from the Chief Secretary requesting us to see him and discuss the situation with him. We did so and during our conversation it was suggested that we should interview the

House at Borsad

A comrade Mohal Lal Pandya

Vallabhbhai after the victory of Borsad Satyagraha

Darbarsaheb Gopaldas A. Desai,
President of Borsad
Satyagraha Committee

Ravishankar Maharaj, Sardar Patel's
"Shanti Sainik"

Leslie O. Wilson, Governor of Bombay, 1923-28

Maurice Hayward, Member Incharge, Home Department, Govt. of Bombay, 1923

Governor. We were not called upon to make any reply to this suggestion, and we had none. Next day Mr. Vithalbhai Patel got a letter from the Chief Secretary, intimating to us that if we desired to see His Excellency who would be glad to see us at 11.00 a.m. next day at the Residency. We accordingly interviewed His Excellency and discussed the whole situation for nearly three hours. We had never made any oral or written request for an interview. But the circumstances under which the interview came about are as mentioned by me above. Secondly, as for the permission, for procession, the statement suggests that we applied for permission, but there was nothing of the kind. My letter to the District Superintendent of Police speaks for itself. It is nothing more or less than a notice or intimation of what we were going to do. In our opinion there is nothing inherently wrong in applying for permission for a procession, but in this struggle the whole issue was absolutely unwarranted and illegal, and any application for permission on our part would be construed, and rightly so by the Government as well as by the people, as a sort of surrender on our part. In fact that was all that the Government wanted us to do and we refused to yield. When Mr. Vithalbhai had his first interview with the Home Member before the Council sitting the Home Member after consulting his other colleagues wrote to Mr. Vithalbhai that the Government had no objection to the passing of a procession if some one on behalf of the Congress Committee approached the District Magistrate in that behalf, and in that event the question of the release of prisoners would be favourably considered. There was no question as to the limit of the number of processionists or the manner in which they should proceed. I am afraid I have not the letter with me when I am writing this, but I have no doubt that the statement made is correct. We at once wrote back to say that we could make no such application to the District Magistrate whose very order has given rise to the Satyagraha movement.

Such was the anxiety of Government to settle matters even before the resolution of the Council. The suggestion in the statement of the Chief Secretary that we applied to the District Superintendent of Police is wholly incorrect and grossly misleading. Thirdly, the statement that we gave an undertaking that prisoners would not take any further part in the Nagpur Flag Agitation except under certain conditions is baseless, and appears to have been deliberately introduced for obvious reasons. Fourthly, there was no undertaking given by the Government to us nor by us to Government on any point. As rightly pointed out by the authors of the joint statement as a result of the interviews we understood the position of the Government and the Government understood us without giving any undertaking by either side.

I would add, in conclusion, that all negotiations and interviews were conducted throughout by Mr. Vithalbhai Patel and lately by both of us when in view of unequivocal statement amounting to an invitation for negotiations made by the Home Member in his speech in Council, the Working Committee authorised us both to do so. All these interviews and negotiations were conducted strictly on the basis of mutual trust and this fact was times without number made clear by each side to the other and there was no question of an undertaking on either side.

But for the fact that the Chief Secretary has chosen to publish a one-sided and distorted account we waive our objection to publication of all (not such of them as they like) letters written by us now in the possession of the Government and we claim that the Government members can have no objection to our publication. Their letters are in our possession.

181

Chief Secretary, Central Provinces to Secretary Home Department on Nagpur Flag Satyagraha

Home Department (Political) File No. 280 N.A.I.
12 September 1923

From A.E. Mathias, Esq., I.C.S., Chief Secretary to Government, Central Provinces, to the Secretary to the Government of India, Home Department, Simla, no. 1278-1287-11, dated Nagpur, the 12th September 1923.

Subject—"Flag" agitation at Nagpur.

I am directed to forward for the information of the Government of India a copy of the Political Department Resolution no. 1262-1057-11, dated the 8th September 1923, on the subject of the "Flag" agitation at Nagpur.

Resolution from A.E. Mathias, Esq., Chief Secretary to Government of the Central Provinces, no. 1262-1057-H, dated Nagpur, the 8th September 1923.

As the Nagpur flag agitation has now ceased, the Government of the Central Provinces considers it desirable to place on record a connected account of the principal events of the last four months and of the action by the Government to maintain order and vindicate respect for the law.

2. A true understanding of this mischievous movement can be gained by contrasting the irresponsible violence of its opening stages with the disavowals published by the leaders at its close. As already announced in this Government's communique of the 28th June, the first aggressive move was made by Bhagwandin, one of the most prominent agitators of the province, when, in a speech delivered on March 23rd, he threatened that a campaign of civil disobedience would be begun in Nagpur in May. Thereafter on the 13th April the attack was taken up by another local leader, Awari, who, in a speech of unusual violence, declared that two lacs of Englishmen must be expelled, and the Government of the Congress established by Satyagraha. He concluded by publicly stating his intention of leading a thousand men into the Civil Station, and the next day marched to the Civil Station at the head of a large and disorderly crowd headed by volunteers carrying national flags and shouting provocative cries. The Local Authorities were thus forced to take action for the maintenance of order, and the procession was

therefore stopped by the District Magistrate and the District Superintendent of Police in person under the authority of Section 30 (i) of the Police Act. Awari, however, insisted on pursuing his disorderly course further into the Civil Station asserting that he could accept no orders but those of his own Government, the Congress. Under the circumstances the Local Authorities decided to prohibit the procession and arrest its leaders.

3. Up to this point but little had been said or heard in Nagpur of the national flag, and, even if Awari's crowd had not carried these flags, the processions would have been dealt with in exactly the same way. From this date, however, the local leaders sought to justify lawless and disorderly conduct under the pretext of asserting the dignity of the national flag. Even after the events of the 14th April and the provocative speeches of the non-cooperators which followed, the Local Authorities made no attempt to interfere with a procession with the flag through that portion of the Civil Station where the public were accustomed in the ordinary course to proceed on business. No objection was accordingly taken to the published route announced by Seth Jamnalal Bajaj for the second procession on the 1st May. It was only when the procession branched off into the purely residential area that the District Magistrate stopped it by the issue of an order under Section 144 Criminal Procedure Code, prohibiting processions without his permission within that area on the grounds that such processions were likely to cause annoyance to the residents and lead to a disturbance of the public tranquillity. This procession under Seth Jamnalal on the 1st May was induced by the District Magistrate to turn back and proceed along its advertised route, but though the order was obeyed on this day it was deliberately disobeyed on the next, the 2nd May, when a third procession returned and crossed the line into the prohibited area. Thereafter day after day parties of varying numbers have sought to enter the prohibited area with the object of breaking the District Magistrate's order, and forcing their own arrest. The local Government then published a communique which stated explicitly that it would not interfere with the use of the Swarajya flag except when it constituted an offence under the Criminal law. As these events have shown, the District Magistrate's order under Section 144 of the Criminal Procedure Code was aimed not against the exercise of any legitimate public right, but against the misuse of the national flag in order to justify the repeated disorder and defiance of the law which ensued daily for the next 3-1/2 months.

4. Numerous volunteers of all ages and castes were brought to Nagpur for the purpose of defying the District Magistrate's order, and when the local and provincial sources of recruitment began to fail, further volunteers were enlisted from the other provinces of India, chiefly Bombay and Madras. The leaders maintained their defiant attitude unchanged until the end of June, and asserted that Stayagraha was justified by "the denial of the elementary right to exhibit the flag, and carry it in peaceful and orderly procession on public roads". No such right ever has been or will be challenged by the Government, and this charge is refuted definitively by the communique of the 1st May. Further the sinister origin of these disturbances is suppressed, and the disorder and civil disobedience

organised and sustained by Awari, Jamnalal, Bhagwandin and others are transmitted into the harmless right to carry a flag in peaceful procession.

5. After the arrest of Jamnalal on the 18th June, representatives of the Working Committee of the Congress took charge of the movement, and disavowals were made of any intention to insult the Union Jack or to cause annoyance to the European residents. Negotiations for a settlement of this agitation were initiated with the Home Member of the Government by Mr. V. J. Patel before the meeting of the Legislative Council at the beginning of August. The position of the Government was explained by His Excellency the Governor in his address to the Legislative Council on the 6th August. He pointed out that the order of the District Magistrate had not prohibited all processions but only processions without his permission; and further declared that the unrestricted right to the use of the public roads without regulation is not permitted in any civilised country. He stated that the local Government regarded the agitation as Civil Disobedience and an attempt to overcome the authority of Government, and that this challenge to lawful authority would be resisted.

On August the 13th His Excellency the Governor granted an interview to Mr. V.J. and Mr. V.B. Patel, under circumstances which have already been made known in the Chief Secretary's communique of the 1st September, in which it was denied that the interview took place at the express invitation of His Excellency the Governor. After subsequent interviews with the Home Member, the Government communicated to Mr. Patel the conditions under which a procession would be permitted within the prohibited area upon application to the Local Authorities. On the 16th August, Mr. V.B. Patel issued a statement, as the authorised representative of the Working Committee of the Congress, that they did not claim the unrestricted right to take processions along the public roads, that the processions were not intended to annoy any section of the public, and that the National Flag was not carried with any intention to insult the Union Jack. The order passed by the District Magistrate of Nagpur prohibiting all processions without his permission within a certain area expired on the 16th August. On the 17th August an order under Section 30(Y) of the Police Act was promulgated by the District Superintendent of Police, Nagpur, prescribing the routes for processions in the city of Nagpur. No procession could therefore pass through the prohibited area covered previously by the District Magistrate's order without the special orders of the District Superintendent of Police. On the morning of the 18th August the following application was made to the District Superintendent of Police:-

To

The District Superintendent of Police, Nagpur.

Sir,

I hereby intimate to you that I propose to organise and take a procession through the city and the Civil lines to-day, the 18th August 1923, at the time, by the routes, and in the manner mentioned in the published notice a copy of which is herewith enclosed for your information.

Yours truly,
VALLABHBHAI J. PATEL

The time, the route, and the manner referred to were the same as those laid down by Government. The route prescribed did not include the strictly residential portion of the Civil Station, the numbers were limited to one hundred, and orderly conduct was required, with no singing of songs or shouting of *jais* beyond the point fixed. This procession was held accordingly, and the conditions duly observed, and thereafter the leaders declared that Satyagraha had ceased. No procession has entered the prohibited area since that date.

6. Having satisfied itself that the agitation had ceased, and having been given an undertaking that the prisoners would not take any further part in the Nagpur Flag agitation contrary to the conditions under which the procession of the 18th August was permitted, the local Government as an act of clemency decided to release the prisoners, except those convicted of offences against the Prisons Act. Most of them are misguided youths with no real knowledge of the movement; and with the cessation of the agitation it was considered that there was no necessity for retaining in prison those who failed to execute bonds under the Security sections of the Criminal Procedure Code.

Throughout this agitation the policy of the Government has remained unchanged. The Governor in Council has insisted on the maintenance of two principles—the first is submission to lawful authority, and the second that no procession can be permitted within the prohibited area without application to the local authorities and due observance of the conditions imposed. Both the above points were satisfied before the procession of the 18th August was allowed. The future policy of the Government will follow the same lines, and any procession such as is calculated to cause annoyance to any section of the public or is disorderly in character will be prohibited.

8. Finally the Governor in Council desires to express his high appreciation of the admirable conduct of all officials upon whom has rested during this trying period the burden of heavy and responsible additional duties. Under the good guidance of the Commissioner, Mr. Clarke, a high standard of duty has been maintained by all ranks. Mr. Clarke was also entrusted by Government with the publicity arrangements connected with the agitation. To the District Magistrate, Mr. H.C. Gowan, I.C.S., the thanks of Government are due for his efficient control, with unfailing patience and sound judgment, of the agitation from its beginning to its close. The Government also desires to acknowledge the good work of the magistrates and the promptitude with which they disposed of their heavy criminal cases. To the District Superintendent of Police, Mr. D.A. Smyth, the City Superintendent, Mr. Sant Singh, and to all ranks of the force under their control, special acknowledgment is due for the excellent arrangements and uniform consideration and good temper with which they have met every call on their energies and self-control. Lastly the local Government desires to acknowledge

the good services of the Jail Superintendent Captain N.S. Jater, D.S.O., I.M.S., and his staff, under trying conditions of exceptional difficulty.

182

Vallabhbhai Refutes C.P. Government's Allegation regarding Permission to Take out a Procession

Navjivan, 13 September 1923

In reply to the communique of the Chief Secretary of the C.P. government:

Whilst I was travelling to Delhi, my attention was drawn to two statements, one issued by Mr. Vithalbhai Patel in concurrence with the Home Member of the C.P. government and another by the Chief Secretary of that government each referring to the various stages of negotiations about the Nagpur struggle. Having read both these statements, I feel bound to explain to the public the real facts as they happened in connection with the so-called negotiations. Unfortunately the whole correspondence which passed between my brother and the Home Member is lying at Ahmedabad, and I shall publish the whole of it at a later stage if the C.P. government challenges any of the statements I am going to make hereunder. I do not desire to controvert all points referred to the statement of the Chief Secretary, but will confine myself to two or three more important of them. I may say at once that I have no quarrel with the statement issued by Mr. Vithalbhai Patel in concurrence with the Home Member. If matters had stood there, probably I should have said nothing but I cannot allow the statement of the Chief Secretary to stand uncontradicted. Both Mr. Patel and the Home Member very rightly publish any account of any of the interviews. The Chief Secretary has however freed me from this obligation and if the government chooses to deny any of the statements, I will make hereunder I propose to publish not only the whole correspondence but also the full account, as far as I remember of the interviews. That no government, least of all Government of India is expected to admit their mistake or confess defeats is understandable. But in this case the C.P. government has gone further and is guilty of breach of confidence by publishing an account of the interviews that they themselves promised to treat as confidential and asked us to treat as such. One might conceive circumstances in which such disclosure may be pardonable. But I least expected that in doing so facts would be distorted and grossly misrepresented. I am sorry for the C.P. government about whom I had carried a somewhat favourable impression. I repeat that I take no exception to the joint statement, but I desire to state my version on two or three points in the statement of the Chief Secretary and would wait to see what the C.P. government has got to say about it.

Firstly, as for the interview with the Governor, Mr. Vithalbhai Patel got a letter from the Chief Secretary requesting us to see him and discuss the situation with him. We did so and during our conversation it was suggested that we should interview the Governor. We were not called upon to make any reply to this suggestion, and we made none. Next day Mr. Vithalbhai Patel got a letter from the Chief Secretary intimating to us that if we desire to see His Excellency he would be glad to see us at 11 a.m. next day at the residency. We accordingly interviewed His Excellency and discussed the whole situation for nearly three hours. We had never made any oral or written request for an interview, but the circumstances under which the interview came about are as mentioned by me above.

Secondly, as for permission for procession, the statement suggests as if we applied for permission. Nothing of the kind. My letter to the District Superintendent of Police speaks for itself. It is nothing more or less than a notice or intimation of what we are going to do. In our opinion there is nothing inherently wrong in applying for taking permission for a procession, but in this struggle the whole issue was absolutely unwarranted and illegal and any application for permission on our part would be construed, and rightly so, by the Government as well as by the people, as a sort of surrender on our part. In fact that was all that the Government wanted us to do, and we refused to yield. When Mr. Vithalbhai had his first interview with the Home Member before the Council sitting, the Home Member after consulting his other colleagues wrote to Mr. Vithalbhai that the Government had no objection to passing of procession if some one on behalf of Congress Committee approached the District Magistrate in that behalf and in that event the question of the release of prisoners would be favourably considered. There was no question as to the limit of number of processionists or the manner in which they were to proceed. I am afraid I have not the letter with me when I am writing this, but I have no doubt that the statement I make is correct. We at once wrote back to say that we could make no such application to the District Magistrate whose very order has given rise to the Satyagraha movement. Such was the anxiety of the Government to settle the matter even before the resolution of the council. The suggestion in the statement of the Chief Secretary that we applied to the District Superintendent of Police is wholly incorrect and generally misleading.

Thirdly, the statement that we gave an understanding that the prisoners would not take any further part in Nagpur Flag Agitation except under certain conditions is baseless and appears to have been deliberately introduced for obvious reasons.

Fourthly, there was no undertaking given by the Government to us nor by us to the Government on any point. As rightly pointed out by the authors of the joint statement as a result of interviews we understood the position of the Government and the Government understood us without giving off any undertaking by either side. I would add in conclusion that all negotiations and interviews were conducted throughout by Mr. Vithalbhai Patel and lately by both of us when in view of the unequivocal statement announcing to an invitation for negotiation made by the Home Member in his speech in the Council, the Working Committee authorised us both to do so. All these interviews and negotiations were conducted strictly on the basis of mutual trust and this fact was times without number made clear by each side to the other, and there was no question of an understanding on either side. But for that the Chief Secretary has chosen to publish a one-sided and distorted account. We have our objection to the publication of all (not such of them as they like) letters written by us and now in the possession of the Government, and we claim that the Government members can have no objection to our publication of their letters in our possession.

183

Vallabhbhai Endorses Resolution[1] on Civil Disobedience Home Deptt. (Sp.) F. No. 355(58)/1923

16 September 1923

"This Congress resolves that a Committee consisting of the following members be formed forthwith to organise an effective campaign of Civil Disobedience and to advise and regulate the action of the provinces organising similar provincial or local campaigns for the speedy attainment of Swaraj, which alone can guarantee the restoration of Mahatma Gandhi and the other political prisoners to liberty, as well as the freedom of the Jaziratul-Arab and a satisfactory settlement of the Punjab wrong."

The Committee is to be composed of Maulana Mohammad Ali, Dr. Kitchlew, Deshbandhu Das, Babu Rajendra Prasad, Mr. Vallabhbhai Patel, Sardar Surendra, Pt. Jawaharlal Nehru and Sjt. Vithalbhai Patel.

Moved by Dr. Kitchlew and seconded and supported by Mrs. Naidu and Deshbandhu Das respectively.

[1]Resolution passed at the Special Session of the Indian National Congress held at Delhi on the 15th September 1923, and three subsequent days.

184

Vallabhbhai Reluctant to Withdraw His Opposition to Council Entry[1] Resolution

Navjivan, 18 September 1923

I support every word that has fallen from the lips of Rajendrababu. My views have not changed and I am firm in my belief. Even so, why have I got up to withdraw my opposition to the idea? You have heard the beautiful idea presented by the gentleman who moved the resolution. You and I know fully well that there could be nobody who is more faithful to Gandhiji, the father of the Non-cooperation Movement, than Maulana Mohammad Ali. I am prepared to give him any help that he wants. I have looked into my heart and found that the least I can do to help him is to withdraw my opposition. He asks me that I must take into consideration the circumstances which are prevailing after two years of his absence. Now he also must have realized the difficulties which those who remained outside faced in that period. I hope that he would have the same feelings towards me as I have towards him. You must have seen that the young Vardhachari looks shattered. I know that this attitude of mine will shatter many hearts. I am not yet convinced that this accord will not deal a mortal blow to non-cooperation. But I do not feel that the future is dark as Mr. Vardhachari does. He thinks that Mohammed Ali will have no leg to stand on in the Kakinada Congress and if the country wants to return to non-cooperation, it will not be able to do so. I believe that if non-cooperation is postponed for some time, it would be beneficial, because the atmosphere is not congenial for it. There are mutual suspicions amongst us and we are now trying to regain mutual love. That is why that we should neither support this resolution nor oppose it. Those who agree with me should follow my lead and do at least that which I am doing. During this period, it was painful for me to oppose the leaders but today when I am giving up that opposition, it is equally painful. I request you to please extricate yourselves from this painful position. I hold Maulana Mohammad Ali responsible to the full. My friends, Jamnalal and G.D. Deshpande agree with me and they have been with me all through my opposition to this idea. I would now resume my seat and say in the end, in clearest terms, that I do not support this resolution nor do I oppose it.

[1]A special session of the Congress was held in Delhi between 15th and 18th September 1923. It passed a resolution to boycott the assemblies. Sardar Patel made a speech withdrawing his opposition to the resolution.

185

G.H.W. Davies, Deputy Secretary, Home Department to William Duke, Under Secretary of State on Nagpur Flag Satyagraha

Home Department (Political) File No. 280, N.A.I., 20 September 1923

From G.H.W, Davies, Deputy Secretary to the Government of India, Home Department, to Sir William Duke, G.C.I.E., K.C.S.I., His Majesty's Under Secretary of State for India, no. 128, dated Simla, the 20th September 1923.

In continuation of the Viceroy's telegram no. 710, dated the 1st September 1923, I am directed to forward for the information of the Secretary of State a copy of Resolution no. 1262-1057-11, dated the 8th September 1923, issued by the Government of the Central Provinces regarding the flag agitation at Nagpur.

Telegram P., from Secretary of State to Viceroy (Home Department), no. 3413, dated the London, the 20th (received the 21st) September 1923.

Reference your telegram of the 1st instant. Nagpur flag incident. Please call for a full report on the whole matter. I should be glad to receive this as soon as possible by mail, with comments of Your Excellency's Government. At present it is not clear whether, when the negotiations were opened, the previous action of the local Government had not already practically defeated the agitation and whether the decision to allow procession even on special conditions is not likely to be generally regarded as a triumph for the flag movement.

I desire, on the my present information, to say that while I recognise the difficulties of local situation, I think that the Local Government should have consulted the Government of India before entering upon negotiations for it must have been obvious that their action would have repercussion far beyond their own provinces. While I am disposed to share the view of Your Excellency's Government on the two points of the second procession which I learn from your telegram of September 8th did not actually take place and release of prisoners these decisions seem to have emerged almost inevitably from negotiations. Obviously permission to hold a procession to celebrate release of prisoners convicted for trying to hold a similar procession was open to construction that Government admitted earlier policy to have been wrong. The essential point however is whether the Local Government was justified in modifying its original attitude which it had very recently justified in the Legislative Council debate.

The Local Government should be informed it is very inconvenient that news of such action should reach the Government of India and myself through the newspapers. It is merely due to accident that Parliament had risen that matter did not immediately lead to very embarrassing criticism here.

I am in the meanwhile deferring reply to your despatch No. 3, dated May 31st but I take this opportunity of saying that resentment expressed by Your Excellency's Government is due to misinterpretation of my suggestion that instructions to District Officers ought to be precise enough exclusive of the possibility of their supposing that they had encouragement of Government for individual action of a kind which the local Governments could not or would not support.

186

Secretary of State Asks for Report on Genesis of Nagpur Satyagraha

Home Department (Political) File No. 280, N.A.I.
24 September 1923

Telegram from the Government of India, Home Department, Simla, to the Government of Central Provinces, Pachmarhi, no.D.-2476-Poll., dated the 24th September 1923.

Secretary of State desires to have by mail full and connected report Nagpur Flag incident. Following are points on which in light of Secretary of State's provisional comments it is desirable that statement contained in Central Provinces Government's Resolution no. 2162-1057-H, dated the 8th September should in particular be supplemented.

(*i*) whether when negotiations were opened previous action of local Government had not already practically defeated agitation;

(*ii*) grounds of local Government for entering on negotiations which must have repercussion beyond their own provinces without consultation of Government of India;

(*iii*) whether decision to allow even on special conditions processions is not likely to be generally regarded as triumph for flag movement, and in particular whether permission to hold procession to celebrate release of prisoners convicted in connection with similar procession was not open to construction that Government admitted earlier policy to be wrong;

(*iv*) grounds of local Government for modifying their original attitude recently justified in Legislative Council.

2. Secretary of State desires Central Provinces Government's attention to be drawn to inconvenience arising from news of such action reaching Government of India and himself through newspapers.

3. Please send report with least possible delay.

187

A.E. Mathias, Chief Secretary, Government of Central Provinces to Secretary, Government of India, Home Department on Nagpur Flag Satyagraha

Home Department (Political) File No. 280 N.A.I. Extracts
1 October 1923

No. 163-1, dated Nagpur, the 1st October 1923.

From—A. E. Mathias, Esq., I.C.S., Chief Secretary to the Government of the Central Provinces, Political and Military Department,

To—The Secretary to the Government of India, Home Department, Simla.

I am directed to acknowledge the receipt of your telegram no. D.-2476-Poll., dated the 24th September, in which it is stated that the Secretary of State desires a full and connected report of the "National" flag agitation at Nagpur. Such a report has already been issued in this Government's Resolution no. 1262, dated the 8th September, but I am directed to supplement it by the following further information, with special reference to the particular points raised by the Secretary of State's comments.

The agitation in connection with the "National" flag commenced at Jubbulpore when the flying of this flag on the Town Hall was prohibited by the District Magistrate under Section 144, Criminal Procedure Code, on the ground that he had received a petition from some 500 residents objecting to such action and that the flying of the flag on the Town Hall would cause annoyance to such persons. A procession carrying the flag was similarly prevented under Section 30 Police Act from entering the Jubbulpore Cantonment area on March the 18th, because it was considered likely to cause annoyance and a breach of the public tranquillity. Thereafter the scene of operations was shifted to Nagpur, the local extremist party deliberately choosing this town in preference to Jubbulpore as more suited to their purpose. With the exception of two or three attempts to fly the flag on the Town Hall, in the course of which fifteen persons were sentenced to periods of imprisonment, there was no further trouble at Jubbulpore.

The salient features of the Nagpur agitation have already been given in the Resolution referred to above. The agitation never received any considerable local support in Nagpur; it failed to appeal to the uneducated, while the more responsible political leaders regarded it from the outset as entirely unjustified; the Swaraj party of the Congress, which had advised entry into the Legislative Councils on the ground that civil disobedience was impracticable and inadvisable, considered the agitation an astute political move directed against themselves. This party, which in this province is strong, threw its influence against the agitation.

By the commencement of June it became apparent that special measures would be needed to counter this new development. After consulting the Government of India, it was decided to arrest the local leaders of the movement for trial under Section 120-B., Indian Penal Code. It was decided at the same time that persons who arrived in Nagpur, with the obvious intention of committing an offence by disobeying the District Magistrate's order, should be arrested under Section 55, Criminal Procedure Code, and called on to give security as not being able to give a satisfactory account of themselves under Section 109, Criminal Procedure Code. Accordingly on the 17th and 18th June four leaders *viz.,* Jamnalal Bajaj, Ibid Ali, Nilkantrao Deshmukh and Bhagwandin were arrested; a general round up of volunteers imported into Nagpur for a special display of civil disobedience on Gandhi day, was carried out early on the 18th June, and 250 arrests were made. On the application of certain residents of the main road along which the processions passed in order to reach the prohibited area, representing that the constant processions caused them serious annoyance, a fresh order under Section 144, Criminal Procedure Code, was issued extending the prohibited area. Instructions were also issued to Deputy Commissioners to prevent the recruitment in their districts of "volunteers" for the Nagpur agitation, by the prosecution of persons attempting to recruit or to incite others to offer disobedience at Nagpur to the District Magistrate's order. These measures were effective in disorganizing the movement for a time, and the supply of "volunteers" was with difficulty maintained.

Efforts however were made to import "volunteers" from other provinces, to secure the formal approval of the Congress, and to get that body to take up the flag movement as an "All-India" matter. These efforts met with success, and on the 6th June the Congress Committee sitting at Nagpur gave its approval to the agitation, instructed other provinces to assist, and directed its working committee to devise ways and means to assist the agitation. Mr. V.B. Patel was entrusted with the general management of the movement on behalf of the Congress Committee. The importance of the Resolution of the Congress Committee was lessened by the fact that the Swaraj party abstained from voting, while the "All-India" flag day arranged for the 18th July was not much of a success. At the same time it must be recognized that the resolution of the Congress Committee meant the financial support of the Congress, and in fact Rs 50,000 were voted to assist the movement. In India it is always possible to obtain volunteers on payment, and the Congress had funds at its disposal sufficient to continue the agitation for an indefinite period. The effect of Congress financial support was at once apparent in the increase in the number of arrests. At the beginning of July arrests averaged from 6 to 8 a day; on the 9th July it increased to 15; between 1st August and 16th August the daily average of arrests was 19. It was the declared policy of the leaders to continue the agitation for a long period by offering for daily arrest small parties of volunteers. The local Government was not in a position to estimate the number of volunteers likely to be recruited from other provinces. Mr. Patel's public statement estimated the number at ten to twelve thousand. Newspapers gave accounts of the organization of parties at various centres, and in particular of women volunteers, with whom it would have been difficult to deal. It therefore seemed probable that the agitation might be continued over a long period, and the local Government had also to take into account the fact that the amendments of the Criminal Procedure Code would shortly come into force, under which it would be possible to award simple imprisonment only for failure to give security in proceedings taken under Section 109, Criminal Procedure Code. But the fact that the agitation might be continued for a substantial period, together with some weakening of the legal position, did not influence the policy of the local Government.

Negotiations for a settlement of this agitation were initiated with the Home Member of the Government by Mr. V.J. Patel before the meeting of the Legislative Council at the beginning of August. The position of the Government was explained by His Excellency the Governor in his address to the Legislative Council on the 6th August. He pointed out that the order of the District Magistrate had not prohibited all processions but only processions without his permission; and further declared that the unrestricted right to the use of the public roads without regulation is not permitted in any civilised country. He stated that the local Government regarded the agitation as Civil Disobedience and an attempt to overcome the authority of Government, and that this challenge to lawful authority would be resisted.

As regards the negotiations with Mr. Patel I am to state that the Government did not enter on such negotiations. It was approached by Mr. V.J. Patel and Mr. V.B. Patel, representatives of the Congress Committee, with a view to ascertaining the conditions in which Government would allow a procession through the prohibited area, and the Government considered that it should not refuse to explain its position to anyone desiring to ascertain it. During the course of the negotiations with the Home Member of the Government, His Excellency the Governor granted an interview to Mr. V.J. and Mr. V.B. Patel on the 13th August, under circumstances which have already been made known in the Chief Secretary's Communique of the 1st September, in which it was denied that the interview took place at the express invitation of His Excellency the Governor. After subsequent interviews with the Home Member, the Government communicated to Mr. Patel the conditions under which a procession would be permitted within the prohibited area upon application to the local authorities. These conditions were settled with the concurrence of the local authorities. Moreover, Mr. Patel gave an undertaking that if this procession was permitted Satyagraha would cease; and that if the prisoners were released they would also abstain from further participation in processions without permission. A further result of these negotiations was that on the 15th August Mr. V.B. Patel issued a statement, as the authorized representative of the Working Committee of the Congress, that they did not claim the unrestricted right to take processions along the public roads, that the processions were not intended to annoy any section of the public, and that the national flag was not carried with any intention to insult the Union Jack. It was considered that this statement materially altered the position.

On the evening of the 17th August the order of the District Magistrate under Section 144, Criminal Procedure Code, expired and as there was no danger of a breach of the peace, it could not be renewed. The same day the District Superintendent of Police issued an order under Section 30 Police Act specifying the roads in the Nagpur Civil Station along which no processions could pass without his permission; the roads specified were those running through the residential portion of the Civil Station. On the morning of the 18th August an application was made by Mr. Patel to the District Superintendent of Police, which has already been published in the Government Resolution, stating the conditions on which he proposed to lead a procession through a portion of the prohibited area. The time, the route and the manner referred to were the same as those laid down by Government. The route prescribed did not include the strictly residential portion of the Civil Station, the numbers were limited to one hundred and orderly conduct was required, with no singing of songs or shouting of *jais* beyond the point fixed. This procession was held accordingly, the conditions were duly observed and thereafter the leaders declared that Satyagraha had ceased. No procession has entered the prohibited area since that date.

The local Government did not consult the Government of India before allowing this procession, because they did not consider that this decision involved any change of the policy followed after consultation with the Government of India, and because the local authorities were alone in a position to judge the local facts upon which the legal position depended. But I am to express the regret of the local Government that in coming to a decision which involved the release of the prisoners, they overlooked the instructions forwarded with your endorsement no. D.-12, dated the 9th February 1923.

The third point is whether the decision to allow a procession even on special conditions is not likely to be generally regarded as a triumph for the flag movement and in particular whether permission to hold a procession to celebrate the release of prisoners convicted in connection with similar processions was not open to the construction that Government admitted the earlier policy to be wrong. In regard to this I am to say that the view that the flag movement has been successful is mainly confined to the extreme section of the Congress, who have grossly misrepresented the facts under which the procession was permitted. The Anglo-Indian press, with one or two exceptions, support the local Government's action (see the leading articles in the *Statesman* of the 12th September and of the *Times of India* of September 10th). The Moderate press considers that the local Government has successfully vindicated its authority. The Swaraj press bitterly attacks the civil disobedience party and considers that Mr. Patel has surrendered abjectly to Government. I am to enclose press cuttings in support of the above statements. After the release of prisoners, the demonstrations in this province were unimportant and generally small. The local Government considers that permission to hold a second procession on the release of the prisoners, on the same conditions as were imposed on the first procession, could not logically nor legally be refused, since there would have been no risk of a breach of the peace or of annoyance to residents. In point of fact permission for a second procession was not sought nor was such a procession held. The local Government understands that on reflection Mr. V.B. Patel decided not take out the second procession because a repetition of the first "funeral" procession would have disclosed the defeat of the flag movement and would have made patent to all that the procession was allowed only under the conditions imposed by the Government, a fact which he has denied but which is admitted in Mr. V.J. Patel's published statement of the 10th September.

ENCLOSURE No. 1 *(Extracts)*
No. 1262-1057-H., dated Nagpur, the 8th September 1923.
Resolution by the Government of the Central Provinces,
Political and Military Department.

As the Nagpur flag agitation has now ceased, the Government of the Central Provinces considers it desirable to place on record a connected account of the principal events of the last four months and of the action by the Government to maintain order and vindicate respect for the law.

A true understanding of this mischievous movement can be gained by contrasting the irresponsible violence of its opening stages with the disavowals published by the leaders at its close. As already announced in this Government's *Communique* of the 28th June, the first aggressive move was made by Bhagwandin, one of the most prominent agitators of the province, when, in a speech delivered on March 23rd, he threatened that a campaign of Civil Disobedience would be begun in Nagpur in May. Thereafter on the 13th April the attack was taken up by another local leader, Awari, in a speech of unusual violence, declared that two lakhs of Englishmen must be expelled, and the Government of the Congress established by Satyagraha. He concluded by publicly stating his intention of leading men into the Civil Station, and the next day marched to the Civil Station at the head of a large and disorderly crowd headed by volunteers carrying national flags and shouting provocative cries. The local authorities were thus forced to take action for the maintenance of order, and the procession was therefore stopped by the District Magistrate and the District Superintendent of Police in person under the authority of Section 30 (i) of the Police Act. Awari, however, insisted on pursuing his disorderly course further into the Civil Station, asserting that he could accept no orders but those of his own Government, the Congress. Under the circumstances the local authorities decided to prohibit the procession and arrest its leaders.

On August the 13th His Excellency the Governor granted an interview to Mr. V.J. and Mr. V.B. Patel under circumstances which have already been made known in the Chief Secretary's *Communique* of the 1st September, in which it was denied that the interview took place at the express invitation of His Excellency the Governor. After subsequent interviews with the Home Member, the Government communicated to Mr. Patel the conditions under which a procession would be permitted within the prohibited area upon application to the local authorities. On the 16th August, Mr. V.B. Patel issued a statement, as the authorised representative of the Working Committee of the Congress, that they did not claim the unrestricted right to take processions along the public roads, that the processions were not intended to annoy any section of the public, and that the national flag was not carried with any intention to insult the Union Jack. The order passed by the District Magistrate of Nagpur prohibiting all processions without his permission within a certain area expired on the 16th August. On the 17th August an order under Section 30 (i) of the Police Act was promulgated by the District Superintendent of Police, Nagpur, prescribing the routes for processions in the city of Nagpur. No procession could therefore pass through the prohibited area covered previously by the District Magistrate's order without the special orders of the District Superintendent of Police. On the morning of the 18th August the following application was made to the District Superintendent of Police:—

To

The District Superintendent of Police,
Nagpur.

Sir.

I hereby intimate to you that I propose to organise and take a procession through the City and the Civil lines to-day, the 18th August 1923, at the time, by the routes, and in the manner mentioned in the published notice, a copy of which is herewith enclosed for your information.

Yours truly,
Vallabhbhai J. Patel

The time, the route, and the manner referred to were the same as by

Government. The route prescribed did not include the strictly residential portion of the Civil Station, the numbers were limited to one hundred, and orderly conduct was required, with no singing of songs or shouting of *jais* beyond the point fixed. This procession was held accordingly, and the conditions duly observed, and thereafter the leaders declared that Satyagraha had ceased. No procession has entered the prohibited area since that date. Throughout this agitation the policy of the Government has remained unchanged. The Governor in Council has insisted on the maintenance of two principles—the first is submission to lawful authority, and the second that no procession can be permitted within the prohibited area without application to the local authorities and due observance of the conditions imposed. Both the above points were satisfied before the procession of the 18th August was allowed. The future policy of the Government will follow the same lines, and any procession such as is calculated to cause annoyance to any section of the public or is disorderly in character will be prohibited.

A.E. MATHIAS,
Chief Secretary to Government, Central Provinces

ENCLOSURE No. 2 *(Extracts)*
Dated Pachmarhi, the 1st May 1923.
Communique by the Government of the Central Provinces

In view of the misunderstanding which prevails in regard to Government's attitude in connection with the use of the "Swarajya" flag, Government considers it desirable to explain its policy in regard thereto.

The local Government has not interfered, and does not propose to interfere, with the use of the "Swarajya" flag except when it constitutes an offence against the criminal law. When it is proposed to fly the "Swarajya" flag or to take it in procession in such circumstances as to be likely to cause a breach of the public tranquillity or cause annoyance to any person lawfully employed, the district authorities will take such action under the law as the circumstances demand to prevent such a breach of the peace or such annoyance. It is undoubtedly the case that any form of disrespect to the Union Jack, the national flag of the British Empire, is deeply resented by some classes of loyal subjects of that Empire.

In accordance with this policy the District Magistrate, Jubbulpore, rightly prohibited the flying of the "Swarajya" flag on the Jubbulpore Town Hall on the occasion of the visit of the Congress deputation. . . .

On the other hand, in Bilaspur, Seoni and other places where it has not yet appeared that the taking of the flag in procession will cause annoyance to any class of persons or will endanger the public peace, the district authorities, consistently with Government policy, have taken no action in the matter.

Moreover, where the circumstances are such as to indicate that a Municipal Committee or other local body has resolved to hoist the "Swarajya" flag over its building, Government is not prepared to tolerate such action. In such circumstances the resolution of the local body will be rescinded and, if in spite of such prohibition the local body persists in such action, Government will mark its disapproval by withdrawing its grants to such local body or taking such other disciplinary measures as it thinks necessary.

N.B. Enclosures No. 3 and 4 deleted.—*Editor*

ENCLOSURE No. 5

Dated 1st September 1923.

Communique by the Government of the Central Provinces

The following statement is published for information. It is reported that in a speech at Bombay on the 18th August in connection with the Nagpur Satyagraha Mr. V.J. Patel stated that "he had gone to the Governor at his express invitation and he wanted to make that point clear". I am directed to deny the accuracy of that statement. The negotiations for a settlement were initiated by Mr. V.J. Patel with the Home Member of the Government. During the course of those negotiations I was approached by certain members of the Legislative Council and it was suggested to me that I should ascertain whether His Excellency the Governor would be prepared to receive Mr. V.J. Patel. Having ascertained from Mr. V.J. Patel that he acquiesced in this suggestion, I agreed to enquire from His Excellency and after doing so, I wrote a letter to Mr. V.J. Patel that if he desired an interview with the Governor, His Excellency would be prepared to receive him at 11 a.m. on Monday the 15th August. The letter is presumably still in Mr. Patel's possession Both the Patel brothers attended Government House at the fixed time and were given an interview by His Excellency the Governor. Other inaccuracies and suppressions of facts have occurred in the accounts of the negotiations, which it may be necessary to correct later.

ENCLOSURE No 6

Mr. Vithalbhai's Statement

The following statement has been issued by Mr. Vithalbhai J. Patel with the concurrence of the Home Member of the Central Provinces Government on the Nagpur Satyagraha movement.

"Numerous enquiries from various parts of the country have been addressed to me asking to publish a brief account of the interviews that I had with the members of the Central Provinces Government and the terms of agreement, if any, reached as a result of these interviews, I have also seen all sorts of conflicting versions appearing in the press in this connection and the public naturally expects me to make some statement on the subject. I, therefore, with the concurrence of the Hon'ble the Home Member of the Central Provinces Government, issue the following:—

"I initiated the negotiations with the Home Member of the Central Provinces

Government after my arrival at Nagpur and before the meeting of the Legislative Council. From the speeches of the official members of the Central Provinces Government in the Council I gathered that there was a genuine desire on the part of the Government also for mutual understanding on the Satyagraha movement. I visited the Chief Secretary and several members of the Legislative Council and was granted an interview by His Excellency the Governor. There were about a dozen interviews at which I found that the Home Member was ready to allow a procession under conditions considered necessary by the Government and which we were prepared to accept as honourable. Mr. Vallabhbhai Patel was present at some of the interviews. We fully understood the position of the Government and I trust Government understood that neither party was to publish an account of the interviews. Under these circumstances the procession of the 18th August passed through the Civil Lines and thus ended the whole trouble."

ENCLOSURE No. 7

(*Press extracts*)

Extract from The Mahratta, *dated the 9th September 1923.*

VICTORY IN A PICKWICKIAN SENSE!

Pandit Motilal Nehru has clearly brought out the real nature of the Nagpur flag affair in one of his speeches. He fully appreciated the devoted self-sacrifice of the workers, but he expressed his regret that he could not pay a similar tribute to the conception itself; nor could he appreciate how the result could possibly be taken as a victory for the Congress. He failed entirely to see what principle had been established and how the country had advanced by the immense sacrifice made. On the contrary, he gave it as his considered opinion that by taking the last procession through the prohibited area with the permission of the authorities and obeying orders of the Police Superintendent about *jais* the organisers of the movement had practically abandoned the first principles of Non-cooperation. The assertion is cruel undoubtedly, but true beyond dispute. All the leaders of the no-change party are making huge efforts to tom-tom this as their victory but a closer scrutiny shows up that the victory claimed is a victory only in the Pickwickian sense. Mr. Vallabhbhai has issued another statement, perhaps to cover with strong words, against the critics of the movement, the ignominy with which the whole affair had to be ended by the underhand machinations of himself and his brother. The statement instead of saving Mr. Vallabhbhai, that tower of truthfulness, lays him headlong on the ground. Mr. Vallabhbhai's love of truth was already published when he point-blank asked a vernacular press representative to contradict the news of his visit with the Governor of the Central Provinces and also when he, being heckled and cornered by the representative, evaded giving a direct answer by such prevarications as, "I did not see the Governor", "I might have seen him in his private capacity" and so on. It need hardly be said that this tergiversation would have better fitted the lips of a professional hypocrite, rather than a truthful, spiritual, self-purified Vallabhbhai.

* * *

In his latest statement this Pecksniff of Non-cooperation has remarked that he would not wait for an invitation if he once understood that the opposite party was anxious to know the other side. Did the Government of the Central Provinces let Mr. Vallabhbhai know that they were sighing for their side being explained to this representative of the Working Committee who was deputed to study the situation? Or did he learn of Government's anxiety through telepathy? But the communique issued by the Chief Secretary of the Central Provinces Government is emphatic on the point. Denying the accuracy of the statement of Mr. V.J. Patel in a public meeting at Bombay that he had gone to the Governor at his express invitation, the communique runs: "The negotiations for a settlement were initiated by Mr. V.J. Patel with the Home Member of the Government. During the course of those negotiations I was approached by certain members of the Legislative Council and it was suggested to me that I should ascertain whether His Excellency the Governor would be prepared to receive Mr. V.J. Patel. . . . Both the Patel brothers attended Government House at the fixed time and were given an interview by His Excellency the Governor". It is for Mr. Vallabhbhai to contradict this assertion or admit that the Central Provinces Government did not seek an interview with the stalwart Mr. Vallabhbhai, nor signify in any way their anxiety to clear their attitude towards the flag affair to this august student of the Satyagraha campaign.

* * *

Like the ignominious surrender of the Satyagraha campaign, the matter of petition to the District Superintendent of Police for permission to conduct the procession also must inevitably stick like a bur to the coat-tail of Mr. Vallabhbhai. It is no use maintaining that a petition for permission was not sent to the District Superintendent of Police. All the conditions were determined previously in a compromise effected between the Government and leaders of the Satyagraha campaign. According to the conditions, the days of Satyagraha, the method, the roads, etc., all such details were settled beforehand and the batch of Satyagrahis submitted to all such restrictions. When, thus, all such humiliating limitations were acceded to and when the batch of Satyagrahis meticulously observed them, it is sheer impudence to aver that the batch passed off without being arrested by the Government. A quarrel ensued between a husband and his wife about painting the walls of their house. The husband wanted the white colour, while the wife had a special liking for grey. In the tussle, the wife got the better of the husband, the walls were painted grey and still the bragging husband boasted that he was successful in the conflict. Those who are in the know are fully well aware that the whole flag affair was puffed up to spite the Swarajya Party by certain honourable gentlemen who have made no secret of their hatred against Maharashtra, that they themselves were not prepared to take part in the Satyagraha and that, when the so-called Satyagraha grew too much for them, they anyhow wriggled out of it by means which are best left unexposed. A movement that was got up by a party with the philanthropic object of putting the opposite party in the wrong box was never likely to be better than what the Nagpur episode has proved itself to be.

Well might Mr. Vallabhbhai and his confreres enjoy the pleasure of being the foolers and the fooled in the Nagpur affair. The Swarajya Party is not spited at all and its weathers are unwrung; but the poor fellows who cut their noses to spite the Swarajya Party must be ruing the evil day indeed!

Extracts from the Central Provinces selections

2. The *Prajapaksha* (Akola) says: From the way in which the Satyagraha struggle has terminated, one is really at a loss to understand whether to call it a success or surrender of the Satyagrahis. It is to be regretted that Mr. Vallabhbhai who spoke so enthusiastically about the flag agitation at the time when he took upon himself the responsibility of conducting it, should have brought about such a dishonourable compromise for the Satyagrahis. As a matter of fact, the Central Provinces Council itself by adopting the flag resolutions made it too difficult for the Government to persist in its policy towards the flag movement. As it was almost impossible for the Government to renew the prohibition order issued by the District Magistrate, Nagpur. Where, then, was the necessity for Vallabhbhai to so impatiently seek a private settlement with the Government? Should his conduct be taken to mean that he anyhow wanted to free himself from the flag bother? Or else, why did he at all frequent the Government House in this connection? If it is his honest conviction that the Government is fully authorised to regulate and control any and every procession, pray why this show of Satyagraha so far? That the flag movement has at last come to an end is a source of relief both to the Government and the Satyagrahis, and the latter have no reason to justifiably claim success for themselves. One thing is, however, clear from what has happened and it is this. The Satyagrahis are not what they profess to be, namely, the advocates of the truth. When Vithalbhai openly announced that his brother Vallabhbhai has interviewed the Governor in connection with the flag agitation, it is inexplicable that our contemporary the *Bombay Chronicle* should have failed to throw light on it! and what surprises us still more is Vallabhbhai's own studious silence over the interview with the Governor! This is love, indeed, for *Satya*—the truth, the very creed of the Satyagrahis!

188

Vallabhbhai Stresses Communal Harmony

The Leader, 6 October 1923

In view of recent deplorable disturbances we the undersigned, Musalmans, Hindus and Sikhs hereby declare that if any individual or group of individuals belonging to any community commits any act of violence against or attacks the person, property or honour of women or place of worship (Mandir, Mosque, Church or Gurudwara etc.) of his neighbours or fellow townsmen or helps those who indulge in such misdeeds, he is, from the religious point of view, guilty of a great sin; and that it is the duty of co-religionists of such offenders to stand up to resist these miscreants and protect those who are so attacked. We further appeal to the followers of every religion that they should act, each towards the other, with mutual toleration and regard for the religious ideas of their neighbours and townsmen.

LALA LAJPAT RAI
VALLABHBHAI PATEL
HAKIM AJMAL KHAN
SWAMY SHRADHANAND
MOTILAL NEHRU etc.

189

Vallabhbhai Protests against Town Planning Scheme[1]

Bombay Chronicle, 9 October 1923

A mass meeting of over fifteen thousand people organised by the Kalupud Seva Samaj was held last evening under the presidentship of Seth Mangaldas Girdharidas to protest against the Town Planning Scheme, number 5, prepared by the present Municipal Committee of Management.

Mr. Vallabhbhai Patel moved a resolution strongly protesting against the declaration of the scheme and the hasty committal of the municipality to a scheme which covered large developed areas inside and outside the city walls and urging the postponement thereof till it was properly scrutinised by the newly elected board which is to come into existence shortly. In the course of his speech, Mr. Vallabhbhai Patel said "I would not have joined in the protest agitations at this stage but for a pamphlet issued by the Chief Officer which misrepresents his own attitude and the attitude of the party in the suspended municipality." In connection with the scheme Mr. Patel clearly pointed out that neither he nor any of his friends were against any well-considered scheme for the city's improvement. They were painfully aware of the necessity of wholesale alteration of the city in the interest of the people, but the present scheme was never considered nor even contemplated by the suspended municipality. It was a gross libel to say that the suspended municipality had lent its support to the scheme in its present form. In fact they merely approved the bare outlines of the rough scheme which merely referred to the demolition of the city walls on the condition of Government agreeing to give the land underneath the walls free of revenue to the municipality. They had also made it clear that, before agreeing to accept the scheme or even part of it, they would like to know the extent of the financial assistance that

Government would give in case of acceptance of the scheme. On both these points replies were received from Government long after the municipality was suspended and they were very unsatisfactory indeed. The present committee of management prepared the whole scheme after the Government replies were received and specially requested the town planning officer to include in the scheme large areas both developed and undeveloped inside and outside the city walls. The late municipality would never have so hastily committed itself to such an ill-considered scheme.

[1]Speech delivered at Ahmedabad on 8 October 1923.

190

Government Concerns Over Anti-Government Activities of Municipalities, Boards & Other Local Bodies

Home Department (Political) Confidential Records N.A.I., 5 December 1923

Demi-official from Sir W. Marris I.C.S., United Provinces, to the Hon'ble Sir W.M. Hailey, K.C.I.E., I.C.S., Member of the Viceroy's Council and In charge Home Department, dated 4th December 1923.

Is there any likelihood that the Home Department will address local Governments about anti-Government political activities on the part of local bodies like Municipalities and district Boards? I spoke to H.E. about it and suggested to him that enquiry on the subject by the Government of India would be useful.

(I am answering this)—

This refers back, I think, to Sir W. Marris' letter 30th March 1923, paragraph 5, to which I replied in the third paragraph of my letter 3rd June 1923.

I have noticed little in recent provincial reports on this subject, save in so far as it relates to attempts to give addresses to the Ali Brothers and similar undesirables. But it is a matter which may at any time assume prominence. The Swaraj Flag demonstration seems for the time to be dead, and it was always to pass an issue that I should doubt if it will be revived. But there are other and graver directions in which well wishers can be harassed, and I think he should make enquiry. We can say that we have noticed references to action taken by local bodies under influences explicitly antagonistic to Government, and should be glad if local Government could give us any information on the subject based on the experience of the last two years. Action of the nature referred to appears to take two directions, demonstratives such as presentations of addresses to ex-convicts or internees, attempts to fly the swaraj flag, exhibition of portraits of Tilak and other opponents of Government, and more serious attacks, such as resolutions in favour of boycotting British or Empire goods, we are not aware whether local bodies have gone further, and committed themselves to action which would harass or discriminate against European ratepayers or persons who are believed to be wellwishers of Government. We should be glad therefore of any material which local Governments can give us as assisting a study of this aspect of the question, and would also inform us of any steps which they have felt it in their power to take in order to meet the undesirable political activities of local bodies.

W.M.H[ailey],—5-12-23.

Draft D.O. submitted for approval.

J. Crerar—13-12-23.

Demi-official letter from the Hon'ble Mr. J. Crerar, I.C.S., Secretary to the Government of India, Home Department to the Chief Secretary of all local Governments and Administrations, etc., no. D.-2909, dated 14th-15th December 1923.

The Government of India have noticed from time to time both in the press and in official reports references to action taken by local bodies under influences explicitly antagonistic to Government and they would be glad to have any information on the matter, based on the experience of the last two years, that the Government of Madras etc./Bombay/you can furnish.

2. Action of the nature referred to appears to take two directions, demonstrations such as presentations of the addresses of welcome to ex-convicts, and ex-internees, attempts to fly the so-called Swaraj Flag, exhibitions of portraits of Tilak and other opponents of Government, and more serious attacks such as resolutions in the favour of boycotting British or Empire goods. The Government of India are not aware whether local bodies have gone further and committed themselves to action which would harass or discriminate against European taxpayers or persons who are believed to be well-wishers of Government. But they would be glad to have any material that is forthcoming to assist them in a study of this aspect of the question, whether the details of any action which the local Government has felt in its/you have felt in your power to take in order to meet the activities referred to.

191

Vallabhbhai Assures People of Victory of Non-violence and Truth

Borsad Satyagraha Bulletin, 5 December 1923

Sardar Vallabhbhai Patel and Darbarsaheb Gopaldas Desai said:

The Government has taken to the path of untruth and immorality. Truth is on your side, and if you observe non-violence, you will certainly be victorious. One who observes truth and non-violence will never be defeated. May God give you the strength to bear sufferings with calmness.

192

Vallabhbhai Condemns Punitive Tax on Some Villagers in Borsad[1]

Navjivan (Supplement), 6 December 1923

1. Bombay Government by its order No.3828 of 25th September has imposed punitive tax of Rs 2,40,074 on 88 villages of Borsad taluka and 14 villages of Anand taluka and additional police has been stationed there. In that connection this Conference resolves that government has failed to protect people from the menace of the dacoits. It is the duty of the government to protect people and to arrange police for that work. Instead of performing that duty, putting false allegation on the innocent people of taluka and imposing fine on them, it is totally an unjust and atrocious act. So this conference advises the people to fight against this injustice, by not paying the fine, and silently suffer the misery, and maintain their self-respect.

2. As news has been received from several places that police have tortured people, so, in order to protect the people from the police excesses, this conference sees the necessity of raising a volunteer corps, and requests the youths of the taluka to join that volunteer corps.

3. Because of less and irregular rains, the crops is only 25 per cent of normal year. Yet the officers of the government present false reports. So the people are asked to be alert.

[1]The resolution passed by Borsad Taluka Conference unanimously on 2.12.23.

193

Vallabhbhai Urges People of Borsad to Get Ready for Final Battle of Swaraj

Navjivan, 6 December 1923

Borsad should consider carefully before it accepts this Resolution. Probably I know Borsad better than anyone of the people present here. I also know the strength of Borsad and also its weaknesses and faults. There are some people here who would try to find fault with the purest of things. All these matters must be carefully considered before a decision is taken.

In addition to the above warning, he said:

After Gandhiji has come out of jail, the country appears to be going downhill which is a matter of deep regret. We must free Gandhiji from all the worries. If we pass this resolution and do our duty without seeking further guidance from the Mahatma, that would result in an end to his worries. My appeal to Gujarat is that it should not bother Gandhiji with his troubles because he has so many other problems to solve.

We are not doing this for any economic benefits but because we want to defend our honour and self-respect and ensure that nobody is able to charge us with being the collaborators of the dacoits. If you love your self-respect, if you are not siding with the criminals, but are innocent and sincere then you must fearlessly decide not to pay this tax.

This struggle began in Borsad and if the people of Borsad withdraw from it, they would be sinning against themselves. The Government documents say that the people of Borsad are cowards, they are emasculated and are the keepers of stolen goods. You must do two or three things so that such allegations can be disproved.

Real Defence

We will have to have at least one or two volunteers in each village to defend the people against police atrocities. These volunteers do not have to take up arms against the police or to abuse them. The only thing they have to do is to send us a report of the happenings there. If the police do not commit any excesses, let the volunteers say so in their report. Secondly, whatever the government might do, let us make it clear that we would not voluntarily pay even one pie of the fine. Take this pledge in the name of God and sincerely resolve to stick to your decision. Do not have a small mind or think of financial benefits. Join this battle from a sense of duty and take it that this is the only way to defend your self-respect.

A government who has been unable to arrest a handful of dacoits is going to arrest you? Is this administration so powerful? What can we do against such a powerful government? If we want to catch the dacoits with police help, would we be able to defend ourselves? The dacoits would snatch away the guns from the police and use them to kill us. What we have to do is to persuade the dacoits to give up violence. This Tehsil has always been a breeding ground of dacoits. The administrative set-up of the government cannot put an end to the dacoits. The only way is that we must reform ourselves and give up a life of ease. We must learn to live hard as the dacoits do. After all, they are also human beings and might have some good qualities. They have been forced to take to dacoities because of persecution by the authorities. They have taken to this way of life out of ignorance. The only way to deal with them is to have volunteers in each village who should overcome them with their selfless service and to improve them. We would have to have many such posts or *thanas.* The way of the gun is the wrong way. The gun is for those who are afraid of death. The police are afraid even though they have guns. The dacoits carry their lives in their pockets and that is why they are not afraid of anybody.

What did the Government do?

Sardar: What would be the population of this village?

A voice from the crowd—13,000

Sardar: Among these 13,000 people how many are the collaborators of the dacoits?

A voice from the crowd—About 10 to 15.

Sardar: The government wants to punish 12,985 persons for the crimes of 15 people. But what has the police been able to do against these 15 persons? It did not arrest either the dacoits or their 15 collaborators. But wants to arrest the common people. This is the type of justice this government believes in. When the Commissioner came here, what did he do? Did the people from the village meet him?

A voice from the crowd—He came to the bungalow, had his dinner and went back.

So, he came, had his dinner and went back. Now when we would advise you not to pay the fine after having gone into the whole question, the officers would say that mischievous people have started the whole thing. Why did we do it? The officers might say that we did it because we had nothing better to do. The Commissioner came for one day and went back but Bhai Mohanlal and Bhai Ravishankar toured all the villages and saw things for themselves. The people are unable to decide whether the dacoit Babar or these vultures of the police are better. In Napa, a policeman hit the cheek of a young boy. Babar may have committed murders but he has not done anything immoral. The policeman who hit the boy has been suspended but has any help been given to that boy?

If the government had announced that in view of the situation prevailing in the area, the special police was needed, but that they did not have any money to pay salaries, we would have collected the money through public donations. But the government chooses to punish us by saying that we are siding with the dacoits. When we are being accused of this, we will not pay a single pie.

Warning

Let us seriously consider the consequences of our struggle. If we have to continue to fight amongst ourselves, let us not engage in this battle against the authorities. Borsad has a heavy responsibility to bear because the other villages will do what Borsad does. If you lose courage, everything would be lost. I think that you have considered the question and made up your minds. I would, therefore, like to know what decision you have taken. Those who do not want to pay this special tax should raise their hands (all present raised their hands).

If this is your view, I would advise you to be very careful and be disciplined. The government men would try to incite a riot. Take care to see that violence is not allowed to be perpetrated under any circumstances. The key to success in this struggle is peace and *ahimsa.*

The amount of fine which each one of you would have to pay is meagre: it is only two or three rupees. After all, we are not beggars that we cannot pay this amount. But the government wants to extort this money on the plea that we are the collaborators of the dacoits. If the government admits that it has no money and it is at the end of its tether, we are prepared to take up the administration ourselves.

Gulab Raja

The *Times* writes in an article: "Mahatma Gandhi's movement has eroded the authority of the government and that is why there are dacoits". But when the dacoit Gulab Raja had started the dacoity, Gandhiji had not come to India. This dacoit was going about trying to murder the Collector, Mr. Wood, who wanted to imprison Gulab Raja. The Collector was camping in Singhlav village. He heard that Gulab Raja was committing dacoities within the borders of Gaikwad with the help of the British Police. The Collector started an inquiry into this. Gulab Raja, dressed in fine clothes and a *zari* turban was standing near the Collector. He said: "I am Gulab Raja." At this Mr. Wood retorted: "How are you going about freely? You should be in chains." Gulab Raja said: "You can do what you can when you catch me. Today I am a king." The Collector later started a false case against Gulab Raja. The Tehsildar incited a trader to abuse Gulab Raja inside the police station. Incensed at this Gulab Raja hit the trader on the head with a brickbat. A case was started and Gulab Raja engaged me as his lawyer. There was nothing much in the case but the Collector spoke to the Senior Judge and had Gulab Raja sentenced to 9 months imprisonment. Gulab Raja got wind of the intention of the Collector and absented himself from the Court the day the sentence was to be announced. From the next day, he intensified his activities resulting in 52 dacoities and 25 to 30 murders. The Police Superintendent, who had harassed Gulab Raja, applied for long leave and went back to England. The Collector was informed everyday that Gulab Raja visited Vallabhbhai, the Lawyer, everyday at his residence. The Collector called me and tempted me with offers of high office if I help the Government to arrest Gulab Raja. I told him: "I know the law and if he comes to visit me I am supposed to inform the authorities because not giving that information is a crime." I advised him that his guns were ineffective and he should have sharp edged weapons. The Collector followed my advice and had double-edged weapons made. Gulab Raja was later on arrested in Gaikwad.

Dacoits in White Caps

A new breed of dacoits has arisen under the leadership of Mahatma Gandhi who have launched this movement. It is a fact. These dacois will go wherever the police are committing atrocities against the people. The youngmen must join our corps of volunteers so that they can be sent to places where the people are being subjected to atrocities by the government.

If the government declares an amnesty, the dacoits would come out tomorrow and surrender themselves. But who believes the word of the government? If the government wants the special police to be posted let them bear its expenses itself. Gaikwad pays for his own police and when we get Swaraj our method of functioning would be entirely different from that of the Britishers. We will have to reform the dacoits. We would have to reform the Patanwadia and Bawaria castes of the district. These people have the strength, the intelligence, but no knowledge. They are not enamoured of thievery but have been placed in this unfortunate position. The volunteers who are following the path of truth should live among those people so that they can be reformed. Those who migrate to the cities after getting education should come back to the villages to serve these people.

Organise yourself and give up jealousies and backbiting. We would win in this battle only if we take it that we are riding the same boat. The government may extract the fine from us by force but we will not voluntarily pay it. You must take firm decision in that regard. If you do so the people from other villages will come and we would be able to persuade them to join this fight.

194

Vallabhbhai Critical of Assembly Entry Decision[1]

Navjivan, 6 December 1923

The very first decision this Council has to take is whether we pay attention to the Congress or to the Assembly. We cannot win this fight unless we take this decision. Thirty three crore Indians are like sheep who are being ruled by a mere two lakh foreigners. The people of India groaning under the foreign heel cannot be liberated by a handful of educated people but by you, the people themselves. It cannot be that a handful of educated persons can defeat the government on its own ground and in its own language. The recent elections have proved this. The only difference is that a different class of people has replaced the members of the Assembly. You have sent them there but before they entered the Assembly, they knew that they would not get anything through the entry into the Assemblies. They have told you that the Assemblies are not the place where *Swaraj* can be achieved but they would replace those people who cooperated with the Government, that they would oust them, have the Assembly disbanded and, thus, adopt a policy of non-cooperation. The Congress does not believe their claim that they can disband the assemblies, but it says that if they believe that they can achieve it, they are welcome to go there. Assemblies, whether they can be disbanded or not, are not our concern. Let's, therefore, forget the Assemblies because they would make us totally powerless. A man who tries to ride two horses eventually falls to the ground and if we do it we would also fall. That is why before we enter the field of battle, we should select one of those horses. A fighter who tries to choose his horse once he has entered the battle is sure to lose. Let us, therefore, see which horse would lead us to Swaraj. Let's enter the battle after having decided whether our own strength would get us Swaraj or the hopes we have from others. Do not hope that once we are in the Assemblies, our taxes would be withdrawn. The Assembly is to meet two months hence but it is a wrong decision to enter it. If you tell the Government clearly that you will not pay for the special police, you would be in direct contact with the Government. That is the real way.

Mahatmaji has shown us the way. After he was jailed, we are beset with doubts whether his way was the right way and that is why we are not able to make any progress. Gandhiji had said that we should stop cooperating with the Government because it functions only so long as we cooperate with it. If the amount of Rs 2.40 lakhs is to be paid by us for the special police, it is our fault. The policemen are our own people. It is our people who inform the Government that we are harbouring the dacoits. The Collector of Kheda is a gentleman from Sind. Now those people who would realise the penalty and then accuse you of harbouring the dacoits are also our own brothers. That is why we must stop cooperating with the government which depends on our help and commits atrocities on us. The educated classes are unable to forget their selfish interests and it is those interests which lead them to help the Government. You are not convinced that you should be slaves. What would you do? The best way for you is to totally boycott foreign textiles because it is the habit of wearing foreign clothes which has made you into slaves. The Englishmen import cotton worth five crores of rupees from India and send us textiles made from that cotton which are worth sixty crores of rupees. The money which they loot from you is utilized to appoint Commissioners and Collectors, to buy guns which are utilized to keep you under their heels. The only way out is that you should wear only those clothes which are made in India. Not only this, you should see to it that the cotton which is produced in your fields is spun by your wives, sisters and mothers and the yarn, thus, produced should be woven into cloth by the weavers in the villages. You should wear only that cloth. If you do that the money of the people will remain with them. When the amount of sixty crores of rupees which goes to England every year is stopped all mischief by the Englishmen would cease. Then there will not be any famines. When there are no famines, the poor people would get sufficient food and there will not be any dacoities. The trouble is that we have left the path of good and taken to the path of evil. Gandhiji has said that we must leave the path of evil and, if we want Swaraj, we should forget about the educated classes being able to help us. That is why he has advised us to adopt the *Charkha.* Gandhiji's message has been heard by all but people have not yet woken up. That is why Gandhiji plies the *Charkha* as he sits in the jail and anybody who comes out of jail carries Gandhiji's message that people should follow his lead. If we listen to him, there will not be any famines, any crimes in this country and *Ramrajya* would come about.

Inquiry

The specific purpose for which this council has been called in a hurry is to discuss the situation created in the Borsad Tehsil. When we return from the

Delhi session of the Congress, we came to know of the policy adopted by the Government in the Tehsil and the Gujarat Provincial Congress Committee asked Shri Mohanlal Pandya and Shri Ravi Shankar to tour the Tehsil, enquire into the circumstances and make their recommendations about what should be done. They have been asked to find out the identity of the dacoits, the reason which forced them to take to dacoities, their *modus operandi,* the reason why the police are unable to apprehend the dacoits and to protect the people against their depredations, why the Government blames the people for the situation, whether the people like the special police or not and whether they are prepared to pay taxes. They have toured each village and have presented their report yesterday. I would inform you of the decision that the Provincial Congress Committee has taken on that report. But before I do so, I would like to know your views. Let me first tell you what these two gentlemen have written in their report. In 1917, a Patanwadia named Babar from the village Golel became a dacoit. In the beginning he committed small crimes. But when the government cannot catch a criminal or metes out a punishment, disproportionate to the crime, then the criminal loses his human qualities and turns into a demon. This is not simple dacoity, this is devilish conduct. The real dacoit is the one in Dhasaka Durbar. That Babar has not yet been apprehended and still indulges in minor crimes. Instead of arresting him, the police reported that the people are collaborating with him. Three years ago, two special police posts were created in Khadana and Jogan villages. The police had said that Patanwadia and Bawaria people of these two villages helped the dacoits. The collective fines were imposed on these castes of the two villages.

The Real Secret

I have received true reports about how the special police "protected" the people. Babar Deva murdered a man named Shivbhai in Jogan village in broad daylight. Even so the police wrote in their report that the people failed to inform it about the dacoits. That man attacked the police personnel in Golel village. How can the special police protect the people under these circumstances? The residents of Khadana and Jogan went to the Collector and told him that they cannot pay the special tax and that they would gladly choose to accept the atrocities committed by the dacoits. The Tehsildar also reported that these people were too poor to pay the tax. The term of the special police was to end on 30th April last. At that time, the Tehsildar gave the opinion that it was not that the people did not want to pay the tax but had no money to pay. He further said that if force was used to realise the amount of the tax, the people would leave their villages. I have got a copy of the report of the Tehsildar with me. But the District Superintendent of Police made a report which was in contradiction of the report of the Tehsildar. He said that the special police posts should be continued. The reason advanced by him for this recommendation was that Babar Deva and his gang had not been arrested, that he had murdered his wife and several other persons in spite of the special police because he was afraid that somebody would inform about him. The police was unable to stop the murders. The other reason advanced by the Superintendent of Police was that the dacoit had murdered Shivbhai in Jogan village in broad daylight, but no eye-witnesses were coming forward and that is why he cannot be brought to book. It is surprising that the police are unable to gather any evidence but expects the people to produce eye-witnesses. The third reason given by him is that the Patanwadia caste people of Jogan harbour the dacoit Babar in their fields and his relatives help him with food and other supplies instead of informing the police about him. The fourth reason adduced by the Superintendent is that Babar comes to Khadana village. The fifth reason is that people of Khadana and other villages never inform the police about the movements of Babar. The sixth reason is that if the special police had not been there, a large number of Patanwadia men would have joined Babar's gang. It is on the basis of such reasons that the Police Superintendent recommends the continuance of the special police posts. When the Collector read this report, he made his own report to the Commissioner. I have a copy of that too. The Collector recommends that the special police posts should be removed from these villages because the police are unable to defend the villagers. But the Collector also says in his report that crimes have increased in the Borsad Tehsil, the number of the dacoits has gone up and that is why some special arrangements will have to be made.

He has further stated that he and the Police Superintendent had discussed this question at a special conference. It appears that this conference is at the root of everything. He says that not only these two villages, many others in the Tehsil refuse to inform the police about the movements of the dacoits. The Collector has also said that those persons who are suspected to have links with the dacoit Babar should be prosecuted under the Land Revenue Act. The Collector says that if the people fail to inform the police about the dacoits, it is because they are afraid. Now look at the Commissioner who makes a fourth report. He does not agree with the three reports. He has, however, agreed with the Police Superintendent and has recommended that the special police should continue to be posted for another year in these two villages and the expenses should be met from the special tax on the people.

Ali Dacoit

It was in June 1923 that a decision was taken to post the special police for one year. How the government changed its opinion and decided to post the police in the village after holding all the castes guilty is not known. I do not have any documents on this question. But one thing is certain which has been told to me by everybody I have met. There is a Muslim dacoit of the name of Ali. When the police were unable to catch Babar, it made friends with Ali. A pact was entered into with the dacoit so that Babar could be caught. The police supplied him with guns, a shameful thing for a government to do. It means that it is not the government, but the dacoits who are ruling this area. The people were subjected to collective fines but now that the government has helped a dacoit with guns,

Government. The local resources for sustaining the agitation were, no doubt, almost, if not wholly, exhausted but the adoption of the movement by the Congress Committee and the support which the Committee succeeded in obtaining for it from extra-provincial sources had undoubtedly given it an impetus the extent and durability of which were then difficult to appreciate. The agitation had assumed more clearly than at any previous stage the aspect of a contest between the Government established by law and the forces organised against it, and His Excellency the Governor justly summed up the position in his address to the Legislative Council in the following words: "The local Government regards this agitation as clearly civil disobedience, an attempt to overcome the authority of Government, and is determined that this challenge to lawful authority, this defiance of the law, should be resisted with all the resources at its command. In this policy it confidently hopes for the support of all law-abiding citizens including the members of this Council."

5. We recognize that the situation had become extremely embarrassing to the local Government and entailed serious dislocation of the normal administration and their desire to terminate it as expeditiously as possible was natural and intelligible; but this result was attained with considerable prejudice to wider considerations. The local Government has adduced a strong body of testimony for the view that public opinion regards the conclusion of the agitation as a victory for Government. In many quarters this was undoubtedly the case, though the structures passed by the Swaraj party on the Gandhiite section, which was responsible for the movement, must be discounted by their mutual animosities which were at that time particularly active. On the other hand, the fact that the Congress representatives were admitted to parley and that terms were concluded with them has been advanced, both at the Congress Session and by the Parbandhak Committee, as evidence that persistent pressure on Government is not devoid of results. As requested in Your Lordship's telegram above quoted, we have pointed out to the Government of the Central Provinces the inconvenience arising from the first intimation of matters of such importance being received by Your Lordship and ourselves from press reports.

We have the honour to be,

My Lord,

Your Lordship's most obedient, humble Servants,

(Signed) Reading.

(Signed) Rawlinson.

(Signed) M.M. Shafi.

(Signed) W.M. Hailey.

(Signed) B.N. Sarma.

(Signed) B.P. Blackett.

(Signed) A.C. Chatterjee.

(Signed) D.T. Chadwick.

198

Secret Police Report on the Activities of Vallabhbhai (Extracts)

Home Department Special File No. 647 of 1924

AHMEDABAD
7th December 1923

To,

The Deputy Inspector-General of Police,
C.I.D., Poona.

RESPECTED SIR,

Mr. Vallabhbhai Jhaverbhai Patel said: "I being a resident of this place my place was in the Reception Committee and some outsider should have been selected for this chair. We must first decide whether we must look towards the Congress or towards the Councils. If you want to liberate the public from the foreign yoke the remedy is not in the hands of a handful of educated men but it is in your hands. Those who have gone in the Councils have gone there with full knowledge that it is not possible to obtain Swaraj from the Councils, but they have gone there to break them. The Congress does not believe in this. So if we believe that we will not gain anything from the Councils we should forget them. We cannot ride two horses at the same time. Councils will sit after two months and the tax will be collected. You say that you will not pay the tax and at that time we come in direct opposition with the Government. We must therefore leave aside the Councils and commence our work. Mahatma Gandhi has shown us the way. He has asked us for non-cooperation with the government. He has asked us not to use the foreign cloth and use the cloth made in this country, he has asked us to use *Charkha* and he is sending the same message from the jail, but we have not been able to carry out the message. The object of calling this Conference is the present situation of Borsad Taluka. Before advising the public of the Taluka how they should act, the Gujarat Prantic Samiti appointed a Committee to enquire into the situation of the Taluka and report the result. Mohanlal Kameshwar Pandya and Ravishankar enquired into the situation and I will place before you their report. One Babar Deva of Gobi became an outlaw for a small offence in 1918 and is still at large. When the police was not able to arrest him, two additional posts were opened at Khodana and Jogan because Dharalas of Jogan, Khodana and Gobi were assisting Babaria. Babar then committed murder of Shivbhai in one of these three villages in broad daylight, and yet the police continued to report that no one was giving them any information of Babar; he then again came on the same village and injured the police. A deputation of Jogan people went to the Collector and said they were unable to pay the tax. The Collector asked a report from the Mamlatdar who reported that the people were unable to pay. The period of the posts was to be over on the 30th April and the Collector asked the Mamlatdar to report whether the period should be extended or not. The Mamlatdar reported that it will not be possible to collect the tax, because the people are poor and if pressure is used to collect it the people will leave the village. The DSP reported that the two posts should be continued. He said in his report that as Babar and his gang were still at large, as Shivbhai was murdered in broad daylight, as Patanwadias of Jogan harbour Babar in their fields and give him every assistance, as the DSP informed that Babar visits Khodana and the people of Khodana do not give any information regarding the whereabouts of Babar and if the additional police were not posted many men of Jogan would have joined Babar, the additional police should be continued. The Collector then sent his report to the Commissioner; he also said in his report that there is no use of additional police, but as the crime in Borsad Taluka is increasing we must do something, and I have asked the DSP to report and it is from this report that the present things have come out. The Collector in his letter to the Commissioner also writes: "Khodana, Jolal and Jogan are not only to be blamed, there might be other villages in the Taluka who might be knowing the whereabouts of Babar, and if we will take tax from these villages many of the villagers will become outlaws. The reason of not giving information to the police is not their sympathy with the outlaws but their fear". When the above report went to the Commissioner he took the third side and I do not know how the Government thought to put the additional police on the whole of the Taluka instead of three villages. Everyone in Borsad talks that Government had to make peace with Alimia and was supplied with gun and ammunition in order to arrest Babar. This is very humiliating. The Government knows how many dacoities and murders he committed after he was given guns. Why did not the Government withdraw the arms or why did it not publish that we have committed a blunder? How is the public to know that Government wants to arrest Babar? Therefore the Government is the most responsible for any wrongs in this Taluka. Now as regards Alimia he was not outlaw from the very beginning, why did not the police arrest him. Now the Government says no one gives information of outlaws. Babar committed 26 murders not one of them was for loot, but all were murdered because he suspected them of giving information against him to the police. How many more the Government wants to be murdered. Babar took away a gun from a First Class Magistrate and the Magistrate saved himself by posing himself as a clerk. The Government knows that the public is innocent but it has no funds. The crime is increasing and its prestige suffers. It cannot take away from you without finding fault with you because here again the prestige comes in. It has therefore accused you of being associates of robbers. Now we have to decide whether we must pay up the tax or not. Representatives of every village have come here. Now want your opinion what you want to do. I also want to tell you that if you want to save Rs 2-8-0 by not paying the tax you must not start the fight; this is a mean idea, but if you want to start the struggle on the principles of self-respect, you may not pay the tax. If you start the struggle beware of men who will try to create trouble what punishment should be awarded to it? Only God can punish such a government. Its prestige is running low and it appears that it is on its last legs. Had this not been so, it would not have been forced to seek the friendship of a murderer. The government knows how that man has utilized the guns supplied by it for committing dacoities and murdering people. The government might claim that it wanted to catch Babar when it entered into a pact with him but the people did not know that this was the purpose. The government should make a public announcement that it has committed a blunder. It is the government which is responsible for all the atrocities committed by Ali on the poor people.

Secondly, that dacoit was not a simple dacoit. In a land dispute he had murdered a lawyer in a village in broad daylight. The scene of the murder was hardly two furlongs from the court but the government was unable to arrest him. When such a person finds that the government is so inefficient and when the government's police helps him, he becomes a confirmed dacoit.

The Condition of the Informers

The government says that the people do not inform the police about the movements of the dacoits. Babaria has murdered 22 persons, none of whom was rich. The murders were not committed by him for purposes of robbery but because he was afraid that they were informers. Now when the government says that people do not inform the police, I would like to ask how many policemen have been killed compared to the 22 villagers who have fallen victim to this dacoit? The dacoit tied a Rawalia, whom he suspected of being an informer, to a tree and nailed him to it. Does the government want more people to suffer the same fate? It is clear that it is dangerous to become an informer against the dacoits. I am reminded of a first class magistrate who met a dacoit while he was coming from Wasad to Borsad. The dacoit slapped him and took away his gun. He had to tell him that he was an ordinary functionary of the government and not a magistrate, in order to save his life. If a government has such magistrates, what right has it got to rule the country or to impose collective fines on the people?

An Insolvent Government

All these things are proof of the fact that it is not the people who are guilty. The government knows this. It has neither the money nor the strength. When the police failed to catch murderers, the princely states in the neighbourhood are able to estimate correctly the efficacy of the police. These villages are on the boundaries of the princely states where there is no special police. The princely states bear the expenses of the police themselves whereas the insolvent Englishmen have to extort money from the people. The government can save its honour only if it can catch the murderers. So long as the murderers are not caught, armed police should be posted in all the villages. The government have, however, no money to pay the salaries of the armed police. The only way for it is to get money from you. For that purpose, they accuse you of being guilty. If the government asks for money on the plea that its treasury is empty, it would lose its prestige.

That is exactly why it blames the people and says that you are siding with the robbers. The question is what we should do under the circumstances.

Some people have been exempted from the collective fines. Who are they? They are the people who have the most to do with these crimes, who help in their commission, they are the persons who have been exempted. It is the duty of the government employees to catch the criminals but they are exempt from collective fines. The second class is that of the priests who, if they are called the collaborators of the dacoits, would take up arms against the government. They have also been exempted. Persons whom these priests have converted into Christians are in a position similar to that in which we find ourselves. The chowkidars and the village headmen have also been exempted even though they are not being bothered by the dacoits. My information is that every chowkidar and Patel knows where Babar is but none of them have the courage to catch him. All these people have been exempted from the fines. Those who go to the Assemblies have not been exempted. They are also the friends of dacoits. The chairman of the Reception Committee was thought fit to adorn a seat in the assembly but he has also not been exempted from this fine.

The Fighting Spirit

Representatives from all the villages have been called here to discuss what we should do to protect our honour under the circumstances. People from all villages have come here. Now we have to decide as to whether we should pay the fine or not. I would like to know your opinion on this question. If it is your view that the fine should not be paid, please consider the consequences. If the consideration is that you would be able to save a sum of Rs 2.5 there is no point in joining battle on this issue. Join the battle only if you think that this government has no right to accuse us of being the friends and collaborators of dacoits and criminals. Then the government might take away Rs 10 instead of Rs. 2, we would not mind. It is better that the dacoits rob us rather than the government takes away Rs 2 from us. Start this struggle only if you think that you are honest, honourable people and you would not accept a certificate of being the collaborators of dacoits and if you tell the government that it can take away the money as the dacoits take it. Gandhiji has taught us to leave untruth, dishonesty and immorality and fearlessly follow the true path. Let me remind you of another thing. When the fight starts, government men and your enemies will persuade you to indulge in violence. Please stay away from it. Remember Gandhiji when you engage in this fight. It is not physical force but courage which will stand us in good stead. Let the government beat us to its heart's content. If you use abusive language or lathis, the government has more force than you can ever muster. The government may not be able to arrest the dacoits but it would immediately arrest you. Greatness does not lie in abusing or beating up somebody, it lies in undergoing pain for the sake of truth. Mahatmaji has undergone many troubles for the sake of truth and is in jail now. That is why people revere him. When a dacoit is hanged, people generally say "good riddance".

If you like these two things, I would like to ask you to raise your hands if you do not want to pay the tax (all representatives raised their hands). Intelligence and wisdom are of little avail when you are faced with force. A weak ruler generally comes to harm. Those who feel that they will not be able to stand against the government and should, therefore, pay this special tax should raise their hands (not a single hand was raised).

A Volunteer Force

We have proof of how honourable is the special police. It has called that chairman of the Reception Committee the elder brother of the dacoit Babar. The dacoit takes away your money but the police are silent spectators to such robbery. You know that it was a member of this special force who hit the cheek of a ten-year old boy in Napa. Even Babaria has not indulged in such things. We have received reports that this police has tried to molest many women. If we have to save the honour of our sisters and daughters, we will have to set this police right. We must have at least one volunteer in every village. I am sure that the people of the village will look after and feed the volunteers. The people who treat thousands of Babars to sweetmeats will not grudge simple food for the volunteers. And the volunteers who are the followers of Gandhi would be content with a few loaves of bread and a little salt. The police knows that it has been posted by the government to punish the people; catching of dacoits is a mere facade. Such a police cannot but commit atrocities against the people. Only yesterday Mr Abbas was told by a government officer that he (the officer) had seen to it that the policemen return the [illegible] they had forced people to give to them. He also advised him that when [illegible] are committed, people should make representations to the [illegible] will tell you that no such representation should be made. It is surprising that you are being asked to make representation against the excesses of the police which has been posted for the specific purpose of seeing that atrocities are not committed. Making representations would be akin to our accepting this police. It is for the government to see that the police does not misbehave. The only representation we can make is to God because we are following the path of truth. We can only pray to God to protect us. Those who think it their duty to side with the people in their hour of travail should give their names to Darbar Gopaldas. So long as this struggle continues, he would be camping in Borsad along with other leaders. The volunteers should inform the leaders about the excesses committed by the police in the villages.

My request to those who have assembled today is to see that those who have been helping the robbers should take a decision today that it is something very bad. A person who does so is a partner in the atrocities on the people. If you have to follow the path of truth, you must give up evil ways and reform your character. People of Bawaria and Patanwadia castes should give up liquor and persuade others too to follow suit. I have received information that the government are thinking of ousting this caste from the Tehsil. If that happens, it would be very bad and a blow to the honour of this district. We must put an end to robbery but a whole caste cannot be banished merely because some of its members commit crimes. Please reform yourself and those who are indulging in evil ways should be told that their excesses will not be tolerated. They should be told to give up evil ways even if the whole caste has to feed them.

Almost half the population in the Tehsil comprises Bawaria and Patanwadia castes. So long as they do not improve themselves the whole district will continue to suffer. It is our job to improve them and to bring them to the right path. If they are shown the right path, they can become cultured and respectable. That is why those who believe in truth should go and stay with them like sadhus. Sadhus are those who truly serve the people and not those only who wear saffron clothes.

I would like to address a few words to the people of Borsad village. If Borsad shows its strength, it would also influence the people of other villages. But the responsibility of the village, where this conference is being held, is the greatest. I would ask you to forget your differences and unitedly join the struggle against the government.

Please stick to the decision we have taken today. Pray to God that He grants us victory in this fight. I also pray that He makes us victorious in this battle for justice.

[1]Speech made by Sardar Patel on 2nd December 1923 at the Borsad Tehsil Council as President.

195

Vallabhbhai asks Government Officers not to Obey Ord[illegible] for Attaching People's Goods

Borsad Satyagraha Bulletin, 6 December 1923

The Government employed Ravanias in the villages. The Government servants asked these Ravanias to carry out part of the unpleasant work of attachments. They were asked by them to enter the houses and to bring out the goods, which would be taken away in attachments. But the Ravanias would not do such work, for they had very close relations with the villagers, generation after generation. If the Government Officers brought pressure on the Ravanias to do the dirty work of the attachments, then they should resign but should not do the work of attachments. Ravanias and other villagers also should not make enmity with the people and they should not join hands with the Government Officers. The villagers should not indulge in improper acts, for no doubt the time would pass away but their good name would be lost.

196

Vallabhbhai Accuses Government of Failure to Protect People and Impose Punitive Tax

Navjivan, 6 December 1923

After a careful study of the report of the Committee, which was appointed to inquire into the reasonableness or otherwise of the imposition of the punitive tax of Rs 2,40,074 on 88 villages of Borsad Taluka and 14 villages of the Anand Taluka, this Committee is satisfied that the Government has proved itself unable to protect the public from dacoits and outlaws. It is the duty of the Government to protect the public and to make adequate police arrangements for the purpose. Instead of discharging this duty of theirs, the Government charged the innocent public falsely with complicity with dacoits and imposed a punitive tax which is wholly unjust and tyrannical. This Committee, therefore, advises the people to fight this injustice, to refuse to pay the tax and, for the sake of their self-respect, patiently to bear whatever hardships they may have to as a consequence.

This fine has been imposed upon the people on the ground that they had been assisting the dacoits. But what fine would it be proper to impose on a Government which assisted the outlaws by giving them guns? God alone can impose an adequate fine for such an offence. The Government must indeed be in a bad way, otherwise why should it have been necessary for it to join hands with a murderer? It is impossible to believe that the Government does not know how many murders and dacoities had been committed by this outlaw after he had been given the weapons. It may be that the Government was quite genuine in its belief that Ali would help them to arrest Babar Deva, but how can people know that was the Government's intention? The Government must now publicly announce that they had committed a mistake. The responsibility for the various atrocities that have been perpetrated by Ali on the poor public rests on the Government.

It is the duty of Government servants to arrest the offenders; they have failed to discharge this duty and yet they have been exempted. Missionaries have been similarly exempted, presumably because if they were described as companions of outlaws, they would oppose the Government with their guns. But the converts, the Christian Dheds have not been exempted. Mukhis and village servants have also been exempted, and yet it is a fact that every village servant and every police official knows quite well where Babar is to be found, though not one of them has the necessary courage to arrest him. While all these people have been exempted, the members of the legislature are treated on a par with the rest of the public as associates of dacoits.

If we oppose this levy for the sake of saving Rs 2-8-0 the conflict would be meaningless. The entire point is we are not companions of thieves and dacoits and the Imperial Government has no right to say so. Only if you feel that way, should you start this fight. It does not matter if the Government takes away your property worth Rs 10 for the recovery of Rs 2. To pay Rs 2-8-0 to the Government for the privilege of being described as companions of dacoits is worse than letting yourselves be robbed by outlaws or dacoits. We are honourable and respectable men and are certainly not associates of robbers.

During the conflict, officers of the Government and your opponents will do their best to tempt you into violent ways but do not allow yourselves to be so tempted. This conflict is going to be conducted along Gandhiji's way. There is no need for either a *dharia* or a stick. We need only strong shoulders. Let the Government strike those shoulders as hard as it likes. If you retaliate whether with abuses or sticks, the Government has ample authority and power to crush you. It is not able to arrest the outlaw, Babar Deva, but it will have no difficulty in arresting you. There is nothing very wonderful in abusing or hitting anybody but there is real greatness in undergoing hardships for the sake of what you regard as your duty.

197

Government of India's Report to Secretary of State on Seditious Character of Nagpur Flag Satygraha

Home Department (Political) File No. 280 N.A.I.
6 December 1923

To

The Right Honourable Viscount Peel,
His Majesty's Secretary of State for India, London

DELHI
6 December 1923

MY LORD,

We transmit herewith the report of the Government of the Central Provinces on the agitation in connection with the so-called Swaraj or National Flag at Nagpur which was required by Your Lordship's telegram no. 3413, dated September 20th, 1923. This report, read with its accompaniment, Resolution no. 1202-1057-11, dated the 8th September 1923 of the Government of the Central Provinces, gives a sufficiently clear and comprehensive narrative of the course of events and in our observations upon it we propose to restrict ourselves to the more important issues affecting the general political situation which emerge.

2. As to the character and design of the agitation there can be no possibility of doubt. Though it originated locally and was ostensibly directed to vindicate the national status of the "Swaraj" flag and to assert the right to hold political

demonstrations in public places, the ulterior object, which was repeatedly avowed, was to constitute it an item in a general plan of civil disobedience, that is, a concerted campaign against the authority of Government. It was in this form and with this intention that it was adopted by the Congress Committee and the Government of the Central Provinces rightly took up the challenge. In view of the fact that the exhibition of the flag was not in itself an offence, their legal position was not an easy one, but, at this stage, they maintained a sound, firm and perfectly consistent policy in regard to the flag processions. Their local officers behaved with remarkable discretion and restraint and were successful in preventing any incidents which could give vitality and substance to what was really a factitious agitation.

3. When matters were in this posture, the Government of India, while advising that action should be primarily directed against the local organization of the agitation and its principles rather than its minor agents, generally approved of the proceedings of the local Government and assured them of support in measures taken to maintain law and order and the authority of Government. The situation was verbally discussed on July 1st by His Excellency the Viceroy and the Honourable the Home Member with His Excellency the Governor of the Central Provinces and the Hon'ble Sir M. Joshi, with special reference to suggestions which had then been made as to the possibility of terminating the agitation on the receipt of certain assurances from its promoters. The views of the Government of India were fully explained by His Excellency the Viceroy and in particular the danger of entering into any form of negotiation was pointed out. In view of this and of the fact that the issues raised had obviously passed beyond the bounds of an incident of purely local concern, we are constrained to express our regret that the local Government should have considered itself justified in taking part in negotiations with the Congress representatives without previous consultation with us. Communications limited to an explanation of the policy and intentions of Government, as already determined and as recently announced by His Excellency the Governor in addressing the local Legislative Council, might have been to good purpose; but the communications actually entered into were liable to the construction of being, and were indeed to some extent in substance, of the nature of negotiations directed towards an agreement or compromise. In particular, whatever passed with regard to the release of prisoners, if not amounting to a definite understanding, was sufficiently tangible to impel the local Government to the conclusion that failure to release could be justifiably regarded as a breach of faith; and we consider that a commitment of this kind, whether implicit or explicit, should not have been made without prior consultation with the Government of India. The result of these proceedings was to present the Government of India with a situation in which any reversal of the action to which the local Government was already committed was clearly impracticable.

4. On the question whether, at the stage when the negotiations were opened, the previous action of the Government had not already practically defeated the agitation, we are disposed to accept the estimate of the Central Provinces

you shall have to be non-violent. I now ask you to raise up your hands those who do not want to pay up the tax (all raised their hands). I have got enough evidence to show what work the additional police are doing in the villages. We shall have to place at least two men in each village where there is the additional police. If we want police protection it is for us to apply and if the Government wants to protect us and if it has no money it must say so openly. The Government must be candid with the people; but here it says you are thieves and robbers; I and many others are of opinion that not a pie should be given to this Government, but this is not the time for it. Now those who are willing to join as volunteers may give their names to Gopaldas. I tell those who are present here that if any of you is in the habit of assisting the dacoits you will go home with a determination not to do it. A rumour has come to my ears that the Government thinks of removing the whole Dharala class from this District to some other place if you do not improve. The greater responsibility is on Borsad who has started the struggle; you will forget your enmities and be united in the common cause."

(Extract of leading article in *Bombay Chronicle,* dated 19-12-1923)

Lawlessness in Borsad

There is no more nauseating cant indulged in by the upholders and apologists of the present system of administration in this country than the claim that it stands between the people and anarchy, with all that it connotes. During recent years, especially, the people of this *country have realised to their cost and shame what the vindication of "Law and Order" by the bureaucracy means.* But the record of the bureaucracy in this respect has, in many ways, been surpassed by its achievement in the Borsad Taluka of the Kaira District and this achievement is not the least of the legacies of misrule and highhandedness bequeathed by Sir Lloyd George to his successor. "Law and Order" has been vindicated with a "thoroughness" out-strafford ing straf ford. And not less "thorough" is the manner in which the people of the Presidency have been kept in the dark about it. On the 3rd instant Mr. Manilal Kothari wired to us a detailed report of the *Borsad Taluka Conference held under the presidentship of Mr. Vallabhbhai Patel.* The message was never delivered in this office and three days later Mr. Manilal was informed that the *message* having been considered *objectionable* has been stopped by the Bombay Telegraph Office under the orders of the Secretary to the Government of Bombay. We have been told that with the introduction of the "Reforms" autocracy has been doomed in this country and that, among other boons, freedom of the Press has been secured to the people. We would ask under what regime except an autocratic one could the freedom of the Press be so flagrantly attacked as to prevent the people from knowing the truth about the grievances of their fellow-countrymen. Why was Mr. Manilal's message considered objectionable by the Government of Bombay? Was it *because* what time *Sir Lloyd George was being feasted and eulogised* by his admirers and flatterers as a great and good ruler, it was not considered convenient that the publication of the woes of the people of Borsad should explode the pretty myth? Will the Director of Information throw light on this mystery ? We draw the attention of His Excellency the Governor to this aspect of the matter as well as the whole question of the sufferings of the people of Borsad Taluka, because careful enquiry will bring home to him what indescribable misery the adherence by Governors to the pernicious tradition of always siding with the officials, whether right or wrong, against the people, has entailed on the latter and what an unbridgeable gulf it has created between them and the Government. The happenings in Borsad Taluka reveal an achievement which, as we have said, in many respects surpasses the normal record of the bureaucracy and it is no wonder Sir Lloyd George dared not face the glare of its publicity.

The tale of woe is briefly told and it is because *Mr. Vallabhbhai Patel* narrated it with effective incisiveness that the message reporting it and the decision of the Borsad Taluka Conference, which, *as result of that speech, resolved not to pay the fine of Rs 2,40,000,* being the amount of expenditure incurred on the punitive police imposed on the people of the whole Taluka, was considered "objectionable". The Kaira District has *for years been the happy hunting-ground of dacoits,* itself a striking commentary on the effective manner in which Law and Order is maintained by the bureaucracy. *In 1917 an outlaw named Babar* made his appearance in the district. He has not yet been captured by the efficient forces of law in the presidency. During these years he has committed untold crimes and atrocities and has *become a terror* to the countryside and even the towns. The *police,* having failed to capture him, covered their inefficiency by the familiar devise of sending panicky *reports against the people charging the latter with complicity in the crimes and* outrages of the outlaw. With the perversity characterising the working of the bureaucratic machinery a punitive police was consequently imposed two years ago on two villages which were alleged to have given shelter to the outlaw. The remedy proved worse than the evil. In one of these two villages Babar murdered one man in broad daylight, when the punitive police instead of arresting him, as with some enterprise it could have done, sought refuge in the pet allegation that the people did not give information against the outlaw. In the other village the punitive police itself was assaulted by the outlaw. The rest of the tale is thus told by Mr. Vallabhbhai Patel:

"The people saw the District Magistrate and said they could not pay the fine. The *Mamlatdar* also reported that it was impossible to realise the fine from people who, not being contumacious, were too poor to pay it. This he said in *his letter P. O.I., 245 dated Borsad 16th February in which he protests against the imposition* of any further burden. "No villager," he said, "seems willing for the continuance of the additional police in the villages." The *District Superintendent of Police disagreed* with this Mamlatdar the man on the spot—and insisted that the impost should be continued. His reasons were that Babar and his gang were still at large, that though Babar killed Shivbhai in broad daylight no evidence was forthcoming! What are the policemen in the village doing? How are the people to furnish evidence, if the police are impotent to do so? The third reason is that Khadana Patanwadias never give information about outlaws, that they on the contrary shelter them and give them food and drink, and so on. One of the reasons is that some of the Khadana Patanwadias would join Babar's gang were not for the check imposed by the special police. The funniest part of the affair is that the *Collector disagreed,* in turn with this Superintendent of Police, and he reported entirely differently to the Commissioner. *His letter too is in my possession.* He was against the continuation of the additional police in either of the villages because "the additional police are useless to prevent" Babar's being sheltered in the villages, but he felt that there was a general increase of crime in the whole of the Taluka, and "every village is directly or indirectly more or less responsible for the general breakdown of order," and so he suggested that *some additional force may be imposed on the whole Taluka* as made by DSP. It seems that consultation is at the back of the impost. I may also add that the Collector admitted that the people do not give information or shelter the miscreants "from fear or from selfish desire to save themselves immediate trouble." *The Commissioner* disagreed with the Collector and the Mamlatdar; he felt that the Superintendent had given solid reason for the continuance of the police in the two villages for another year and issued orders accordingly. That was in June. How all of a sudden in *October Government resolved to impose the police on the whole Taluka passes comprehension. I have not these communications* in my possession. But I am sure about my facts. Every one I have met has told me what has happened.

In no other country would an outlaw be allowed to run amuck for so long a time as Babar has been allowed *thanks to the inefficiency of the police,* and the failure to capture him within a short period would be met with the instant dismissal of all the responsible officials. But in this bureaucrat-ridden country if the police fails to perform its duty, the *people are made the scapegoat* and in this case the impotence of the authorities to protect the person and property of law-abiding people is attempted to be ascribed *to the lack of co-operation on the part of the people* who are charged with refusing to give information or evidence. But how baseless is this patently ridiculous charge is proved by the admission of the apologists of the officials themselves apart from the evidence of the Collector himself who reported that the people did not give information and sheltered the miscreants "from fear or from the selfish desire to save themselves immediate trouble." The correspondent of the *Times of India* writing the other day said: "It is stated that his (Babar's) hatred against police informers is so intense that he does not spare even his nearest relatives." Surely, the man who will not spare even his nearest relatives will give no mercy to others. And, as the record shows, Babar has to his credit 22 murders. Not one of these 22 victims was a rich man and Babar murdered them because they were informants and he crucified one of them to a tree with a view to strike terror into the hearts of the helpless and distressed people, and yet there are responsible officers of the Government who dare assert that the people do not give information and on whose advice *Government have punished the people of the whole Taluka by imposing a punitive police on them. This is not all. Mr. Vallabhbhai Patel, in his speech, charged the authorities with having sought the aid of another outlaw to get rid of Babar and provided him with arms and ammunition. If the allegation is true, there could be no greater proof of the inefficiency of the police.* But under the present dispensation, it seems to be nobody's business to remove this blot on the police administration. The police can do no wrong. Neither can its efficiency be impugned. So the helpless, unprotected people must have the insult of a baseless charge against them added to the injury done by the outlaw, not to speak of the reported pinpricks administered by the punitive police itself. They have in a Conference resolved upon refusing to pay the fine. *There has been no enquiry made by the "Ma-Bap" Government as to* why the people have been driven to resort to this extreme step. But the fiat has gone forth, the fine must be realised. The realisation has already commenced with the attachment and sale of the moveable property of the villagers and according to reports we have received, the latter have even been threatened by the officials with attachment and sale of their lands. Evidently there is lawlessness rampant in the Borsad Taluka. But we may well ask: On whose part is that lawlessness?

199

N.D. Commissioner's Rejoinder to DM.'s Confidential Report

Home Department Special File No. 647 of 1924

AHMEDABAD
20th December 1923

HOME DEPARTMENT,

Submitted to Government. Mr. Kirpalani has very clearly stated his views and I offer my comments upon them after full personal discussion with him.

2. Mr. Kirpalani is of opinion that for the present we should ignore the hostile propaganda of the political agitators even if it takes the form of inflammatory speeches by prominent and influential political leaders openly advising the public at large to disobey the orders of Government and to obstruct their execution by every means in their power short of actual violence. He argues that there is a better chance of eventually collecting all the police charges if we refrain from prosecutions and confine ourselves to the steady and constant pressure of ordinary administrative measures directed against the defaulting villagers.

3. If this fails he says we can resort to "strong measures" hereafter but if we resort to strong measures now they may also fail and they may lead us on into an agitation and a struggle of unknown and incalculable dimensions—the end and result of which it would be difficult to foresee.

4. I do not agree with these views. The seditious and anti-Government propaganda in Borsad has been inspired by and is largely led by men who are the avowed enemies of Government. Their incitements to civil disobedience are particularly dangerous in a Taluka with the terrible crime record of Borsad. The mischief which they have already done is clearly described in Mr. Kirpalani's letter. In my opinion they are not in the least likely to relax their efforts as time

goes on. On the contrary they will redouble and intensify them for purpose of fostering and strengthening feelings of hatred and contempt against Government and its officers. Bitter experience in the past has shown that in the face of such an agitation the friends of Government cannot be rallied or persuaded to come out into the open. Government will be discredited, its officers will be discouraged and the administration will be paralysed.

5. Especially I do not agree with Mr. Kirpalani's statement that *"our primary object is to collect the tax"*. That is a purely secondary object. Our primary object was and is to put an end to a pandemonium of atrocious crime in the Borsad Taluka and to purge it of murderous outlaws and their shelterers and supporters. A good beginning has been made. There has been no serious crime in the Taluka since the outside police came in.

But the political agitation is now to a great extent paralysing the police because the people are being taught and encouraged to boycott them. If this is to go on, the police might as well be withdrawn for it is not worth while keeping them in the Taluka, if they are to serve no purpose beyond assisting in the collection of the cost of their own Upkeep. I learnt personally from the District Superintendent of Police that the higher police officers have already had to give up as hopeless several promising clues and lines of investigation because of the altered attitude of the people.

6. Further I understand from the District Magistrate that he now feels doubts about the expediency of proceeding with the policy of deportation of selected members of the criminal tribes in the district. He thinks that the deportations would add fresh fuel to the smouldering discontent which has been aroused by the political propaganda.

I do not think that it can be argued that the deportations of these criminals is less necessary now in the interests of the public peace than it was 2 months ago. It is true that this was recommended then as an emergency measure and the emergency has been partially and for the time being met by the introduction of the outside police. But the additional police will sooner or later be removed and I do not think that the deportation policy should be abandoned or postponed until another emergency arises.

I do not think that we should abandon or postpone this measure because of the opportunities it will give for hostile misrepresentation.

7. For these reasons I think that Government should, if advised that a good case can be made out, at once order the prosecution of the political leaders who have been preaching and organizing civil disobedience and should deal similarly with any others who may be tempted to take their places.

Other means may be found for controlling smaller and less influential men without making the mistake of crowding out jails and lockups with inconsequential numbers of prisoners.

8. But this policy once adopted must be steadily pursued even if an uproar is raised like the uproar of Nagpur and even if the Borsad Taluka should attract volunteers and agitators from all over India.

Commissioner, N.D.

200

Vallabhbhai Condemns Government Atrocities in Borsad and Anand

Navjivan, 9 December 1923

Government imposed the tax of two and a half lacs on the innocent people of Anand and Borsad, and has sent additional police force in about one hundred villages. The people have decided to launch Satyagraha against this action of the government.

The police force sent to villages is brought from outside. Some of the policemen there have started committing atrocities on the people. People who were victims of the atrocities of the bandits. Few have become the victims of the atrocities of the police. In the villages the people have not the vigour to combat the atrocities of the police, women are molested, yet because of ill fame people do not desire that such incidents be reported.

Village revenue officers have been ordered to confiscate the properties and those who do this job quickly have been promised rewards. As this is a year of drought, the people have been doubly harassed. Government was already angry, and now God also has been displeased.

In this miserable condition, it is absolutely essential that we should stand by people and share their miseries. The young men of Gujarat have got this opportunity to serve the people. Young men of Gujarat who rushed to Nagpur (to take part in flag Satyagraha) should not leave the miserable people of their province unattended. Darbar Gopaldasbhai, who erected a Satyagraha camp in Borsad, is staying there. Those volunteers who want to work in Borsad taluka should send their application immediately to the Secretary of the Provincial Congress Committee. For this struggle money will be required. I desire that Gujarat will provide necessary money for Satyagraha struggle. Those persons who want to help are requested to send their contribution to Gujarat Provincial Congress Committee. Struggle has begun, therefore immediately help is needed.

201

Vallabhbhai's Appeal for Funds for Borsad Satyagraha

Navjivan, 9 December 1923

We will require money for this struggle. I desire that only Gujarat will procure the money required for Borsad Satyagraha. Those who want to contribute should send their contribution to Gujarat Provincial Congress Committee. Struggle has started, and therefore help is required quickly.

202

Vallabhbhai Advises Borsad People to Refuse to Pay Fine[1]

Navjivan, 9 December 1923

Government is bound to protect you. Government collects excessive tax from you to maintain police and the army, yet it is not able to protect you from the atrocities of murderers and dacoits. Gaikwad Government has increased its police force to protect its subjects, but has not fined the people. Our Government has accused you of helping the dacoits, imposed a fine of two and a half lac rupees on you and increased police force. It is better to die than to pay the fine and being labelled as the collaborator of dacoits. Your representatives met at the first conference held at Borsad and have pledged not to pay the fine. You adhere to your pledge and preserve your self-respect. Government as usual will be angry with you, will start terrorising you and attach your property, it will take away your cattle. For a rupee or two it will confiscate goods worth tens of rupees. You bear that plight silently and bravely, but do not give a pie to the men of the government. Do not indulge in any kind of violence. Ways of the Government are immoral and devoid of truth, on your side is truth and if you are non-violent, victory is yours. Person who practises truth and non-violence is never defeated. Let God give you strength to suffer hardships and misery.

[1]Bulletins were issued from Borsad Satyagraha Camp to boost the spirit of the people, and to see that they are not misguided. This Satyagraha bulletin was issued under the joint signature of Vallabhbhai and Darbat Gopaldas.

203

"Congress and Not Councils are Our Saviour"—Vallabhbhai

Bombay Chronicle, 12 December 1923

We have to consider first which is to be our saviour, the Congress or the Councils. I may tell you that you need not depend on handful of educated men who claim to represent you, and to deliver you from the bondage of another handful that governs three hundred million people as so many sheep. A band of such educated people used to play chess with the bureaucracy on a board arranged by the latter according to its own will. You have removed that band and placed another instead. But they have gone in not professing to gain anything from, but to destroy, the Councils. The Congress does not believe that they can do it, but has allowed such of them to go in as insisted. We are not concerned with whether they break them or not. Let us be sure that the Councils cannot help us. You cannot ride two horses at a time. Let us decide before going to the field of battle

205

Vallabhbhai Condemns Forced Labour

Borsad Satyagraha Bulletin, 20 December 1923

Barbers, potters, Vaghris, Dheds and such humble brothers should give up the age-old system of forced labour. The very Government Officers, who used to take forced labour from these people, were breaking the Government laws. When people have to do forced labour, their personality remained suppressed and that they brought up their children in slavery. It was painful to hear the contemptuous language of other people when these persons were addressed. No one should do any forced labour, but if they so wished they might do some work in a voluntary capacity. In any case they should not do any forced labour. It was a matter of great joy that the artisans of many villages had given up forced labour and that they had to be congratulated for that. The friendly relationship of give and take should be continued in the villages. The people should do all the work of the village, but they should not do any work of the Government Officers. If they were to ask the *Mukhis,* the *Matadars,* to do the forced work in connection with the *Chora,* they should refuse it. If the *Mukhis* and the *Matadars* refused to do forced labour then the Government servants would try to intimidate these people. They would threaten them, abuse them and even harass their children and women. But they should not be afraid of the Government. They should be prepared to bear peacefully whatever *zulum* might be forced on them by the Government officers and should give complete information of these *zulum* of the Government servants to the Satyagraha Camp at Borsad.

206

Vallabhbhai Condemns[1] *Punitive Tax Imposed by Government*

Bombay Chronicle, 21 December 1923

In a lecture he delivered at Bhetasi before he left for Bombay, Mr. Vallabhbhai Patel declared:

If the Government would withdraw from this taluka I promise to capture the dacoits within 15 days from today. Whence they have sprung? They are, after all, our countrymen. As long as the police is impotent they will plunder us. We shall have to summon requisite courage and fearlessness should we think of escaping from danger.

The police have been baffled by the dacoits and a gang of them have been infesting the taluka for half a dozen years. If a few dacoits are captured others spring up and the trade of plunder and highway looting goes on merrily, openly and in broad daylight as a Bania's trade in jaggery and candy; and no one, the worse for it, but the poor villagers who are buffers between the marauders, plunderers and an unsympathetic Government. "Who can save us from this?" was their cry and to their joy the White Cap has befriended them. The insistence with which the leaders are inculcating the principle of non-violence is noteworthy. I quote the following from a bulletin issued over the signature of Mr. Gopaldas Desai:

"Do not interfere in the work of the police. Do not get infuriated or excited even when your dearest articles are attached. No *dharias* or sticks are to be used in this movement of Satyagraha. This is to be particularly borne in mind. The key to our success lies in absolute control over thought, word and action."

After my investigations and close contact with a large number of workers and people I have come to the conclusion that there is not a man or woman in Borsad who does not regard the poll-tax as an outrage on his or her self-respect.

[1]Speech delivered at Borsad on December 21.

207

Vallabhbhai's Rejoinder to Government

Extract from Bombay Chronicle, 27 December 1923

TO THE EDITOR OF "THE CHRONICLE".

Sir,

We congratulate you for having compelled Government to take you in their confidence about their case regarding "lawlessness" in Borsad. But we feel bound to raise our protest against the way in which the Government have tried to throw dust in the eyes of the public and we must make our charge against them absolutely clear.

2. Mr. Gennings refers to so called "confidential official documents improperly and illegally obtained" by one of us. We can only assure you that these *documents,* however, "confidential" they may be, were so relevant that the formidable array of those with which the Director of Information has endeavoured to enlighten you and we should have failed in our duty if we had not exposed the hollowness of the Government case as revealed by admissions of their own officers. We are, however, in a position to show that the documents that the Director of Information has ventured to publish believing them to be harmless also help to give away the whole Government case.

3. We may accept that the Superintendent of Police who has signed the impressive document on which the Director of Information relies is an officer with a distinguished record. But we are afraid the record was won by him elsewhere than the field of Kaira, and he has not been long enough to give evidence of that

record except perhaps in the preparation of that document of 77 paragraphs—a document based on the reports of officers who were solely responsible for the maladministration of the past several years. We do not know the order that he and his gallant band have restored, but if any it is due to a variety of causes for which Government can take no credit whatsoever. One of them is the capture of the dacoit Ali which we make bold to say was not due to the bravery of the police, *and another is the capture of Mirkhan by Baroda State police.* A third reason is the posting of the Satyagraha volunteers in the Taluka which has gone a great way to relieve the distress. But any relief or restoration of order for which the Government can take any credit is more than counter-balanced by the disorder and misery caused by the punitive police imposed on the Taluka, and the abnormal concentration of police force in one part of the District has rendered other parts insecure.

4. We see that the Director of Information has accepted the charge of inefficiency of the police, but has tried to make it out as the result entirely of the lack of will on the people's part to support the police and of the lack of courage to help themselves. A study of the report of the Superintendent of Police will demonstrate the utter worthlessness of the excuse. It should be observed that the report relates to the whole district and no less than a score or more of the cases described are of events that happened in Talukas other than Borsad. We shall only point out the numerous instances in which the people have only tried to help the police, but have risked and lost their lives.

It is the Taluka of Borsad which was the scene of these deeds of daring which the Commissioner of the Division described as one in which the failure on the part of the people at large to give information or cooperation to the police has been "conspicuous". If the record given above is one of "demoralisation" and "lack of will to help" a fresh dictionary will have to be issued by the Director of Information.

To these records of brave resistance we shall only add the cases of scores of villages which have out of their own strength remained immune from the attacks of dacoits and marauders and which because of the organised defence they are capable of putting up with that they were free from the scourage of the punitive police and even of the assistance of the ordinary police which claims to afford them protection.

In concluding this paragraph we shall only make a passing reference to the plea of the Director of Information that the people should have been capable of greater resistance because of the "lethal weapons" that the villagers have always ready to hand. What shall we say regarding the prowess of the policemen who inspite of their swords and guns have not been able to capture dacoits who escaped in one instance because it was dark, or in another because the way lay through surrounding fields and standing crops, whilst the poor villagers were fighting. For all they were worth with their "lethal weapons" against dacoits armed with "guns, dharias, bows and arrows".

5. But the Director of Information would even acquit the people of the charge of deliberate failure to inform the police, if his Govt. can find the wherewithal to pay for the cost of the punitive police. "The only question" says he, "is whether the police force should be paid for by the public of the whole Presidency or by the inhabitants of the small tract whose lawlessness had rendered them necessary." The only question is not that. The only question is whether a people should be condemned unheard, whether the character of a vast majority of the peaceful inhabitants of a taluka should be so shamelessly impugned: The only question is not that. The only question is whether a Government that admits (para 3 of D.S.P.'s report) that the continued success of the dacoits depredations has "completely cowed down the law abiding sections of the district" can conscionably punish the section cowed down.

6. But we have touched only the points raised by the Director of Information's reply. Whilst he has questioned our right to publish certain damaging documents he is indifferent to the most serious charges that we have made against them. Why is it that whilst so many informers have been shot or murdered in cold blood, no police has been touched? Why is it that inspite of so many informants having been murdered, the police up to a few days ago failed to capture the arch dacoits? *The charge of the public against Government is that they allied with a dacoit who was known to be a murderer, provided him with arms and ammunition and allowed him to go unchecked on his career of murder and loot.* They have come to believe that all cooperation with such a department of police was futile.

The Government have been culpably indifferent to the charge we have noted above. Whilst all the documents published and unpublished are contrived to throw the whole blame on one dacoit Babar Deva and on the socalled "demoralised" public, no mention is made of that miscreant Ali in any one of these reports though his career of crimes has been no less dastardly than his brother dacoit. It is we repeat with all the emphasis that we command a guilty silence. The last though not the least charge, which has also been left unanswered is that the *Government imposed the police, knowing that it was useless to do so, and that the public did not need it. The District Magistrate in his letter no. 184, 13th April 1923, one of the confidential documents we have "illegally" obtained* was emphatically of opinion that the "continuance of the additional police is not desirable in either of the villages", that "the police parties never move out of the village, and their presence does not reduce the number of men otherwise required for the police of the Taluka", that they do not even serve the purpose of preventing crime, as the murder of Shivbhai in Jogan in daylight proves, to say nothing to the attack made on the similar police parties in Gold". He also frankly confessed that "from the application I have received and from the statements of a deputation of the non-Dharala residents of Jogan who recently came to see me, it appears that they do not need such protection (i.e. the protection of the punitive police), and would much prefer to be without the police altogether than to have to pay for them."

7. The question then, the public will ask, is where shall we fix the responsibility

for the general state of criminality in the District we are here concerned with that in the Taluka, and what has been done to remedy it. We have not the slightest doubt that the Govt. have to thank themselves for it, that they are reaping what they have so sedulously sown. They have chosen to fix the label of criminal on a virile, industrious agricultural community and having once condemned it, they have daily driven it to a life of despair by the measures they have devised out of their own desperation. Their most handy weapons have been the Criminal Tribes Act and the notorious security of the Criminal Procedure Code which are so framed as to lend themselves to almost indefinite abuse, or which an ingenious overzealous officer finds easy to abuse. "Well thought out and carefully calculated solutions were suggested to meet the situation," and these receive the strong support of several district magistrates, but mourns the officer, "unfortunately for various reasons they were negative and so owing to continued criminality on the part of the Dharalas the work of reiterating these proposals like a penelope's web continues". While one officer is prepared to admit that the "ultimate cause of this abnormal amount of crime is partly an economic one", he feels, "it is not one that can be easily removed," another thinks that the attention shown to these people have not been adequate, that the leniency with which they have been treated upto now has been utterly misplaced, and that "in lieu of improving them the half-hearted and completely inadequate *hazri* measures taken up under the Criminal Tribes Act have resulted in their retrogression" and consequently presses for measures "indicative of determination and strength" under the Criminal Tribes Act. "It will now generally be admitted" says the D.S.P. "that after nearly a decade's trial this *hazri* measure has borne enough fruit in the shape of increased crime." The remedy has been worse than the disease, but rather than radically alter the remedy it has been always thought proper to intensify it. If person aggravates the malady, one way is to make the dose stronger, and despatch the patient, another is alter the dose altogether and put him on the way to recovery. It was no wonder that proposals for a more determined use of the Criminal Tribes Act were long negatived. It is a wonder that they should have been countenanced at all.

If anything was needed to complete the ravages of the application of the Criminal Tribes Act, the security sections supplied it. Imagine a district in which in one single year there should have been no less than 1800 cases under the security sections. What is the poor wretch to do if he is to be put into jail on the slightest suspicion? Better, he thinks, to court jail by defiant crime than to be ever the object of police suspicion and police attentions. The economic aspect has never been faced and the District Magistrate fears that it may not be possible to face it at all. Even temporary relief as suspension of payment of land revenue in a year of failure of monsoon has been so frequently denied and a Deputy Secretary to Government naively suggests "that the force to be employed should be as strong as the general population can pay for" not under usual conditions, not if they can afford but "under pressure"! In almost every year of famine there is the cry of "false annawarnees" and the full measure of revenue is exacted where it should not be.

Having refused to face the economic aspect of the case, and having been unable to tackle the question of moral reform of the community the Government have naturally not looked beyond the limits of the Criminal Tribes Act and the security sections and the final desperate act has been the imposition of punitive police. As has been noted above the District Magistrate was of the opinion that the punitive police had failed to serve any useful purpose and that no villager wanted it. But the police was imposed with a vengeance and the people are not yet free from their oppression.

8. We do not think we need discuss here what in our opinion would be the proper solution of the case. We shall only say that the little experiment of posting trained experienced Satyagraha volunteers in every village of the Taluka who will take to every home the message of non-violence, truth and Khaddar, is already proving successful and if the Government retires, as we think it ought, with good grace, from the area, we shall galdly share with the people of the village the responsibility to keep peace and order.

9. It is beyond our purpose here to narrate the long tale of woe of the Borsad peasantry, the way in which the punitive police has terrorised them, the way in which attachments are carried out, and how the life of the people has been rendered insecure by those who profess to keep them in security. We can only describe that condition of things as atrocious.

10. It has been our duty in the circumstances detailed in the foregoing paragraphs to advise the vast majority of the innocent people of Borsad to refuse to pay the unwarranted impost and to resist with all their might and power of endurance the attempt to cast an unmerited slur on their character.

Yours, etc.
VALLABHBHAI PATEL
MAHADEO DESAI
Wadi Junction, on way to Coconada, DE

208

Vallabhbhai Feels Swarajya Meaningless if People Continue Wearing Foreign Cloth

Stray Bulletin, 31 December 1923

If India secures Swarajya and if, at that time, Indians are seen wearing foreign cloth, that Swarajya will be like dust; under such Swarajya the poor people will be suffering oppression like that of the present day. Mahatma Gandhi has imagined Swarajya in a different way. In this idea of Swarajya, the poor will enjoy happiness and peace.

209

Vallabhbhai Accuses Police of Helping Dacoits

Stray Pamphlet, 1923 (Abstract)

We have seen things for ourselves in a great many villages and have made careful and detailed enquiries. We are satisfied that by far the greater part of the police is completely innocent. The outlaws commit robberies at night; the police commit robberies during the day, and on top of it all, the people are being dubbed collaborators of dacoits. The people maintain that the police is dishonest; it gives to the outlaws guns and ammunition, and fills its own pockets by sharing in the looted property.

210

AICC Members Elected from Gujarat including Vallabhbhai

According to the report of Shri Ganesh Vasudev Mavalankar and Shri Acharatal Chunilal Sheth who were election officers, undermentioned twelve members are declared elected to AICC for the year 1923-1924.

1. Shri Vallabhbhai Jhaverbhai Patel
2. Shri Gopaldas Ambaidas Desai
3. Shri Chandulal Manilal Desai
4. Shri Abbas S. Taiyabjee
5. Shri Mahadev Haribhai Desai
6. Shri Manilal Vallabhji Kothari
7. Shri Fulchand Babuji Shah
8. Shri Kalidas Jaskaram Jhaveri
9. Shri Amrutlal Dalputhbhai Sheth
10. Shri Imam Abbas Kadar Bavalzir
11. Shri Devdas Mohandas Gandhi
12. Shri Mohandas Kameshvar Pandya

President
VALLABHBHAI JHAVERBHAI PATEL

(13) *Paragraph 37:* Babar took a revenge on a public informer and inflicted deadly wounds on him.

(14) *Paragraph 58:* A potter was hit in his chest most brutally, not because he has money, but either he must have been informer, or he must have shown courage to resist them.

(15) *Paragraph 60:* They were killed because they were suspected to be informers.

(16) The people of Sunva came out and they chased Babar Deva.

(17) *Paragraph 71:* Three vegetable vendors were attacked and shot dead. (Of course not because their chest was loaded with money.)

4. Now in these cases many points deserve our attention.

(*a*) The report from which all these cases have been extracted was specially prepared to prove that the necessity of stationing of punitive police there, and so it does not consider the fact that large number of people had informed the police or shown the courage to combat the dacoits.

(*b*) In the report the cases in which informers have informed the police, but the police had not taken any action, are not considered at all.

(*c*) The head of the information department had as a correspondent of *Times of India* had referred to some special cases in last October, but there is no mention of those cases in this report. "Babar does not leave the informers without taking revenge", and "he is so much exasperated towards police informers, that he does not leave their near relatives unpunished." In such atmosphere also people have shown courage to give information to police. In the report there is also a reference to Babar Deva's killing his mother and uncle because he suspected that they have given information to the police about him.

These acts of bravery have taken place in the Borsad taluka about which the Commissioner has said that "common people here have no tendency to inform or help the police". If what has been said above is a proof of people's lack of bravery and a desire not to help the police, then the head of information department should prepare a special dictionary and publish it.

There are many incidents when people have fought bravely with the dacoits. Besides that there are instances when several villages have bravely defended themselves, and depended upon their own strength. As these people are in a position to defend them in an organised manner, they want to be free from the trouble not only of the punitive police but of the ordinary police who claim to defend them.

Before ending this Chapter it is necessary to refer to one argument of the head of the department of information. He says that as people had *lathis* and *dharias* (a spear-like weapon) they ought to have fought with the dacoits. Now what to say about the bravery of policemen who had rifles and swords but could not arrest the dacoits? Once dacoits escaped because it was dark. Once a dacoit was going through the fields full of crops and so police could not arrest him. But in spite of police inaction, poor villagers who had *lathis* were already fighting with the dacoits who were equipped with guns, rifles, bows, arrows, and other deadly weapons.

5. But if the government could have solved the problem of getting money for the maintenance of punitive police, then the head of the information department was ready to exonerate people from the charge of intentionally not giving information to the police. He says: "Only question is this expenditure of police should be given by the people of the whole presidency or the people of the trouble spot who have compelled the government to station additional police force?" But that is not the question. Question is whether to punish the people before hearing their complaints? Whether to cast aspersion on majority of peace loving people? Now the question is that the Government which itself admits (see report of DSP, para 3) that because of the continuous victory of the dacoits, the law-abiding people had been suppressed. Whether to brutally punish such suppressed people?

6. We have taken only the points which arise from the reply of the head of the information department. He objects to our publishing some letters which were going against them, and which we had no right to publish. But he is silent regarding the serious charges which we have levelled against him. So many informers were killed, they were shot, but nothing has been done to the police. There must be some reason behind it. So many informers were killed, but how is it that police have not been able to arrest the main dacoits? People accuse the government that it has joined hands with dacoits who have committed innumerable murders; it provided them guns and explosives, and allowed them loot and murder undisturbed. Now people are convinced that it is useless to cooperate with such police.

The Government does not reply to our charges mentioned above. In all the letters of the government—open and secret—dacoit Babar Deva and valourless people are blamed. But there is no reference to Ali who has not committed less number of murders than Babar Deva, in a single letter. We boldly say that in this silence of the government there is something ominous. Government has not replied to our another serious charge. Our charge is that government knew that it was useless to keep punitive police, and the people had no need of them. Yet it took the burden upon itself. District Magistrate in his letter no. 184 dated 13th April 1923—which is one of the illegally secured secret letter—he says, "It is my definite opinion that there is no need to keep additional police in any of the two villages." "Police party does not go out of the village, and because of that there is no reduction in the number of police which is normally kept in the taluka." Again this additional police is not helpful in containing the crimes. In Jogan Shivbhai was murdered in broad daylight and in Golel police party was attacked. These are some of the instances. He has frankly admitted "from the applications which I have received, and from the meeting which I had with the delegation of the communities other than that of Patanwadia and Baria of Jogan I have come to the conclusion that they do not need such protection—means punitive police protection—and they would prefer to have no police than to deal with police.

7. Now the people ask "Who is responsible for the crime polluted atmosphere in the district or taluka?" We have not an iota of doubt and Government itself is

solely responsible. It is reaping what it has sown. It labelled as criminals people of a community who are industrious, powerful, and who are engaged in the work of agriculture. It defamed them, humiliated them day in and day out, and brought them to the brink of frustration. The enforcement of Criminal Tribes Act, and to give bail according to Criminal Procedure Code are cheap and easy equipments in the hands of government at present. The structure of that law is such that one can misuse it as he likes, and some over-enthusiastic officers do not fail to misuse the law. That very officer says in exasperation "After having deeply thought about the situation, and after serious calculations some remedies are suggested. Many district magistrates also gave strong support. Yet because of various reasons our scheme was not accepted, and on the other side the criminal activities of Patanwadia and Bawria communities continued, hence these recommendations have to be presented again and again." Some officer is ready to confess, "The main reason of this unusual circumstances is economic", but he feels that it has no easy remedy. Another thinks "We did not pay proper attention to them, and the mildness shown towards them was misplaced" and "Instead of reforming them, action was taken against them according to Criminal Tribes Act, comprising of their daily report to the police station was half-hearted, and improper, as a result they have gone more and more backward . . ." and therefore the officer insists "such remedy should be found out under Criminal Tribes Act, which might indicate our strength and determination." D.S.P. says that "now it is generally accepted that the remedy of their reporting at the police station has been found completely ineffective." We say that he is mistaken. From that remedy, the hike in criminal activities has resulted. Here medicine has been proved more dangerous than the malady, and instead of changing the remedy, efforts have been made to make it more and more stringent. If because of poisonous medicine the disease spreads like wild fire, then one remedy is to increase the dose and kill the patient and the other is to change the medicine, and cure the patient. There is no wonder that remedies under Criminal Tribes Act were discarded long back, wonder is why those remedies were accepted again?

When Criminal Tribes Act was applied terrorism was let loose, and what was left unfinished was finished by the bail clause. Imagine a district where during one year there were 1800 prosecutions under the bail clause. Slightest doubt, and a person would be dumped in the jail. What can poor man do under such circumstances? He will think that it is better to confront the police and go to jail than remaining under the vigil of police. Nobody has thought of improving their economic condition. District Magistrate thinks that it is not possible to do anything in the matter. Even in the drought year tax relief is denied; and the deputy secretary is mean enough to suggest that as much "military force should be stationed there as the people can afford the burden of expenditure"—not what people can pay in normal circumstances, but what can be forcibly collected from them. In the years of drought also there are complaints that there are false assessments and full land tax is collected even from the places where it ought not to have been collected.

Thus the government had denied to find out any treatment for the removal of poverty, and it has no moral courage to improve their moral standard; and so it has to hide itself in the hedge of Criminal Tribes Act and bail clause, and as a last resort it took no steps of stationing punitive police.

As stated above, the opinion of the District Magistrate was that it was no use stationing additional police force. Village people do not need that police force. But police force was deployed there as an act of revenge, and people are not free from its atrocities.

8. We do not feel that we should discuss here about the possible solution of this problem. We will only say that our experience of putting trained satyagrahi volunteers in every village is yielding fruits. They propagate the message of non-violence, truth and khadi in every home. If the government leaves this region—we wish that it should honourably leave the region—we will gladly take the responsibility of maintaining peace and order in the region.

9. It is beyond our object to describe how the people of Borsad taluka are terrorised, how the additional police is committing atrocities on them, how the attachment is being resorted to, and how the authorities devour them in the name of protecting them, we will only use the word most tragic for it.

10. We think it as our sacred duty to ask the innocent people of Borsad that under prevailing circumstances described in details in the above paragraphs, not to pay this senseless tax, and assimilating all their strength and endurance, fight out, and to wipe out the stigma on their character.

[1]Government had issued a white paper regarding the satyagraha of Borsad. In that paper some charges were made against those who conducted Satyagraha movement. Vallabhbhai Patel and Mahadev Desai had sent their reply to the Editor of *Bombay Chronicle* on 23 November 1923.

214

Vallabhbhai Exposes Conflict among Swarajya Party Leaders

Sevak, 8 January 1924

That the Swarajya Party is suffering from too many leaders is gradually being borne out by the turn events that are gradually taking. The recent meeting of the Central Council of the Swarajya party in Cocanada in which important resolutions regarding the conduct of the Swarajya members in the Council and the Assembly were passed was very poorly attended, and if attendance be a test of the party's enthusiasm for the cause which it represents, it can be fairly said that the Swarajist ideals have already lost their charm for most of its members. In the circumstances under which the sitting of the General Council was held it is nothing strange that its resolution should fail to enforce that respect and obedience which is its due. Thus we are told that the Swarajya Party in the Punjab has decided to sit on the Standing Committees in spite of the Central Council resolution to the contrary. Madras also has raised her voice of protest against the Central Council decision. Mr. Satyamurti altogether denies that the Central Council passed a resolution asking the Swarajya party members in the Madras and Punjab Council to abstain from participating in the proceedings of the Council and Mr. Satyamurti contends that resolution involving such momentous consequences can be passed only after full consultation with provincial parts. While the Punjab has thus coolly ignored its resolution, it must be said to the credit of Madras that it has at least the courtesy to make a formal protest. That a bewildering confusion of thought now reigns supreme in the ranks of the Swarajya party has, by this time, been made quite evident. It remains to be seen how far the party will succeed in maintaining coherence and cohesion in its ranks amidst such conflicting views and tendencies.

215

People of Borsad Deserve to be Congratulated

Young India, 10 January 1924

It is not in a vainglorious spirit that we should offer our congratulations to the people of Borsad and their leaders. Let us thank God in all humility that in this trial He has given us a speedy victory. The justice of the cause, the simple and manly programme of suffering that was adopted and above all the absolute determination of the people unalloyed by any mental reservation to carry it out to the bitter end have brought victory as a natural and necessary consequence. The triumph of justice and the success of satyagraha are one and identical. The people of Borsad have won because their cause was absolutely true and just. Satyagraha is admissible and possible only where the cause is true and just. In other cases it will only be a base imitation and no better than physical violence. It may seem to succeed for a time but is bound ere long to wither away. But where the cause is just as at Borsad success is certain. The government of Bombay deserve to be congratulated for quickly realising this. They have put aside their prestige and proceeded bravely to set things in order. The victory of satyagraha is complete where even the vanquished does not feel the sting of defeat but feels that he is acting solely under the compelling force of justice. We too shall not wrongly stress our triumph but offer thanks for justice.

The penal cess is cancelled and the cost of the special police is to be part of general administrative charges. This being done it becomes more easy for all to consider whether the special force is necessary and if so whether the men and officers now employed are efficient. When once a man or government makes up its mind to be just and is on the path of right conduct there is every hope of complete reforming.

It is too much to expect so great and sudden a change in the mentality of government as is involved in a radical reform of the criminal race. But as a special case if definite and liberal terms are offered as an ultimatum it is possible that the absconding criminals of Borsad may prefer surrender to living a continual life of hunted boars. The gallows need not be the only solution for error on the part of brave and capable human beings. The chain of wrong on either side complicates the issue. But if we look back to the history of any crime we generally reach a point where a strong human motive which may not be justification but is certainly a moral explanation calls for human solution instead of the all too easy remedy of the hangman's rope.

216

Babar Deva[1] Dacoit Surrenders to Police due to Efforts of Vallabhbhai

Bombay Chronicle, 10 January 1924

From Kaira accept the Ram Ram of Babar Deva. I did not give trouble to any body without any reason. Now I am not doing the business of dacoity. I have left dacoity. It is true that by my name other dacoits commit dacoity and loot the people. But I request you not to get cheated by those dacoits. I came to Kaira for the last two days to see the Collector at evening, but the Collector Saheb was at Borsad. Convey my Ram Ram to Shri Vallabhbhai-Bapu.

Yours
BABAR DEVA

[1]A notorious dacoit came to be known during Borsad Satyagraha in 1923, later on adopted the Gandhian path of non-violence as a consequence of inspiration received from Sardar Vallabhbhai Patel.

217

Vallabhbhai Advises His Friends to be Graceful in Victory

11 January 1924

DEAR GOPALDASBHAI AND MOHANLAL PANDYA,

Bhai Bhaskar[1] has just brought your lecture as well as your pamphlet. I am on the horns of a dilemma. I feel that these two articles are not in harmony with the principles for which we fought, and the occasion of our victory. A true Satyagrahi does not make the opponent feel the pinch of defeat. If we can do that then only it can be said that we have understood the spirit of Satyagraha. I have a strong fear that if we publish these articles we will lose the greatness of our victory. So, it is with intense pain that, in spite of my deep feelings for you, I do not send them to the press, but will keep them with me. I am dead sure that after some time, you will be convinced about the truth of my advice. On this occasion we should not say a word against Government officers. It will be a graceful act. We have simply to examine our weaknesses, and go on experimenting on the ways of uplifting people that will be true celebration of victory.

In tomorrows musical programme only hymns, befitting the occasion, like, "Only he knows, what it is to pine for meeting the Lord",[2] should be sung. I have confidence that you will act according to my advice. More when we meet.

VALLABHBHAI PATEL

[1]Dr. Bhaskar Patel, afterwards Prohibition Minister of Bombay Presidency.
[2]Dhana Bhagat's hymn. *Ashram Bhajnawali,* Navjivan, Ahmedabad.

218

Vallabhbhai Congratulates People of Borsad and Government on Withdrawl of Punitive Tax

Bombay Chronicle, 14 January 1924

The following statement under the signatures of Mr. Vallabhbhai Patel and Mr. Gopaldas Desai has been published:

The Borsad Satyagraha was inaugurated by the Gujarat Provincial Congress Committee on the 1st of December last by the following resolution:

This Committee after considering the report submitted by the Sub-Committee to inquire into the punitive police and the tax of Rs 2,40,074 imposed on the inhabitants residing in 84 villages of the Borsad Taluka and 14 villages of the Anand Taluka, and after further hearing the Sub-Committee on the situation which has arisen in the Talukas in consequence of the impost, resolves that the impost is entirely unjust and oppressive, inasmuch as the Government which has failed in its function to protect the people from the oppressions of the dacoits, has wrongly aspersed the character of the innocent people and shifted its guilt on them. The Committee therefore, advises the people in these villages to resist this injustice by refusing to pay the impost and by peacefully putting up with all the suffering consequent on the refusal.

The representatives of each and every community of people of the said villages, in a conference assembled on the next day, welcomed the Resolution. The local officers in their turn immediately started on making recoveries by all sorts of measures, and all the revenue and the police officers were ordered to leave their ordinary work and to busy themselves entirely with recovery work. The punitive police was also brought into aid. The limit of the law was transgressed, and considerable harshness was resorted to in attachment proceedings. Valuable articles were attached for recovering trifling amounts. Even milch cattle were not spared.

Speaking at considerable length at a meeting of the volunteers in the evening at the Satyagraha Camp, Mr. Vallabhbhai asked them to stick to their work of carrying out the constructive programme. He said he did not disguise his joy at the great work they were doing in the villages. But it would not be enough if they now stopped that work. They must get on with it till the great battle of Swaraj was won. Nothing would please the Mahatma more than their silent, unassuming work in villages.

[1]Speech delivered at Borsad on 12 January.

220

Vallabhbhai Applauds People's Sacrifices during Satyagraha and Outlines Future Course of Action[1]

Navjivan, Special issue, 17 January 1924

Now there can be only one duty for you. If you have achieved real victory, you give up looking at the weaknesses of the government, and think about your own weaknesses. You have achieved everything that you wanted to achieve in the struggle. Now you have no small quarrel against the government. It is true that the big struggle which is being fought in the whole country has not yet ended, but till we achieve the strength to achieve our objective through that struggle, and till we are ready for confrontation till then we should not look at its weaknesses. In order to launch a final struggle against the government, it is necessary to quickly examine our own weaknesses and remove them. That it is our immediate task.

During a short span of one month you have sacrificed much, you have shown much courage. You have stood united, and struggled enthusiastically, as a result you got everything that you wanted. It has not been achieved, because of mine, Darbar Saheb's or Pandyaji's intellectual skill, but because we have followed the path shown by our master, and greatest saint of the modern times who is languishing in jail.[2] We have yet to repay his due to our master. We have only paid the interest of our debt, and till we repay the debt we have to hang our heads in shame. We have forgotten him and his work. Otherwise, how would the problem of dacoits cropped up? If we had learned the lessons he had taught us, if we had assimilated his ideas, then the dacoits would not have been amongst us. Therefore, let us now recapitulate what we have forgotten, and examine our weaknesses and remove them.

Wind up Sweetly

Our fight is over, so whatever yet remains in winding up operations should be done with as much sweetness as possible. Some of you might have paid the fine out of fear. Some of them might have voluntarily given the facilities for attachment, but you give up the idea of either punishing or harassing them. If they are excommunicated take them back in the community fold. You must have generosity to assimilate the victory you have won in the battle. Let God give you good sense of protecting the weak and assure them that they have nothing to be afraid of.

I know that you are going to celebrate your victory. Let the celebration be there, but I advise you to invite even those who were responsible for attaching your property, and let them also take part in celebration. Our fight is not that of a devil, therefore when the enemies have laid down their arms, you be friendly with them, and you invite policemen also to take part in the celebration. If any of your act irritates them, or terrifies them, then stop doing that. You are now not fighting with him, and hence we should not do anything which might irritate our own brethren. Be friendly with police, village officers, record keepers and government messengers, and give up the attitude of an adversary. Forget about the attachment done by them, whatever they have done is due to their desire to play two roles, obeying government orders and to satisfy the people and their task was difficult, so there cannot be anything else but generosity towards them.

Land Tax

About land tax payment we held inquiry about the crops in this *taluka* of the district. Rain was scanty and the crops grown are less than thirty to twenty-five per cent of the normal year. In such circumstances according to the land tax rules Government has no right to recover the land tax. We have to think about this problem.

The second matter we have to think about is whether the Government withdraws the fine imposed for additional police and what measures to take if it is not prepared to rescind its order then are we to pay the fine?

Third question is, till greater complaints are still there—because of which we have launched Satyagraha against it—are we to pay land tax or not? We have to think about these three topics.

Out of these, last topic is very serious. Till we have strength to take that step, till our weaknesses are removed, we cannot think about. When we are not able to walk, if we try to run, it is like taking a suicidal step.

In the second complaint as we have received justice is not there. Therefore, as crops are much less we have to decide whether to pay tax or not. I have inquired into the matter and some persons also have told me that there is possibility that Government genuinely might have miscalculated in the assessment. We have differences with government about it, and it is but natural that government assessment is from the angle of tax collection, while our assessment is from the angle of not paying the tax. This difference of opinion is bound to be there. But if we do not pay tax this year, next year we shall have to pay double amount of tax. We have fought one battle. So it is not proper to fight a second battle in the current year. At present it is necessary that we stabilise the advantage we got by fighting the battle. Therefore, my advice to you is to pay the tax, as ordered by the Collector. Everybody accepts the advice which is congenial, but when you will be able to accept uncongenial advice, then only establishment of *Swaraj* is possible. If you act according to our advice, which is to your liking then we are fallen. You assure the Government that our fight is just.

Some officers have doubted that there is no record of the attached goods. There are no *panchnamas* and therefore at the time of return of the attached goods people will harass the government, but I tell you that you take the goods which government returns. That behoves you. It is not befitting Satyagrahis to quarrel for trifling matters.

Create Pious Atmosphere

First thing is that robbers and dacoits can not stay amongst us. This does not mean that we beat them and drive them out, but in our village such a religious and pious atmosphere should be created that such persons would get nervous to commit antisocial acts. Men and women of this place should be so religious-minded that those such people would be afraid of God. Such people should be put on the right track. We tell moneylenders of this place that you have suffered most because of loot, and if the atmosphere does not change in future also you will suffer most. Therefore take interest in such work where looting will be impossible. You continue your business with clean heart, and examine the causes of people's anger. Government's police won't be able to protect you. They will only, after the crime is committed to take notes, and to get proofs from you. You will not be able to get any benefit but you will be loser thereby. Howsoever good an officer might be but the system of the government is such that he will not be able to protect you. Therefore, if you do not fear God, and go on extracting money from the poor, you shall have to suffer. In your dealing with the poor be God-fearing, take minimum of profit, and give up the idea of exploiting them. Nobody likes to commit crime or dacoity, but one indulges in such things being exasperated by the atrocities of moneylender. They must be consoled, and we have to see that they are prevented from indulging in criminal activity.

What to Tell Dacoits

I do not know as to how many dacoits are still there amongst you. They are not afraid of guns but they are afraid of your unity. They know that when all the communities stand united, it is difficult for them to encroach. If any of you who is present here happens to be their friend, they must be persuaded to give up their activities.

If I happen to see a dacoit I will tell him this, "Your life is not worth living. You will die on gallows, by bullets, by a fall, but one day you are surely going to die. After having committed so many sins, go to the police station, or Government bungalow, and confess your crimes, and express regret, so that your sin might recede. Nobody can hide himself when the messengers of death come. They find him even though he hides in any corner of the world. Confessing your crime, and then to die on gallows is real act of bravery. Simply hiding yourself is cowardice." You deliver this message of mine if you happen to see them, and if you arrange our meeting, I will tell them what I have said.

Congress Work

Now I want to tell you about other works to be done. We have abundant Congress work. If the people of Borsad taluka have understood the significance of Satayagraha struggle, they should enrol themselves as members of the Congress. Just anybody who was above sixteen years old was considered eligible for government fine. Similarly, everybody who is above eighteen years old should enlist his name, and be eligible for *Swaraj*. Yearly membership fee is four annas, and the funds are to be utilised in their own villages. In order that proof can be had from the records of the Congress, as to who wants to attain Swaraj, who are on the side of Gandhiji, every man and woman of eighteen years age should go to Satyagraha camp and enlist their names. The other thing is that henceforward you should not go to courts or police stations, but if necessary go to Satyagraha camp. Do not complain, do not quarrel, should not file false law suits, prepare false documents, because all that is dirty work. Those who have understood the significance of *Satyagraha* do not heed Government courts or pleaders. Leave the lure of police stations and courts, and when by mistake any dispute arises, appoint wise people to settle the disputes justly, and even then the dispute is not solved, then go to the *Satyagraha* camp.

I want ladies to understand this. Those of your menfolk who have gone to the court, and impoverished themselves, quarrel, commit murders, mortgage their lands. So do not let them climb the steps of court room, do not show them the house of a lawyer. The other day a person had come to me to take my advice regarding the appeal for his relative who was sentenced to three years. He sold all his land and paid the lawyer's fee and now he wants the appeal to be filed *gratis.* Where there is no place for religion, what is the use of appeal on charity basis? I told him, "Go to your home and count beads".

There are hundreds of such cases, in which both the sides are ruined. Why we need courts of the government which we have discarded? In court you are asked to take an oath that by God, you will tell the truth, and yet people there tell nothing but untruth. So why go to the court and be irreligious?

Is Love True or Momentary?

I leave behind Satyagraha camp. Darbar Saheb, Mohanlal, Ravishankar, and others will stay here. You make proper use of them. You have shown immense love, but whether it is true or momentary, whether there is any selfish motive in it or not, is to be tested now. When I make you fight the government you shower affection on us, but when I make you fight your weaknesses, then your love will be put to test, and it will be known whether it is true or not. If you will be united, non-violent, give up drinking alcohol, then you shall not have to fight with the government. Government is illusion, a castle of winds, a bubble of water, if we know it, it will at once burst. But there are layers on our eyes, and therefore we have not known it. Therefore, I say that make good use of the workers who are staying here.

Stop Troubling Others

Now the last thing. As you were troubled by the atrocities of the government, similarly others also were troubled by your atrocities. They also find your action equally troublesome. Therefore, don't misuse power. I have been informed in Asod village, twenty people who have paid land tax, have been excommunicated. It is bad. It is atrocious. Do not misuse the properly arranged order of the village or the community and goodness will improve those who have weaknesses. If we want them to be good, we shall have to be more good. If we are not good to them, they will helplessly go to the government. Everybody has not the strength which we have. We must inculcate it in them. Generate fearlessness in them, and untie the bondage of harassment. Give them their independence back. If we are unjust, we cannot ask others to be just to us. Those who have been lost their way should be forgiven. Be friendly to them. If you do all this, then I pray that God may give you strength, to start a big struggle in whole of Gujarat during the time of paying tax.

[1]On the 12th January the victory celebrations of Satyagraha movement were held in a most enthusiastic atmosphere. People from the villages had flocked to take part in the celebrations. Out of about thirty thousand people assembled about seven thousand might be ladies, one can see the joy of victory in the eyes of each one of them. Sardar Vallabhbhai Patel delivered a thought-provoking speech, to a huge assembly in which he put a special stress on future programme.

[2]Mahatma Gandhi.

221

Vallabhbhai Advises People of Borsad to remain Humble in Victory[1]

Navjivan, 17 January 1924

During the short struggle lasting about a month you have given evidence of the spirit of sacrifice, courage, unity and enthusiasm which is unique. It is because of this that you have got what you wanted. It is not because of the sagacity shown by Darbar Sahib, Pandyaji or I, but because you followed the path shown by our guru and the great seer who is in jail. We have to repay the debt we owe to him; what we have done so far is only pay the interest. So long as you and I are not able to repay the principal sum, we would have to be humble. We have forgotten him; had that not been so there would have been no talk of the dacoits. It is necessary, therefore, that we refresh our memories, indulge in introspection and get rid of our weaknesses.

I have come to know that you want to celebrate your victory. Go ahead and do it by all means but please do not forget to invite those who carried out the attachments of your properties. Ours is not an evil battle and when the enemy has surrendered to us, let us be magnanimous, show our love towards him and invite the police to the public meeting you propose to hold.

Advice to Pay Land Revenue

Now there is only one thing we have to decide. The harvest has been poor and the question is whether you pay the land revenue or not. I have gone into the question and people have told me that there was probably a mistake in estimating the value of the crop. There are differences of opinion between us and the authorities on this and it is but natural that we differ. The Government base their estimates on the need to collect land revenue and we on the basis of our desire to evade payment of the same. These differences would persist. But if we do not pay the land revenue this year, the amount payable next year would be double of what we pay this year. We have fought one battle this year and may not be able to engage in another. It would not be proper to do so. What we need at the moment is to consolidate the gains of our victory. I would, therefore, advise you to please follow the orders that the Collector might issue on this subject. Land revenue should be paid promptly. Everybody listens to advice which he wants to hear, but we can win the battle for swaraj if we can follow an advice we do not like. If you accept a thing which you like and nothing else it would lead to a fall. Convince the Government that you would fight a just battle.

What of the Dacoits?

I do not know how many among you are dacoits. They were not afraid of guns, but your unity has subdued them. They understand that if there is unity among all the eighteen castes, they will not be able to make any inroads. If there are any among you who side with the dacoits, they should tell them to give up their evil ways. If I happen to meet a dacoit, I will tell him: "Fie on you and the way you live! You will die either by a bullet or on the gallows, but die you must. You have committed too many sins and should now repent, go to police station, admit your crimes so that the burden of sin is reduced to some extent. The messenger of death is one being whom you cannot avoid or escape. He would find you in the thickest of jungles. Only the brave would admit their sins and go to the gallows with a smile on their lips. Running away from your actions is nothing but cowardice." If you happen to meet such persons please give them my message. If you arrange my meeting with them, I would tell them myself.

Is it True Love or a Passing Fancy?

I am going away from the satyagraha headquarters, but Darbar Sahib, Mohanlal, Ravi Shankar and others would remain here. I tell you to make good use of their services. Now is the time when your love for us would be tested and we would find out whether it was true love or a passing fancy. You show your affection when I ask you to fight the authorities, but when I put you to fight your own weaknesses, I would find out whether it was true love. If you remain united, follow the principles of *ahimsa* and swear off liquor, you will never come to a pass when you have to fight the authorities. The Government is as ephemeral as a water bubble. The moment you realise this the bubble would burst. But there is a veil over our eyes and we are unable to recognise it for what it is. That is why I say that you must accept the services of gentlemen who are staying behind.

Stop Atrocities

One last thing—the atrocities committed by the Government pained you. Remember that if you are unkind or unjust towards others they would be similarly pained. Do not, for God's sake, misuse your power. I have come to know that the villagers of Asodar have turned out 20 persons who had paid Government dues. Now this is bad; it is a kind of atrocity. Do not misuse the village or the caste for such purposes. Those who are weak can be brought to the true path through kindness. If we want to improve them we should first improve ourselves. If we do not improve ourselves they would become weak and surrender to the authorities. Everybody cannot be as strong as we are. That strength has to be generated. Spare them the terror and pardon them. Return their liberty to them. If we are ourselves unjust we cannot demand justice from others. Pardon those who make mistakes. If you do this, we would start another movement at the time of payment of land revenue in Gujarat. I pray to God that He gives you enough strength to behave in a just and moral way.

[1]Speech made at a public meeting held at B'orsad on 12th January 1924, to celebrate the victory of the Borsad Satyagraha.

222

Secretary (Home) Bombay Government on Vallabhbhai's Activities in connection with Borsad Satyagraha

Home (Political) 19 January 1924

MY DEAR CRERAR,

I am desired to submit my report for the fortnight ending the 15th January 1924.

2. *Political*—The Satyagraha campaign in the Borsad taluka in connection with the recovery of the cess imposed to meet the cost of the additional police force was brought to an end with the decision of Government to remit the cess. The decision was received generally with feelings of relief and gratitude rather than with jubilation under sense of any popular victory. At a congratulatory meeting held at Borsad on the 12th, at which about 20,000 people from the surrounding villages were present, Vallabhbhai Patel, who led the movement for the non-payment of the cess, in expressing the gratitude of the people to His Excellency the Governor for his personal interest in bringing about a happy settlement, said that either side had an equal claim to victory, and called for the rehabilitation of good feeling between the people and Government servants of the taluka. He finally advised them to pay up the land revenue: "We should be as

which we shall ride. Do not hope to get the impost removed through the Council. The Council will sit two months hence. If you tell the Government that you do not want to pay the fine, you will get into direct touch with them. That direct touch is the horse you will ride and not the horse of the Council.

Mahatmaji showed us the right way, viz., Non-cooperation. You know that we ourselves are responsible for the impost of Rs 240,000, the policemen are our men, the men who have reported to Government that you have harboured dacoits and outlaws are our men, even the present Collector is our man, and the men who will come to realise the fine will also be our men. These men cannot non-cooperate for sheer selfishness. Let us then non-cooperate. You can easily do so, you can easily spin your own yarn and weave your own cloth, produce your own food and refuse to provide Government the wherewithal to pay its Collectors and Commissioner. Immediately you have done so, these people will have ceased to tyrannise over us, our famines will cease, and the dacoities also will cease.

Immediately after the Delhi Congress the Provincial Committee came to know of the Government action in the matter and deputed Mohanlal Pandya and Ravishankar to investigate it, and to report as to who were the outlaws, why they have turned outlaws, what sort of crime they commit, who are their victims, how the police tackles the situation, whether the people like the punitive police, whether they are prepared to pay the impost. They went about from village to village and have submitted their report. It seems from their report that an oulaw named Babar made his appearance in Golel in 1917. He indulged in petty crimes in the beginning. When the Government fails to detect crime or imposes on a wrong-doer punishment out of proportion to his crime the man turns into a brute. Babar has been at large all these years and has committed numerous crimes. . . . In Golel the outlaw assaulted the punitive police. The people saw the District Magistrate and said they could not pay the fine. The Mamlatdar also reported that it was impossible to realise fine from people who not being contumacious were too poor to pay it. . . . The District Superintendent of Police disagreed with the Mamlatdar and insisted that impost should be continued . . . The funniest part of the affair is that the Collector disagreed, in turn, with this Superintendent of Police, and he reported entirely differently to the Commissioner. . . It seems that consultation is at the back of the impost. I may also add that the Collector admitted that the people do not give information or shelter the miscreants "from fear or from selfish desire to save themselves immediate trouble." The Commissioner disagreed with the Collector and the Mamlatdar! He felt that the Superintendent had given solid reasons for the continuance of the police in the two villages for another year and issued orders accordingly. That was in June. How all of a sudden in October Government resolved to impose the police on the whole Taluka passes comprehension. I have not these communications in my possession. But I am sure about my facts. Every one I have met has told me what has happened. There is a Musalman outlaw abroad named Ali. When Babar could not be got hold of, the police made friends with this new genius, sought to get rid of an outlaw with the help of an outlaw, and provided him with arms and ammunition. Oh the pity and the shame of it! The Government ceased to rule making room for the outlaw. Who is going to punish the Government for having leagued with this outlaw? God alone. Government surely know what a number of murders and dacoities this Ali has committed having been armed by the Government itself. No doubt its intention was to catch Babar through Ali, but how are the people to know? I hold the government responsible for all the misdeeds of that miscreant Ali. . .

The only reason assigned by Government for punishing a whole people is that they do not provide information or evidence. Let us see how far this is true. Babar has to his credit 22 murders; not one of them was a rich man. He has not murdered his victims for the mere fun of it. He murdered them as they were the informants. If after 22 such informants were murdered, the Government seriously argues that the people do not give information, shall we ask how many policemen were murdered? An informant was crucified to a tree by Babar. How would Government have to suffer the fate of this informant? An informant's job is no easy job then. A first class magistrate was waylaid by the outlaw on his way from Wasad to Borsad. The outlaw gave a smack on his face, and wrested his rifle from his hands. The poor fellow had to represent that he was an ordinary clerk and not a magistrate, to escape with his life. A Government with such a magistracy has no title to exist, has surely no title to punish a people.

All it reveals that the Government knows that the people are innocent. But the Government has no money. It still wants to hold its head erect before the native States in the vicinity. Those States have imposed on their villages additional police to protect them from those very outlaws, but they have not taxed their "raiyats". Government must ape those states and impose the police, but money it must find out of the people's pockets. Well, if it wants money, let it beg of us. But why should they cast a slur on our name, why should they asperse our behaviour, treat us as criminals and extort the cost of the police as fine.

What then should you do? I say that there are some exceptions. Those who can be charged with the utmost complicity in the crimes are exempted, viz., the Government servants. My information is that every petty village officer knows the whereabouts of these outlaws, but is afraid of them. We may note that even the new M.L.C. is not exempted from the fine. What a curious commentary on the Government which thought our Reception Committee Chairman good enough to be elected to the Council, but not good enough to be exempted from fine!

Let us then make up our minds. Do not for a moment think you are fighting for the paltry amount of Rs 2-8-0. If you do so, the sooner you pay the fine the better. You are fined because of complicity in crime, because you shelter the outlaws, because you are their friends. I ask you to fight only if you are convinced that no power on earth has the right thus to impugn your character. Let us plainly tell the Government that we are honourable men of character, we shall not sign certificates of our bad behaviour with our own hands. We refuse to pay the fine. You might plunder us if you like, like the outlaws, and realise the fine. That is Mahatmaji's way. Fight the fine then like his men—his men do not need a stick or a *dharia,* they need brave backs to receive blows. Do not be tempted into anger, do not be tempted into violence, for the tempter will be there. Now then I ask you if you are prepared to fight raise your hands.

One thing more. Complaints have reached me that the punitive police is oppressing you, that they are plundering your fodder, that they have not even hesitated to molest our sisters. A Government servant told Mr. Jyabji yesterday that steps are immediately taken whenever such complaints come: the people should only put in complaints. I ask you not to put in such complaints. The police is imposed to prevent "zoolum", and you have to complain against their own zoolum! We shall not recognise this police. Let us have our own Volunteer Corps. I ask you to raise a corps from amongst you. I ask young men to give their names to Darbar Saheb Gopaldas.

I appeal to all such present here, as have ever helped the dacoits in any way to realise that it is a hateful thing. I ask them to give up that nefarious business. I ask "Dharalas" amongst you to give up drink. I may warn you that Government thinks of removing you from the District and penning you up in a criminal settlement. That will be a sorry plight indeed. I ask you each and all to reform yourself, and let not a whole people suffer for the misdeeds of a few ruffians.

204

Vallabhbhai Congratulates People of Alarsa and Khedasa for Keeping Peace[1]

Navjivan, 16 December 1923

Just now I have received the news by wire that twenty people of Alarsa and six of Khedasa are arrested. Side by side I have also received the news that all of them are cheerful and there is peace there. I do not have information as to crime they have supposed to have committed, for which they have been arrested. But I congratulate the people of those two villages for having a privilege being first to offer their sacrifice in this fight.

This is only the beginning. We shall have to sacrifice many people in this fight. Our victory depends on our ability to suffer miseries, and being peaceful. There is no happiness without misery. The misery which is willingly suffered always produces good result. Our reputation lies in going to jail with a smile. Giving money because of the fear of being jailed, and becoming the companion of dacoits is an act of which we should be ashamed. May God give you power to suffer misery and to adhere to non-violence.

[1]Government attachment activities were in full swing, yet people did not lose courage. So under some excuse it arrested and imprisoned people. In such conditions also Vallabhbhai gave this message to the people to stand firm.

211

Vallabhbhai Advises Maniben to put up Bravely with Circumstances[1]

Sardar Ki Seekh

AHMEDABAD

DEAR MANIBEN,

From your letter it appears that you are still suffering from fever. I think that if you are at peace with yourself, you would recover quickly. Keeping awake at night means that your mind is not at peace. This leads to constipation. I think that your worries are without any foundation. It is strange that after having been educated, you have failed to have a happy disposition. It appears to me that if you start thinking of the unthinkable, it leads to mental anguish. Whatever the reasons for your worries, you should tell me. One must not have a disposition which would give pain to oneself and those around one. Poverty is not something at which one should be sorry. If we have accepted poverty voluntarily or if there is sudden adversity, we should be able to face it happily.

With blessings,

Yours affectionately,

[1]The probable date is 1923.

212

Vallabhbhai Advises Maniben not to Feel Perturbed over Gandhiji's Fast

Sardar Ki Seekh[1]

DEAR MANIBEN,

If you are unhappy on Bapu's hunger strike, I can understand it. But when we follow Gandhiji, we must understand that sometimes his actions are such that we cannot normally understand them. That is the difference between ordinary people and Bapu. If sometimes we are unable to understand what Bapu is doing, we must have the faith that whatever God does is for the best. And then, we cannot doubt that whatever Bapu does is with a clear conscience and for the good of the country. His whole life is dedicated to the country. If God wills Bapu will come out of this ordeal safe and sound. Half the period of the hunger strike is over and the other half would also be completed if one believes what the doctors are saying. There is no reason, therefore, to worry about this. If we face such a thing in the future, we should not be nervous about it. We must be sure that Bapu takes every action after considering all the circumstances. The result is always in the hands of God, because man proposes and God disposes. But even if the result of some good action is not good, so what. This thing should be taken into consideration by people who are in jails and they should not worry about those who are outside jails. This both of you should understand. Who knows what we would have to do in future and face many kinds of troubles. We should, therefore, happily accept the troubles that fall on our head in jail.

. . . By the time you get this letter, the period of Bapu's fast would be about to end or would have ended. But you should remember for the future and that is why I am writing these lines to you. Only those are fit to go to jail who would not let the events outside affect their health. We have to do our duty and nothing more.

Bapu's penance should teach us only one thing and that is that we must purify ourselves. We must consider how far we can purify ourselves and become more proficient for the service of the country. One does not have to think of or do anything else.

With a father's blessings,

Yours

[1]The probable year is 1923.

213

Vallabhbhai's Rejoinder to Government's White Paper[1] *on Borsad Satyagraha*

Bombay Chronicle, 23 November 1923
Navjivan, 6 January 1924

Mr. Gennings alleges that one of us had obtained some so-called secret government circulars illegally and unjustly. In that matter we can assure him though the circulars were secret, but were very important for this case. Director of Government's information department has tried to enlighten you by long list of circulars, which he has flunged on you. But if we do not publish more important letters and circulars, in which Government's misdeeds are acknowledged, we will fail in our duty. Yet if we are in a position to show from the contents of the letters which government has published thinking that those letters are not damaging such things which will explode the ground below the government's feet.

2. We might accept the bundle of documents on which that the head of information department relies is signed by a police superintendent who might be very well known officer. But we are afraid that he must have earned name not in Kheda but in some part of the region. He has just come in Kheda, and had not enough time to earn a name. That he has prepared a white paper containing

seventy seven paragraphs, might be considered a work enough to earn a name, but which is the base of that document? Of course that officer who is responsible for fears of misrule one does not know what kind of peace his bourgeois squad has established. But even if some kind of peace is restored, then the reason for it were quite different. Government cannot take credit for it. About Abas' arrest, we boldly say that he has not been arrested by the efforts of police. Then Mir Khan is arrested by Gaikwad police, and other reason is that satyagrahis have been stationed there. If government deserves any credit for restoration of peace, then it is the stationing of additional police force in whole of the taluka, but because of their presence the disturbance and terrorism which are generated justifies everything. Again when if police force of different regions is thus stationed in one region, naturally the security of other regions is put in jeopardy.

3. The head of the information department should acknowledge the incompetency of police, but he has tried to show that the people were not willing to help the police, nor the people had the courage to defend themselves, which resulted in the deteriorating situation. From the report of the Police Superintendent the falsity of this type of reasoning can be proved. It is to be remembered that the report covers the entire district, and from the cases, and the cases stated therein, about twenty are from other talukas than Borsad. We are here referring to such cases where people have tried to help police, not only that but they have taken risks of various types and have lost their lives.

(1) *Paragraph 6:* Report of District Police Superintendent. Poor man who was tied to the tree, nailed, and shot by bullets was an informer.

(2) *Paragraph 7:* The murder was a result of the deceased relative's helping the police.

(3) *Paragraph 9:* One Muslim had given the evidence against the dacoits, so his nose was cut and he was set free.

(4) *Paragraph 10:* The deceased was a witness in a murder case.

(5) *Paragraph 12:* Babar killed Bukor suspecting him to have helped the police.

(6) *Paragraph 13:* People of Betva village came out to resist the dacoits, but dacoits fired and killed two people.

(7) *Paragraph 14:* One Patidar took the risk of combating the dacoits, he was knifed.

(8) *Paragraph 18:* Babar Deva killed a police informer in Bankteda.

(9) *Paragraph 29:* Dacoits with deadly weapons attacked four villages—all of Borsad taluka but the "attackers" had to run away.

(Of course not because they were prompted by goodness but the people knew that wisdom is better than bravery.)

(10) *Paragraph 32:* As the people gathered together and so two shots were fired. (Had the people assembled there for fun?)

(11) *Paragraph 34:* Four villages were attacked, but only one person was wounded and one home looted.

(12) *Paragraph 37:* One tailor went to fight with the dacoits, and as a result of his taking the risk he was seriously wounded.

Notices to confiscate land were issued. By a sheer abuse of authority several people were rushed into jail on false complaints or trumped up charges. To fight this oppression, the Satyagraha camp established stations in various villages, and posted volunteers there to help the people in non-violent suffering. The suffering came in as an unexpected event. Every village resolved not to pay the tax, and each vied with the other frustrating the efforts of *Zabti* (confiscation) officers. Mahajans advised shop-keepers to close their shops, and they implicitly obeyed, keeping their shops closed by day and doing their business by night. The poor practically left their homes, and with their cattle repaired to the fields. All forced labour was refused, the headmen and the *ravanias,* and even some men of the punitive police disobeyed orders to carry to Police Stations the articles attached. Some of the headmen even resigned their posts. The women beat even the men in their enthusiasm; they buried their metal pots and pans and began using earthen vessels, they fasted by day and cooked and fed and drew water by night. As a result a month's labour on the part of the attachment officer failed to recover even the cost of the recovery proceedings. No one turned up to bid for articles put to auction.

This severe penance melted the heart of Government. The new Governor deputed the Home Member Sir Maurico Hayward to make enquiries on the spot. He visited Borsad and met several leading men of the Taluka. They told him their tale of woe with firmness and with courage. The Home Member stopped all attachment proceedings, and returned to Bombay having promised to place the result of his inquiry before Government. As a result the Government issued a Press Note withdrawing the Punitive Tax.

The Borsad Satyagraha now comes to a close. Truth and non-violent suffering have triumphed once more. It is a matter of relief that the quickness of the triumph is in consonance with the justice of our cause. It is a unique triumph in as much as it is a triumph for both parties. Government have admitted their mistake with courage and candour. In doing so they have abandoned the traditional way of sticking to prestige, and absolved themselves from the crime of condemning an innocent population unheard and of oppressing them. In thus embracing truth, they too have triumphed. We should be failing in our duty if we did not congratulate most heartily the new Governor, Sir Leslie Wilson, on the great moral courage he has shown.

Our triumph does not consist in our having secured from Government the remittance of the tax and in their restoration to us of the articles attached, nor even in their decision to meet the cost out of the general revenue. We have indeed triumphed in that the Government has withdrawn the charge against us. But, we shall have truly triumphed only when we have realised the magnitude of the triumph and are able to contain it. Government always hesitates to admit its mistakes. It believes that the State would be jeopardised by even a legitimate surrender to people fighting an injustice with pure weapons. This is the first time that Government has not hesitated openly to admit its mistake and repair it, and in yielding to the just demands of the people has recognised that a movement of peaceful non-payment of taxes is constitutional. We feel that rather than give any verbal assurance we should prefer to demonstrate by future conduct that this goodness of Government will not be abused. It depends on the local officers, no less than on the people to preserve intact the grace and dignity with which this struggle has been concluded. It was natural that high-handedness in attachment proceedings should have embittered both the parties. Some headmen had to send in their resignations and there was evident damage to property. Several people have been wrongly proceeded against. We hope that each party will close the chapter with goodwill, and behave in a spirit of "forget and forgive." We have ourselves severely criticised the police. But it was no pleasure to us to do so. We have no ill-will against the Police Department or anyone of its officers. We think ours is a common function. The object of the Police as well as of us is to serve the people and to afford protection to them. Government have tried their methods on the *Dharalas* for years together, but they have succeeded in achieving only the contrary result. We do not doubt the intentions of Government but the result, they will recognise, has been contrary to their intention or expectation. We submit that this oppressed community should be dealt with sympathy and forbearance. We were deeply pained not to find a word of sympathy in all the Government correspondence that has been published or in their Press Note, for families of a number of unfortunate people who have lost their lives in helping in the arrest of a couple of dacoits and muderers. We are sorry to have had to say this in reply to the last paragraph in the Government Press Note.

We congratulate the people of the Taluka on the courage and patience with which they have suffered. We also congratulate the volunteers on the perseverance and determined courage with which they have served the people of the Taluka, and on behalf of the people of Borsad, we express our thankfulness for all the help, direct or indirect, rendered to them by the Press and the public.

We now feel thankful to announce that the Borsad Satyagraha comes to a close. Let God be thanked in full measure for this triumph of truth and non-violence.

VALLABHBHAI J. PATEL
GOPALDAS AMBAIDAS DESAI

219

Vallabhbhai Advises Peasants Not to Pay Taxes till Withdrawl of Punitive Tax by Government

Bombay Chronicle, 16 January 1924

Among those who were present in the meeting were Mr. Vallabhbhai Patel, Mr. Gopaldas Desai, Srimati Bhakti Devi, Mr. Mahadeo Desai, Mr. Jerajani,

Mr. Narhari Parikh and his brother, Mr. Gokuldas Talati, Mr. Lakhmidas Purshottam, Mr. Fulchand Shah and Dayalji Desai.

Vallabhbhai's Speech

"Do not be intoxicated with the joy of the present success. Do not get into the habit of finding out mistakes of your rulers. Learn to see your own error and your own shortcomings." This was the burden of his speech, and the audience followed him with rapt attention. He said that he was advised by some people to launch Satyagraha in regard to the postponement of paying land revenue for that year. He was for the time being against such a proposal. They should not talk of big things till they were prepared for the requisite sacrifice. He knew that the rains were not satisfactory and the people had a bad year. It was not advisable, however, he continued, to enter into a struggle with the Government immediately after the government had yielded to their point of view. He therefore advised the people to pay up their revenue without delay.

It was their duty, he said, to make all dacoities in the Taluka impossible. The unity which was the result of Satyagraha should be maintained and nothing should be done in villages or towns which would jeopardise the brilliant unanimity at present witnessed, in the whole taluka. He observed that the religious atmosphere was due to the unsparing efforts of volunteers and it was their duty to maintain the same atmosphere and enable the youngmen to press on with their constructive work. Examining the cause which led the illiterate people to take to dacoities, he advised the rich among them to treat the poor with justice and humanity. The rich *sahukars* must give up aiming at getting rich at the cost of the life-bloods of the poor peasants. These peasants when they became desperate through poverty rushed to dacoities as a madman rushed down a precipice. If these rich men went on with their extortion unconcernedly relying on police protection he warned them that they would live to repent it. Continuing, he said his advice to the poor was to earn their bread by the sweat of their brows. That was the only honest way for a man. He added that he was going to give the *Dharalas* of the whole Taluka, the same advice at three places where big conferences of the *Dharalas* were invited. To the dacoits he had a word to say. He advised them most sincerely to give up their nefarious activities. The right course for Baba Deva and men of his ilk, he said, was to surrender to the police. That was the way they could embrace a manly death. He advised the people to repulse the attacks of the dacoits by preserving unity among themselves and by opposing them tooth and nail when they approached their villages.

Speaking on the constructive programme before the country, he said that it was an extremely easy thing for them to avoid going to law-courts. There were volunteers working in the whole Taluka and they should avail themselves of their presence to get their quarrels settled without incurring any expense whatever. He impressed upon them in a very effective way why they should immediately set to work to abolish untouchability and make their villages self-sufficient in point of clothing.

quick to pay it up as we were slow in paying up the additional tax: you must swallow this bitter pill I am giving you."

Considerable general anxiety was felt when it became known that Gandhi had been removed to hospital suffering from appendicitis. There is a warm feeling of gratitude at his successful operation and the care, attention and consideration he is receiving at the hands of Government. On the other hand, Gandhi's illness has redoubled the popular demand for his release on his recovery.

The news of the remission of the unexpired portion of the sentence of transportation for life passed upon Vinayak Damodar Savarkar and of his release was received very quietly, any tendency to make political capital out of it having been forestalled by the conditions which he agreed to and even more by his full acknowledgment of the justice of his trial and sentence. This acknowledgement has roused some anger in extremist circles and has been described by some of the papers as a "shocking admission". It is reported that Kelkar and some of his other friends in Poona, whom he visited on release, intend trying to get the conditions imposed upon him removed after he has had complete rest for six months.

The Poona City Municipality has passed a resolution deciding on the boycott of goods manufactured in the British Empire.

3. *Labour*—As reported in paragraph 3, sub-paragraph 2, of my last letter, the Committee of the Bombay Millowners' Association held a meeting on the 7th instant at which the present state of the cotton mill industry was reviewed and the questions of short time and a cut in wages were fully discussed. It was definitely decided that no reduction in wages should take place at present but that the question of organised short-time should be considered again in two months' time. It is anticipated, however, that several large groups of mills will shortly go on short-time as there is nothing to prevent the mills acting independently of the Association in this respect. Mr. N.N. Wadia, who is not a member of the Association,—a split having occurred over the double shifts introduced by him in his mills during the boom period,—but who exercises considerable influence in the mill industry here, has already put up a notice for a five-days' week in his mills, the Spring and Textile Mills. His action has been followed by the Hongkong Mill. The present situation in the mill industry has been brought about not by trade depression so much as by the high price of raw cotton consequent upon limited supplies and the fact that many of the mills were caught "short".

223

Gandhi's Programme Pragmatic: Vallabhbhai's Call to People of Borsad

Navjivan, 20 January 1924

When I returned from Nagpur little did I realise that God would give such a beautiful opportunity to the people of Gujarat. By following the orders of Gandhiji while he was among us they have shown that there is life yet in the province of Gujarat. Darbar Sahib and I wrote the message after having carefully considered what Gandhiji would have done after having fought such an important battle. If we have understood the true spirit of Satyagraha, we should be humble and free from vanity. If that is not so we would be guilty of haughtiness. This was very clear to me and that is why we used sweet words in the circular we issued.

Let us for the moment forget about our fight with the Government. So long as we do not have the strength to engage in a final battle with the authorities we should not think of any confrontation. If circumstances compel us, we will not run away from a fight, but would not start a fight without due and sufficient reason. I have thought over his matter and have come to the conclusion that given the present circumstances we cannot afford to launch our battles again and again. How the battle, the final battle will begin is known to nobody. They know that Gandhiji has shown them the way, but do not appear to be able to follow it. Leaders in the Congress and outsiders talk of constructive work and civil disobedience, but I have no faith in them. They, themselves, have no faith and when the leaders are without faith, we would surely lose the battle. It appears to me that our struggle will not be over till we follow the path shown by Gandhiji. The Government have tested our strength in the Borsad satyagraha. It knows that it would lose sooner or later and tried to cut down its losses. If we engage in a battle without the type of which we gave proof of in Borsad, we would surely lose the battle.

Bapu has given us the responsibility for Bardoli, the programme for which was fashioned by him on the basis of his experience. Many people feel that his approach is not pragmatic, but I disagree with them. What Bapu says is purely pragmatic. I am proud of the fact that probably none of you is as pugnacious as I am, but still I stop others because we suffer from many weaknesses. I do not want to lose a single soldier now that the battle is over. If Darbar Sahib or I had been arrested during the movement, we would have accepted it as normal, but if somebody is arrested because he gives evidence of anger we may not be able to pocket it. That would be sheer suicide. We must not waste our strength without sufficient reason. Now is the time when we can imbue the people with the enthusiasm which pervades our souls. This battle has shown the people that they can fight the Government. In the last battle the Government would use every ounce of its strength. Our rulers are traders and, hence, very clever. Only a trader or a merchant can subdue them. That is why God has sent us a leader who is a trader by birth. Even if we implement 75 per cent of the programmes he has suggested to us we would be victorious in the final battle too.

When zeal is needed in a battle, you can find many soldiers. A man may turn into a good fighter in a state of inebriation, but rare is the individual who can engage in an insipid enterprise. Others just run away. You who have tasted the inebriation of battle should now turn to constructive work, which may look insipid, but which has a permanent value. Centres for carrying on the work should be established throughout the Tehsil. We have to get inside the minds of the people; will have to find the reasons for the crimes; will have to see that all liquor shops are closed; will have to wipe the crime graph from this area and totally boycott imported textiles. All this would be possible if we use the weapon which Gandhiji has fashioned. That is why I tell all the workers that if you are truly Gandhiji's disciples you will not leave your place. You shall not run away from your responsibilities. Do not be under the impression that I am less tired than you are. It was this feeling which had led me to exhort you for a battle on the larger scale in Dakor two years ago. But I was dismayed to find that the whole thing was slipping from our fingers; discord raised its ugly head everywhere and there was no place for a big battle. Let us be ready to go before Bapu without a sense of shame. When he comes back we might sit and take it easy. Today is the time for action. I give you one year's time. If within that period of time we are able to do what I said earlier we should, namely, lock up the courts, close all liquor shops, establish *panchayats,* wipe crime from the area and make *khadi* popular among the people, we would be strong enough to challenge the Government for the big battle.

224

Vallabhbhai's Anxious Enquiries about Gandhiji's Health in Jail

Bombay Chronicle, 26 January 1924

. . . while the conditions under which Mahatmaji was confined since the middle of April last were undoubtedly good, it is remarkable that his health had been gradually failing. During June and July last year, he was seriously ill, and a medical examination by the jail authorities showed that he had an attack of dysentery. At this examination, Col. Maddock also appears to have been present, and I believe Mahatmaji was given some injections. What reports were made to the Government regarding Mahatmaji's health, I do not know; but there is no doubt that one or two reports were submitted to Government about that time. Subsequently, Mahatmaji does not seem to have recovered at all, but began to lose weight in an alarmist degree. He used to have sudden rises of temperature and this seems to have been invariably set down to fever. When Mahatmaji's weight was reduced to as low as 95 lbs., his friends and relatives, who were in a position to know, got alarmed, and my friend, Mr. Vallabhbhai Patel, wrote a letter to the Jail Superintendent, and a copy thereof was sent to the Chief Secretary to the Government of Bombay, as Mahatmaji's case was directly under the Government—requesting for a chart of Mahatmaji's temperature during a given time, so that independent medical men, who had been acquainted with the previous history of his health might form their own opinion of the case and inform the parties vitally interested in the health of Mahatmaji accordingly. I have made enquiries of Mr. Vallabhbhai and learnt that the letters in question were both sent, and Mahadeo Desai confirmed that statement, telling me that he himself posted the letters. Mr. Vallabhbhai has also promised to let me have a copy of the letters as soon as convenient. The Director of Information denies the fact of any letter having been received either by the Chief Secretary to the Government or by the Jail Superintendent. I thought I had been guilty of a little confusion when I spoke to the Director of Information some days ago on the subject of Mahatmaji's illness and treatment but I have since learnt that Mr. Vallabhbhai Patel has received no sort of answer from the Government or the Jail Superintendent. Mr. Gennings maintained that no letter was received for an examination of Mahatma's health by private medical men as I had put it to him, would he maintain that no letter was received asking for a chart of Mahatma's temperature and does the blame lie at the door of our erratic Postal Department? and convinced that some sort of letter was sent to the two officials mentioned and no reply was vouchsafed to the sender.

But all the same, have the people not asked assurance from time to time from the Government that Mahatmaji was in good health and that there was no cause for anxiety. Even as early as the last week of December 1923 such an assurance was given, and it is difficult to imagine how all of a sudden appendicitis could have developed in Mahatmaji, considering that, since some time in November last, Mahatmaji had been "experimenting in his diet" and had been living only on milk for over a month. Why Mahatmaji reduced himself to living on milk and abandoned it only after a great deal of entreaty on the part of Col. Murray would form an interesting chapter of jail history, but I regret I cannot at present go into this matter. Suffice it to say, Mahatmaji had been suffering from temperature of a hectic type, which usually is symptomatic of the formation of pus in some part of the body. There were several other symptoms also, which, if they had been intelligently studied, might have given cause for serious reflection to the Government and the medical authorities.

225

Vallabhbhai's Appeal for Donations

Bombay Chronicle, 12 February 1924

The trumpet call of Mahatmaji has through the mercy of Providence been sounded once again. It is a call for cementing an indissoluble union between all communities, and to a fulfilment of the constructive programme. It is an appeal which must go home to the heart of every Indian who desires Swaraj and every one who loves Mahatmaji. Whilst I ask all Gujaratis to do their full share in those two items I appeal to all Gujaratis, in and outside Gujarat, to give a further indication of their intense love for Mahatmaji by every one or such as can do so by contributing a sum not less than Rs 10, so as to enable Gujarat to present him with a purse which may be worthy of his service to them. I do not think it is too much to expect from all the Gujarati speaking population in and outside India to get together a sum of Rs 10 lakhs.

Please permit me to appeal through your columns to every Gujarati reading your paper to help in making up the purse so that the sum may be presented to him when he arrives in Ahmedabad early next month.

226

Vallabhbhai to Narhari on Confrontation between Adivasis and Local People of Surat

Sardar Shrino ke Vishista aur Anokhe Patra-2

AHMEDABAD
15 February 1924

DEAR NARHARI.

I received your letter today on my return for a four day tour of the Borsad Tehsil. I was afraid of a confrontation between the Kaliparaj[1] and the Ujaliparaj,[2] but had never even dreamed that we would be involved in the fight. We will have to pay for the hurry. Even the Ujaliparaj suffers from ignorance in addition to selfishness. We cannot remove it in haste. Please continue to keep me informed of the day to day happenings.

How painful is it to see such things happening in Borsad which we wanted to make into a harbinger of Swaraj. It would pain Bapu no end. It is all God's will. Who knows that something good might come out of it.

May God make you successful in your enterprise. Vande Matram.

Yours,
VALLABHBHAI

[1]The original inhabitants of Surat District in Gujarat were called Kaliparaj.
[2]Ujaliparaj meant non-adivasis.

227

Vallabhbhai Urges Hindu-Muslim Unity

Navjivan, 17 February 1924

After two years we have been again fortunate to hear Mahatmaji's nectar like words. It is the greatest grace of God. There is no doubt that the nectar will rejuvenate us. We were pining for Mahatmaji's return. It is to be seen whether we are ready to assimilate the nectar infected by him.

The Hindu-Muslim unity which Mahatmaji witnessed two years ago is in shambles today and hence Mahatmaji's heart bleeds. He lives for cementing that unity, and that is the only thing which will give him mental peace. Fortunately for Gujarat the lack of that unity is not seen here, and so Gujarat has little to be ashamed of in comparison with other provinces. But Gujarat can nicely divert that unity in constructive channels.

Gujarat should prepare three such fields of constructive programme, that Gandhiji might find it difficult to select any one out of those three and conduct experiment in that field. We have to create such a situation.

But besides this I expect more from Gujarat which is very dear to Gandhiji. Gujarat has not much to do regarding Hindu-Muslim unity in comparison with other provinces, so Gujarat has much scope for diverting its energy in other programme. Every Gujarati living in India and abroad should decide to donate ten rupees as a token of his or her love for Gandhiji, then we can place heap of money at his feet. But I know that all Gujaratis cannot afford to donate that amount. Yet we are in a position to get one lac Gujaratis, who by their contribution can give a total of ten lac rupees. There are also rich Gujaratis who can contribute one lac each and ten lacs can be easily collected. But I am requesting ordinary Gujaratis—poor Gujaratis who are dear to Gandhiji. The purse that is to be presented to Gandhiji will contain contributions of Hindus, Muslims, Parsees, Christians, as well as cooperators, non-cooperators, Government servants and private individuals, because Gandhiji is equally loved by everybody. Ten lac rupees is only a small token of our love for Gandhiji. Should not the Gujaratis call that much amount to offer at the feet of Gandhiji when he comes to Gujarat? I desire that every reader who reads this appeal to send his contribution of ten rupees to the Secretary of the Gujarat Provincial Congress Committee.

228

Vallabhbhai's Appeal to Gujaratis to Collect Funds, Spin Khadi for Gandhi Jayanti

Navjivan, 24 February 1924

Gandhi month has started. Time will run fast, so today's work cannot be postponed for tomorrow, and if possible tomorrow's work also should be completed today. Bharat Khadi Mandal wants this month to be observed as Gandhi month. There cannot be any need to recommend khadi to Gujarat. We earnestly hope that after the Gandhi month is over, shortly the land of Gujarat will be sanctified by the return of Gandhiji. So, those who have not yet discarded foreign cloth, should discard in this month and be prepared to welcome Gandhiji.

But if we really want to observe this month as Gandhi month, then all the days, hours, and every moment should be owned by Gandhiji. We should not have any right over them. Our this month's earning should be dedicated to Gandhiji, i.e. Gandhiji's work, then it will be considered as a real celebration. Every spare moment of this month should be devoted to spinning, and the thread should be offered to Gandhiji, only then it will be a real celebration of Gandhi month. On the occasion when Gandhiji again sanctifies the land of Gujarat, it has been decided to collect ten lacs of rupees in guise of his reception. So for Gujaratis Gandhi month is like killing two birds with one stone.

The joy of the people of Ayodhya who were suffering from the pangs of separation knew no bounds on the day Ramachandra returned to Ayodhya on the completion of the period of banishment. Similar day is coming nearer to Gujaratis. Such a day comes only once after centuries, and it is the duty of every Gujarati to remember the day eternally. I wish that Gujaratis will not fail to send their earnings of Gandhi month to the Secretary, Gujarat Provincial Congress Committee, as a mark of the remembrance.

I had asked for one lac Gujaratis who will donate ten rupees each, but it does not mean that those who can afford to donate more should donate only ten rupees. I have received several letters from poor Gujaratis. They are not in a position to give ten rupees yet their devotion to Gandhiji is boundless. The value of a pie of those pure hearted persons is much higher than the value of lac of rupees of a millionaire. For those people we cannot fix any minimum. Such poor Gujaratis can send whatever amount they wish and it will be received with thanks.

Gujarat's capacity to manage also will be put to test. I am sure that every Gujarati will contribute something in this fund. But we can get full benefit of such a tremendous goodwill only if we have fool-proof machinery of management of the funds. For this at every place their should be responsible volunteers. If one thousand enthusiastic industrious and honest Gujaratis sacrifice some of their time and shoulder the responsibility of collecting one thousand rupees each, then our task will be easily accomplished much earlier. I hope that one thousand Gujaratis will easily come forward to take up this work, those who want to recruit themselves as volunteers should get a certificate from Gujarat Provincial Congress Committee.

229

Vallabhbhai to Maniben Expressing His Deep Anguish over Her Sadness

Sardar Shrino Patro-3

AHMEDABAD
31 March 1924

MY DEAR DAUGHTER MANIBEN,

You must have received the letter despatched yesterday. I have heard that after going there[1] you started crying. Bapu has enough worries, then why add more? Until now I was not worried about you at all, but since last three or four months, your indifference is worrying me. Dahyabhai also is unhappy. You do not tell me what you should have told. When I ask you, you do not speak anything. When I go on asking you begin crying and complain against me. I am unable to understand as to what you are complaining about.

I can't crack jokes with you, as I do with a child. Yet, if I am not speaking to you, according to me you are much at fault than myself. I tried my best. I am now tired and your complaint against me stands, besides on your side there is the power of crying. The result is I accept my defeat. I am ready to have frank talks with you but not prepared to tolerate your crying. Your brother[2] is also very unhappy and we are unable to understand this change in your behaviour.

When you were travelling in Madhya Prant[3] you were freely moving about, and you were freely, sometimes overfreely, talking to everybody. All that is changed, and though now there is nothing else except your grievance against me, you do not speak with anybody, not even with your brother, and day and night you weep bitterly and making everybody unhappy, what does all these mean? I hear that there also you wept and therefore I am deeply pained. I am ready to give you peace as far as I can, but you must correct your mistake. As I try to make you understand you get more stubborn. I feel that it is mere childishness. So try to recover as early as possible, and after that we will compare each other's faults, and decide as to who is how much at fault. I hope that there also you won't do anything which might hurt anybody, and you also won't entertain unhappy thoughts.

Uncle[4] might be coming there often. Nowadays I am afraid to write to you. You might doubt the sincerity of my writing and if you see in it my fault then there will be difficulty. Even then I write to you what is right according to me. But that should not lead you to think that I want to chide you. I simply want to impress upon you that you have no reason to be unhappy. You are happy in every way. Even then if mind is not healthy then even in happiness one sees unhappiness. Even I do not talk to Dahyabhai more than I talk to you. Yet he knows that I love him, and he does not hesitate to say what he wants to say. I want to see both of you happy. I don't desire anything else.[5] If you are unhappy, then where am I to go? We will talk about it at length after you become alright.[6] I wish that you will empty your heart to Bapu. You will get peace in abundance.[7]

I wish to come there in middle of May. Just now I am deeply engrossed in work. Brother is cheerful. That's all.

Bapu's blessings

[1]At that time Maniben had gone to Juhu to stay with Gandhiji for some time.

[2]Dahyabhai.

[3]For propagating flag satyagraha at Nagpur.

[4]Vithalbhai Patel.

5Vallabhbhai lost his wife when he was thirty four. Yet he did not entertain the idea of marrying again to make children happy.

[6] At that time Maniben was suffering from constipation and slow fever.

[7]Maniben might be twenty-two years old at that time. She had lost her mother in childhood. Thereafter Sardarshri had gone to England for study of law. Only when he started practising in Ahmedabad in 1913, then only Maniben must have heaved a sigh of relief. But from 1917 onwards Sardar's whole life took a turn, and father and daughter's staying together became less and less. Being motherless, she could not get opportunity to talk about her problems to her father, so Maniben sometimes was tense. But in a short time she extricated herself from that situation. Graduated in 1925 from Gujarat Vidyapith, she courted arrest several times in 1930, 1933, 1938-39, 1940 and 1942. Nominated to the Congress Working Committee by P. D. Tandon, she was a member of Parliament from 1952 to 1980.

230

Villagers Dissatisfied with M.L.C.s and Request Vallabhbhai to Lead Them

Jayakar Collection N.A.I., March 1924-1927

Resolution on the subject of Enhancement of Revenue in Bombay Presidency

March 1924—The Legislative Council passed by a majority a resolution to the effect that a Committee be appointed to consider the question of bringing the process of revising the land revenue under closer regulation and to report on the nature and form of the legislation to that end, and that *no revision be proceeded with, and no new rates be levied till the said legislation was brought into effect.*

March 1927—The Legislative Council passed by a majority of 52 against 29 resolution to the effect that Government give immediate effect to the preceding resolution by introducing necessary legislation making provision for giving retrospective effect to the legislation, *and pending such legislation to issue orders to the revenue authorities not to collect assessment enhanced in revision after March 1924.*

Enhancement of Revenue and Constitutional Agitation

Report of the Settlement Officer suggesting enhancement in the assessment of the Taluka published in 1926. Series of articles in the Press criticising the Report in detail, and petitions and memorials protesting against the proposed enhancement. Revision Settlement enforced in July 1927. More petitions and memorials from the bulk of villages in the Taluka. Gujarat members of the Bombay Council wait in deputation to the Governor and have conferences with the Revenue Member, without avail.

Some of the workers in Bardoli Taluka, with representative people from Bardoli, meet Sjt. Vallabhbhai early this year with a request to come and lead an agitation. He refuses to interfere with the M.L.Cs who were then interesting themselves in the situation.

In February another deputation of workers in Bardoli waits on Sjt. Vallabhbhai and represents that their M.L.C. advisers could help them no more and that they had themselves referred them to Sjt. Vallabhbhai.

231

Vallabhbhai Feeling Worried about Maniben's Health

Sardar Shrino Patro-5

AHMEDABAD
April 1924

MY DEAR DAUGHTER MANIBEN,

I roamed about in Kadi for a week. I returned today only. From your letter it appears that your slow fever still persists. I think that if you keep peace of mind you will recover soon. Insomnia is indication of disturbed mind. Insomnia causes constipation also. I think your anxieties are baseless. How is it that after having so much of education one cannot live cheerfully. I think useless and undesirable imagination creates misery. If there is any reason you must tell me about it. Our nature should not be such that all the persons surrounding us become unhappy and we also become unhappy. Poverty is not a thing to be miserable about. Self-imposed poverty begets special type of misery; one must be more happy about it. Yet our poverty is not of the type which can make us unhappy and we invite sufferings. You must be getting peace while staying with Bapu.[1]

If you do not listen to anybody it is obstinacy. Such obstinacy is no good. I am not blaming you. I want to see you peaceful.

You must write to me daily about your health. Dahyabhai is well. Remember me to Devdas.[2]

VALLABHBHAI's blessings

[1]At the time Maniben was staying with Bapu at Juhu.
[2]Gandhiji's youngest son.

232

Vallabhbhai Advises Maniben to Remain Calm and Happy

Sardar Shrino Patro-3

AHMEDABAD
4 April 1924

MY DEAR DAUGHTER MANIBEN,

Received your letter.

Continue writing to me about the effect of Vaidya's medicine. No medicine will be effective unless you have faith. Therefore, do not lose faith in medicine, and don't think that this medicine will not cure me. Only after taking medicine with full faith in its curability effect will be discernible. If you have no faith the medicine does not become effective. You must have full faith in your mind that you are going to be cured.

If mind is uneasy, medicine becomes ineffective. Therefore, day and night you must be cheerful. Anxiety or continuous thinking disturbs the sleep, which results in ill-health. There is no doubt about it. The atmosphere there is such that even a morose person becomes cheerful. Therefore I think that you will have a happy time there.

Now forget the past, and think about as to what is to be said or done.

You are not at all at fault. Circumstances were such that you were not able to have a frank talk with me. But what of that? Yet by mistake we have not done anything wrong. So why worry? How can innocent child like you can be guilty? Only your shedding of tears there and other places makes me and others unhappy, and people think that I might be harassing you, or they might think that your behaviour is childish. Both these situations are undesirable. You must regain your former courage and happiness. I have nothing else to say.

I am not unaware that you had bitter dose of miseries. Yet you won't have the idea of misery from step mother. That's why many people have to suffer many other greater miseries than the separation of mother. We should remember that God has bestowed us with many other kinds of happiness, for which we have to thank Him and be happy.

To remember and to be unhappy for the miseries for which there is no remedy, means despising the other happinesses bestowed upon us by God. If you be cheerful you will recover soon.

Both the brothers are happy.

Respected Ba is leaving day after tomorrow. That is all.

Bapu's blessings

233

Vallabhbhai to Maniben to Keep Faith in God

Sardar Shrino Patro-3

AHMEDABAD
7 April 1924

MY DEAR DAUGHTER MANIBEN,

One can understand nervousness caused by prolonged illness but the miseries are test of our patience. When you feel uneasy, pray to God. He is the giver of happiness and unhappiness. We should think about the misery of all those persons more miserable than us and thank God for happiness He has bestowed on us. We have lots of happiness and there is bound to be some sort of unhappiness. If we only think about unhappiness and forget the happiness which He has bestowed than it's betrayal of God. Therefore we should keep in mind our happiness and be more happy.

I had a boil on my forehead. It was operated three days ago. Now the wound has healed, and now everything is almost normal.

When you are being treated by *Vaidya,* then why have you gone to the hospital? The medicine started some days ago should be continued, only then you will be able to know whether you will be cured or not. Servants' taunting has pained you. You must forget all that. We must keep in mind as to what misery is there to be a servant. Getting angry and scolding is not the way to reform the servants. We must pity them. Yet you will find some servants who will misuse your compassion. Such servants should be sacked, but you cannot quarrel with them. Only experience will make you understand this. In childhood I had such habit, but experience changed me and similarly you will also be changed. That's all.

Bapu's blessings

234

Vallabhbhai to Maniben Inquiring about Her Health

Sardar Shrino Patro-3

AHMEDABAD
10 April 1924

DEAR DAUGHTER MANIBEN,

I met Dada Saheb[1] and Ba. I am yet to get news about your health, which may relieve me of anxiety. If there is anything worth knowing in the X-ray report of Dr. Dalai Saheb let me know. As you have been dieting your weight might be decreasing. You must be feeling weak. Yet you must act according to the instructions of the doctor or *Vaidya,* who is treating you. So for some time you shall have to wait with patience and without being perturbed and observe the changes taking place.

I am extremely pleased to know that you have gained peace of mind and I am sure that though weakness might increase, yet you shall have good results within a short time.

Day after tomorrow I am going to Bhavnagar. I have received a wire from Tayabji Saheb.[2] So I must go. Bhaktiben[3] is coming here tomorrow. She will stay here for a day and next day she will go to Anand.

Keep your mind peaceful and be cheerful.

Bapu's blessings

[1]G.V. Malavankar, well known barrister of Ahmedabad, close associate of Sardar Patel, Speaker of Central Assembly (1946-50). Speaker of First Lok Sabha in 1952.

[2]Abbas Tayabji. After retiring from Baroda as Judge, he joined Gandhiji and devoted himself to the service of the nation. He was President of Khedi District Congress Committee.

[3]Wife of Darbar Gopaldas, took part in national struggle. Amongst the women who took active part in freedom struggle, Bhaktiben holds a high position.

235

Vallabhbhai to Maniben Expressing His Happiness over Her Health

Sardar Shrino Patro-5

AHMEDABAD
12 April 1924

MY DEAR DAUGHTER MANIBEN,

Received your letter. I am going to Bhavnagar this evening. Mahadevbhai is also coming with me.

Don't worry about home. I am relieved of the anxiety, because you have attained peace of mind. I am sure that within a short time you will be relieved of pain, and once that process starts you will recover your health soon.

Bhaktiben[1] is coming here this evening. She will stay with us tonight. Tomorrow she will leave for Anand.

Dahyabhai and Chhotu[2] are well. Poor Chhotu's eyes are weak. Today I got a note from the doctor. He writes that for one year he has to stop reading, and should not do anything which might strain his eyes. The boy is very sober, but poor boy has this trouble. It seems in future he will suffer from eye disease.

Do not worry about this place.

Bapu's blessings

[1] Wife of Darbar Gopaldas. Well known political and constructive worker.
[2]Chhotubhai Patel, Sardar's nephew.

236

Vallabhbhai to Maniben on Bhavnagar Ruler's Unhelpful Attitude

Sardar Shrino Patro-5

AHMEDABAD
1 April 1924

MY DEAR DAUGHTER MANIBEN,

Yesterday I returned from Bhavnagar, Mahadevbhai was with me. There the State does not give permission to hold conference, and there is no other go than holding a conference. So, it appears that we shall have to fight with the State.

I think that your health must have been improved. Since how many days you have been taking medicine prescribed by Vaidya?

Darbar Saheb[1] and Abbas Saheb have returned back from Kathiawad. Darbar Saheb is elected President of some conference to be held at Santa Cruz. I have heard that he is going there on 19th. He will see you if he comes there.

Here Dahyabhai and Chhotu are well.

I am in sound health. That's all.

Bapu's blessings

[1]Darbar Gopaldas Desai, ruler of a small state "Oasa" in Saurashtra. Joined National Movement. Imprisoned several times. Deprived of his state.

237

Vallabhbhai on Differences among Congress Leaders during Gandhiji's Imprisonment

Sardar Shrino Patro- V

30 April 1924

REVERED BAPUJI,

Yesterday I had written a letter to Maniben. After receiving your letter today I have written another letter to her. I will definitely do everything in my power. But I think her fault is greater than mine. I called her and tried hard to know her mind, but instead of replying she continued crying, and so I am tired. I think that this change in her nature is recent, but she won't accept it, and if we tell her about her, she will begin to cry. So now only after her recovery frank talks can be had. I desire to have a very frank talk with her, but she keeps mum and so it becomes difficult to know her misery. I do not talk much with Dahyabhai, yet I can see through his heart, and he is able to see my abundant love for him. Change in nature of Maniben is since last three or four months. But looking to her mental conditions I am afraid to tell that it is defect. If you think proper please write to me about her reactions of my letter.

Leaders have come to you. From their talks you must have got the idea of our plight after you were jailed.[1] With you they have got their work done by sycophancy, but you can understand how they made us extremely miserable. You were released because of God's grace or our good luck. Otherwise God knows what miseries the present Congress President would have inflicted on us.

Will you regain your former health? I think that it will be better to look after

Gujarat only. At present we shall have to allow others to go their own way.

Vallabhbhai's pranam

[1]During this time Pandit Madan Mohan Malviya, Lala Lajpat Rai, Pandit Motilal Nehru and other leaders had seen Bapuji, and had consultations with him regarding entry into legislatures.

[2]During 1922-24 when Bapuji was in jail, there was a conflict amongst the leaders regarding non-cooperation and council entry.

238

Vallabhbhai to Maniben Not to Travel in IIIrd Class if Health does not Permit

Sardar Shrino Patro-3

AHMEDABAD
1 May 1924

MY DEAR DAUGHTER MANIBEN,

I knew from Mahadevbhai's letter that you and Pranjivan[1] have reached Surat.[2] I was pleased to know that though you travelled in IIIrd class, your journey was not difficult. It was not necessary to take such a risk, one has to incur necessary expenses for maintaining health. If we try to economise then ultimately it proves to be expensive. I think as Durgaben[3] and Pragjibhai are there you will have a good time.

Even then the peace solely depends on you than any other means. If we restrain our mind from indulging in useless thoughts and try to keep it cheerful then we can be happy under any circumstances. If mind becomes weak then even there is allround happiness one feels unhappy. I think that your mental burden has become light and now in congenial atmosphere and good company, you will recover quickly.

Revered Kasturba also wants to come and stay there for some time. You must write a letter to Nanduben. That poor lady loves you like her own daughter, and doctor also loves you intensely. It is not good that you do not write to them.

Bapu's blessings

[1]He joined the struggle of Indians in South Africa under the leadership of Gandhiji. When Bapu returned to India Pragjibhai also returned to India and served the nation as Gandhiji's soldier.

[2]For going to Hajeera.

[3] Wife of Mahadevbhai Desai.

239

Vallabhbhai to Maniben regarding Her Health

Sardar Shrino Patro-3

AHMEDABAD
12 May 1924

MY DEAR DAUGHTER MANIBEN,

I am going to Borsad[1] today. Mahadevbhai is with me. Jamnalalji[2] is coming to Borsad. I will return from there on 16th morning.

Mahadevbhai will come to Hajeera on Sunday. Mostly Kanuga[3] will come with them. Nothing is decided about me.

Doctors opine that there is no constipation. So, after some time there will be no fever.

Chhotu is coming to Borsad with me. We are all happy. So also you might be. That's all.

Bapu's blessings

[1]On 13th May Gujarat Political Conference was held at Borsad. The fight for removal of Criminal Tribes Act fought under the leadership of Sardar, resulted in glorious victory and so the entire Borsad Taluka was rejuvenated. In such circumstances a conference was held at Borsad. Side by side anti-untouchability and Thakar Conferences were also held.

[2]Jamnalal Bajaj, rich businessman, follower of Mahatma Gandhi, treasurer of Indian National Congress for years. He had liberally donated for constructive and cow protection work.

[3]Dr. Balvantrai Kanuga.

240

Vallabhbhai Advises Maniben to Stay at Sabarmati

Sardar Shrino Patro-5

AHMEDABAD
19 May 1924

MY DEAR DAUGHTER MANIBEN,

Received your letter. Doctor's opinion and Pragjibhai's[1] utterances indicate that climate there[2] has definitely improved your health. If it is so, then there is no reason why you should hurry. Heat here is unbearable, and the water here also causes indigestion. So it would be better if you stay there till the end of the month.

Bapu also is coming at the end of the month.[3] So if you stay there till then, it would be better for your health.

Mahadevbhai had wired Swami[4] to stay there[5] for a week. But Swami is not here. Mostly he will come tomorrow. Then I will ask him and let you know.

Is Durgaben[6] keeping good health there?

If there is no special inconvenience, what is the reason for your hurry? That's all.

Bapu's blessings

[1]Pragjibhai Desai. He has joined the struggle of Indians in South Africa, conducted by Gandhiji. When Bapu returned to India he also returned and engaged himself in national service as Bapu's soldier.
[2]Of Hajeera.
[3]In Sabarmati Ashram.
[4]Swami Anand.
[5]In Hajeera.
[6]Mahadevbhai's wife.

241

Vallabhbhai to Maniben Expressing Happiness over Improvement in Her Health

Sardar Shrino Patro-3

AHMEDABAD
21 May 1924

MY DEAR DAUGHTER MANIBEN,

Don't be in a hurry to walk too much. One must exert according to one's energy. Increase of two seers (4 pounds) is good.

Every malady can be compared with the flood. It comes like a speed of the horse and leaves like a speed of an ant. Howsoever impatient we might be it leaves when it is time for it to leave.

Here it is so hot that even a healthy person gets uneasy. Your hurry indicates that now you are fed up of the place. As Pragjibhai and others have gone you might be feeling lonely. Stay there as long as possible.

It is useless to stay there if your mind is not cheerful.

Bapu is coming on 19th.[1]

Bapu's blessings

[1]From Bombay to Ahmedabad.

242

Vallabhbhai's Rejoinder to Government on its Apathy to People of Kaira and their Sufferings

Young India, 13 September 1924

(Joint statement of Vallabhbhai Patel and Mahadev Desai addressed to the Editor, the *Bombay Chronicle,* on 23rd December 1923, in reply to the allegations of the Government.)

1. Mr. Gennings refers to the so-called "confidential official documents improperly and illegally obtained" by one of us. We can only assure you that those documents, however, "confidential" they may be were the most relevant ones in the case—even more relevant than the formidable array of those with which the Director of Information has endeavoured to enlighten you and we should have failed in our duty if we had not exposed the hollowness of the Government case as revealed by admission of their own officers. We are however in a position to show that the documents that the Director of Information has ventured to publish believing them to be harmless also help to give away the whole government case.

2. We may accept that the Superintendent of Police who has signed the impressive document on which the Director of Information relies is an officer with a distinguished record. But we are afraid the record was won by him elsewhere than on the field of Kaira and he has not been long enough to give evidence of that record except perhaps in the preparation of that document of 77 paragraphs—a document based on the reports of officers who were solely responsible for the maladministration of the past several years. We do not know the order that he and his gallant band have restored but if any it is due to a variety of causes for which Government can take no credit whatsoever. One of them is the capture of the dacoit Ali which we make bold to say was not due to the bravery of the police and another is the capture of Mir Khan by Baroda state police. A third reason is the posting of the Satyagraha volunteers in the Taluka which has gone a great way to relieve the distress. But any relief or restoration of order for which the government can take any credit is more than counterbalanced by the disorder and misery caused by the punitive police imposed on the Taluka, and the abnormal concentration of police force in one part of the district has rendered other parts insecure.

3. We see that the Director of Information has accepted the charge of inefficiency of the police. But has tried to make it out as the result entirely of the lack of will on the people's part to support the police and of the lack of courage to help themselves. A study of the report of the Superintendent of Police will demonstrate the utter worthlessness of the excuse. It should be observed that the report relates to the whole district and no less than a score or more of the cases described are of events that happened in Taluka other than Borsad. We shall only

point out numerous instances in which the people have not only tried to help the police, but have risked and lost their lives:

(1) *Para 6.* DSP's Report. The unfortunate man who was crucified to a tree and riddled with bullets was an informer.

(2) *Para 7.* The murder in the case was the outcome of assistance rendered to the police by the deceased man's family.

(3) *Para 9.* A Mahomedan who had given evidence against dacoits was attacked and left with his nose severed.

(4) *Para 10.* The deceased was a witness in a murder case.

(5) *Para 12.* Babar shot Bakore in cold blood suspecting him of being in league with the police.

(6) *Para 13.* At village Bedwa the dacoits met with resistance they fired at the villagers, killing two.

(7) *Para 14.* A Pattidar villager who had the "temerity to oppose the dacoits" was stabbed with a knife.

(8) *Para 18.* Babar Deva murdered a police informer at Banjeda.

(9) *Para 20.* Four villages, all in Borsad Taluka, were raided by dacoits armed with deadly weapons but the "raiders decamped". (Surely not out of goodwill, but because they saw that discretion was the better part of valour.)

(10) Para *32.* "The people having collected, two shots were fired." (Did they collect there to witness a *tamashal*)

(11) *Para 34.* Four villages were raided but there was only one case of assault and one of extortion.

(12) *Para 37.* Babar wreaked vengeance on a police informer who was brutally wounded.

(13) *Para 37.* "A tailor opposed the dacoits and as a result of his temerity received several wounds."

(14) *Para 58.* A potter was cruelly stabbed in his chest surely not because he was rich, but because he was either an informer or because he dared to offer resistance.

(15) *Para 60.* Suspected informers done to death.

(16) *Para 61.* The villager of Sunav "turned out and followed" Babar Deva.

(17) *Para 71.* Three vegetable sellers were attacked and shot dead certainly not because their treasuries were full.

Now there are several points worth noting regarding these cases. They are taken from a report specially prepared to make out a case for the imposition of punitive police and which takes no count of the numerous people who furnished information or dared to resist the dacoits and laid down their lives. The people have dared to give information in spite of the fact "Babar swears vegeance against his informants," and "It is stated that his hatred against police informers is so intense that he does not spare even his nearest relatives." Reference is made therein to the way in which Babar Deva murdered his mother and his uncle whom he suspected of having given information against him.

It is the Taluka of Borsad which was the scene of these deeds of daring which the Commissioner of the Division describes as one in "which the failure on the part of the people at large to have given information or cooperation to the police has been conspicuous." If the record given above is one of "democratisation" and "lack of courage" and "lack of will to help" a fresh dictionary will have to be issued by the Director of Information.

To these records of brave resistance we shall only add the cases of scores of villages which have out of their own strength remained immune from the attacks of dacoits and marauders and which because of the organised defence are capable of putting up with that they were free from the scourge of the punitive police and even of the assistance of the ordinary police which claims to afford them protection.

In concluding this paragraph we shall only make a passing reference to the plea of the Director of Information that the people should have been capable of greater resistance because of the "lethal weapons" that the villagers have always ready to hand. What shall we say regarding the prowess of the policemen who in spite of their swords and guns have not been able to capture dacoits who escaped in one instance because it was dark or in another because the way lay through surrounding field and standing crops, whilst the poor villagers were fighting. For all they were worth with their "lethal weapons" against dacoits armed with "guns, dharias, bows and arrows."

5. But the Director of Information would even acquit the people of the charge of deliberate failure to inform the police, if his government can find the wherewithal to pay for the cost of the punitive police. "The only question", says he, "is whether the police force should be paid for by the public of the whole presidency or by the inhabitants of the small tract whose lawlessness had rendered them necessary." The question is not that, the only question is whether a people should be condemned unheard, whether the character of a vast majority of the peaceful inhabitants of a Taluka should be so shamelessly impugned, the only question is whether a government that admits (Para 3 of DSP's report) that the continued success of dacoits' depredations has "cowed down the law-abiding sections of the district" can conscionably punish the section cowed down.

6. But we have touched only the points raised by the Director of Information's reply. Whilst he has questioned our right to publish certain damaging documents he is indifferent to the most serious charges that we have made against them. Why is it that whilst so many informers have been shot or murdered in cold blood, no police has been touched? Why is it that in spite of so many informants having been murdered the police upto a few days ago failed to capture the arch dacoits? The charge of the public against Government is that they allied with a dacoit who was known to be a murderer. Provided him with arms and ammunition and allowed him to go unchecked on his career of murder and loot. They have come to believe that all cooperation with such a department of police was futile.

The government have been culpably indifferent to the charge we have noted above whilst all the documents—published and unpublished—are contrived to throw the whole blame on one dacoit Babar Deva and on the so-called "demoralised" public, no mention is made of that miscreant Ali in any one of these reports though his career of crimes has been no less dastardly than his brother dacoit. It is we who repeat with all the emphasis that we command a guilty silence. The last though not the least charge which has also been left unanswered is that the government imposed the police knowing that it was useless to do so, and that the public did not need it. The District Magistrate in his letter No. 184, 13th April 1923—one of the confidential documents we have illegally obtained—was emphatically of opinion that "the continuance of the additional police is not desirable in either of the villages", that "the police parties never move out of the village and their presence does not reduce the number of men otherwise required for the police of the Taluka", that "they do not even serve the purpose of preventing crime as the murder of Shivbhai in Jogan in daylight proves to say nothing of the attack made on the similar police parties in Golel." He also frankly confessed that "from the application I have received and from the statements of a deputation of non-Dharala residents of Jogan who recently came to see me it appears that they do not need such protection" (i.e., the protection of the punitive police) and "would much prefer to be without the police altogether than to have to put for them."

7. The question then the public will ask is where shall we fix the responsibility for the general state of criminality in the District—we are here concerned with that in the Taluka, and what has been done to remedy it. We have not the slightest doubt that the Government have to thank themselves for it, that they are reaping what they have so sedulously sown. They have chosen to fix the label of "criminal" on a virile, industrious agricultural community and having once condemned it they have daily driven it to a life of despair by the measures they have devised out of their own desperation. Their most handy weapons have been the Criminal Tribes Act and the notorious security of the Criminal Procedure Code which are so framed as to lend themselves to almost indefinite abuse or which an ingenuous overzealous officer finds easy to abuse. "Well thought out and carefully calculated solutions were suggested to meet the situation and those received the strong support of several district magistrates but", mourns the officer, "unfortunately for various reasons they were negatived and so owing to continued criminality on the part of the Dharalas the work of reiterating these proposals like a penelope web continues." While one officer is prepared to admit that "ultimate cause of this abnormal amount of crime is partly an economic one", he feels, "it is not one that can be easily removed," another thinks that "the attentions shown to these people have not been adequate that the leniency with which they have been treated up to now has been utterly misplaced," and that, "in lieu of improving them the half hearted and completely inadequate Hazri measures taken up under the Criminal Tribes Act have resulted in their retrogression," and consequently presses for "measures indicative of determination and strength" under the Criminal Tribes Act. "It will now generally be admitted", says the DSP "that after nearly a decade's trial this Hazri measure has proved completely abortive." We think the officer is mistaken. The measure has borne enough fruit in the shape of increased

crime. The remedy has been worse than the disease but rather than radically alter the remedy it has been always thought proper to intensify it. If poison aggravates the malady one way is to make the dose stronger, and despatch the patient, another is to alter the dose altogether and put him on the way to recovery. It was no wonder that proposals for a more determined use of the "Criminal Tribes Act" were long negatived. It is a wonder that they should have been countenanced at all.

If anything was needed to complete the ravages of the application of the Criminal Tribes Act, the security sections supplied it. Imagine a district in which in one single year there should have been no less than 1800 cases under the Security Sections! What is the poor wretch to do if he is to be put into jail on the slightest suspicion? Better he thinks to court jail by defiant crime than to be ever the object of police suspicion and police attentions. The economic aspect has never been faced and the District Magistrate fears that it may not be possible to face it at all. Even temporary relief as suspension of payment of land revenue in a year of failure of monsoon has been too frequently denied and Deputy Secretary to Government naively suggests that the force to be employed "should be as strong as the general population can pay for"—not under usual conditions not if they can afford—but "under pressure"! In almost every year of famine there is the cry of false annawarnees and the full measure of revenue is exacted where it should not be.

Having refused to face the economic aspect of the case and having been unable to tackle the question of moral reform of the community the government have naturally not looked beyond the limits of the Criminal Tribes Act and the Security Sections and the final desparate act has been the imposition of punitive police. As has been noted above the District Magistrate was of the opinion that the punitive police had failed to serve any useful purpose and that no villager wanted it. But the police was imposed with a vengeance and the people are not yet free from their oppression.

8. We do not think we need discuss here what in our opinion would be the proper solution of the cases. We shall only say that the little experiment of posting trained experienced Satyagraha volunteers in every village of the Taluka who will take to every home the message of non-violence, truth and khaddar is already proving successful and if the government retires as we think it ought with good grace from the area we shall gladly share with the people of the village the responsibility to keep peace and order.

9. It is beyond our purpose here to narrate the long tale of woe of the Borsad peasantry the way in which the punitive police has terrorised them, the way in which attachments are carried out and how the life of the people has been rendered insecure by those who profess to keep them in security. We can only describe that condition of things as atrocious.

10. It has been our duty in the circumstances detailed in the foregoing paragraphs to advise the vast majority of the innocent people of Borsad to refuse to pay the unwarranted impost and to resist with all their might and power of endurance the attempt to cast an unmerited slur on their character.

243

Vallabhbhai's Clarion Call to Villagers to be Bold and Courageous[1]

Navjivan, 17 September 1924

An innocent child purified the atmosphere of this place by singing *bhajan,* so I want to say few words at this place after praying to God, and by saying words I want to shake your hearts. All of you have showered profuse love on us, but we do not cherish mad love; we are not fools, we know fully well our value and our limitations. As you are soaked with sins and weaknesses so are we. When you fold hands before us, it is not because of us, but you fold hands because we are trying to serve you according to our limited intellect and energy following the footsteps of the greatest man of the world, who is sitting in Yervada jail. You do not fold hands before us but you are folding hands before him. You value us because we are doing our work in his name and today I want to say few words to you in his name.

We fought fierce battle with government. If you believe that the fight was for removal of the Haidiya tax (tax on the people who are announced by the government as people of the criminal tribe) of two and a half rupees, then you are mistaken. That time circumstances were such that we had no other recourse but to fight. We fought for removal of the unbearable blot on you on account of your being declared as criminals. But don't you think that we are interested in fighting. If the Government reverses its wrong steps, then I would wish to serve you peacefully with government's cooperation. But if the government does not mend its ways, then I will fight with it till my last breath. Government has accepted its error, and so, we would not take its name till a similar occasion arises. It is foolish to see the fault of others till we are full of sins, weaknesses and filth. Government has accepted its mistake that you are not bandits nor you give them refuge. But in the decision of the government there is one other thing, which pains me immensely.

Government proclaimed you as innocent in its resolution but it has termed you as cowards. It has said that you have been terrified. The mischief mongers have terrorised you. Having heard this, I am as much pained as when I read the orders regarding additional police force. If bandits can move freely amongst you, loot you, torture you, attack moneylenders, and you run away like mute animals, then how are you going to fight with government to get Gandhiji released? Everybody praises you seeing your height, your stout body, your faces, but if your heart is that of a goat then I don't want your friendship. I am a companion of the brave.

When we call you *Dharala* you get angry. But on government records you have been dubbed as persons hiding their real identity. Your complete history, your dynasty is that of robbers and dacoits, that is government's charge. Till that black spot is there, life should not be worth living for you. Crimes are committed in your regions which are not your work, but it is the work of scoundrels, and therefore government withdraw punitive tax. But, police force is still stationed there. Will the additional police force be able to protect you? We are fools to have allowed the police force to be continued staying here. Police with guns are more afraid of dacoits than you. I demand courage of gunless, white-capped Ravishankar Maharaj. I have appointed him *Fozdar* (Police Officer) of eighteen villages of a seashore. I have warned 20,000 men and women there, that if they loot anybody, commit robbery, molest any woman then first thing I will do is to break the head of Ravishankar, then break my head and then the head of Darbar Saheb. Your such sins tarnish the name of Mahatma Gandhi. When Mahatma Gandhi fought battle on this land five years ago, it was not a battle of a violent form. You were asked to fight so that you can become brave. You can become desparate. If you go to the ruffians who move about in your villages, and fight with them, then the ruffians will be unnerved. See how the government has climbed down? We had no guns, no swords, but we had truth on our side. That is why government had to lay down arms. If you take that weapon, the dacoits and robbers shall have to lay down their arms. If you are not prepared to be brave you see him, though he might be your real brother, father, or husband. Forsake him. Not only that you do not give shelter to the robbers, but you also should not keep stolen goods.

If anybody from you knows Babar Deva, and if you have occasion to see him or talk him tell him that his insurgence is not real insurgence. To run about with gun and to loot and kill innocent persons is not insurgence. Real insurgent does not need any weapon. Real insurgent is the Darbar of Dhasa, of Mahatma Gandhi. A person who harasses unarmed people, loots the rich, and commits murder, is a curse to the society. How can we call such a person brave?

If the entire community decides to restrain him from committing dacoity, then though the police of the government might be entirely corrupt or bad, if the entire community decides that, for one man the entire community is, earns blasphemy, then you must inform him. "If you have courage then give seven days notice to government telling it, I have wandered for seven years, but you have not been able to arrest me. But today I have known God, I am neither afraid of your punishment, nor of police, arrest me within seven days, otherwise I myself present myself to police". In doing so is real bravery. Otherwise tell him that hanging rod is already there. One day you shall have to die the death of a rabid dog. He can escape from the clutches of police, but he can't escape from the claws of the police of God. Therefore, give public apology to the community, and stop being criminal before God.

If you want my love, you shall have to give me some promises. You put complete faith in us. Similarly, a situation is created when we also can put complete faith in you. I will come to you after a month. There should not be any crime during the month, nobody goes to the wine shop, and give up drinking, within a month such a situation should be created that rich man's child can go about tossing rupees in his hand, and a woman can fearlessly move about in dark night—if you create such situation, I will believe that you are going to contribute your mite in Gandhi's work.

You have no right to marry and produce cowards, no right to live. You take a vow today that you won't tolerate bandits and dacoits, you will fight with them and lay down your lives while fighting, but won't allow anybody to be robbed, and injured.

I don't want to wash dirty linens of the police, but I want to say that in this taluka there were no policemen. They were the companions of robbers. You did not help them, but you cared for your own safety. You allowed your neighbour to die when he was dying, and shut your doors. Such cowardice will not help you to get Swaraj, and we want to establish *Ramrajya,* we want to know God. That is like walking on the edge of the sword. It is easy to cheat dacoits, easy to cheat the government, but you can never cheat God.

Today I say to the government but you have been taking measures which are bound to fail. Your actions will make robber a looter, and looter a dacoit. Man gets more tired of living. The measures to reform the robbers are not the measures which they have undertaken. The way of reforming the robbers is the way of God, way of ethics, the way of religion. The measures taken by the government make persons who are not criminals indulge in crimes, and criminals escape. The real way of reforming criminals is to win their confidence, and to make them your kith and kin. The real temple of God is human body. It is covered with illusion. One has to keep the body as pure as possible and I want to do that by making friendship with you.

For this I am going to beg. My first begging is that you give up drinking. This government has given facilities to you to drink because they have no plan to make you religious. I request you in front of this temple that if you are sitting here with sincerity, then take a vow that you will never go to wine shops. Let those of you who rent their houses to wine dealers, take a vow that they will burn their houses, but will never rent the houses to wine dealers. My second begging is that do not tolerate the robbers. Drive him out as soon as possible. (After this lecture of Sardar was over people in thousands took a vow in front of Ranchodji's idol.)

[1]Lecture delivered by Vallabhbhai in Beas village on 14 January 1924 after the victory celebrations of Borsad Satyagraha.

244

Mahadev to Vallabhbhai on Gandhiji's Displeasure

Sardar Shrino Patro

DELHI
22 October 1924

REVERED BROTHER,

Excuse me for not writing to you regularly.

Reading your letter gave me an idea of your mental condition. When I was with you, I used to share your worries and contribute a little not by helping you, but talking to you and sitting with you. Now that situation also is not there. Whatever happens to Hindus and Muslims in Gujarat, Bapu is not worried as long as you are there. If riot spreads when you are there Bapu will think that it was impossible for you to prevent it.

My anxiety and misery are boundless . . . has written a long letter to Bapu, in which he writes, "How can you tolerate those persons who like you, filling the pages of *Navjivan* with your praises. . . . We want advice, we don't want to be bored by your eulogies." After reading the letter I bitterly wept before Bapuji. People defame our good intentions also in such a manner? I told Bapu that "if my writings harm you then I will stop writing". Bapu said, "I do not think like that. You continue writing as you do. It is usual for people to level charges. How can we please all?" I am tired by that personal utterances in which he acts to be smart. People are eager to know everything regarding Bapu, then what else am I to write? Write about quarrels? Discussion of scriptures? And whom do I eulogise? I am describing only the force of love. If you find anything improper in my writings please let me know. Bapu's health is improving. Now he will be able to take his normal food. But he has not the energy to move about. Permission regarding Kohat[2] has not been received as yet.

MAHADEVS
Pranam

[1]During this time Gandhiji had undertaken 21 days fast for communal unity.
[2]There were communal riots in Kohat in those days. Bapu wanted to go there for establishing peace.

245

Vallabhbhai Urges Gujaratis Not to Rest Content with Their Performance in Spinning

Navjivan, 9 November 1924

Last month in competition with Andhra we won. Was it an accident? Could it be that Andhra had undervalued our capability, and it was mistaken. Whatever it might be we should not be mistaken in our estimate of the capability of Andhra. All the provinces which had competed with Gujarat are in an advantageous position. The population of Andhra and Bengal is many times more than Gujarat. In both the provinces spinning is an ancient industry. Not only that there *Charkhas* were plying even before the emergence of khadi movement. We are new recruits, yet because we are trained by a teacher like Gandhiji, we have been able to keep our heads aloft.

Constant effort is needed to maintain our progress in this field. The workers of Gujarat—really speaking Maha Gujarat—have to be cautious. It is not too much to expect a larger number of spinners from Kathiawar (Saurashtra). Why should all the districts of Gujarat not fall in line with Kheda district? It is not at all impossible. But before it happens it is important that the stronger districts increase the number of spinners and continue their efforts to reach to the goal set up by Gandhiji. Gandhiji has impartially blessed all the provinces, yet if Gujarat is unsuccessful Gandhiji will consider himself responsible for it.

15th is coming nearer and nearer naturally we expect that all the 1700 spinners young and old who took part in the competition last month should take part in this month's competition also. If we do not cross the number of 1700 then we will be considered unfit for participating in the competition.

Not a single spinner—that one who knows spinning—should not fail to send his or her contribution. Those who desire to learn spinning should immediately put his or her desire into practice; and alert workers should provide all the facilities to them. Then the follow up work will be done automatically. In Gujarat the number of women spinners is 265, which is more than the total number of women spinners of all the provinces. It is a very hopeful sign. Women have always played a predominant role in national activities. Even in Muslim spinners Gujarat comes third in comparison with other provinces. A little effort will bring Gujarat at the top. Last month Maha Gujarat spun 44 lac yards, which is double than the quota of Andhra and four or five times than the quota of other provinces.

Thus will the province which is ahead of other provinces in many respects will lag behind in the number of spinners?

246

Vallabhbhai Asks Villagers to Shun Police (Extracts)[1]

Navjivan, 17 December 1924

It is shameful that 1800 people from your village go to jail for failing to give security for good behaviour. Your having born is futile. In such condition your life is just like dying. Either all of you die or all of you improve. I want you to fight with Government. I want to die for you. But only if you are going to change your living style, if you are going to be brave and by my fighting you are going to be benefited. My master from whom I have learned something has taught me the art of fighting. He told me to fight for truth, fight to make people brave.

I want to say to the Government "Not only that I do not want your additional police but I do not want even a single police. We will make our own arrangements. If you bring your disputes to Darbar, stop committing theft, and do not use foul language, the government, police stationed will automatically close down."

[1]From the speech at the public meeting at Alarsa before reaching Borsad.

247

Vallabhbhai Proud of Dharala[1] Community

Navjivan, 17 December 1924

You do not like to be called Dharala. So now I will like to call you Kshatriya, but till you do not act in a manner like Kshatriya how can you be given the name of Kshatriya? You must have acted like Kshatriya. When you rescue somebody, who is injured, who is being looted or save some lady who is molested. Then in that case I will be proud of being your friend. But today I am ashamed of your actions, and your community is earning a bad name. I fought the battle not for moneylenders but for you.

[1] After the festival of the termination of Borsad fight, Vallabhbhai Patel took a round of some villages of Borsad Taluka, and he tried to divert the energy generated by the fight in taluka towards the freedom struggle. This speech was delivered in Anklav village, while going from Borsad to Raas. It was mainly addressed to people of Bawaria and Patanwadia communities.

248

Vallabhbhai to Mathuradas[1] on Congress Organisation

Sardar Ki Seekh

BORSAD
30 March 1925

DEAR MATHURADAS,

We should not forget our allegiance to our organisation. Its mistakes would gobble it up. If it makes another mistake, it would fail to continue.

Vande Matram,

Yours,
VALLABHBHAI

[1]Mathuradas Trikaunj, a well-known freedom fighter, close lieutenant of Sardar Vallabhbhai Patel, imprisoned several times, took part in Bardoli Satyagraha in 1928.

249

Vallabhbhai Appeals to People for Celebration of South Africa Day

Navjivan, 11 August 1925

As per resolution of All India Congress Committee a public meeting of the citizens of Ahmedabad will be held on Sunday 11th October at 9 p.m. in Manek Chowk Tilak Maidan in order to back the Indians of South Africa on whose heads a sword is hanging, and also to give them moral support. All are requested to attend the meeting.

250

Vithalbhai to Vallabhbhai asking for Advice on Purchasing Car

Sardarshri Ke Vishista aur Anokhe Patra-2

BOMBAY
10 October 1925

DEAR VALLABHBHAI,

I have not received any reply to my letter and fail to understand the reason for your silence. From 1st December I shall be staying in Delhi.[1] After I reach there all preparations should be made. Bhai Manilal Kothari will have to make all the arrangements, as I shall be unable to look after these things. He should also arrange for a cook one week before and reach Delhi.

I have not yet bought a motor car and some people are advising me that I should do so in Delhi. Please let me know what Manilal thinks about it.

Yours
VITHAL BHAI

[1]Vithalbhai Patel had been elected for the first time the President of the Central Assembly, an important event in the history of India.

251

Vallabhbhai Advises Maniben to Live Amicably with Her Sister-in-law

Sardar Ki Seekh

BHUJ (KUTCH)
25 October 1925

DEAR DAUGHTER MANIBEN,

We have reached here safely.[1] We will be here in Kutch till 7.11.25.1 have decided to reach Ahmedabad on seventh morning.

You live amicably with Yashoda.[2] You should overlook each other's faults. If the people come to know that you have strained relations with your sister-in law, it presents a bad picture of both of you, and our family. If you want to serve the people then you shall have to come in contact with people of different temperaments. So you have to be generous and learn to tolerate misbehaviour of others and this lesson has to be learnt from your own home. If you cannot live affectionately with members of your family, then it will be difficult to do public service. How can that house be happy where members of the family quarrel with each other? That is why you must learn to live amicably. Everybody is not of the same temperament.

Inquire about Bhurubhai's[3] health.

Take care of your health. Dahyabhai is also well.

Bapu's blessings

[1]Gandhiji had started this tour from 22nd October. In the tour Sardar and Mahadevbhai were with him.

[2]Sardar's daughter-in-law.

[3]Indranandan Thakor, son of Balwantrai Thakor, and editor of *Prajabandhu* and *Gujarat Samachar* was ill at that time.

252

Vallabhbhai to Maniben on His Tour Programme

Sardar Shrino Patro-5

AHMEDABAD
5 December 1925

DEAR DAUGHTER MANIBEN,

Received your letters written from Poona and Bombay. I was pleased to receive the news that you have safely reached Poona.[1] I am thinking of sending Dahyabhai and your sister-in-law[2] to Delhi for some time, because your uncle[3] has invited them.

Tomorrow I am going to Dholka with Bapuji. I will be there only for a day.

You must have by now well settled there. Live amicably with everybody. Write to me if you want me to do anything for you there. Do not entertain unhappiness. Let me know if you want anything and I shall get it for you.

Bapu's blessings

[1]In Sevasadan, Poona.

[2]Dahyabhai's wife Yashodaben.

[3]Vithalbhai Patel who was elected as Chairman of Central Legislature, a prominent Congress Leader, Member Congress Working Committee for several years; General Secretary, Indian National Congress (1923), took active part in Nagpur Flag Satyagraha (1923), and in Borsad Satyagraha (1924), died on 11 November 1933.

253

Vallabhbhai on Vithalbhai's Grand Style of Living

Sardar Shrino Patro-3

AHMEDABAD
17 December 1925

DEAR DAUGHTER MANIBEN,

Received your letter. Prabhakar the younger son of Dr. Kanuga died yesterday after a week's illness. It is but natural that Nanduben is terribly shocked. Sumitra[1] also is crying bitterly. Doctor is very courageous. Write a letter of condolence to Nanduben.

I am thinking of going to Kanpur[2] from here on 23.12.25. Motiben[3] has been engaged. Her marriage is to be arranged in the beginning of January after the plenary session of the Congress. Smt. Bhaktiben will stay here only. If you wish to see Nanduben then you do come here without any hesitation.

Bhai and Bhabhi[4] (brother and his wife) have gone to Delhi. Your poor Bhabhi feels lonely, and she is not comfortable there. Uncle's style of living is lordly. So I don't know what sort of cooking arrangement is there.

I am in good health.

Blessings
BAPU

[1]Sumitra Desai, daughter of Vijayagauri Kanuga.

[2]For Kanpur session of Indian National Congress.

[3]Daughter of Laxmidas Ashar.

[4]Dahyabhai and Yashodaben, first wife of Dahyabhai. Both of them on the invitation of Vithalbhai Patel had gone to Delhi to stay with him for some days.

254

Punitive Tax Imposed on Certain Villages in Borsad[1]

1925

The total annual expenditure, which was to be incurred in employing police in the areas enumerated below to protect people from so called "dacoits" was estimated at Rs 2,40,315. Since this entire amount was to be recovered from the people residing in that area, with very few exemptions, the Department of Finance did not have any objection to incurring the expenditure. The Department of Finance considered that during the year, the expenditure which was to be incurred on this account was estimated at Rs 1,00,000. The Commissioner, Northern Division, communicated to the Government that the entire estimated amount could probably be recovered before the end of the financial year 1923-24. The Department of Finance took the view that some funds would be necessary for the payment of the salaries etc., after the end of the month, since the recoveries of the punitive police tax from the people residing in that area might take some time for collection.

A special allotment of Rs 1,00,000 was required to be made available from the reserve funds, which were at the disposal of the Department of Finance, as this entire amount would ultimately be deposited in the Government Treasury. The Department of Finance took the decision to obtain orders from His Excellency, the Governor of Bombay, for making the allotment for this purpose from the reserve funds of the Department.

The scheme covered the following villages:

VIRSAD POLICE STATION

1. Padra
2. Sunav
3. Piplav
4. Isnao
5. Palaj
6. Israwa
7. Ranjipura
8. Bhawanipura
9. Amod
10. Pandoli
11. Khadana
12. Jogan
13. Dawalpura
14. Rupiapura
15. Lakadpura
16. Virol
17. Dantali
18. Wadadia
19. Virsad
20. Khanpur
21. Gold
22. Shijpur
23. Bamanwa
24. Mahi

KATHANA POLICE STATION

1. Jantral
2. Benejda
3. Khantnal
4. Vatra
5. Ralaj
6. Ras
7. Divel
8. Kanbha
9. Kathana
10. Dali
11. Kalu
12. Kankapora
13. Badalpur
14. Dehvan
15. Gorva
16. Kathal
17. Gajna
18. Salol
19. Umlao
20. Pilodra
21. Wadeli
22. Wachhiel
23. Amiad

BORSAD POLICE STATION

1. Santokpura
2. Bochasan
3. Dabhasi
4. Kasari
5. Borsad
6. Nisraya
7. Vasna
8. Alarsa
9. Khedasa
10. Khothiakhol
11. Sherdi
12. Davol
13. Bodal
14. Pamol
15. Dehmi
16. Naman
17. Singlao
18. NapaWanto
19. Dhobikui
20. Dhundhakua
21. NapaTalpad
22. Dedarda
23. Vehra
24. Ashi
25. Surkuva

ANKLAV POLICE STATION

1. Kasumbed
2. Harkhapura
3. Khadol
4. Kaldari
5. Asodar
6. Ambav
7. Kantharia
8. Bhetashi Baria
9. Umeta
10. Bhetashi Talpad
11. Bhanpur
12. Ambali
13. Mojkuva
14. Kanwadi
15. Anklav
16. Amrol
17. Asarwa
18. Sankhiad

ANAND TALUKA POLICE STATION

1. Karamsad
2. Sandesar
3. Meghwa
4. Gana
5. Waskhilia
6. Jitodia
7. Khandhli
8. Navli
9. Napad Wanto
10. Napad Talpad
11. Vadod
12. Hadgod
13. Jahangirpura
14. Adas
15. Wasad
16. Sarsa
17. Vehra
18. Khankuwa
19. Lambhwel

MATAR TALUKA POLICE STATION

1. Khanpur
2. Gorad
3. Jisika
4. Chikhlia
5. Moraj
6. Ramangam
7. Paryaj
8. Sinjiwada
9. Dewataj
10. Bheleda
11. Saela
12. Adeva
13. Valatri
14. Chanor
15. Shekhapur
16. Cimbhasi
17. Vasai
18. Ranesar
19. Dethli
20. Nandali
21. Khandhli
22. Laval
23. Maliataj
24. Sinheldi
25. Alindra
26. Sandhana

[1]*The Indomitable Sardar and the Triumph of Borsad* by S.K. Kshirsagar.

Glossary

Ahimsa	Non-violence, Gandhiji's weapon of love for mass action.
AICC	All India Congress Committee.
Akali Dal	Religio-political organization of the Sikhs.
Akalis	Belonging to Akali Dal.
Anasakti	Mental quality of detachment.
Annawarenees (also *Ennawarnees*)	Person who has no claimant to his property after his death.
Ashram	Literally hermitage, a place for penance and spiritual pursuit, here Gandhiji's community of workers engaged in constructive and national work.
Atira	Ahmedabad Textile Industries Research Association.
Bandobast	Arrangement, management, order, control.
Bapu	Literally father, a generic term to denote respect to elders, a term widely used in India for Mahatma Gandhi.
Begar	Forced free labour.
Bhadarwa	The last but one month of the year, according to the Hindu calendar, comes at the end of the rainy season and just precedes the onset of winter.
Bhagwadgita, the	The Song Celestial, highly philosophic poem laying emphasis on the selfless view of life and action.
Bhajan	A devotional song.
Bhakta	Devotee, disciple.
Bhartiya Vidya Bhawan	Literally, the seat of Indology; the name of K.M. Munshi's University founded by him for the spread and propagation of India's religious, cultural and literary heritage in tune with modernity.
Brahmin	One belonging to the priestly class.
Brahmisthiti	The state attuned with Divinity.
C.D.O.	Civil Disobedience Movements alias non-violent or Satyagraha Movements of Gandhiji to resist British rule in India.
Charkha	Spinning-wheel.
Charkha Jayanti	Yearly celebration of spinning movement.
Charkha Sangh	Spinners' Association, the All-India body that Gandhiji had formed in 1925 to provide employment to the starving millions of India.

Chawl	Locality.
Chela	Disciple, follower, student.
Chaddar	Bedspread.
Chowpatty	Public square.
Constructive Programme	Gandhiji's eighteen-fold programme for India's resurgence.
Dal	Pulse—uncooked or cooked.
Darbar	Court.
Daridra Narayana	The God of the poor: symbolically, God in the form of the poor and the distressed.
Darshan	Glimpse.
Dewan	Adviser, Prime Minister of the erstwhile Princely State.
Dharala	A backward class of people who once owned considerable land and are now largely landless.
Dharma	Duty, religious injunction, in wider sense religion.
Dharmaraja	A prince of virtue, the first among the five Pandavas.
Dhed	A caste of untouchables in Gujarat.
Dharmashala	A charitable travellers' home.
Dhoti	Indian loin-cloth.
Doblas	A backward class, usually landless agricultural workers of Gujarat.
Fakir	A man of renunciation.
Firka	Sub-taluka.
Farman	An edict or administrative order.
Gaddi	Post, position, throne.
Gandhi Smarak Nidhi	Gandhi National Memorial Trust
Garasias	A class of landholders then prevalent in Saurashtra drawing their source of income from the sweat of peasants.
Ghee	Clarified butter.
Goonda	Miscreant, rowdy, hooligan.
Goontha	Fortieth part of an acre.
Goshala	A cow-dairy.
Gujarat Sabha	A political body then generally wedded to moderate school of thought before it was converted into Gujarat Provincial Congress.
Gujarat Vidyapith	The National University, Ahmedabad, which Gandhiji founded in 1920.
Guru	Preceptor, spiritual guide.
Gurudevdatt	The divine precentor Dattatfava.

Gyana Yogi	One who pursues the path of knowledge with yogic discipline.
Harijan	Literally, man of God, the term used by Gandhiji in relation to one-time secluded sections of the Society.
Harijan Sevak Sangh	An association for the service of Harijans which Gandhiji founded in the thirties.
Hinayana	The doctrinal cult of Buddhism.
INA	Indian National Army; a military corps raised by Netaji Subhas Chandra Bose for India's liberation during World War II.
Individual Satyagraha	Gandhiji's Satyagraha campaign of 1940 through satyagrahis of his choice to protest against Britain's war-effort in India.
Inquilab Zindabad	Long live Revolution.
INTUC	Indian National Trade Union Congress
Jagirdar	A landlord possessing hereditary rights.
Jallianwala Bagh Memorial	A memorial to the massacred men and women of India who had fallen victims to British guns and bayonets at a mass meeting on Jallianwala Bagh grounds on 13 April 1919.
Janaka	A hoary king of Mithila (Bihar) known for his wisdom and renunciation.
Janamashtami	A Hindu festival in celebration of Lord Krishna's incarnation.
Japti	Confiscation of property, etc., in defiance of non-payment of taxes, etc.
Jathas	A group of people, gathering, an attacking party.
Jowar	Coarse tropical grain.
Kali Ma fa	The Goddess Kali—The Divinity of Prowess.
Kaliparaj	A backward community in Gujarat.
Karma Yogi	Believer in the path of *karma-action* with selflessness.
Khadi	Hand-spun and hand-woven cloth.
Khadi Mandal	Organization for the propagation of spinning-wheel.
Khadi Pracharak Mandal	The organization for the spread and popularization of Khadi.
Kheda Campaign	No-tax Campaign of the peasants of Kheda in 1917; it was Gandhiji's first Satyagraha Campaign in India.
Khichadi (*kichari*)	A dish of pulse and rice cooked together.
Kirpan	A small dagger, used as a religious symbol by Sikhs.
Kirti Mandir	Gandhiji's memorial at Porbandar.
Kisan	Peasant, agriculturist, farmer.

Kshatriya	One belonging to warrior class.
Kumkum	A red-coloured dust used as auspicious mark on forehead by Hindu women, also being used on ceremonial occasions.
Kurta	Shirt, here loose garment especially of the North Indian type.
Lathi	Cudgel, wooden stick.
Lokasevak	Literally, a servant of people.
Mahal	A smaller administrative unit, then a Taluka of Gujarat.
Mahalkori	The administrative head of the Mahal. His functions and powers correspond to those of Tehsildar.
Maharaja	The ruler of a former Indian State of bigger territory.
Mahatma	Literally, high-souled person, a title bestowed on Gandhiji by Indian people.
Mahavidyalaya	A centre of higher education, college.
Mahayana	Another Buddhist cult laying emphasis on the propagational aspect.
Mai	A cotton type used in a spinning-wheel.
Mamlatdar	Revenue Collector in a taluka.
Mandal	Association, gathering.
Matador Patel	A village official with certain revenue duties.
Mazdoor	A labourer, a worker.
Mohalla	Locality.
Mohar	Coin, seal.
Moksha	Salvation, self-realization, freedom from the bondage of birth and death, the state of eternal bliss.
Mukhi	Mukhi means village Chief like a Patel.
Namaskar	Obeisance, salutation.
Narva	A system of land tenure peculiar to this part of Gujarat.
Nawab	A petty ruler, a landlord.
Nizam	A Muslim ruler; here reference is to ruler of the old Hyderabad State.
Nirvan	Buddhist term of non-duality, the state of absolute peace.
Non-violence	Literally, non-killing; Ahimsa which along with Truth formed the *summum bonum* of the philosophic view of Gandhiji's positive force to resist tyranny and injustice; love-force.
Paddy	Standing rice-crop.
Panch Pyaras	The five chosen.

Panchyat	Literally, the rule of the five—the village elders; the rule of the village republic, a system of village governance peculiar to Indian traditions.
Pandal	Temporarily erected shed for public gatherings and ceremonials, etc.
Paramdham Ashram	Literally, the abode of higher pursuit, Shri Vinoba's ashram at Paunar.
Pardah	Literally, a curtain; a curtain-like garment to loosely enwrap face and bodily parts.
Parshuram	Seer of Ramayana age possessing super-human valour.
Patidar	Landholder, agriculturist.
Pepsu	Erstwhile Patiala and East Punjab States Union.
Praja Mandal	The term then applied to people's organizations in Indian States.
Pranam	Salutation, obeisance.
Pundalik	A saint of Maharashtra who attained realization through devotion to parents.
Puni	Carded cotton roll.
Qaumi Ekta	Communal unity.
Raj	Rule, sovereignty, kingdom.
Raja	A king, ruler, prince.
Rajghat	A place of Gandhiji's shrine at New Delhi.
Rajpramukh	The titular or rather the constitutional head of the interim Unions of States after Independence.
Rajput	A warrior, one belonging to the martial race.
Rama Raj	Literally, the rule of God, Righteousness; Gandhiji's conception of an ideal non-exploitative human society wedded to Truth, Non-violence and Brotherhood.
Razakars	The volunteers of Ittehad-ul-Musilmeen.
Rishi	Seer, prophet, man of penance.
Roti	Indian bread.
RSS	Rashtriya Swayamsevak Sangh; an association founded by Dr. Hedgewar to inculcate discipline and solidarity among Hindus.
Ryot	People, subject, ruled.
Sadhu	A saint, a man of religion.
Sanyas	Renunciation from worldly affairs in sole pursuit of Divinity.
Sanyasini	Nun, recluse.
Sardar	Leader, captain.
Sarvarajochhetta	Uprooter of kings.

Satyagraha	Literally, insistence on truth; Gandhiji's weapon of truth and love for mass action.
Satyagrahi	A believer in satyagraha.
Sepoy	Soldier, policeman.
Servants of India Society	The Society founded by the late G.K.Gokhale for preparing lifelong workers devoted to the cause of Mother India.
Shawl	A loose covering over body.
Shravana	*A* month of Indian year; a unique character in the epic Ramayana known for his matchless devotion to parents.
Shloka, Sloka	Verse, couplet.
Sthitaprajna	The man of equipoised mind.
Swaminarayana sect	A Guru cult in Gujarat, worship its founder as God incarnate.
Swaraj	Self-rule, Independence; according to Gandhiji's conception, social, economic and political independence in the true sense of the term.
Swarajists	Those wedded to Council Entry programme during twenties.
Talati	An important village revenue officer concerned with the collection of land revenue.
Taluka	Taluka or Tehsil is an administrative unit of varying sizes, but usually extending over a few hundred square miles in area and containing a number of villages and one or two towns of population exceeding 10,000.
Talukdar	A holder of a taluka generally applied to a special class of landholders.
Taqavi	Taqavi means loan or advances given to cultivators for purchase of seeds, bullocks, reclamation of land, wells etc. These loans are repayable in easy terms and carry low interest.
Thana	A police station, a boundary post, a check-post.
Vad	The second half of Indian month.
Vaghari	*A* backward sect of Gujarat which work on the land.
Veth	Forced free labour.
Verandah	*A* ground-floor balcony.
Vishnu	The second among the trio of Gods symbolizing protective facet of the Supreme.
Yogi	One who practices Yoga, i.e., spiritual, mental and bodily discipline for self-realization.
Zamindar	Absentee landlord.
Zamindari	Absentee landlordism.
Zulum	Atrocities, repression.

Chronology*
(1875-1950)

1875 October 31	Vallabhbhai Jhaverbhai Patel born at Nadiad town in Kheda district of Gujarat. Mother: Ladbai, Father: Jhaverbhai, a peasant holding 10 to 12 acres of land. Follower of the Swaminarayan Sect. Believed to have participated in the Great Revolt of 1857.
	Took education at his own village Karamsad, at Petlad, Nadiad and Baroda.
1891	At Petlad, he lived in a group of four or five students; walked to Karamsad once a week, brought supplies and cooked food by himself.
1893	Married Zaverba of village Gana, 4 miles from Karamsad, at the age of 18.
1897	Passed the Matriculation Examination from Govt. High School, Nadiad, at the age of 22.
1900	Borrowed books from friends and passed the District Pleader's examination.
	Started legal practice at Godhra in July.
1902	Proceeded to Borsad for legal practice. Won laurels as an accomplished criminal lawyer.
1903 April	Daughter Maniben was born.
1905	Decided to proceed to London to study at the bar. However. he decided to stay back on brother Vithalbhai's persuasion. Underook to run his brother's household during his absence.
1905 November 28	Son Dahyabhai was born.
1909 January 11	Wife Zaverba expired in Bombay. He was arguing a case when he received the telegram conveying news of her demise. Received the telegram, read it and coolly pocketed. Argued out his case patiently. Broke the sad news only after the hearing was over. Stood firm against insistent proposals for remarriage in spite of young age and comfortable financial position.

*Based on Babubhai J. Patel's *Sardar Vallabhbhai Patel: His Life and Times,* 1986; and Yashwant Shejdiwala's *Sardar Shatabdi Samaroh Granth,* 1976.

1910 August	Proceeded to London for qualifying at the bar. Used to walk about 9 miles everyday to read at the Middle Temple Library.
1912	Completed his study in 10 terms instead of 12 terms. Passed his examination in the first class and was awarded a scholarship of 100 guineas per year for 3 years. Left for home on the day following the convocation in view of his children's tender age.
1913 February 13	Reached Bombay. Declining the offer of professorship at Government Law College, Bombay, settled at Ahmedabad. Established flourishing practice as an eminent lawyer in a short time.
1914	Father Jhaverbhai died at the age of 85.
1915	Became a member of the Gujarat Sabha, a political body established in 1884 and began his public career.
1916	Came in contact with Gandhiji. Participated in the Lucknow Session of the Congress as a representative of the Gujarat Sabha.
1917	Was elected to the Ahmedabad Municipal Board. Was re-elected unopposed, his first election having been declared void.
	As a Chairman of the Health Committee, undertook relief work in connection with fighting the scourge of plague, then raging in the city.
	Was impressed by Gandhiji's readiness to court imprisonment in his espousal of the cause of poor peasants of Champaran. Was also inspired by Gandhiji's address to the princes at Benares.
	Participated in the first Gujarat Political Conference at Godhra.
	Accepted responsibility as the Secretary of the Gujarat Sabha. Opposed forced labour system.
1918	Extended cooperation to Gandhiji in the mill-workers' movement at Ahmedabad.
1919 April	Led the Khaira Peasant Movement successfully. Led a huge procession at Ahmedabad in protest against the Rowlatt Bills. Handled open sale of banned literature, like the *Hind Swaraj* and the *Sarvodaya.*
	The *Satyagraha Bulletin* was published.

Disturbances broke out in Ahmedabad on receipt of news of Gandhiji's arrest. Martial Law was declared. Extended support to the authorities in quelling disturbances and restoring peace. In spite of this the riot cess was recovered from him by auctioning his sofa. Government tried to cancel his *Sanad* on grounds of his support to the anti-Rowlatt Act satyagraha. But the judge did not approve the charge in view of his faith in truth and non-violence. This decision made it easier for lawyers and barristers to participate in the civil disobedience movement.

1920 — Following the declaration of non-cooperation and the five-point boycott programme gave up legal practice and adopted simple mode of life.

Collected a fund of Rs 10 lakhs from Gujarat for the Tilak Swaraj Fund in pursuance of the Nagpur Congress Resolution. He also fulfilled the targets of enrolling ten lakh members of the Congress and introducing spinning wheel on mass scale within three months.

In collaboration with Gandhiji decided to establish Gujarat Vidyapith for imparting national education.

Was elected Chairman of the GPCC (Gujarat Provincial Congress Committee) as formed under the new constitution of the Congress.

Elected Chairman of the Reception Committee for the 36th Session of the Congress held at Ahmedabad. The session for the first time adopted simplicity and arranged Indian style of sitting on the floor. It also insisted on the use of *khadi* all through. Thereafter, a hospital was set up on this ground.

1922 — In conformity with the Congress resolution of non-cooperation and the five-point boycott programme, grants-in-aid from the Government were refused. Schools were started by the people's primary education committee. Thereby set up an example how a municipality could effectively implement the programme of non-cooperation.

The Government superseded the Municipal Board of Ahmedabad.

1923 — Master-minded the Nagpur Satyagraha and upheld the right to honour the National Flag.

1923 December — Led Satyagraha to protest against the punitive tax imposed upon the people of Borsad and Anand talukas on the charge of harbouring the dacoits. The Government was eventually compelled to withdraw the tax within 37 days of the no-tax campaign.

1924	Won majority for the Congress Party in the elections to the Ahmedabad Municipality and was elected its President. Got a Harijan candidate elected as a member of that municipality.
1927	Gujarat was faced with unprecedented floods. Organised extensive relief for the flood affected people and saved Gujarat from a great calamity.
1928 April 28	Resigned from the Presidentship of Ahmedabad Municipality following differences over the appointment of the Chief Officer.
	Proceeded to Bardoli the same night. Galvanised the peasants of Bardoli to protest against an arbitrary increase in land revenue and launched a *satyagraha.* The peasants did not yield even though Government confiscated their land, property, crops and cattle. The Government had to yield to the demand for appointment of an Inquiry Committee to review the increased land revenue. The success of the Bardoli Satyagraha infused confidence in launching a nation-wide non-violent movement for independence.
	Endeared himself as the Sardar, the leader, in the hearts of the people.
	Was hailed as the victor of Bardoli in the Calcutta Session of the Congress and honoured with the title of 'Sardar'.
	Elected President of the Maharashtra Political Conference held at Poona.
	Toured Maharashtra to rouse public opinion against increased land revenue and untouchability.
1928 March	Elected President of the Kathiawar Political Conference held at Morbi.
	Became President of Tamil Nadu Political Conference. Toured Tamil Nadu, Karnataka and Bihar.
	Withdrew his name in favour of Jawaharlal Nehru, proposed for the Presidentship of the Lahore Session of the Congress.
1930 January	Gandhiji announced the programme of Dandi March to defy the Salt Law.
1930 March 7	Was arrested at village Ras in the Khaira district in the first leg of this tour which was undertaken with a view to rouse the conscience of people in favour of the historic struggle that was to follow Gandhiji's Dandi March.
	Imprisoned at Sabarmati (March 7 to June 26). Started fast to get 'C' class diet like other prisoners rejecting 'A' class diet to which he was entitled.

	The people of village Ras decided not to pay land revenue. They resorted to an exodus. The peasants of Borsad, Bardoli, Jalalpur talukas of Gujajrat and two talukas of Karnataka also emulated their example.
1930 June 26	Released from jail.
	Congratulated the peasants of Gujarat and Karnataka for their sacrifice.
1930 June 30	Following his arrest, Motilal Nehru, who was officiating as Congress President in absence of Jawaharlal Nehru who was imprisoned, Sardar was nominated as the President of the Congress.
1930 August 1	Arrested and sentenced to nine months' imprisonment, when the Working Committee joined a procession in Bombay on Tilak anniversary.
1931 January 26	Released from the prison.
1931 March 29	Elected President of the 46th Session of the Congress to be held at Karachi.
1932 January 4	Arrested at Bombay. Detained at the Yeravda Central Prison with Gandhiji.
1932 November	Mother Ladbai expired at Karamsad.
1933 October 22	Elder brother Vithalbhai died in Switzerland; his body was brought to Bombay—refused to be released on conditional parole to be able to participate in his brother's funeral.
1934 January 14	Released unconditionally from the prison on account of a nose ailment.
1934 May	Elected Chairman of the Congress Parliamentary Sub-Committee.
	The Congress having decided to participate in the elections to the Central Legislative Assembly, undertook tours for election campaigns.
1935 January 9	Resigned from the presidentship of the Gujarat Provincial Congress Committee. Successfully handled the anti-plague operation in Borsad taluka.
1936	Collected Rs 49,000 for the Harijan Fund in just two days at the instance of Gandhiji.
	Elected Chairman of the Congress Parliamentary Sub-Committee. Maulana Azad and Dr. Rajendra Prasad were the other members.

1937	Organised election campaigns for the Provincial Legislative Assemblies.
	Congress Ministries were formed in seven provinces. Established discipline and fidelity to the Congress.
1938	The Session of the Congress was held at Haripura in Surat district under the guidance of Sardar.
	Hand-pound rice and flour, indigenously extracted oil and cow's milk and ghee were made use of in preparing food to be served to the thousands of delegates and visitors at the time of this Session.
	The students of Gujarat undertook the entire conservancy work including cleaning of latrines.
	The women of Gujarat who had been specially trained looked after various services and arrangements.
	The session also resolved to permit Congress workers to carry on agitation for the establishment of responsible government in their states.
	Became President of the Bhavnagar Session of the Kathiawar Political Conference.
	Made settlement between the Thakore Saheb of Rajkot and the State Praja Parishad.
1939 January 26	Gandhiji undertook a fast from March 3 to 7 at Rajkot upon the Thakore Saheb committing a breach of agreement.
1940 November 18	Arrested at Ahmedabad in the individual *satyagraha* launched to protest against the war and uphold the freedom of speech.
1941 August 20	Released from the prison following an ailment of intestines.
1942	Participated in talks with Sir Stafford Cripps.
1942 August 8	"Quit India" Resolution was passed in the Bombay Session of the AICC.
1942 August 9	Arrested under the Defence of India Rules. Detained along with his Congress Working Committee colleagues in the Ahmednagar Fort.
1943 June 15	Released from the prison after 1,040 days of imprisonment.
	Participated in Simla Talks by Indian leaders with Viceroy Lord Wavell which failed due to Jinnah's insistence to accept Muslim representatives nominated by the Muslim League only.
	Took over responsibility for elections to Central and Provincial Legislatures.

1946 February	Persuaded naval ratings at Bombay to resume duties.
1946 May 5	Talks with the Cabinet Mission at Simla.
	Congress resolved to join the Viceroy's Executive Council and form the Interim Government.
1946 September 2	Joined Interim Government as Home Minister. Suggested appointment of a tribunal to settle the dispute between the Muslim League and the Congress.
1947 June 3	Declaration of Partition of India and transfer of power on August 15.
1947 June 14	The Congress endorsed the decision to divide the Punjab and Bengal and the formation of Pakistan.
1947 July 5	A separate Ministry of States was formed under Sardar.
	Persuaded the princely States to sign the stand-still agreement and instrument of accession within a short period of six weeks. Thus he consolidated the country as one nation for the first time in the history.
1947 August IS	India achieved independence. Sardar sworn in as India's first Deputy Prime Minister and Home Minister.
1947 September 30	Successfully dissuaded the Sikhs from the path of violence, taking revenge upon Muslim refugees crossing over to Pakistan, reminding them that it may not be forgotten that the Sikh religion was born to protect the weak. *Kirpan* is not meant for killing those who seek your protection. Thus, provided security of life and liberty to the Muslim refugees.
1947 November 9	Ignored Lord Mountbatten's advice to refer the Junagadh issue to the UNO and persuaded the Government of India to accept the accession of the Junagadh State in his own way.
1947 December 14	The process of merger of Native States commenced with the merger of Ajaygadh and other Eastern States into Orissa.
1947 December 15	Agreement signed to merge Chattisgarh and other States into Central Provinces.
1948 February 15	The United State of Kathiawar was inaugurated. Thus began the process of the formation of unions of princely States.
1948 April 7	The Rajasthan State comprising Jodhpur, Jaipur, Bikaner, Jaiselmer, Udaipur, Bharatpur and others was formed.
1948 April 22	Agreement signed to form a union of Gwalior, Indore and 25 States of Madhya Bharat.
1948 June 1	Kutch became a centrally administered state.
1948 July 15	The Union of PEPSU comprising Patiala and East Punjab States was formed.

1948 September 13	Police action was launched against Hyderabad following outbreak of violence and eventual threat to the security of the country.
1948 September 17	The Government of India took control of Hyderabad.
1949 January	Decision was taken to merge the Baroda State with the Bombay State.
1949 February 24	The Nizam received the Sardar with folded hands at the Begumpet airport during the latter's visit to Hyderabad.
1949 April 13	Decision taken to form a union of Travancore and Cochin States.
1949 May 1	Merger of Baroda State with Bombay.
1949 May 15	The Nawab of Rampur signed the agreement to merge the State with Uttar Pradesh.
	The Nawab of Bhopal signed the instrument of accession. 1949 June 1 Bhopal became a Centrally-administered State.
1949 Oct 7-Nov 15	Officiated as Prime Minister during Jawaharlal Nehru's absence on tour abroad.
1950 May 19	Visit to Kanyakumari.
1950 September 20	Participated in the Nasik Session of the Congress.
1950 September 22	Advised the workers of Gujarat to concentrate on the Constructive Programme and also to strengthen the hands of Jawaharlal Nehiu.
1950 October 31	A purse of Rs 15 lakhs was presented to him by the citizens of Ahmedabad on his 75th birthday anniversary. The Sardar made over this amount to the Gujarat Pradesh Congress Committee.
1950 November	Expressed his displeasure with the Chinese interference in Tibet. Also dropped a hint at the possibility of China attacking India.
1950 November 15	Fell ill at Delhi. Health deteriorated despite treatment.
1950 December 12	Shifted to Bombay.
1950 December 15	"Friday—breathed his last at 9.31 a.m.
	Cremation at the Sonapur, a common man's crematorium at Bombay.
1950 December 28	Ashes were immersed in the holy confluence of Prayag.

Index

Vaikunthbhai Patel